Codesign

Codesign

Computer-Aided Software/Hardware Engineering

Edited by

Jerzy Rozenblit
The University of Arizona
Tucson, USA

Klaus Buchenrieder
Siemens AG
Munich, Germany

IEEE
PRESS

The Institute of Electrical and Electronics Engineers, Inc., New York

This book may be purchased at a discount from the publisher
when ordered in bulk quantities. For more information contact:

IEEE PRESS Marketing
Attn: Special Sales
P.O. Box 1331
445 Hoes Lane
Piscataway, NJ 08855-1331
Fax: (908) 981-8062

Printed in the United States of America
10 9 8 7 6 5 4 3 2 1

ISBN 0-7803-1049-7

IEEE Order Number: PC4028

Library of Congress Cataloging-in-Publication Data

Codesign: Computer-aided software/hardware engineering / edited by Jerzy
    Rozenblit, Klaus Buchenrieder.
        p. cm.
    Includes bibliographical references and index.
    ISBN 0-7803-1049-7
    1. Computer-aided software engineering.   2. Computer engineering.
I. Rozenblit, Jerzy.   II. Buchenrieder, Klaus.
QA76.758.C675   1994
004.2′—dc20   94-22820
                                                                  CIP

Contents

Preface

This book addresses an emerging paradigm of computer-aided software/hardware engineering (CASHE) codesign. The goals of this design technique are optimized functionality of heterogeneous systems and reduced system development time. To accomplish these goals, system modeling techniques must not presuppose an implementation of various components in hardware or software. Subsequent design refinement of hardware and software components should be performed concurrently, which requires appropriate coordination and consistency control methods. Furthermore, mixed hardware/software specification, modeling, simulation, and verification techniques should be available to the designer.

The key to a unified codesign process is the concurrent pursuit of software and hardware threads in the design process. Decisions made in one thread can significantly affect the other. Therefore, planning, scheduling, and synchronization of design activities should be ensured through well-defined task, flow, and design data management techniques provided by a CASHE framework. Whereas most computer-aided design tools and methods have been very successful in supporting hardware or software design functions, the tools treat the two domains as separate entities. A salient requirement in a codesign system is that both functions be integrated to support the design of a complete system. New approaches that take this distinct, integrative approach are emerging.

The material presented here provides a comprehensive review of work in software/hardware codesign. The contributions originate from the presentations and discussions at the First International Workshop on Software/Hardware Codesign (CODES), held in Grassau, Germany, in May 1992. The workshop, organized under the auspices of the

International Federation for Information Processing (IFIP) and supported by Siemens Corporation, brought together leading experts in the field from academia and industry.

The resulting book is organized as follows: Part I begins with formal methods and modeling concepts and techniques to aid codesign. A number of chapters follow that discuss specific methods and languages for system partitioning and synthesis.

The focus of Part II is the development of computer-aided environments to support the codesign methodology. Systems for specifications, architecture, simulation, and data management are presented. The book concludes with three case studies, presented in Part III. The studies are a telephone channel simulator, a telephone exchange design, and application-specific controllers in mechatronic systems.

The organization of the text conforms to a generally accepted view of design in which formal methods should underlie the specification of system models. Languages are then used in frameworks and environments to develop computer-based system prototypes.

The book was written as a reference for scientists and practicing design engineers. It is the first comprehensive monograph on the subject of codesign. It can be used as a textbook for students in courses and seminars on digital systems design, systems engineering, and concurrent design. The chapters are self-contained so the material can be used selectively. Readers who are more practically inclined may wish to peruse Parts II and III first. Those who wish to gain a better understanding of the underlying formal design principles are encouraged to begin with Chapters 1 through 6.

We gratefully acknowledge the collaboration of workshop organizers and participants. Siemens Corporation in Munich provided funds for the workshop. Professor Dr. Hörbst and Dr. Klugmann were instrumental in planting the idea and ensuring corporate support. Markus Zolg, Alexander Sedelmeier, and Christian Veith spent innumerable hours helping to plan the meeting, reviewing the abstracts, and making all logistic arrangements—to them our special thanks. Teija Hohl lent her talents to assist in the initial cover design.

We are also grateful to the editorial staff of the IEEE Press. Russ Hall's intuition and foresight was invaluable in getting this project off the ground. Denise Gannon coordinated and supervised the production process. Her professional expertise and guidance helped greatly along the way.

Jerzy Rozenblit
Klaus Buchenrieder

Tucson and Munich

Contributors

Edna Barros Departamento de Informatica, Cidade Universitaria, PO Box 7851, Recife 50732-970, Brazil

Juergen Bortolazzi Computer Science Research Center, Electronic Systems and Microsystems Department, Forschungszentrum Informatik, Haid-und-Neu-Str. 10–14, 76131 Karlsruhe 1, Germany

Djamel Boussebha L.E.R.I., Parc Scientifique George Besse, 30000 Nimes, France

Raymond Boute Deptartment of Computer Science, University of Nijmegen, The Netherlands. *Present address:* Department of Information Technology, University of Ghent, Sint-Pietersnieuwstraat 41, B-9000 Ghent, Belgium

Manfred Broy Institut für Informatik, Technische Universität München, Arcisstr. 21, W-8000 Munich 2, Germany

Klaus Buchenrieder Corporate Research and Development, Siemens AG, ZFE BT SE 52, Otto-Hahn-Ring 6, 81739 Munich, Germany

Reinhard Bündgen W. Schickard Institute for Informatics, Universität Tübingen, 72076 Tübingen, Germany

Gisbert Dittrich Fachbereich Informatik, Universität Dortmund, PO Box 500, W-4600 Dortmund 50, Germany

M. D. Edwards Department of Computation, University of Manchester Institute of Science and Technology (UMIST), Manchester M60 1QD, United Kingdom

D. Gareth Evans Department of Computation, University of Manchester Institute of Science and Technology (UMIST), PO Box 88, Manchester M60 1QD, United Kingdom

John Forrest Department of Computation, University of Manchester Institute of Science and Technology (UMIST), Manchester M60 1QD, United Kingdom

Munish Gandhi Computer Science Department, Indiana University, Lindley Hall, Bloomington, IN 47405-4101, USA

Norbert Giambiasi L. E. R. I., Parc Scientifique George Besse, 30000 Nimes, France

P. Gillard Department of Computer Science, Memorial University of New Foundland, St. John's, Canada, A1C 5S7

M. Glesner Institute for Microelectronic Systems, Darmstadt University of Technology, Karlstr. 15, D-64283 Darmstadt, Germany

H.-J. Herpel Kernforschungszentrum Karlsruhe GmbH, PMT-PL, PO Box 3640, D-76021 Karlsruhe, Germany

R. B. Hughes Abstract Hardware Ltd., Brunel University, Howell Building, Uxbridge, Middlesex, UB8 3PH, United Kingdom

Ahmed A. Jerraya TIMA/INPG, 46 Avenue Felix Viallet, 38031 Grenoble Cedex, France

Asawaree Kalavade Department of Electrical Engineering and Computer Sciences, University of California at Berkeley, H178 Cory Hall, Berkeley, CA 94720, USA

Wolfgang Küchlin W. Schickard Institute for Informatics, Universität Tübingen, Sand 13, 72076 Tübingen, Germany

Edward A. Lee Department of Electrical Engineering and Computer Science, University of California at Berkeley, H178 Cory Hall, Berkeley, CA 94720, USA

Peter Mertens Siemens AG, ZFE BT SE 42, Paul-Gossen-Str. 100, D-91050 Erlangen, Germany

Derrick Morris Department of Computation, University of Manchester Institute of Science and Technology (UMIST), Manchester, M60 1QD, United Kingdom

Klaus D. Müller-Glaser Computer Science Research Center, Electronic Systems and Microsystems Department, Forschungszentrum Informatik, Haid-und-Neu-Str. 10–14, 76131 Karlsruhe 1, Germany

G. Musgrave Abstract Hardware Ltd., Brunel University, Howell Building, Uxbridge, Middlesex, UB8 3PH, United Kingdom

Petra Nauber Fraunhofer-Institute of Microelectronic Circuits and Systems, Grenzstr. 28, D-01109 Dresden, Germany

K. O'Brien TIMA/INPG, 46 Avenue Felix Viallet, 38031 Grenoble Cedex, France

Fredrik Östman ELLEMTEL Telecommunication System Laboratories, PO Box 1505, S-12525 Älusjö, Sweden

K. C. Posch Institute for Applied Information Processing and Communications Technology, Graz University of Technology, Klosterwiegasse 32, A-8010 Graz, Austria

Edward Robertson Computer Science Department, Indiana University, Lindley Hall, Bloomington, IN 47405-4101, USA

Wolfgang Rosenstiel W. Schickard Institute for Informatics, Universität Tübingen, Sand 13, W-7400 Tübingen, Germany

Jerzy W. Rozenblit Department of Electrical and Computer Engineering, The University of Arizona, Tucson, AZ 85721, USA

Klaus Scherer Fraunhofer-Institute of Microelectronic Circuits and Systems, Grenzstr. 28, D-01109 Dresden, Germany

A. Sedlmeier Corporate Research and Development, Siemens AG, ZFE BT SE 52, Otto-Hahn-Ring 6, 81739 Munich, Germany

Jørgen Staunstrup Department of Computer Science, Technical University of Denmark, Building 344, DK-2800 Lyngby, Denmark

Yankin Tanurhan Computer Science Research Center, Electronic Systems and Microsystems Department, Forschungszentrum Informatik, Haid-und-Neu-Str. 10–14, 76131 Karlsruhe 1, Germany

Lars Taxen ELLEMTEL Telecommunication System Laboratories, PO Box 1505, S-12525 Älusjö, Sweden

C. Veith Corporate Research and Development, Siemens AG, ZFE BT SE 52, Otto-Hahn-Ring 6, 81739 Munich, Germany

Gerd vom Boegel Fraunhofer-Institute of Microelectronic Circuits and Systems, Grenzstr. 28, D-01109 Dresden, Germany

N. Wehn Institute for Microelectronic Systems, Darmstadt University of Technology, Karlstr. 15, D-64283 Darmstadt, Germany

INTRODUCTION

Codesign: An Overview

Klaus Buchenrieder
Corporate Research and Development
Siemens AG
Munich, Germany

Jerzy W. Rozenblit
Department of Electrical and
Computer Engineering
The University of Arizona
Tucson, Arizona, USA

Abstract: We introduce codesign and its fundamental issues. Basic definitions and tenets of the field are given. We then discuss concepts, techniques, and methods that are essential for support of system specification, development, simulation, and design verification activities. Current state-of-the-art codesign methodologies are addressed. We introduce a model-based codesign approach that favors late hardware/software partitioning. A framework for embedding codesign techniques in a larger design context, namely, computer-aided software/hardware engineering (CASHE), is stipulated. We conclude by stipulating measures to assess the utility and effectiveness of codesign methodologies.

1 BASIC CONCEPTS

Codesign is often referred to as the "integrated design of systems implemented using both hardware and software components" [1]. Hardware/software (HW/SW) codesign is predominant in the engineering of tightly coupled systems with hardware and software modules interacting to solve a certain task. Such systems are not new. However, methodologies that concurrently apply and trade off design techniques from both spectra are only now emerging [2–4]. The growing interest in codesign stems from several reasons [5]. First, advances in enabling technologies such as new system-level specification and simulation environments, soft-prototyping techniques, formal methods for design and verification, high-level synthesis, and the emergence of computer-aided design (CAD) frameworks, have opened new venues for codesign. Second, the increasing diversity and complexity of applications employing embedded systems demands advanced design methods for the development of both software and hardware. Third, the need for a decreased cost in the design and test of HW/SW systems is imperative in today's competitive commercial markets. More than ever, optimization of cost and performance and a significant reduction in the product-to-market time is vital in high technologies.

HW/SW codesign is different from conventional approaches in that it continuously relates the hardware development cycle to the software one. Hence, decisions made at the hardware design spectrum significantly affect software design activities and vice versa. In codesign, the entire problem is treated as a whole. The "co" means primarily *together*. However, it also expresses a design flow that is properly coordinated; a joint effort among designers from different areas. The effort is inherently concurrent in that the majority of all design steps are carried out in parallel by a team that guides, coaches, and supervises the design process. Ideally, several teams of experts develop system components rapidly and resolve problems in a timely manner. Although few codesign environments utilize parallelism, many experts in the field are confident that exploiting concurrency among design threads and tools will result in significant gains [6]. In fact, frameworks extended by design flow management and decision support modules can facilitate enhanced planning and maximized utilization of existing tools for HW/SW codesign [7–10].

In the last two years, codesign has become increasingly recognized. A number of workshops have been dedicated exclusively to the field. The International Federation for Information Processing (IFIP) has sponsored codesign workshops in Europe. In the United States, two meetings have been held under the auspices of the IEEE.

Research contributions have begun to appear in archival literature. The September 1993 issue of *IEEE Design and Test* [5] contains a series of articles that address the modeling and methodological issues as well as specific applications. Thomas *et al.* [4] present a behavioral model for mixed systems and its utility in a codesign methodology. Gupta and DeMicheli [11] focus on cosynthesis issues for digital systems. Kalavade and Lee [12] demonstrate an application of a codesign approach to digital signal processing. Smailagic and Siewiorek [13] discuss a case study on the design of a "wearable" computer.

IEEE Computer has introduced a new section called "Computing Practices." Recent articles in this section are exclusively dedicated to codesign. Kuman *et al.* [14] present several codesign concepts, including a model for evaluating hardware/software alternatives and an integrated HW/SW model that supports representations at different levels of details. Wenban *et al.* [15] describe a HW/SW codesign process for translating communication protocol specifications written in Promela into implementations consisting of both custom hardware and software. Gupta *et al.* [16] analyze the performance of mixed systems and argues the robustness of the codesign practice. Woo *et al.* [17] use functional specifications to examine automatic repartitioning during design.

Several domains such as embedded, real-time, and reactive systems are the application areas for which HW/SW codesign techniques are most beneficial. They are beneficial because the increasing complexity of advanced systems combined with technological advancement requires new design methods and integrated tool environments. As an example, consider heterogeneous systems or components that contain analog as well as digital components for control or signal processing. Time-continuous and time-discrete components clearly require different design methods and tools in the transformational process from a specification into a working prototype. The integrative HW/SW codesign approach supports this process and allows us to extend the application domain by mechanical components. Novel work in the area of embedded controllers in mechatronic systems and "smart I/O" is presented in Part III of this book.

2 TECHNIQUES AND METHODOLOGY

Traditionally, heterogeneous systems design is based on multiple, subsequent HW/SW development steps in which designers refine specifications and construct a prototype. Based on experiments and system profiling, functionality is moved from software to hardware and vice versa in each iteration. Codesign, as practiced today, relies heavily on techniques and methods that have been successfully applied in the past. New contributions to the field are being made in the areas of intertool communications, tool-to-tool interfaces, development of HW/SW partitioning schemes, and enhanced framework technologies. We now describe the traditional codesign approach.

2.1 Conventional Approach

The generic framework techniques facilitate tool encapsulation and integration as well as management support for coordinated, coached, and cooperative design. Figure 1 depicts a typical series of processes and activities in a codesign methodology. This view reflects the approaches recently presented in the literature.

2.1.1 Analysis of Constraints and Requirements

In this step, the basic system's characteristics are defined based on the user's and customer's specifications. Project objectives, constraints, and requirements as stipulated by the client often lack coherence and completeness. Hence, the constraint and requirement analysis step helps to uncover inconsistencies and to pinpoint missing information. Typical design facets captured in the analysis step include marketability based on the study of consumer expectations, real-time performance requirements, realization technology, programmability, power consumption, product size, nonrecurring costs (development), recurring costs (manufacturing), environment in which the product is to be used, reliability, maintenance, design evolution, and recycling costs.

2.1.2 System Specification

The system specification is the results of the analysis step. It is a formalized specification suitable for electronic processing from which a designer derives and develops modeling algorithms. Such algorithms may be simulated using rapid prototyping tools based on state charts [18,19] or queuing models for a performance-oriented simulation. The development step typically involves a combination of experimentation, empiricism, and educated guessing. The simulation is, in fact, the first opportunity for system designers to demonstrate the idea to both the management and marketing project staff.

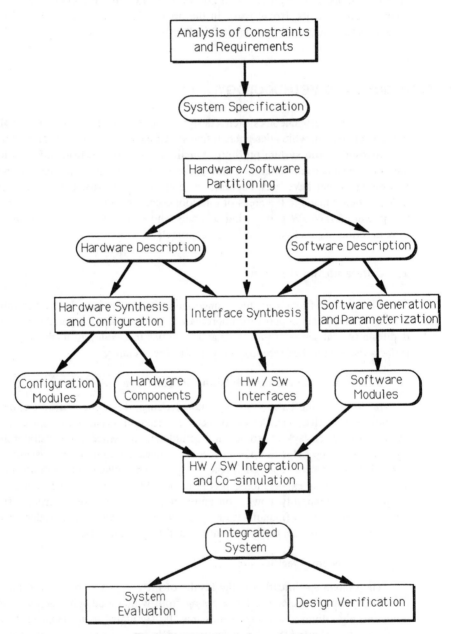

Fig. 1: Conventional codesign methodology

2.1.3 Hardware/Software Partitioning

The central problem of HW/SW codesign is the partitioning phase where a system designer or a tool decides which components of the system will be realized in hardware and which will be implemented in software. Systems design starts with a modeling step, in which the designer expresses the system's behavior formally (e.g., with parallel random access machines that encapsulate state diagrams and time-continuous transfer functions [20]). Depending on the underlying theoretical model, the level of abstraction, and the integration strategy, several estimation and analysis methods are available [21]. Most often, deterministic or statistical techniques as well as profiling methods are applied to obtain a meaningful HW/SW split [22]. Among the possible partitioning schemes—derived mostly from related areas such as VLSI design—deterministic, statistical, benchmarking, and profiling techniques are most popular. Deterministic estimation requires a fully specified model, with all data dependencies removed and all costs of components known. This method leads to very good partitions, but fails whenever data items are unavailable. Statistical estimation, based on the analysis of similar systems and certain design parameters, is then required.

An application considered for implementation might require just the opposite HW/SW split. Then, the profiling technique generally yields better results because system partitions can be determined even when strongly data-dependent execution conditions exist. Typically, profiling techniques rely on the examination of control and data flow within an architecture to determine computationally expensive parts destined for a hardware realization.

Fully automatic system partitioning is not possible yet. The requisite estimation and analysis tools to support partitioning are only now being developed. At best, users may obtain some assistance from automatically derived estimations in guiding their intuition. This is currently satisfactory but not sufficient for industrial applications. Therefore, much attention must be focused on partitioning methods and tools for industrial use.

System partitioning can be performed on different levels of abstraction or at different stages in the design process [23]. When we carry it out on a high level, partitioning is synonymous with the domain binding of modules. This binding step can be performed either early or late in the design process. Strategically, early binding is currently preferred in industry because the entire development cycle can be preplanned and design decisions are eased. This, however, requires that only few or no customer-induced changes are allowed in the design cycle. In contrast, late binding would allow for better solutions with respect to product performance and the treatment of moving target problems when change requests from consumers are frequent.

2.1.4 Hardware Synthesis and Configuration

In the hardware synthesis and configuration step, a hardware platform that executes the code produced in the software generation step is designed (this is a view that presumes early software generation). It is constructed from the hardware description obtained during partitioning. Synthesis involves technology binding by translation (mapping) of hardware descriptions such as VHDL, hardware C, HDL, etc., into physical units [24]. In the synthesis process, functionality is realized as hardware, for example, a single or connected processors. Actually, this choice determines the selection of the code generator in the SW generation step and affects the execution speed of the generated code. It also eases the dynamic configuration process of hardware and readily available components from the existing design libraries. Naturally, most of the hardware is constructed with synthesis tools [24–29].

Besides mere selection of hardware components, programmable devices, such as FPGAs and configurable coprocessor logic, require additional code. Configuration software for hardware modules, that is, FPGA, dynamic CLB logic, and ASIC setups, stems simply from synthesis. Additionally, dynamically configurable coprocessors also receive in-line code from within software generation. Software components depend on decisions made after partitioning and, therefore, the software generation step is dependent on the decisions made in the early phases of hardware synthesis. As an example, consider the word length of a data-path architecture, the coprocessor chosen, or the performance requirements of hardware. These are attained only after a certain register size has been selected.

Hardware configuration is not limited to programmed arrangement of logic functions on the gate and logic level. Knowledge-based configuration techniques can also be applied to construct the hardware platform in the codesign process [30]. Modules of different complexity, from simple logic blocks to processor arrangements, and granularity, ranging from behavioral processor cores to complex processor arrangements, are stored in a knowledge base. An inference engine selects, based on specifications of the required hardware platform, appropriate components from the base and constructs the hardware.

2.1.5 Software Generation and Parameterization

In the software generation and parameterization phase, software modules are generated for the synthesized and configured hardware (here an opposite view is taken; hardware is assumed be generated prior to software). Proper interaction of the components of the hardware and software is ensured by a scheduler that is implemented in either the hardware, software, or both. For this reason, all prototyped codes have to be enriched only with scheduling routines to become production codes. Because software generation depends on the hardware platform and its architecture, specific target architectures are chosen. This allows for the use of standard code and hardware component libraries. Modules from these libraries then need only be parameterized for specific design needs.

2.1.6 Interface Synthesis

Interface synthesis provides a means of hardware and software synchronization [31,32]. Typically, signal exchange (HW), semaphore (SW), or interrupt driven schemes are employed in this phase. Implementations range from custom logic to dynamically configurable logic devices. Some approaches have incorporated a central scheduler (in SW) that sends signals to invoke HW processes.

2.1.7 Hardware/Software Integration and Cosimulation

The problem of HW/SW integration and cosimulation is dual to partitioning and is equally difficult [16]. It leads to a working prototype that can either be physically built or eventually exercised on a heterogeneous system simulator. Hardware/software cosimulators, not commercially available yet, must run objects (modules) produced during software generation on simulated hardware platforms [2]. Cosimulation tends to be extremely time consuming and several measures for speeding up the process are common. Abstract processor models instead of gate-level equivalents at the behavioral level help to speed up the simulation process [33]. Simulation engines that allow for higher simulation speeds are available at industrial research laboratories. There, the general approach to cosimulation is to dedicate several, interacting simulators to the problem. However, the Babylonian language phenomenon experienced by using several distinct simulators from different domains and application areas has negatively affected many researchers in the area.

2.1.8 Design Verification

Design verification ensures that the system produced as a result of the design process meets the original specifications [34,35]. Usually, verification is carried out at the level of a simulated design system model rather than a physical prototype.

In what follows, we advocate a more advanced codesign methodology that is a precursor to what we term a computer-aided software/hardware engineering approach. Our approach is illustrated in Figure 2.

2.2 Model-Based Approach

We contrast the methodology depicted in Figure 2 to the conventional view shown in Figure 1. Traditional approaches to codesign favor early partitioning, especially in industry. The reason for this is the ability to plan all steps of the product development cycle at the beginning of the design process.

Late partitioning or binding, however, can help to find better solutions with respect to the treatment of moving target problems, product performance, and product cost minimization. In our proposed approach, we suggest a refinement that warrants late technology assignment from a validated system model of the desired granularity. This strategy fosters component reuse regardless of their technology. We feel that this leads to a significant reduction in design cost and to faster development. As depicted in Figure 2, the system model obtained in the modeling step is refined in a stepwise fashion to a validated system model by an iterative process. The recurrence, compared with the other approach, does not affect the allocation of technology. This is especially advantageous when large designs are undertaken, since any reallocation (or shift from SW to HW and vice versa) requires numerous changes to the interfaces. This not only affects performance but also the system's behavior.

Next, we proceed to characterize the elements of our approach that augment the codesign methodology discussed when describing Figure 1.

2.2.1 Modeling

Fundamental to the proposed codesign methodology is the use of modeling [36]. We interpret the real system as a source of observable data [37]. In a modeling enterprise, a model is a set of instructions for generating behavioral data. Valid model-generated data should be equivalent to real-system data, or actually to a subset of it, because we cannot possibly build models accounting for all input/output behavior of the real system. Thus, we construct models that correspond to a set of questions, objectives, and purposes for which a design modeling effort is undertaken. Models are then constructed at the level of

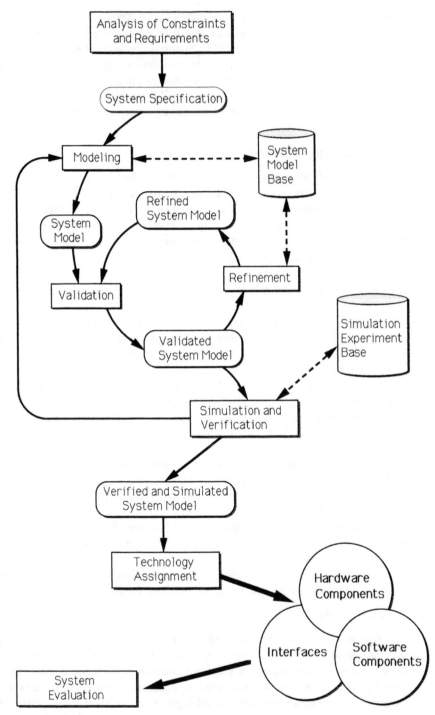

Fig. 2: A model-based codesign approach

abstraction that correspond to those questions. We interpret a simulator as a computational process that generates data given suitably encoded model instructions.

The use of adequate models facilitates transitions across levels of abstraction. In the modeling step, system components, descriptive variables, and component interaction are described at a behavioral level. Specific mathematical formalisms (e.g., discrete event specifications, finite state machines, etc.) may be used as a vehicle for model specification. Because models encode behavior (they are interpreted as design "blueprints"), no decisions need to be made concerning the realization of the components at this stage of the design process.

We exploit the concepts of modularity and hierarchy. More specifically, we attempt to construct models from elementary building blocks that are connected into larger blocks in a hierarchical fashion. It is only then feasible to specify models in a formally oriented manner. (Otherwise the formal complexity would be difficult to manage.)

2.2.2 System Model Base

A system model base is a collection of model components that can be used in modeling a system to be designed. The models stored in the model base serve as a repository of knowledge about existing designs. As designs are modified, augmented, and refined, new models units are stored for potential future reuse.

2.2.3 Validation

We say that a model is *valid* (with respect to design specifications) if the model instructions can generate input/output behaviors consistent with those we have specified for the system being designed.

2.2.4 Refinement

In the refinement step, a validated system model is refined into one with a higher resolution. Typically, model decomposition into elementary submodels is carried out here. Model component couplings and interactions are defined as well.

2.2.5 Simulation

As stated earlier, simulation is a process that generates data given encoded model instructions. Simulators should be verified. By verification, we mean a process of ensuring that the design data are correctly generated by the device called a *simulator*. Simulator-produced data are used to evaluate the proposed design solutions.

2.2.6 Simulation Experiment Base

It is easy to conceive that any real system can be analyzed (or designed) from a perspective that involves a multiplicity of objectives. This implies that the objectives orient the model building process by helping to demarcate the system boundaries and to determine the model components of relevance. The role of the objectives is equally important in the process of specifying the experimentation aspects for the models that have been perceived for the real system. The key concept in this process is that of experimental frame, that is, the specification of circumstances under which we can observe and experiment with a model (or the real system).

The experimental frame definition reflects the objectives of modeling by subjecting the model to input stimuli, observing reactions of the model by collecting output data, and controlling the experimentation by placing relevant constraints on values of the designated model state variables. The data collected from such experiments serve as a means of evaluating the proposed design solutions with respect to the specifications.

Notice that we make a clear distinction between what drives the model, what is observed as its output, and the model itself. On no account should we incorporate such elements in the model itself. If we follow such a clear distinction, a model can be instrumented with different experimental frames, each corresponding to a particular performance specification.

2.2.7 Technology Assignment

Technology assignment is not as limited as the target architecture bound partitioning schemes used in most existing systems today. This is because the implementation independence of the design persists up until this very step. The components of the validated system model can be bound to modules of a possibly different technology.

The interfaces and their synthesis are again central to technology assignment. In fact, the dual steps of partitioning and integration have now been replaced by a stepwise refinement procedure. This procedure is based on an abstract behavioral model and an interface synthesis step. The problem as such has not become easier; however, the design task is more tractable in that smaller, validated objects are coupled and synchronized through well-defined interfaces. These interfaces are generated based on component interrelations derived from the refined model. Depending on the technology choice, either signal exchange, interrupt, or other synchronization means are chosen. In our proposed codesign methodology, alternative designs can be evaluated with respect to various criteria, for example, the allocation (binding) of behavioral models or functionality to action modules (HW, SW, interfaces). This assignment step is guided by the performance estimation results obtained in the previous simulation step.

In the next section, we argue that codesign should be subsumed by a larger framework that will incorporate advanced methods and concepts from the broad area of CAD.

3 COMPUTER-AIDED SOFTWARE/HARDWARE ENGINEERING

In the last several years, we have witnessed a proliferation of electronic design automation tools and systems that integrate them in what is typically termed *computer-aided design* (CAD) frameworks [8]. The CAD Framework Initiative (CFI) views a framework as a collection of extensible programs/modules used to develop a unified CAD system [38–40]. It provides the following definition [41]: "A CAD framework is a software infrastructure that provides a common operating environment for computer aided design (CAD) tools. A framework should enable users to launch and manage tools; create, organize, and manage data; graphically view the entire design process; and perform design management tasks such as configuration and version management. Among the key elements of a CAD framework are platform independent graphics and user interfaces, inter-tool communications, design data and process management, and database services."

The existing VLSI CAD systems and those being developed incorporate many of the framework tenets, for example, tool control, configuration and version management, etc. However, they are not tailored to handle the characteristics inherent to codesign. Current design systems solve problems only in a single domain and a global perspective is still missing. Few tools are designed for interaction with environments or other tools for HW/SW cross specification, development, simulation, integration, and test.

Our fundamental supposition is that advanced computational tools are of limited effectiveness without a reliable design decision support methodology to induce a systematic handling of the multitude of goals and constraints impinging on the codesign process. Hence, we postulate that codesign tools and techniques must be subsumed by an approach that we term *computer-aided software/hardware engineering* (CASHE).

We advocate that a CASHE framework should incorporate advanced concepts such as design flow and task management, concurrent engineering techniques for conjoint design, conventional decision support systems (DSSs), and symbolic expert systems techniques. In our previous work [42], we have developed concepts for prototyping designs through knowledge-based simulation design techniques. As briefly discussed in the previous section and in [43], this approach focuses on the development of simulation models comprising the characteristics of the system being designed. Models, developed at various levels of abstraction and granularity—this, for example, facilitates postponing partitioning decision—constitute reusable modules that populate the model base. Similarly, experiments populate simulation experiment databases for cross checking of model compliance with design specifications, constraints, and requirements. In our framework, we provide expert systems-based techniques for the generation and evaluation of alternative design solutions and strategies.

We envision the need for an integration of model-based concepts with a CAD framework technology. Frameworks provide a supportive infrastructure for the codesign process in that they facilitate communication among many design representation mechanisms, design management tools, various design tools, and designers [9]. Communication between tools and data requires exchangeable data formats or a common design representation. Homogenous frameworks are built around a set of established design tools or a VHDL language core and are often based on an existing design technology or environment. Another approach, the so-called heterogeneous frameworks, allows for a wide variety of design tools and languages. This requires numerous translators between design tools embedded within the framework for the exchange of design data. In the industry, large investments have been made in design tools and training of people who use these tools. Codesign frameworks should incorporate diverse design tools without limitations on the design languages used.

4 CONCLUSIONS

In closing, several critical needs of codesign are identified. We believe researchers and practitioners will focus on these issues in further advancing the field. To better understand and assess the benefits and effectiveness of codesign, we must accomplish the following:

- We must design new systems and build more working prototypes. It is necessary to develop and apply theoretical models for HW/SW codesign (at both the system and the process level).
- We should look more closely at the partitioning problem and apply successful partitioning methods from other design domains, that is, VLSI design or operations research, to high-level system partitioning.
- We should not develop new tools! Instead, we should use what is available and develop new design techniques.
- We must convince management that HW/SW codesign is beneficial.

To accomplish the last desideratum, potential payoffs of codesign must be clearly shown. We relate such payoffs to the following factors: The cost of correcting design errors increases by about a factor of 10 from each phase of the realization process to the next. As the number of reusable (soft and hard) components increases, the design and development costs decrease. Therefore, codesign frameworks and environments must operate on and employ highly reusable models and databases.

Fully parallel design threads facilitate faster design and fewer errors. This significantly decreases time to market. Continuous cross-checking and cross-simulation unveil problems early in the design process. Correcting the problem of a poor match between a SW and a HW component is at least three orders of magnitude more costly than redesign at a higher, model-based level of abstraction.

The performance of existing systems and environments should be improved. Current combinations of CAD tools are often too slow. Design formats are often incompatible and the number of interfaces and translators is high and too costly to maintain.

Even though some recent applications have demonstrated the utility of codesign [13,44], the user-friendliness of design aids has not been shown for a wide enough class of applications. Development of codesign systems requires significant effort and cost and related tools and technologies are not yet mature. The existing demonstrators have not convincingly shown the benefits of employing HW/SW codesign techniques. Managers who are responsible for adopting new design paradigms, techniques and tools are often driven by factors that can be measured in monetary terms. Hence, codesign will become reality as soon as corporate entities recognize its full benefits.

REFERENCES

[1] P. Subrahmanayam, "Harware-Software Codesign: Cautious Optimism for the Future (Hot Topics)," *IEEE Computer,* 26(1), pp. 84–85, 1993.

[2] D. Becker, R. K. Singh, and S. G. Tell, "An Engineering Environment for Hardware/Software Co-simulation," in *Proc. 29th Design Automation Conference,* Anaheim, CA, USA, June 8–12, IEEE Computer Society Press, Los Alamitos, CA, 1992, pp. 129–134.

[3] A. Antoniazzi and M. Mastretti, "An Interactive Environment for Hardware/Software System Design at the Specification Level," *Microprocessing Microprogramming,* 30, pp. 545–554, 1990.

[4] D. Thomas, H. Schmit, and J. Adams, "A Model and Methodology for Hardware-Software Codesign," *IEEE Design Test Computers,* 10(3), pp. 6–15, 1993.

[5] W. Wolf, "Special Issue on Hardware/Software Codesign," *IEEE Design Test,* September 1993.

[6] K. Buchenrieder, "Codesign and Concurrent Engineering," *Computer,* pp. 85–86, January 1993.

[7] K. Chandy, "A Framework for Hardware-Software Tradeoffs in the Design of Fault-Tolerant Computers," in *Proc. AFIPS Fall Joint Conference,* C. Ramamoorthys, Ed., Part I, 1972, pp. 55–63.

[8] D. Harrison *et al.,* "Electronic CAD Frameworks," *Proc. IEEE,* 78(2), pp. 393–417, 1990.

[9] M. B. Srivastava and R. W. Brodersen, "Rapid-Prototyping of Hardware and Software in a Unified Framework," in *Proc. International Conference on Computer-Aided Design,* Santa Clara, CA, November 1991, vol. 1, IEEE Computer Society Press, pp. 152–155.

[10] D. W. Franke and M. K. Purvis, "Hardware/Software Codesign a Perspective," in *Proc. 13th International Conference on Software Engineering,* Austin, TX, USA, May 13–16, 1991, vol. 1, IEEE Computer Society Press, Order No. 2140-02, Cat. No. 91CH2982-7, pp. 344–352.

[11] R. Gupta and G. DeMicheli, "Hardware-Software Cosynthesis for Digital Systems," *IEEE Design Test Computers,* 10(3), pp. 29–41, 1993.

[12] A. Kalavade and E. Lee, "A Hardware-Software Codesign Methodology for DSP Applications," *IEEE Design Test Computers,* 10(3), pp. 16–28, 1993.

[13] A. Smailagic and D. Siewiorek, "A Case Study in Embedded-System Design: The VuMan 2 Wearable Computer," *IEEE Design Test Computers,* 10(3), pp. 56–63, 1993.

[14] S. Kuman, B. Johnson, J. Aylor, and W. Wulf, "A Framework for Hardware/Software Codesign," *IEEE Computer,* 26(12), pp. 39–45, 1993.

[15] A. Wenban, G. Brown, and J. O'Leary, "Codesign of Communication Protocols," *IEEE Computer,* 26(12), pp. 46–52, 1993.

[16] R. K. Gupta, C. N. Coelho Jr., and G. De Micheli, "Synthesis and Simulation of Digital Systems Containing Interacting Hardware and Software Components," in *Proc. 29th Design Automation Conference,* R. Werners, Ed., Anaheim, CA, USA, June 8–12, 1992, IEEE Computer Society Press, Los Alamitos, CA, pp. 225–230.

[17] N. Woo, W. Wolf, and A. Dunlop, "Codesign from Cospecification," *IEEE Computer,* 27(1), pp. 42–47, 1994.

[18] D. Harel, "Statecharts: A Visual Formaliser for Complex Systems" in *Science of Computer Programming,* pp. 231–274, 1987.

[19] D. Harel, A. Naamad, H. Lachover, A. Pnueli, R. Sherman, A. Shtul-Tauring, and M. Trakhtenbrot, "Statecharts: A Working Environment for the Development of Complex Reactive Systems," *IEEE Trans. Software Eng.,* 16(4), pp. 403–414, 1990.

[20] K. Buchenrieder, A. Sedlmeier, and C. Veith, "HW/SW Co-Design with PRAMs Using CODES," in *Proc. 11th IFIP WG10.2 International Conference on Computer*

Hardware Description Languages and their Applications—CHDL '93, D. Agnew, L. Claesen, R. Camposanos, Eds.; sponsored by IFIP WG10.2 and in cooperation with IEEE COMPSOC, 26–28 April 1993, North Holland, 1993, ISBN 0-444-81641-0, Ottawa, Ont., Canada; *IFIP Transactions A* (Computer Science and Technology) vol. A-32, pp. 65–78.

[21] C. U. Smith, F. A. Geoffrey, and J. L. Cuadrado, "An Architecture Design and Assessment System for Software/Hardware Codesign," in *Proc. 22nd Design Automation Conference*, Las Vegas, Nevada, USA, June 23–36, IEEE Computer Society Press, Order No. 635 (microfiche only), 1985, pp. 417–424.

[22] F. Vahid, "A Survey of Behavioral Level Partitioning Systems," University of California/Irvine, 1991.

[23] E. Lagnese and D. Thomas, "Architectural Partitioning for System Level Synthesis of Integrated Circuits," *IEEE Trans. on CAD*, 10(7), pp. 847–860, 1991.

[24] D. Gajski, *Silicon Compilation*, Addison-Wesley, Reading, MA, 1988.

[25] G. DeMicheli, in *IEEE Design Test*, pp. 37–53, 1990.

[26] R. Camposano, in *High-Level Synthesis*, W. Wolf, Ed., International Series in Engineering and Computer Science, Kluwer Academic Publishers, Boston, 1991.

[27] R. Walker, in *A Survey of High-Level Synthesis Systems*, R. Camposano, Ed., International Series in Engineering and Computer Science, Kluwer, Academic Publishers, Boston, 1991.

[28] R. K. Gupta and G. De Micheli, *IEEE Design and Test of Computers*, 10, pp. 29–41, 1993.

[29] M. Edwards, *Automatic Logic Synthesis Techniques for Digital Systems*, Macmillan New Electronic Series, Macmillan, Basingstroke, Hampshire, 1992.

[30] W. Birmingham, in *Automating the Design of Computer Systems: The MICON Project*, D. Siewiorek and A. Gupta, Eds., Jones and Bartlett, New York, 1992.

[31] E. Barros and W. Rosenstiel, *A Method for Hardware/Software Partitioning*, COMPEURO, 1992.

[32] P. Chou, R. Ortega, and G. Boriello, "Synthesis of Hardware/Software Interface in Microcontroller-Based Systems," in *Proc. International Conference on Computer Aided Design*, November 1992.

[33] W. Billowitch, "Simulation Models Support HW/SW Integration," *Computer Des.*, 1, p. 31, 1988.

[34] M. Altmae, L. Taxen, P. Gibson, and K. Torkelsson, "Verification of Systems Containing Hardware and Software," in *Proc. 2nd Conference on VHDL Methods*, 1991, pp. 149–156.

[35] L. Philipson, "Multilevel Design and Verification of Hardware/Software Systems," *IEEE J. Solid State Circuits*, 25(3), pp. 714–719, 1990.

[36] G. Estrin *et al.*, "SARA: Modeling, Analysis and Simulation Support for Design of Concurrent Systems," *IEEE Trans. Software Eng.*, SE-12, pp. 293–311, 1986.

[37] B. Zeigler, *Theory of Modelling and Simulation*, Wiley-Interscience, New York, 1976.

[38] J. Bhat and F. Taku, "A Seven-Layer Model of Framework Functionality," *Electron. Eng.,* pp. 67–73, September 1990.

[39] A. Graham, "CFI: Towards a Broad, Standard Framework," *IEEE Spectrum,* 29(11), p. 40, 1992.

[40] D. Holden, "CFI Fills Tech Slot to Prove Long-Term Role," *Electron. News,* 38, p. 22, 1992.

[41] L. Maliniak, "CAD Frameworks Ride a Rough Road to Success," *Electron. Des.,* 40(16), p. 36, 1992.

[42] J. Rozenblit, "Design for High Autonomy," *Appl. Artificial Intell.,* 6(1), pp. 1–18, 1992.

[43] J. Rozenblit and B. Zeigler, "Knowledge-Based Simulation Design Methodology: A Flexible Test Architecture Application," *Trans. Soc. Computer Simul.,* 7(3), pp. 195–228, 1990.

[44] G. DeMicheli and Giovanni, "Extending CAD Tools and Techniques: Hardware–Software Codesign," *IEEE Computer,* 26(1), pp. 85–87, 1993.

PART I

Formal Methods, Models, and Languages

Many formal techniques exist to support specification and design of hardware or software. However, such techniques typically apply to homogenous components (i.e., either only hardware or purely software). This section presents formal methods and modeling concepts that attempt to assist in the design of heterogeneous components by taking a more holistic, integrative approach.

The first three chapters have a strong theoretical flavor. Büngden and Küchlin, the authors of Chapter 1, discuss the term-rewriting framework and demonstrate how it can be used for specification and verification of systems embedding both hardware and software components. They demonstrate the underlying formalism, apply it to simple design case studies, and show how the term-rewriting–based induction can be used to verify design specifications. In Chapter 2, Boute introduces a declarative formalism for codesign. He argues that the formal facets of hardware design are more general than those that can be expressed by programs and, thus, it is necessary to devise mechanisms for expressing nonexecutable descriptions (e.g., mathematical equations in unsolved form). Broy describes concepts and techniques for the specification and refinement of networks of interacting components in Chapter 3. The techniques are the basis for design and development of distributed interactive systems.

Chapters 4 through 12 provide insight into the modeling facet of codesign. Evans and Morris give an overview of the purpose and method of dynamic modeling of embedded systems. An example of a PABX telephone exchange is given to illustrate the basic modeling concepts, techniques, and tools. Staunstrup develops a codesign model that employs a language to describe computations at an abstraction level that transcends any specific commitment to hardware or software.

In Chapter 6, Dittrich uses hierarchical Petri nets as a formalism underlying functional representation and design specification modeling. He emphasizes the expressive power of this approach, especially when applied to modeling of complex, large-scale, concurrent systems. Jerraya and O'Brien describe a design representation language called SOLAR (Chapter 7). The language is the foundational basis for a design environment that combines computer-assisted software engineering (CASE) and integrated circuit CAD techniques.

Chapters 8 and 9 address the time issues in modeling of mixed hardware/software systems. Gillard and Posch structure timing events hierarchically. They discuss an object-oriented implementation of their approach and demonstrate the underlying concepts with an example from cryptography. Boussebha and Giambiasi focus on timing verification of VHDL-based behavioral hardware specifications. Shoham's logic is used as a vehicle for temporal verification. A "verifier" system was implemented in Common Lisp with an object-oriented layer. The systems compares favorably with other existing verifiers.

The next two chapters discuss partitioning techniques in HW/SW codesign. Hughes and Musgrave (Chapter 10) present data and control flow graph partitioning based on a formal logic calculus. A different partitioning approach based on the concept of UNITY is given in Chapter 11. This approach, presented by Barros and Rosenstiel, facilitates problem specification at a high level of abstraction for which only the logical aspects (e.g., nondeterminism, asynchronous behavior, etc.) have to be addressed.

This part of the book concludes with the chapter by Forrest on the implementation of heterogeneous systems using an object-oriented paradigm.

CHAPTER   1

Term Rewriting as a Tool for Hardware and Software Design

Reinhard Bündgen   Wolfgang Küchlin
W. Schickard Institute for Informatics
Universität Tübingen
Tübingen, Germany

Abstract: We give an overview of how term-rewriting techniques can be used for the specification and verification of both hardware and software. In particular, we cover recent significant advances in the theory of term-rewriting–based induction and we point out how some of the new techniques can be used for the task at hand.

1 INTRODUCTION

To verify hardware or software formally we must have a precise (formal) specification $\mathscr{S}$ at hand; we call this the *formality requirement*. Other components in the design process are the design $\mathscr{D}$ itself and the implementation $\mathscr{I}$ of the designed system. Automated proofs initially verify properties of $\mathscr{S}$. In order for these properties to hold also for $\mathscr{D}$ and $\mathscr{I}$, strong links must exist between $\mathscr{S}$ and $\mathscr{D}$ and $\mathscr{I}$. In this chapter, we assume that $\mathscr{D} = \mathscr{S}$, and that $\mathscr{D}$ can be automatically compiled into $\mathscr{I}$ with preservation of all verifiable properties of $\mathscr{S}$. Therefore, every property that can be proven true about $\mathscr{S}$ must also be true about the implementation.

Because of the formality requirement, it is, in principle, impossible to verify formally that an implementation meets informal design specifications. Formal verification is therefore frequently used to prove that two different specifications $\mathscr{S}_1$ and $\mathscr{S}_2$ of the same Boolean function F are equivalent (see, e.g., [1]). In this chapter we also discuss the additional approach of *plausibility checking*. We assume that the designer starts with $\mathscr{D} = \mathscr{S}$, and that $\mathscr{I}$ can be correctly compiled from $\mathscr{D}$. The designer checks whether the formal design $\mathcal{D} = \mathcal{S}$ captures his or her intentions by proving a set of theorems $\mathcal{T}$, which should hold if the design is right. In some sense, $\mathcal{T}$ reflects a set of secondary design properties that must follow from the primary design specifications if the design is right.

Our choice of $\mathcal{D} = \mathcal{S}$ places some formal restrictions on $\mathcal{D}$, but it also makes it easy to connect a theorem prover to the design process. As formal language we choose the language of *term equations*. This language has already been widely used for software specification in the area of algebraic data type specification [2,3]. It has also been used for hardware specification purposes [4], and it is very closely related to the intermediate hardware specification format of *net lists*. Under some additional restrictions, which are usually fulfilled in our application to design verification, term equations can be interpreted as rewrite rules. A term-rewriting system can then execute the computations prescribed by the equations, thus serving as a rapid prototyping system. Simulation of the designed system by symbolic execution then serves as another plausibility check. Although it may be impractical to simulate long computations in this high-level way, it is frequently possible to check system behavior for nonstandard or trivial inputs.

For these reasons we maintain that term equations are an interesting design language for hardware/software codesign and verification. It remains to be seen whether the language is really convenient for large-scale practical use. But in any case more abstract specification languages can probably be compiled into term equations, from which verification could then proceed.

In this chapter, we give an outline of the potential of "pure" term-rewriting techniques, and especially of recently enhanced techniques for rewrite-based induction, as a tool for hardware and software design. The use of term rewriting for hardware verification goes back to at least 1987 [1], and rewrite-based theorem provers such as Larch continue to be in use for this purpose [5]. However, the former approach does not use induction at all, and the latter [6] uses extended rewrite rules and does not use certain recent induction methods such as advanced ground-reducibility tests.

As we see later, the use of induction has a number of advantages over the use of standard equational reasoning. Term-rewriting–based induction goes back to the famous paper by Musser [7], which was motivated by the need for software verification. At first, however, the technique bore so little resemblance to traditional induction methods that it was termed *inductionless induction*. Therefore, it was quite unclear how traditional knowledge in either term rewriting or automated induction could be used to lift some of its restrictions. For example, because there was no concept of an induction variable, no traditional heuristics [8] could be employed to find "the variable to induct on" and thus to guide the proof.

Then, classical term-rewriting theory took a significant step forward as the standard completion proof procedure was generalized and reinterpreted as a *proof transformation process* which gradually transforms equational proofs into reduction or rewrite proofs [9–12]. As a side effect of this new completion theory, *confluence criteria* could now be used to omit the generation of some lemmas or *critical pairs*, and thus to speed up the completion process. It was, however, unclear how these advances could be carried over to inductionless induction. Furthermore, inductionless induction came under criticism for requiring unnatural preconditions and, consequently, for being unwieldy and weak [6].

In due time, however, inductionless induction was generalized in a way similar to that of general completion. Let us just mention two developments out of many.

First, generalizing results of Huet and Hullot [13], Jouannaud and Kounalis [14] (J-K) noticed that a term-rewriting–based induction prover could be obtained by adding a test for ground reducibility to the Knuth-Bendix completion procedure. Ground reducibility, called quasireducibility in [14] J-K, tests whether all ground (nonvariable) instances of a term are reducible. The prover starts with a (ground) confluent rewrite system $\mathscr{S}$, which produces a unique normal form for each class of ground terms in the equational theory $\mathscr{S}$. Now a theorem T holds in the initial model of $\mathscr{S}$, if $\mathscr{S} \cup T$ has the same congruence classes of ground terms as $\mathscr{S}$. This is proved by completing $\mathscr{S} \cup T$ while checking that T, and all new rules introduced during completion, are ground reducible. The main problem with the J-K procedure was that it produced far too many lemmas and frequently did not terminate even in cases where simple proofs existed. Also, the J-K quasireducibility test was still rather crude and inefficient, and there was still no notion of an induction variable or position.

Later, Fribourg [15] noticed that the overlap positions used in completion to generate lemmas are connected with the notion of an induction position. He proved that certain induction positions, and hence the lemmas produced from them, are redundant. Consequently, his streamlined version of the J-K procedure terminates more often, and its proofs can be guided by selecting induction positions.

In an independent development [10], the newly developed proof transformation view of completion was being applied to the J-K induction method. Proof transformation theory explains how the completion procedure transforms general equational proofs into rewrite proofs. As a by-product, it also succinctly justifies the use of *confluence criteria*, which had been carried over from Gröbner basis theory to reduce the number of rules generated in general completion [9,16]. The main observations are very simple. First, because we are interested in the ground term model, ground confluence is all that is really needed in the J-K method. Second, every important notion of the general completion method has a straightforward analog on the ground level: *ground* reducibility, *ground* critical pairs, *ground* confluence, etc. In [17], general proof transformation and ground proof transformation theory were developed side by side. In particular, *ground* confluence criteria were derived that completely covered, and even generalized, Fribourg's theory of omitting certain derivations in the J-K algorithm. The correctness of this theory follows by direct analogy to the correctness of the general proof transformation theory.

A ground confluence criterion can be obtained as a side effect of the J-K ground reducibility test. A slightly extended procedure can determine which subset $\mathscr{S}' \subseteq \mathscr{S}$ of the initial specification rule set is sufficient to show ground reducibility of a term t, and at which positions in t the rules of $\mathscr{S}'$ would have to be applied. Then those positions form a set $\mathscr{P}$ (frequently a singleton) of induction positions, and it is sufficient for an induction proof to consider the lemmas produced by overlapping $\mathscr{S}'$ and t at those positions; all other lemmas produced using other rules or other positions are redundant. Incidentally, the different overlaps correspond to a case distinction of the kinds of ground terms that could be substituted at the induction position. Of course, there may exist many pairs $\langle \mathscr{P}, \mathscr{S}' \rangle$ of positions and rules. In this case, we may alternatively select one of the pairs to continue the proof. The main limitation of this technique is that currently it can only handle case distinctions whose cases are expressible by the patterns on the left-hand sides of rewrite rules.

Thus, we have a mathematically precise notion of an induction position, and the necessary information can be computed by the extended ground reducibility test of [18]. This development placed great importance on the ground reducibility test, and there is now a growing body of work on how to make the test more efficient [18–23]. To test a term t for ground reducibility, we must have a finite description of the infinite set of ground terms that could be substituted for the variables in t. This description can be in the form of a grammar, or in the form of a finite, but representative, "test set." In any case, this description of the irreducible ground terms admitted by a set of rewrite rules $\mathscr{S}$ can now also be used to provide another plausibility test for $\mathscr{S}$ as a specification. If there are irreducible expressions such as $+(0, 0)$, then we probably forgot to specify how to evaluate the $+$ function in this case. In our experience, this check works well for the "fringe" cases of a specification, where arguments are 0, *undefined*, or the like.

This new procedure was termed *inductive completion* because of its close similarity to general completion. Today, inductive completion stands out as a method that has both strong and precise theoretical foundations *and* a perspicuous relationship to traditional notions of induction, such as induction variables and heuristics and how to find them.

2 FORMAL BACKGROUND

In this section, we present a rather brief introduction to term-rewriting systems and completion procedures. The interested reader is advised to consult [24], [25], or [26], for more comprehensive introductions.

TERMS.   A term is made up of *variables, constants,* and *function symbols* (*operators*). Each variable and each constant has a *sort* (type) associated with it and each function symbol f has fixed rank, result sort, and argument sorts; usually we denote by $f : s_1 \times \cdots \times s_n \to s$ that the result sort of f is s and the i'th argument of f has sort s_i. Terms are defined recursively: All variables and constants are terms of their respective sorts. If $f : s_1 \times \cdots \times s_n \to s$ is a function symbol and $t_1, \ldots, t_n$ are terms of sorts $s_1, \ldots, s_n$, respectively, then $t = f(t_1, \ldots, t_n)$ is a term of sort s. Nothing else is a term. A term without variables is a *ground term*. The set of constants and function symbols together with the sort information is called the *signature* $\mathscr{F}$.

The basic operations on terms are instantiation and tests for (structural) equality, matching, and unification. A term t' is an *instance* of t if it can be obtained by substituting terms for the variables in t; it is a *ground instance* if it is in addition a ground term. A term s *matches* another term t if all variables in s can be *substituted* by terms such that the new *instance* of s is equal to t. Two terms s and t *unify* if their respective variables can be substituted in such a manner that s and t have a common instance.

RULES.   A *rewrite rule* is a pair $l \to r$ of terms. It may be applied to *reduce* a term t if t contains an instance of l. Then t reduces to t' where in t' this instance of l is replaced by the corresponding instance of r. For example, $f(g(1, y))$ reduces to $f(f(1))$ by applying the rewrite rule $g(x, y) \to f(x)$. A set of rewrite rules is a *term-rewriting system* $\mathscr{R}$. A term t is *reducible* by $\mathscr{R}$ if there is a rule in $\mathscr{R}$ that can reduce t;

otherwise, t is *irreducible*. Similarly, t is *ground reducible* if all of its ground instances are reducible. A term-rewriting system $\mathcal{R}$ should have the *termination property*. That is, starting with any term t there is no infinite sequence of reductions using rules from $\mathcal{R}$. The termination property of a term-rewriting system is undecidable in general, but there are powerful criteria to ensure this property; see [27] for an overview. A second important property of term-rewriting systems is *confluence*. When reducing a term t by a confluent term-rewriting system, the sequence of the rule applications does not matter: If a term is reachable by one sequence, it is reachable by any other sequence as well. A terminating *and* confluent term-rewriting system is called *canonical*. For canonical term-rewriting systems each term eventually reduces to a unique and irreducible *normal form*. Similarly, a term-rewrite system is *ground confluent* and, respectively, *ground canonical,* if the preceeding properties hold for all ground terms.

EQUATIONAL PROOFS.   An equation is a pair $s = t$ of terms. Equations may be applied to terms both from left to right and from right to left. Thus $s = t$ corresponds to the (nonterminating) term-rewriting system $\{s \rightarrow t, t \rightarrow s\}$. An *algebraic specification* $\mathcal{A} = \langle \mathcal{F}, \mathcal{E} \rangle$ is a signature $\mathcal{F}$ together with a set of equations $\mathcal{E}$ between terms over $\mathcal{F}$. (Sometimes we only mention $\mathcal{E}$, and $\mathcal{F}$ is understood to contain the operators ocurring in $\mathcal{E}$.) According to a theorem of Birkhoff [28], all equations $s = t$ valid in an algebraic specification can be derived by repeatedly applying equations from $\mathcal{E}$ to s and t. A sequence of equation applications $s =_{\mathcal{E}} \ldots =_{\mathcal{E}} t$ is called an *equational proof* of $s = t$. If the equations in $\mathcal{E}$ can be oriented into a set of rewrite rules $\mathcal{R}$, the equational proof $s =_{\mathcal{E}} \ldots =_{\mathcal{E}} t$ corresponds to a *back-and-forth* proof, say, $s \leftarrow_{\mathcal{R}} \ldots \leftarrow_{\mathcal{R}} \cdot \rightarrow_{\mathcal{R}} \ldots \leftarrow_{\mathcal{R}} \cdot \rightarrow_{\mathcal{R}} t$, in which the direction of rule application is exhibited. Because of a complete lack of guidance, back-and-forth proofs cannot be constructed efficiently in practice.

The significance surrounding canonical term-rewriting systems is that they admit very simple proofs, which can be constructed efficiently. If $\mathcal{R}$ is canonical, then every equation $s = t$ in the corresponding equational theory $\mathcal{E}_{\mathcal{R}}$ does not only have a back-and-forth proof, but it also has a *V-form* proof $s \rightarrow_{\mathcal{R}} \ldots \rightarrow_{\mathcal{R}} \cdot \leftarrow_{\mathcal{R}} \ldots \leftarrow_{\mathcal{R}} t$ as well. Hence $s = t$ can be efficiently proved by reducing s and t to their respective normal forms, and $s = t$ holds if, and only if, the normal forms of s and t are syntactically equal. This special kind of an equational proof is also called a *reductional,* or *rewrite, proof.* The significance of the *Knuth-Bendix completion procedure* [29] is that it compiles a given set of equations $\mathcal{E}$ into an equivalent canonical term-rewriting system $\mathcal{R}$. It does so by systematically producing new rules, called *critical pairs,* which are valid equational consequences of $\mathcal{E}$ and are hence sometimes interpreted as lemmas. If the Knuth-Bendix completion procedure terminates, then the resulting canonical term-rewriting system $\mathcal{R}$ provides a decision procedure for all equations in the theory described by $\mathcal{E}$.

INDUCTION PROOFS.   Theorems proved by equational proofs (or rewrite proofs) hold in *all* models of $\mathcal{E}$. This includes so called *nonstandard models,* which, as their name implies, are of mostly theoretical interest. In practice, we are usually interested only in standard models, which consist of elements that can actually be constructed using the operators (and constants) of the specification; that is, we are interested in the *term model.* In the term model, irreducible ground terms correspond to *data items,* such as 0, succ(0), . . . in Example 1. Reducible ground terms correspond to function calls or expressions that can be evaluated, such as $+(0, \text{succ}(0))$ in Example 1. Terms with variables correspond to patterns of ground terms, such as succ(x), which denotes all terms whose top operator is succ.

Our interest in specific models leads to a more specific interpretation of the variables and therefore more equations may be valid than in the general equational theory. In Example 1, commutativity of + does not hold in general under the usual Peano axioms. When we postulate some nonstandard number a that cannot be expressed as a successor of 0, no axioms are available that could be used to prove even $+(0, a) = +(a, 0)$.

EXAMPLE 1

$$\mathscr{F} = \begin{cases} 0: & \rightarrow \text{INT} \\ \text{succ}: \text{INT} \rightarrow \text{INT} \end{cases}$$

$$\mathscr{E} = \begin{cases} +(0, y) & = y \\ +(\text{succ}(x), y) = \text{succ}(+(x, y)) \end{cases}$$

□

To be a little more precise, we are really interested in whether an equation $s = t$ holds for all *distinct* data objects. Our intended model is the *initial model* [3], which is isomorphic to the classes of $\mathscr{F}$-ground terms modulo $\mathscr{E}$. In Example 1, we want to know if $+(x, y) = +(y, x)$ holds in the model 0, succ(0), succ(succ(0)) .... Some distinct terms such as 0 and $+(0, 0)$ are $\mathscr{E}$-equal and hence belong to the same ground term congruence class modulo $\mathscr{E}$, which represents only one data object. We can work with these term classes if we can work with unique representatives, which we also take to represent the data object, such as 0 in Example 1. Clearly, it is sufficient to consider only the irreducible ground terms as representatives, but in general two different $\mathscr{R}$-irreducible ground terms, such as $+(1, 0)$ and $+(0, 1)$, may be equal in the equational theory $\mathscr{E}_{\mathscr{R}}$ and denote the same data object. With a ground canonical rewrite system, however, the irreducible ground terms are isomorphic to the initial model: Every distinct data object is uniquely represented by an irreducible ground term.

INDUCTIVE COMPLETION.   Equations that hold only in the initial model cannot be proved by equational proofs alone: Structural induction over the term structure is necessary. Induction proofs in equational specifications can be performed by *inductive completion procedures* such as those in [14,17,30]. Inductive completion is a specialization of the general Knuth-Bendix completion procedure. Whereas general completion attempts to transform every equational proof to a rewrite proof, inductive completion attempts this only for proofs containing no variables. In addition, every new rule (new lemma) introduced by the process is subjected to a so-called *consistency test*. It checks whether the left-hand side of the rule is ground reducible by $\mathscr{R}$; in this case it is impossible that the new rule reduces one of the unique representatives of $\mathscr{E}_{\mathscr{R}}$ classes. Note that a rule R may pass the test and still be inconsistent with the inductive theory of $\mathscr{E}_{\mathscr{R}}$. However, if there is an equational proof using R that equates two distinct irreducible ground terms s and t, inductive completion will eventually produce an augmented system $\mathscr{R}'$ under which there is even a rewrite proof $s \rightarrow_{\mathcal{R}'} \dots \rightarrow_{\mathcal{R}'} \cdot \leftarrow_{\mathcal{R}'} \dots \leftarrow_{\mathcal{R}'} t$. Hence, at least s or t must have become reducible in this process. Conversely, if inductive completion stops with a system $\mathcal{R}'$ in which every newly introduced rule passes the consistency test, the set of irreducible ground terms, and hence the initial model, of $\mathcal{R}$ and $\mathcal{R}'$ is the same. If inductive completion already started with a ground confluent axiom system, a theorem is actually inconsistent with the axioms if the consistency check fails, that is, a theorem may be disproved. The ground proof transformation theory of [17] develops *ground confluence criteria* as special cases of the general confluence criteria to reduce the number of critical pairs (lemmas) needed for inductive completion. The reduction is significant because in many cases inductive completion now terminates where it previously did not.

Previous inductionless induction methods also required the axiom system to be confluent, and this was a point of much criticism [6]. Therefore, we would like to emphasize two points. First, it is significantly less restrictive that we now only require *ground confluence* of the specification. If a specification is not ground confluent, there is most likely something wrong to begin with, because there is one expression (without variables) that can be evaluated in two ways yielding two different results. Second, it is easy to see [31,32] that even the ground confluence requirement can be lifted if we only wish to prove theorems and not disprove them. This implies that we can trust any proof of the inductive completion method. Only if the consistency check ever fails do two potential outcomes result: If the initial specification was indeed ground confluent, then the theorem is disproved because it equated two data items that were not equal under the specification alone. If the initial specification was not ground confluent, then the outcome is *don't know*, because the inconsistency may either be like that in the first case or it may be a consequence of completing the specification as a side effect of the proof.

THE THEORY AC.   There are two important equations that, taken together, cannot be part of any canonical term-rewriting system of the simple type discussed so far. These are the associativity and commutativity laws:

$$\mathcal{E}_{AC} = \begin{cases} f(x, y) & = f(y, x) \\ f(f(x, y), z) & = f(x, f(y, z)) \end{cases}$$

To incorporate knowledge of the associativity and commutativity of certain functions (*AC operators*) in a term-rewriting environment the basic operations of matching and unification must be performed *modulo AC*, that is, the AC knowledge must be built into these procedures. A generalized completion procedure that can handle AC operators was proposed by Peterson and Stickel [33]. References [14] and [30] show that AC completion procedures can also be specialized to inductive AC completion procedures.

3 DESIGN AND VERIFICATION OF SOFTWARE

To design and verify software using equations, we may specify the behavior of our functions by a description of the argument types and by a set of equations describing (recursively) which function calls are equal to (i.e., evaluate to) which data objects. This leads to an *algebraic specification* $\mathcal{A} = \langle \mathcal{F}, \mathcal{E} \rangle$ of an abstract data type, which is expressed by a finite signature $\mathscr{F}$ and a set of equations $\mathscr{E}$ over first order terms that must be satisfied [2,3]. Example 2 shows the algebraic specification for Ackermann's function.

EXAMPLE 2

$$\mathscr{F} = \begin{cases} 0: & \to \text{INT} \\ \text{succ}: \text{INT} & \to \text{INT} \\ \text{ack}: \text{INT} \times \text{INT} & \to \text{INT} \end{cases}$$

$$\mathscr{E} = \begin{cases} \text{ack}(0, y) & = \text{succ}(y) \\ \text{ack}(\text{succ}(x), 0) & = \text{ack}(x, \text{succ}(0)) \\ \text{ack}(\text{succ}(x), \text{succ}(y)) & = \text{ack}(x, \text{ack}(\text{succ}(x), y)) \end{cases}$$

□

If the set $\mathscr{E}$ can be oriented into a terminating set of rewrite rules $\mathscr{R}$, then $\mathscr{R}$ can be used as a functional program; $\mathscr{I} = \mathscr{R}$ is an implementation of $\mathscr{S} = \mathscr{E}$. If $\mathscr{R}$ does not terminate, some expression evaluations take forever. If $\mathscr{R}$ is not ground confluent, then the result of some expression evaluation depends on the evaluation sequence chosen; the data item denoted by the expression has several different representations. If $\mathscr{R}$ is canonical, then $\mathscr{R} = \mathscr{I}$ implements all consequences of the specification $\mathscr{S} = \mathscr{A} = \langle \mathscr{F}, \mathscr{E} \rangle$; we can prove all equations that are valid in all models of $\mathscr{E}$ using rewrite proofs. Otherwise, an equivalent canonical term-rewriting system may be generated from $\mathscr{E}$ using a completion procedure.

However, as discussed in Section 2, only the *initial model* of $\mathscr{A}$, which is isomorphic to the set of ground term classes modulo $\mathscr{E}$, is significant from the programmer's point of view. Only objects described by ground terms will be manipulated by the program, and only equalities between ground terms are of interest. To prove the theorem

$$e : +(x, +(y, z)) = +(+(x, y), z)$$

it is therefore sufficient to show this equality for all ground instances of e. Interpreting an equation like this means that e is an *inductive theorem:* Usually, some kind of induction over the term structure is needed to prove e. Proving inductive theorems is in general a very hard problem, which is undecidable in many theories and beyond the scope of simple rewrite proofs. Given a term-rewriting system, inductive theorems can in many cases be proven by an adaptation of the Knuth-Bendix completion procedure, a so-called *inductive completion procedure.* In fact, the abstract data type approach to software specification [2,3] was the original motivation for the work in term-rewriting based induction [7,34].

Recall that the main difference between the original completion procedure and its specialization to prove inductive theorems is a consistency check and a possible restriction of the critical pairs to be computed. To perform the consistency check, a characterization of the set of irreducible ground terms is necessary. Since the irreducible ground terms represent the objects that we accept as results of our program, this characterization provides valuable feedback as to whether our specification really specifies what we wanted to speccify. The latter was actually recognized in the algebraic specification field before ground reducibility tests were developed for induction; the property of a function to be specified for all parameter combinations was known as *sufficient completeness* [35–39,41].

With the tools provided by term rewriting, software design and verification may proceed along the following lines.

1. Specify your program as abstract data type $\mathcal{A} = \langle \mathcal{F}, \mathcal{E} \rangle$, providing a signature $\mathcal{F}$ and a set $\mathcal{E}$ of equations.

2. Complete $\mathcal{E}$ using the Knuth-Bendix procedure. This yields, on success, a canonical term-rewriting system $\mathcal{R}$.

3. Analyze the set of ground terms that are irreducible with regard to $\mathcal{R}$. If there is an irreducible ground term t' that is not acceptable as a result of the program, then the specification of the abstract data type is wrong or incomplete! Correct your specification (analyzing what your program does with input t' will give you a clue about what is wrong with the specification) and continue with step 2.

4. Verify your specification by proving all theorems that are essential for your data type. If this cannot be done by a rewrite proof, try to prove it using an induction proof. If a theorem does not hold, the specification is wrong. If the inductive completion procedure disproves a theorem, it will find a counter example, that is, an instance of the theorem that does not hold in the initial model of $\mathcal{A}$. This counterexample provides a clue about what is wrong with the specification. So if the theorem is refuted, correct your specification and continue with step 2.

5. The specification is correct with regard to your requirements (theorems).

Let us demonstrate this procedure by a small but nontrivial example. We want to specify a stack over the two elements 0 and 1. We will need element constants 0 and 1, a constant nil, and operations push, pop, and top. Encoding our knowledge of stacks into equations leads to the following algebraic specification:

SPECIFICATION 1

$$\mathcal{F}_{\text{stack0}} = \begin{cases} 0: & \to \text{EL} \\ 1: & \to \text{EL} \\ \text{nil}: & \to \text{STACK} \\ \text{push}: \text{EL} \times \text{STACK} & \to \text{STACK} \\ \text{pop}: \text{STACK} & \to \text{STACK} \\ \text{top}: \text{STACK} & \to \text{EL} \end{cases}$$

$$\mathcal{R}_{\text{stack0}} = \begin{cases} \text{pop}(\text{push}(e, s)) \to s \\ \text{top}(\text{push}(e, s)) \to e \end{cases}$$

The term-rewriting system $\mathcal{R}_{\text{stack0}}$ is complete. If we apply to this specification the ground normal form analysis described in [22,40] and implemented in the ReDuX term-rewriting laboratory [42], we get as a result the following context-free grammar, which accepts (and hence characterizes) the set of irreducible ground terms:

$\langle EL \rangle \quad ::= 0 \mid 1 \mid \text{top(nil)} \mid \text{top}(\langle POP(R) \rangle)$

$\langle STACK \rangle ::= \text{nil} \mid \text{pop(nil)} \mid \text{push}(\langle ELEMENT \rangle, \langle STACK \rangle) \mid \text{pop}(\langle STACK \rangle)$

$\langle POP(R) \rangle ::= \text{pop(nil)} \mid \text{pop}(\langle POP(R) \rangle)$

Equivalently, a finite set representing the irreducible ground terms may be computed:

$$\{0, 1, \text{nil}, \text{top(nil)}, \text{pop(nil)}, \text{push}(e, s), \text{top(pop}(s)), \text{pop(pop}(s))\}$$

Therefore, our specification allows stacks like pop(nil) and elements like top(nil), top[pop(nil)], etc. This is certainly not what we intended to specify. We forgot about some inputs for which top and pop should be undefined. So we have to fix our specification and after some cycles of respecification and correction we may end up with the following complete algebraic specification:

SPECIFICATION 2

$$\mathscr{F}_{\text{stack1}} = \begin{cases} 0: & \to EL \\ 1: & \to EL \\ \text{errel}: & \to EL \\ \text{nil}: & \to STACK \\ \text{error}: & \to STACK \\ \text{push}: & EL \times STACK & \to STACK \\ \text{pop}: & STACK & \to STACK \\ \text{top}: & STACK & \to EL \\ \text{goodstack}: STACK & \to STACK \\ \text{if}: & STACK \times EL \times EL & \to EL \end{cases}$$

$$\mathscr{R}_{\text{stack1}} = \begin{cases} \text{push}(e_1, \text{error}) & \to \text{error} \\ \text{push}(\text{errel}, s) & \to \text{error} \\ \text{pop(nil)} & \to \text{error} \\ \text{pop(error)} & \to \text{error} \\ \text{pop(push}(0, s)) & \to s \\ \text{pop(push}(1, s)) & \to s \\ \text{pop(push}(\text{errel}, s)) & \to \text{error} \\ \text{goodstack(error)} & \to \text{error} \\ \text{goodstack(nil)} & \to \text{nil} \\ \text{goodstack(push}(0, s)) & \to \text{goodstack}(s) \\ \text{goodstack(push}(1, s)) & \to \text{goodstack}(s) \\ \text{goodstack(push}(\text{errel}, s)) & \to \text{error} \\ \text{if}(\text{nil}, e_1, e_2) & \to e_1 \\ \text{if}(\text{error}, e_1, e_2) & \to e_2 \\ \text{if}(\text{push}(e_1, s), e_2, e_3) & \to \text{if(goodstack(push}(e_1, s)), e_2, e_3) \\ \text{top(error)} & \to \text{errel} \\ \text{top(nil)} & \to \text{errel} \\ \text{top(push}(e_1, s)) & \to \text{if(goodstack}(s), e_1, \text{errel}) \end{cases}$$

This specification is not confluent yet. If we complete $\mathcal{R}_{\text{stack1}}$ using the Knuth-Bendix procedure, the rule

$$\text{if}(\text{goodstack}(s), \text{errel}, \text{errel}) \rightarrow \text{errel}$$

is added, the rules

$$\text{pop}(\text{push}(\text{errel}, s)) \qquad \rightarrow \text{error}$$
$$\text{goodstack}(\text{push}(\text{errel}, s)) \rightarrow \text{error}$$

are deleted, and we get the following term-rewriting system:

SPECIFICATION 3

$$\mathcal{R}_{\text{stack2}} = \begin{cases}
\text{push}(e_1, \text{error}) & \rightarrow \text{error} \\
\text{push}(\text{errel}, s) & \rightarrow \text{error} \\
\text{pop}(\text{nil}) & \rightarrow \text{error} \\
\text{pop}(\text{error}) & \rightarrow \text{error} \\
\text{pop}(\text{push}(0, s)) & \rightarrow s \\
\text{pop}(\text{push}(1, s)) & \rightarrow s \\
\text{goodstack}(\text{error}) & \rightarrow \text{error} \\
\text{goodstack}(\text{nil}) & \rightarrow \text{nil} \\
\text{goodstack}(\text{push}(0, s)) & \rightarrow \text{goodstack}(s) \\
\text{goodstack}(\text{push}(1, s)) & \rightarrow \text{goodstack}(s) \\
\text{if}(\text{nil}, e_1, e_2) & \rightarrow e_1 \\
\text{if}(\text{error}, e_1, e_2) & \rightarrow e_2 \\
\text{if}(\text{push}(e_1, s), e_2, e_3) & \rightarrow \text{if}(\text{goodstack}(\text{push}(e_1, s)), e_2, e_3) \\
\text{if}(\text{goodstack}(s), \text{errel}, \text{errel}) & \rightarrow \text{errel} \\
\text{top}(\text{error}) & \rightarrow \text{errel} \\
\text{top}(\text{nil}) & \rightarrow \text{errel} \\
\text{top}(\text{push}(e_1, s)) & \rightarrow \text{if}(\text{goodstack}(s), e_1, \text{errel})
\end{cases}$$

An automatic ground normal form analysis of $\mathcal{R}_{\text{stack2}}$ by the ReDuX system yields the following grammar[1] describing the set of $\mathcal{R}_{\text{stack2}}$-irreducible ground terms:

$$\langle \text{STACK} \rangle \quad ::= \text{nil} \mid \text{error} \mid \text{push}(1, \langle \text{PUSH}(A, R) \rangle) \mid$$
$$\text{push}(0, \langle \text{PUSH}(A, R) \rangle) \mid \text{push}(1, \text{nil}) \mid \text{push}(0, \text{nil})$$

$$\langle \text{PUSH}(A, R) \rangle ::= \text{push}(1, \langle \text{PUSH}(A, R) \rangle) \mid \text{push}(0, \langle \text{PUSH}(A, R) \rangle) \mid$$
$$\text{push}(1, \text{nil}) \mid \text{push}(0, \text{nil})$$

$$\langle \text{EL} \rangle \qquad ::= 0 \mid 1 \mid \text{errel}$$

---

[1] This grammar can be further simplified.

ReDuX also produces the following set of terms, corresponding to the grammar, which represent the induction bases (ground terms) and induction steps (nonground terms) needed in a proof by structural induction:

$$\{\text{nil}, \text{error}, \text{push}(1, \text{push}(e, s)), \text{push}(0, \text{push}(e, s)), \text{push}(1, \text{nil}), \text{push}(0, \text{nil}), 0, 1, \text{errel}\}$$

This term-rewriting system matches our intention. Stacks are either empty (nil) or are obtained by pushing a 0 or a 1 on a correct stack. There are two error states: an error stack occurring whenever we try to pop an empty stack and an error element occurring whenever we try to take the top of an empty stack. Now we can prove equations that hold in $\mathcal{R}_{\text{stack2}}$.

EXAMPLE 3

We want to prove the theorem

$$\text{top}(\text{pop}(\text{push}(e, s))) = \text{if}(\text{goodstack}(\text{push}(e, s)), \text{top}(s), \text{errel})$$

This theorem cannot be proved using a rewrite proof because both sides of the equation are irreducible. However, the equation holds for all its ground instances and can be proved using the ReDuX prover, which is based on the inductive completion theory developed in [17]. During the inductive completion process the following lemmas will be proposed and proved automatically:

$$
\begin{aligned}
\text{if}(\text{goodstack}(s), \text{top}(s), \text{errel}) &= \text{top}(s) \\
\text{if}(\text{goodstack}(s), \text{if}(\text{goodstack}(s), 1, \text{errel}), \text{errel}) &= \text{if}(\text{goodstack}(s), 1, \text{errel}) \\
\text{if}(\text{goodstack}(s), \text{if}(\text{goodstack}(s), 0, \text{errel}), \text{errel}) &= \text{if}(\text{goodstack}(s), 0, \text{errel}) \\
\text{if}(\text{goodstack}(\text{push}(e, s)), \text{if}(\text{goodstack}(s), e, \text{errel}), \text{errel}) &= \text{if}(\text{goodstack}(s), e, \text{errel})
\end{aligned}
$$

□

4 HARDWARE DESIGN AND VERIFICATION

Hardware can often be specified by functional equations, and it was shown by Buchenrieder [4] that these specifications can also be compiled into time- and space-efficient VLSI circuits. These functional equations are very similar to term-rewriting systems in that they normally equate first-order terms; however, built-in knowledge about Boolean operators is assumed.

We want to consider pure logic circuits, and circuits consisting of logic gates and flip-flops controlled by a single clock where in each cycle the signals must be buffered in a flip-flop. All such circuits can be specified by term-rewriting systems and thus the methods presented in the last section can be applied to verify hardware designs.

The circuit descriptions in textual form, which are often the (intermediate) results of hardware design tools, may already be similar to equations. Here we want to discuss how a subset of net lists in the Berkley Logic Interchange Format (BLIF) [43] can be translated into an algebraic specification.

4.1 Pure Logic Circuits

First we must encode the properties of the Boolean operators. Therefore, the signature must contain a function symbol for each Boolean operator and two constants for the signal values low and high.

EXAMPLE 4

$$
\mathscr{F}_{\text{Bool}} = \begin{cases}
L: & \to \text{SIGNAL} \\
H: & \to \text{SIGNAL} \\
\neg: \text{SIGNAL} & \to \text{SIGNAL} \\
\vee: \text{SIGNAL} \times \text{SIGNAL} & \to \text{SIGNAL} \\
\wedge: \text{SIGNAL} \times \text{SIGNAL} & \to \text{SIGNAL} \\
\supset: \text{SIGNAL} \times \text{SIGNAL} & \to \text{SIGNAL} \\
\equiv: \text{SIGNAL} \times \text{SIGNAL} & \to \text{SIGNAL} \\
\oplus: \text{SIGNAL} \times \text{SIGNAL} & \to \text{SIGNAL}
\end{cases}
$$

□

Given such a signature the operators can be defined for all argument values by appropriate rewrite rules.

EXAMPLE 5

$$
\begin{aligned}
\wedge(L, x) &\to L \\
\wedge(H, x) &\to x
\end{aligned}
$$

□

Such a specification of the Boolean operators is incomplete in that we assume properties of the operators to hold which cannot be proved by rewrite proofs. As a matter of fact, induction proofs are needed to prove these properties.

EXAMPLE 6

Given the specification of $\wedge$ in Example 5 there is no way of proving $\wedge(x, y) = \wedge(y, x)$. However, one can verify that this equation holds whenever x and y are substituted by ground terms.

□

Because inductive proofs are rather expensive compared to rewrite proofs, it is preferable to have a term-rewriting system that produces unique normal forms for any Boolean formula. Such a term-rewriting system exists. It was first presented by Hsiang [44] and uses implicit knowledge about the associativity and commutativity of the operators AND ($\wedge$) and EXCLUSIVE-OR ($\oplus$). The resulting normal form is the so-called *reduced exclusive-or normal form,* which was known before as Stone polynomials [45] and is often called the Reed-Muller expansion by hardware designers. The term-rewriting system producing the reduced EXCLUSIVE-OR normal form is shown in Specification 4.

SPECIFICATION 4

$$\mathcal{R}_{\text{xnf}} = \begin{cases} \vee(p,q) & \to \ \oplus(\wedge(p,q), \oplus(p,q)) \\ \supset(p,q) & \to \ \oplus(\wedge(p,q), \oplus(p,H)) \\ \equiv(p,q) & \to \ \oplus(p, \oplus(q,H)) \\ \neg(p) & \to \ \oplus(p,H) \\ \oplus(p,L) & \to \ p \\ \oplus(p,p) & \to \ L \\ \oplus(q, \oplus(p,p)) & \to \ q \\ \wedge(p,H) & \to \ p \\ \wedge(p,p) & \to \ p \\ \wedge(q, \wedge(p,p)) & \to \ \wedge(q,p) \\ \wedge(p,L) & \to \ L \\ \wedge(p, \oplus(q,r)) & \to \ \oplus(\wedge(p,q), \wedge(p,r)) \end{cases}$$

A BLIF-net list describing a logic circuit consists of a list of entries, each of which describes a logical function. An entry starts with a function specification of the form

$$.\text{name } X_1 \ldots X_n Y$$

which specifies the names of the input variables $X_1, \ldots, X_n$ and the output variable Y. The function definition is a list of m lines of the form

$$x_{i_1} \ldots x_{i_n} y_i$$

for $1 \le i \le m$ where the x_{i_j} are one of 0, 1, or − (don't care). Such a BLIF entry defines the functional equation

$$Y = \bigvee_{i=1}^{m} \left(\bigwedge_{j \in \{k | x_{i_k} = 1\}} X_j \wedge \bigwedge_{j \in \{k | x_{i_k} = 0\}} \neg X_j \right)$$

To specify the functions in a net list, one constant for each logic variable occurring in the net list must be added to $\mathcal{F}_{\text{Bool}}$ and one rewrite rule for each function definition must be added to $\mathcal{R}_{\text{xnf}}$.

The use of EXCLUSIVE-OR normal form-based term-rewriting systems for hardware specification has already been presented in [1]. The authors of this article use a refutation technique proposed by Hsiang [44] in order to perform resolution-like proofs by completion. In a refutation technique, the converse of the theorem is added to the specification, and the theorem holds if an inconsistency (in our case the equation $L = H$) is then derived. One problem with this approach is that none of the intermediate results produced even by a successful proof can be retained for future use, because they were obtained from an inconsistent system. Usually, intermediate results in a proof are useful lemmas, which may be used to shorten future proofs or which may give additional hints about the specification. Proofs by inductive completion are an alternative to these refutation proofs, and here all lemmas derived during a successful proof are valid theorems as well.

Let us close this section with a few remarks on the advantages and disadvantages of using term-rewriting systems with or without built-in knowledge of associative and commutative operators. Term-rewriting systems modulo associativity and commutativity are a very powerful tool. Thus many equations can be proved using simple AC rewrite proofs and only few induction proofs are needed. On the other hand, they need expensive basic operations (equality tests, matches, unifications) both with regard to their computational complexity [46] and the cost of implementing the algorithms. It may be possible to find specializations that improve on the general procedures for the special application of hardware design verification (see also [44]). Another possibility is to use Buchberger's algorithm for multivariate polynomials over $\mathbf{Z}/(2 \cdot \mathbf{Z})$ modulo $\{x^2 - x \mid x$ is an indeterminate$\}$ in order to compute the EXCLUSIVE-OR normal form [47]. Pure term-rewriting systems without built-in knowledge of associative and commutative operators are based on rather easy and fast basic operations. Their disadvantage is that they offer a rather weak calculus and that we may have to perform many induction proofs. A good combination of both techniques is an open field of research.

4.2 Synchronous Circuits

When specifying synchronous circuits, all logic variables must be considered to be functions of time. If all events are controlled by a single clock, time may well be modeled by the natural numbers asuming that all states are reset at a well-defined point in time (t_0).

Flip-flops (we assume clocked D flip-flops) have one input and one output, each of which is a function of time such that the output at time $t + 1$ equals the input at time t or its negation. Therefore, the *abstract concept* of a flip-flop or a functional unit containing flip-flops must be described by higher order functions. This may be one reason why higher order theorem provers like HOL [48] are often the first choice for the automation of hardware design verification. But for hardware specification and verification, the *abstract concept* of a flip-flop is not really needed. All we need are *concrete instances* of flip-flops, which can be specified using pure first-order terms as shown next.

To specify a synchronous circuit, we need a many-sorted algebra with two sorts. One sort SIGNAL for objects of a Boolean type and a sort TIME to describe the time by natural numbers. The sort SIGNAL contains the constants L and H and all Boolean connectives described in Section 4.1. There is a constant 0 of sort TIME and a unary function symbol $s :$ TIME $\rightarrow$ TIME, which denotes the successor (time step) function. All logic variables become unary function symbols of sort SIGNAL, that have arguments of sort TIME.

The net list specification in BLIF of the types of flip-flops we can handle looks as follows:

```
.latch  I  O  i
```

where I is an input variable, O is an output variable, and $i \in \{0, 1\}$ is the initial value of O. In some cases, unknown or don't care initial values may also be admissible. Such a latch description is translated into two rules. One, depending on the value of i, describing the initialization (reset state)

$$O(0) \to L \quad \text{or} \quad O(0) \to H$$

and one describing the function of the flip-flop

$$O(s(t)) \to I(t)$$

Thus, each instance of a flip-flop is fully defined by its input and output variables and its initial value. The full equational circuit specification consists of the signature described, the rewrite rules for the logic connectives ($\mathcal{R}_{xnf}$), and the rules extracted from the function and latch definitions of the net list.

4.3 The Hardware Design Cycle

Given a hardware specification by equations and rewrite rules, its verification consists of the same steps as the verification of software. We must complete the equations and rules, analyze their ground normal forms, and prove essential theorems using either rewrite or inductive proofs. Note that in the ground normal form analysis step the constants L and H should turn out to be the only irreducible constants of sort SIGNAL. Otherwise we will have logic variables in our circuit that are undefined for some points of time. Analogously, irreducible ground terms of sort TIME must be of the forms 0, $s(0)$, $s(s(0))$, ... Whenever we detect an unexpected object, such as a logical value other than L or H, or a theorem that is invalid in the specification but reflects a desired property of the design, we must correct the specification and repeat the verification process.

The kind of theorems one wants to prove are manyfold. First one can try to verify all kinds of relations among logic variables whether they are time dependent (e.g., the period of a counter) or not [e.g., idempotency of a function $f : f(x, x) = x$]. The latter ones can often be proved using rewrite proofs, but showing that an equation holds for all points of time normally requires induction over time.

Another reason why one would like to prove theorems stems from the way circuits are designed. Even though there may be an adequate equational specification for the functionality of a design there may be design tools that need another form of input than equations, or parts of a circuit must even be designed by hand. Then it is important to check whether the specification extracted from the net list corresponds to the original specification of the expected functionality of the circuit.

The third important application of the proof step arises if a part of a circuit is replaced by a different realization of that part. Then one would like to prove that the two circuits realize the same function by proving that their respective equational specifications are equivalent.

Let us look at a small example, which already shows the aspects of software or hardware design and verification dicussed earlier. We consider a 2-bit counter whose most significant bit is stored in a logic variable B and whose least significant bit is stored in A. The BLIF-net list for such a 2-bit counter may look as follows:

```
.latch    A      T2     0
.latch    B      T3     0

.name     CIN    A      T1
11        1
.name     CIN    A      T2
10        1
01        1
.name     T1     B      T3
10        1
01        1
.name     CIN
          1
```

To translate this net list into an algebraic specification, we must add operators for A, B, $T1$, $T2$, $T3$, and CIN to $\mathcal{F}_{\text{Bool}}$ and add the rules associated with the functional specification to $\mathcal{R}_{\text{xnf}}$. Since we want to show a relation between the 2-bit counter and the integer division by 2, we also add to the specification a function symbol $\frac{1}{2}$ and rules describing the function of $\frac{1}{2}$:

SPECIFICATION 5

$$\mathcal{F}_{\text{count2}} = \mathcal{F}_{\text{Bool}} \cup \begin{cases} 0: & \to \text{TIME} \\ s: & \text{TIME} \to \text{TIME} \\ \frac{1}{2}: & \text{TIME} \to \text{TIME} \\ A: & \text{TIME} \to \text{SIGNAL} \\ B: & \text{TIME} \to \text{SIGNAL} \\ T1: & \text{TIME} \to \text{SIGNAL} \\ T2: & \text{TIME} \to \text{SIGNAL} \\ T3: & \text{TIME} \to \text{SIGNAL} \\ \text{CIN}: & \text{TIME} \to \text{SIGNAL} \end{cases}$$

$$\mathcal{R}_{\text{count2}} = \mathcal{R}_{\text{xnf}} \cup \begin{cases} \frac{1}{2}(0) & \to 0 \\ \frac{1}{2}(s(0)) & \to 0 \\ \frac{1}{2}(s(s(t))) & \to s(\frac{1}{2}(t)) \\ A(0) & \to L \\ A(s(t)) & \to T2(t) \\ B(0) & \to L \\ B(s(t)) & \to T3(t) \\ T1(t) & \to \wedge(\text{CIN}(t), A(t)) \\ T2(t) & \to \vee(\wedge(\text{CIN}(t), \neg(A(t))), \wedge(\neg(\text{CIN}(t)), A(t))) \\ T3(t) & \to \vee(\wedge(T1(t), \neg(B(t))), \wedge(\neg(T1(t)), B(t))) \\ \text{CIN}(t) & \to H \end{cases}$$

Completion (modulo AC) of $\mathcal{R}_{count2}$ yields this canonical term-rewriting system:

SPECIFICATION 6

$$\mathcal{R}_{count2^*} = \mathcal{R}_{xnf} \cup \left\{ \begin{array}{ll} \frac{1}{2}(0) & \to 0 \\ \frac{1}{2}(s(0)) & \to 0 \\ \frac{1}{2}(s(s(t))) & \to s(\frac{1}{2}(t)) \\ A(0) & \to L \\ A(s(t)) & \to \oplus(H, A(t)) \\ B(0) & \to L \\ B(s(t)) & \to \oplus(B(t), A(t)) \\ T1(t) & \to A(t) \\ T2(t) & \to \oplus(H, A(t)) \\ T3(t) & \to \oplus(B(t), A(t)) \\ CIN(t) & \to H \end{array} \right.$$

Thus, the functions $T1$, $T2$, $T3$, and CIN are actually obsolete because they can be replaced by equivalent expressions, that is, these correspond to auxiliary logic variables that are not really needed to describe the circuit. The set of ground terms that are irreducible by $\mathcal{R}_{count2^*}$ can be described by the following context-free grammar:

$$\langle SIGNAL \rangle ::= L \mid H$$

$$\langle TIME \rangle \quad ::= 0 \mid s(\langle TIME \rangle)$$

and the finite set of ground terms presenting the induction bases and steps is

$$\{L, H, 0, s(0), s(s(0)), s(s(s(t)))\}$$

This means that all logic variables are defined for all points in time because the only irreducible ground terms of sort SIGNAL are L and H. By the same argument, our specification of the time is correct because the irreducible ground terms of sort TIME are 0 or an arbitrary number of s stacked over a 0, which is isomorphic to the natural numbers (i.,e. our choice for modeling the time in a synchronous circuit). Now we can prove some interesting theorems about our circuit for a plausibility check.

EXAMPLE 7

Let us prove that the value of A is the same every other clock cycle, that is, $A(s(s(t))) = A(t)$. $A(s(s(t)))$ reduces to $A(t)$ and therefore the theorem holds.

$\square$

EXAMPLE 8

Now we want to prove the same for B: $B(s(s(t))) = B(t)$. $B(s(s(t)))$ reduces to $\oplus(B(t), H)$. Thus, the new equation $\oplus(B(t), H) = B(t)$ can be derived. Together with $B(0) \to L$ the equation (critical pair) $L = H$ will be deduced, which is clearly a contradiction, and, therefore $B(s(s(t))) = B(t)$ does not hold. This is certainly a correct answer if B is the most significant bit of a 2-bit counter.

□

EXAMPLE 9

In a 2-bit counter, B should have period 4: $B(s(s(s(s(t))))) = B(t)$ can be demonstrated by a rewrite proof.

□

So far our equations were simple, that is, a rewrite proof was sufficient to prove them. The next equation describes an arithmetic relation between A and B that can only be proved by induction.

EXAMPLE 10

B is half as fast as A, where half is taken modulo 2. This can be expressed by the equation $B(t) = A(\frac{1}{2}(t))$. Both terms are irreducible. The inductive completion procedure will propose the new lemma $A(\frac{1}{2}(s(t))) = \oplus(A(\frac{1}{2}(t)), A(t))$ and show that both the original equation and the lemma are inductive consequences of $\mathcal{R}_{count2^*}$.

□

5 CONCLUSION

We have discussed the state of the art in term-rewriting–based induction, which is now significantly more powerful than its origins in inductionless induction. We then showed to what extent pure term-rewriting techniques can be useful for hardware and software design verification. Equational (algebraic) specification techniques have the potential to serve as a design and specification language in both fields; in the hardware area, net lists can also be translated into equational specifications. Standard term-rewriting systems can then execute the specifications symbolically, providing rapid prototyping, and term-rewriting–based induction can be used to verify properties of the specifications. In addition, an automated analysis of the ground-term algebra corresponding to the specification gives valuable feedback about missed subcases in the specification of functions.

It appears to us that a common specification language with an attached verification tool should be an important step toward a practical system for hardware and software codesign.

ACKNOWLEDGMENTS

We are indebted to Klaus Buchenrieder and Udo Kebschull for many critical hints and helpful discussions. Nicholas Nevin implemented a first version of the hardware design verification system, using a Gröbner basis technique to verify Boolean equivalences. This work, which is part of his Ph.D. thesis research at The Ohio State University, provided us with an invaluable set of initial examples.

REFERENCES

[1] Mandalagiri S. Chandrasekhar, John P. Privitera, and Kenneth W. Conradt, "Application of Term Rewriting Techniques to Hardware Design Verification," in *24th ACM/IEEE Design Automation Conference*, pp. 277–282, ACM/IEEE, 1987.

[2] John Guttag, Ellis Horowitz, and David Musser, "Abstract Data Types and Software Validation," *Comm. ACM*, 21, pp. 1048–1064, 1978.

[3] Joseph A. Goguen, J. W. Thatcher, and E. W. Wagner, "Initial Algebra Approach to the Specification, Correctness, and Implementation of Abstract Data Types," Chap. 5 in *Data Structuring, Current Trends in Programming Methodology*, R. T. Yeh, Ed., Vol. IV, Prentice Hall, Englewood Cliffs, NJ, 1978.

[4] Klaus J. Buchenrieder, "A Standard-Cell Placement Tool for the Translation of Behavioral Descriptions Into Efficient Layouts," PhD Thesis, The Ohio State University, 1988.

[5] Jørgen Staunstrup, Steven Garland, and John Guttag, "Mechanized Verification of Circuit Descriptions Using the Larch Prover," in *Theorem Provers in Circuit Design*, V. Stavridou, T. F. Melham, and R. T. Boute, Eds., Vol. 10 of *IFIP Transactions A*, Nijmegen, Netherlands, pp. 277–299, Elsevier, Amsterdam, 1992.

[6] Stephen J. Garland and John V. Guttag, "Inductive Methods for Reasoning about Abstract Data Types," in *Proc. 15th PoPL*, pp. 219–228, San Diego, California, ACM SIGACT-SIGPLAN, New York, 1988.

[7] David R. Musser, "Proving Inductive Properties of Abstract Data Types," in *Proc. 7th PoPL*, Las Vegas, Nevada, pp. 154–162, ACM, New York, 1980.

[8] Robert S. Boyer and J Strother Moore, *A Computational Logic*, Academic Press, Orlando, FL, 1979.

[9] Wolfgang Küchlin, "A Confluence Criterion Based on the Generalised Newman Lemma," in *Proc. European Conference on Computer Algebra, Volume II: Research Contributions*, Vol. 204 of *LNCS*, pp. 390–399, Springer-Verlag, Berlin, 1985.

[10] Wolfgang Küchlin, "Equational Completion by Proof Transformation," PhD Thesis, Swiss Federal Institute of Technology, Switzerland, June 1986. (Also as Equational Completion by Proof Simplification, Report 86-02, Mathematics, ETH Zürich, May 1986.)

[11] Deepak Kapur, David R. Musser, and Paliath Narendran, "Only Prime Superpositions Need Be Considered in the Knuth-Bendix Completion Procedure," *J. Symbolic Computation*, 6(1), pp. 19–36, 1988.

[12] Leo Bachmair and Nachum Dershowitz, "Critical Pair Criteria for Completion," *J. Symbolic Computation*, 6(1), pp. 1–18, August 1988.

[13] Gérard Huet and Jean-Marie Hullot, "Proofs by Induction in Equational Theories with Constructors," *J. Computer Sys. Sci.*, 25, pp. 239–266, 1982.

[14] Jean-Pierre Jouannaud and Emmanuel Kounalis, "Proofs by Induction in Equational Theories without Constructors," *Info. Computation*, 82, pp. 1–33, 1989.

[15] Laurent Fribourg, "A Strong Restriction of the Inductive Completion Procedure," *J. Symbolic Computation*, 8(3), pp. 253–276, September 1989.

[16] Franz Winkler, "A Criterion for Eliminating Unnecessary Reductions in the Knuth-Bendix Algorithm," Technical Report 83-14.0, CAMP, Universität Linz, Austria, May 1983.

[17] Wolfgang Küchlin, "Inductive Completion by Ground Proof Transformation," Chap. 7 in *Rewriting Techniques,* H. Aït-Kaci and M. Nivat, Eds., pp. 211–244, Academic Press, New York, 1989.

[18] Reinhard Bündgen and Wolfgang Küchlin, "Computing Ground Reducibility and Inductively Complete Positions," in *Rewriting Techniques and Applications,* N. Dershowitz, Ed., Vol. 355 of *LNCS,* pp. 59–75, Springer-Verlag, Berlin, 1989.

[19] Hubert Comon, "An Effective Method for Handling Initial Algebras," in *Algebraic and Logic Programming,* J. Grabowski, E. Horowitz, and W. Wechler, Eds., Vol. 343 of *LNCS,* pp. 108–118, Springer-Verlag, Berlin, 1988.

[20] Grigori A. Kucherov, "A New Quasi-Reducibility Testing Algorithm and Its Application to Proofs by Induction," in *Algebraic and Logic Programming,* J. Grabowski, P. Lescanne, and W. Wechler, Eds., Vol. 343 of *LNCS,* Springer-Verlag, Berlin, 1988.

[21] Deepak Kapur, Paliath Narendran, and Hantao Zhang, "Automatic Inductionless Induction Using Test Sets," *J. Symbolic Computation,* 11, pp. 83–111, 1991.

[22] Grigori A. Kucherov, "On Relationship Between Term Rewriting Systems and Regular Tree Languages," in *Rewriting Techniques and Applications,* Ronald V. Book, Ed., Vol. 488 of *LNCS,* Springer-Verlag, Berlin, 1991.

[23] Reinhard Bündgen and Hasko Eckhardt, "A Fast Algorithm for Ground Normal Form Analysis," in *Algebraic and Logic Programming,* H. Kirchner and G. Levi, Eds., Vol. 632 of *LNCS,* pp. 291–305, Springer-Verlag, Berlin, 1992.

[24] Gérard Huet and Derek C. Oppen, "Equations and Rewrite Rules: A Survey," Technical Report CSL-111, SRI International, Stanford, 1980.

[25] Nachum Dershowitz, "Completion and Its Applications," Chap. 2 in *Rewriting Techniques,* H. Aït-Kaci and M. Nivat, Eds., pp. 31–85, Academic Press, New York, 1989.

[26] Nachum Dershowitz and Jean-Pierre Jouannaud, "Rewrite Systems," Chap. 6 in *Formal Models and Semantics,* Vol. 2 of *Handbook of Theoretical Computer Science,* Elsevier, New York, 1990.

[27] Nachum Dershowitz, "Termination of Rewriting," *J. Symbolic Computation,* 3, pp. 69–116, 1987.

[28] Garret Birkhoff, "On the Structure of Abstract Algebras," *Proc. Cambridge Philos. Soc.,* 31, pp. 433–454, 1935.

[29] Donald E. Knuth and Peter B. Bendix, "Simple Word Problems in Universal Algebra," in *Computational Problems in Abstract Algebra,* J. Leech, Ed., Pergamon Press, New York, 1970.

[30] Gérard Huet and Jean-Marie Hullot, "Proofs by Induction in Equational Theories with Constructors," in *Proc. 21st FoCS,* Lake Placid, NY, pp. 96–107, IEEE, New York, 1980.

[31] Dieter Hofbauer and Ralf-Detlef Kutsche, "Proving Inductive Theorems Based on Term Rewriting Systems," in *Algebraic and Logic Programming,* J. Grabowski, E. Horowitz, and W. Wechler, Eds., Vol. 343 of *LNCS,* pp. 180–190, Springer Verlag, Berlin, 1988.

[32] Uday S. Reddy, "Term Rewriting Induction," in *10th International Conference on Automated Deduction*, M. E. Stickel, Ed., Vol. 449 of *LNCS*, pp. 162–177, Kaiserslautern, Germany, Springer-Verlag, July 1990.

[33] G. Peterson and M. Stickel, "Complete Sets of Reductions for Some Equational Theories, " *J. ACM*, 28, pp. 223–264, 1981.

[34] Joseph A. Goguen, "How to Prove Algebraic Inductive Hypotheses Without Induction, with Applications to the Correctness of Data Type Implementations," in *Proc. 5th CADE*, Vol. 87 of *LNCS*, pp. 356–373, Les Arcs, France, Springer Verlag, Berlin, 1980.

[35] John Guttag, "Abstract Data Types and the Development of Data Structure," *Comm. ACM*, 20(6), pp. 396–404, 1977.

[36] Tobias Nipkow and G. Weikum, "A Decidability Result About Sufficient Completeness of Axiomatically Specified Abstract Data Types," in *Sixth GI Conference on Theoretical Computer Science*, Vol. 145 of *LNCS*, pp. 257–268, Springer-Verlag, Berlin, 1982.

[37] Emmanuel Kounalis, "Completeness in Data Type Specifications," in *Proc. European Conference on Computer Algebra, Volume II: Research Contributions*, Vol. 204 of *LNCS*, pp. 348–362, Springer-Verlag, Berlin, 1985.

[38] E. Kounalis and H. Zhang, "A General Completeness Check for Equational Specifications," in *Proc. Hungarian Conference of Computer Science*, pp. 348–362, 1985.

[39] Hubert Comon, "Sufficient Completeness, Term Rewriting Systems and 'Anti-unification'" in *8th International Conference on Automated Deduction*, J. Siekmann, Ed., Vol. 230 of *LNCS*, pp. 128–138. Springer-Verlag, Berlin, 1986.

[40] Reinhard Bündgen, "Term Completion Versus Algebraic Completion," PhD Thesis, Universität Tübingen, Germany, May 1991. (reprinted as report WSI 91–3).

[41] Deepak Kapur, Paliath Narendran, and Hantao Zhang, "On Sufficient-Completeness and Related Properties of Term Rewriting Systems," *Acta Info.*, 24(4), pp. 395–415, 1987.

[42] Reinhard Bündgen, "The ReDuX System Documentation," Technical Report 91–5, Wilhelm-Schickard-Institut, Universität Tübingen, Germany, 1991.

[43] University of California at Berkeley. *Berkeley Logic Interchange Format (BLIF)*. Unpublished system documentation.

[44] Jieh Hsiang, "Topics in Automated Theorem Proving and Program Generation," PhD Thesis, University of Illinois at Urbana-Champaign, 1982.

[45] M. H. Stone, "The Theory of Representations for Boolean Algebras," *Trans. American Math. Soc.*, 40, pp. 37–111, 1936.

[46] Deepak Kapur and Paliath Narendran, "Matching, Unification and Complexity—A Preliminary Note," *ACM-SIGSAM Bull.*, 21(4), pp. 6–9, November 1987.

[47] Deepak Kapur and Paliath Narendran, "An Equational Approach to Theorem Proving in First-Order Predicate Calculus," in *9th IJCAI*, Los Angeles, CA, 1985.

[48] Michael J. C. Gordon, "HOL: A Proof Generating System for Higher Order Logic," in *VLSI Specification, Verifications and Synthesis*, G. Birtwistle and P. A. Subrahmanyam, Eds., pp. 73–128. Kluwer Academic Publishers, New York, 1988.

CHAPTER 2

A Declarative Formalism Supporting Hardware/Software Codesign

Raymond Boute
Department of Computer Science
University of Nijmegen
Nijmegen, The Netherlands

Abstract: Two common pitfalls are pointed out: the assumption that hardware can be understood satisfactorily as "programs on silicon," and the idea that all formal hardware or software descriptions should be executable. We argue that relevant phenomena in hardware are more general than can be reflected by programs, and that formalisms for reasoning about them must allow the usage of nonexecutable descriptions (e.g., mathematical equations). Conversely, in any formalism providing this degree of generality, the particular case of computational processes and the programs describing them can be handled very conveniently.

Funmath (*Fun*ctional *math*ematics) is a formalism for supporting theory development, analysis, and design for hardware and software systems. The full language has a *declarative* interpretation (only), and can be used for mathematical modeling and for pure behavioral specification. The subset *Reals* (*Real*izable *s*ystems) has an additional interpretation expressing realizations of systems and circuits, and the subset *Comma* (*Com*putational *ma*thematics) has an additional interpretation as a functional programming language.

The basis of Funmath is *functional* because this is most convenient for *transformational reasoning*. Ensuring close notational similarity to the "common" language of pure and applied mathematics was a major design goal. This is achieved by the orthogonal combination of only four basic language constructs: identifier, (function) application, tuple denotation, and a generalized form of lambda abstraction. The first three also support a description style without variables.

Such surprising simplicity was made possible by the underlying semantic principle, namely, the uncompromising unification of lists, sequences, tuples, and functions, with the Funmath generalized Cartesian product as a matching type definition operator. The use of Funmath for specification and transformational reasoning in hardware and software design is illustrated by means of two representative examples.

1 INTRODUCTION

1.1 Problem Statement

Most present-day hardware description languages are strongly inspired by programming languages. They offer constructs that, when interpreted by a simulator (as opposed to a silicon compiler), coincide with the usual constructs for sequential programming. Through the constructs that reflect the inherently parallel nature of hardware, they support parallel programming as well. Finally, they also provide the data types common in programming languages, and even some additional ones (e.g., *signals* in VHDL-VHSIC Hardware Description Language). All these observations would suggest that hardware description languages are actually very suitable for hardware/software codesign.

However, this is not the case, and the reason is rather ironic: hardware description languages (HDLs) inspired by programming languages are quite suitable for programming, but are not fully adequate for hardware description. Indeed, as other authors have also pointed out, a program does not reflect well what goes on in a circuit. The processes in continuous time are more general, as can be seen from their mathematical models, than computational processes. Computational processes are meant here in the precise sense of the theory of computation, and hence constitute exactly the processes that are expressed by programming languages.

Furthermore, because these HDLs allow algorithmic descriptions only, they express realizations rather than specifications. This requires the hardware specifier to make design decisions, which can render the description overspecific in comparison with a pure (input/output or black-box) specification. Even worse is that such design decisions are based on programming considerations rather than on hardware considerations. In the very worst case, the hardware designer must have detailed knowledge of the silicon compilation process if he or she wants to influence the optimality of the resulting circuit via the source program. The term *simulation program* more accurately characterizes such a description.

Similar observations hold for software specification: Languages restricted to executable expressions impose prior design work to bring proper specifications into executable form. Hence the term *executable specification* is highly misleading, because it represents the inability to express the intermediate results of this design work within the language as an advantage. The term *rapid prototyping* more accurately characterizes the derivation of such a description.

1.2 Rationale for a Solution

To unify hardware and software successfully, their differences must be recognized right from the start. More specifically, it is most advantageous to consider both design fields as particular instances of the more general framework that, in applied science, already serves as the common basis for systems theory and signal processing. In this framework, computations and algorithimic processes very naturally fit into discrete systems theory. In the epistemological sense, they constitute the particular case, which is exactly the opposite of the "programs on silicon" view.

Second, any formalism for hardware/software codesign should allow for nonexecutable expressions (implicit functions, equational definitions, and so on). This does not mean that the opportunities for automated support are reduced, rather the opposite. Apart from "trivial" forms of automated support such as parsing and editing, one can imagine a wide variety of nontrivial support activities such as type checking, supervision of transformations (checking, making suggestions, archiving), theorem proving (verification, derivation of properties), and symbolic equation solving (computer algebra). The degree to which any of these particular forms of support can be automated depends, of course, on the state of the art.

1.3 The Proposed Formalism

By the term *formalism* we mean a *language* or notation together with a style of *reasoning* to be supported by that language.

Funmath (*Fun*ctional *math*ematics) is a formalism supporting anaysis, design, and theory development for hardware and software systems. Obtaining wide applicability while keeping the language small is made possible through Funmath's support of multiple interpretations:

1. The full language has a declarative interpretation (only), i.e., it allows forms that need not have an operational interpretation (in the sense of being executable or describing the structure of a circuit), yet are mathematically meaningful. It is essentially a streamlining of the "common" language of (pure and applied) mathematics that keeps its notation fully recognizable. The proposed solution to these seemingly conflicting requirements turns out to be surprisingly simple, due to the notion of *function* as the basis for the language. Various traditionally monolithic and mutually unrelated *ad hoc* notations are reconstructed from a limited number of smaller functional entities, combined with higher order functions.

2. The *Reals* (*Real*izable *s*ystems) subset supports a multiplicity of models for systems and circuits, ranging from structure (interconnection of subsystems) to various static and dynamic behavioral models in discrete and continuous domains (time and value). Reals is a Funmath data type that can be seen as a system description language. As a language, this data type has no preconceived semantics; instead, we have uncommitted types and operators to which multiple system semantics can be attached that use the full (declarative) language itself as the metalanguage.

3. The *Comma* (*Com*putational *m*athematics) subset is a ful-fledged functional programming language. In principle, it consists simply of the executable part of the full language.

The style of reasoning for which this language is intended is transformational, and mostly even equational, i.e., based on equality and substitution.

The definition phase of the Funmath language is nearing completion. It has undergone some streamlining and simplification since earlier introductions [1,2]. A precursor of the Reals subset, named Glass [3], has been fully defined and implemented in the context of a four-year Esprit project [4]; this language and its environment have been available in the public domain since 1991. The precise characterization of the Comma subset and its implementation are tasks planned for the near future.

1.4 Relation to Other Formalisms

The origin of Funmath lies in the analog domain, in particular, in describing continuous as well as discrete models for Glass. This has influenced the most crucial design decisions, the main one being the unification of lists, sequences, tuples, and functions, with the functional generalized Cartesian product as a matching type definition operator. Correspondingly, the use of higher order functions subsumes the various traditional abstractor notations for summation ($\Sigma_{i=0}^{n-1} x_i$), quantification ($\forall x : X . P$) and so on.

In spite of these different origins and entirely independent evolution, a strong similarity exists with certain aspects of the Veritas [5] and Nuprl [6] languages. With Veritas, the similarity is not restricted to the logical basis (classical rather than intuitionistic), but also includes some more detailed design decisions, such as the important role of dependent types, and truth values constituting a subtype of natural numbers. For Nuprl, the basis is different (constructive set or type theory, Martin-Löf style), but otherwise there are many practical similarities, such as the use of dependent Cartesian products for defining abstract algebras. As a specification language, Funmath also meets the objectives of the Z notation [7].

However, in comparison with these languages, the structure of Funmath is considerably simpler and more orthogonal, and thought was given to continuous domains right from the start, rather than as an afterthought.

The Reals subset provides all the expressive power of complicated HDLs such as VHDL, but without being restriced to a single predefined behavioral model such as the discrete event similation model of the VHDL *signal*.

The Comma subset is semantically similar to the functional programming languages Miranda [8], but has a richer and more orthogonal system. It also has a growth potential within Funmath because it can attach operational interpretations for parallel programming or logic programming to some of the purely declarative constructs of the full language.

1.5 Organization of This Chapter

Sections 2, 3, and 4 present the main aspects of the Funmath declarative language. Section 5 introduces some conventions regarding specification and transformational reasoning. Section 6 illustrates the use of Funmath for verification using a software example. Section 7 illustrates its use in transformational reasoning using a hardware example. Section 8 presents some conclusions regarding its relevance to hardware/software codesign.

2 GENERAL PRINCIPLES

2.1 Choice Between Two Options in Functional Language Design

An important decision regarding the means of expression in functional languages is whether to use constants and application only or to include variables and abstraction as well.

The use of constants and application only is illustrated in languages for purely foundational purposes such as combinator terms [9], in HDLs such as μFP [10], in Ruby [11] and the analog circuit description subset of FUNDS [12] (an early precursor of Glass), and in programming languages such as FP [13] and the so-called Bird-Meertens formalism [14]. Advantages are elegance of expression (at least for "regular" mathematical, hardware, or software structures) and conceptual simplicity. Disadvantages are that the expressions may become unwieldy for irregular structures (unless new *ad hoc* combinators, combining forms, etc., are introduced), and that the definition of the higher order functions themselves is most conveniently done by using variables anyway, even if they are often technically hidden at the metalevel.

The use of variables and abstraction is illustrated in languages for purely foundational purposes such as lambda terms (Church) [15], in HDLs such as Glass [3], and in programming languages such as Miranda [8]. The more general "bridging" properties of the scoping rules for variables give such languages an advantage when describing less regular structures. A major disadvatage is the significantly more complicated language design.

In designing Funmath, the decision was made at the earliest stage *not* to exclude variables and abstraction, so that new operators can be defined conveniently within the language, rather than at the metalevel only, as in FP. However, the advantages of a style without variables become increasingly apparent through its use, which is facilitated by a suitable collection of general-purpose operators introduced in Section 4.

2.2 Types, Functions, and Relations in Funmath

For expository purposes, we let $\mathcal{U}$ denote the type of all objects (including types and functions), $\mathcal{T}$ the type of all types, and $\mathcal{F}$ the type of all functions.

At this stage, *types* can be thought of as sets in a liberal sense, keeping in mind that suitable precautions or restrictions may be desirable to avoid the known paradoxes [16]. Type theory [17–19] and variants of set theory [20] offer a variety of solutions for this issue, without affecting the essence of the intended use of types in Funmath. Stratification as in Veritas currently appears to be the most likely candidate. However, the final choice has been postponed because the first priority in the design of the language is to obtain clear and succinct forms of expression based on the requirements derived from the envisaged applications areas so as to determine *what* is necessary and useful, before deciding *which* foundational models best satisfy these needs.

This unconventional attitude was possible because the essential principles turned out to be largely insensitive to the availability of a precise notion of type.

Now let A and B denote arbitrary types. A *function* from A to B is a mathematical object characterized by two elements: its *domain* (A), and its *mapping,* which associates with every element of A exactly one element of B. Two functions are *equal* if they have the same domain and the same mapping. A *codomain* for a function is a set containing the function's range and hence it need not be unique.

A *relation* in Funmath is a function with codomain $\mathbb{B}$ (the set of truth values 0 and 1). Using infix notation for a relation R between two types, aRb is just a function application, rather than an abbreviation for $(a, b) \in R$, as would be the case with the traditional definition. With this convention, all relational calculi of interest to hardware and software design can be expressed in Funmath without any change in notation. Furthermore, relations enjoy all privileges of functions. The unnecessary distinction between a relation and its characteristic function also disappears. A *predicate* is a relation operator.

3 THE LANGUAGE PROPER: FOUR WAYS TO DENOTE MATHEMATHICAL OBJECTS

Funmath essentially consists of only four constructs, constituting four ways of denoting mathematical objects. Everything else, in particular the various operators introduced in Section 4, is defined within the language itself using only these constructs, together with a (still preliminary) convention for operator overloading and polymorphism. The four constructs are identifier, application, tuple, and abstraction. The first three support the style without variables, whereas the fourth is useful for defining the operators themselves and for supporting the style with variables.

3.1 Identifier

An *identifier* designates a mathematical object by its name. An identifier is either a *constant* (discussed next) or a *variable* (always part of an abstraction, discussed in Section 3.4). An identifier designating a function is called an *operator.*

Among the *primitive constants* are the names for the universes $(\mathcal{U}, \mathcal{T}, \mathcal{F})$ and for associated functions, such as the set membership operator $\in$, the function domain operator $\mathcal{D}$, and the function range operator $\{-\}$. The latter two are operators from $\mathcal{F}$ to $\mathcal{T}$. If f is a function, then $\mathcal{D}f$ denotes the domain of f, and $\{f\}$ denotes the range of f. Incidentally, the singleton set containing just x is denoted by ιx, as in [20]. The empty set is denoted by $\emptyset$, and the function with empty domain by ε (called the *empty function*).

Primitive constants are also the names for basic types (e.g., $\mathbb{B}$ for Booleans, $\mathbb{N}$ for naturals), for basic values (e.g., 0, 1, 26.53, π, e), and for operators over them ($\wedge, +, \cdot$).

New constants are introduced by definitions of the form

$$\textbf{def } a : A \textbf{ with } P$$

introducing the new constant a satisfying $a \in A \wedge P$, where P is a proposition. The part $a : A$ is called the *type declaration* and P is called the *defining proposition.* To avoid confusion: $a : A$ *introduces* an identifier, *binds* it in the context (global for a constant, local for a variable), and states that a is in A, whereas $a \in A$ just states that the (already-bound) identifier a is in A.

In a definition, both *existence* and *uniqueness* of the object are required. This constitutes a proof obligation for the definer. Otherwise the definition is said to be *incorrect* and the constant is said to be *ill defined.* For example:

def $a : \mathbb{N}$ **with** $a^2 = 9$	correct (1 solution)
def $a : \mathbb{R}$ **with** $a^2 = -9$	incorrect (0 solutions)
def $a : \mathbb{C}$ **with** $a^2 = -9$	incorrect (2 solutions)
def $double : \mathbb{Z} \to \mathbb{Z}$ **with** $double\ n = 2 \cdot n$	correct (1 solution)
def $\sqrt{} : \mathbb{N} \to \mathbb{R}$ **with** $(\sqrt{n})^2 = n$	incorrect (∞ solutions)
def $\sqrt{} : \mathbb{N} \to \mathbb{R}$ **with** $(\sqrt{n})^2 = n \wedge \sqrt{n} \geq 0$	correct (1 solution)

As a matter of convenience, in function definitions, the defining proposition is implicitly quantified over the variable occurring in the argument position, e.g., n in the preceding examples. Explicit quantification is discussed soon.

As a matter of style, observe that a definition proceeds by successive refinement: the type declaration (down to a set) and the defining proposition (down to the intended object). It is important to distribute information in a clear way over these two steps.

3.2 Application

An application is a notation for designating a mathematical object as the image of some suitable object under some suitable function. For instance, using the correctly defined constants *double* and $\sqrt{}$ of the preceding subsection, $\sqrt{4}$ denotes the number 2 whereas $\{double\}$ denotes the set of even numbers.

The default syntax for application is prefix notation, namely, the image of x under f is denoted by fx, where f and x may be any of the four constructs.

However, as in mathematics, we shall freely introduce and use operators with other affix conventions such as infix (e.g., $3 + 7$) and postfix (e.g., $3!$). In that case, the affix conventions for the operator are established when the operator is introduced, using dashes [21] to indicate the argument position(s) with respect to the operator. The indexing of the dashes corresponds to the order of the domain denotations in the type expression in a fairly straightforward fashion, illustrated by the following example but not further elaborated here:

$$-_0 \$ \begin{array}{c} -^1 \\ -_2 \end{array} -_3 : A \to B \to C \to D \to E$$

Dashes with equal index or without index correspond to components of a same tuple (Cartesian product domain), with the positions ordered from left to right and from top to bottom.

3.3 Tuple Denotation

A tuple denotation denotes a function whose domain is a sufficiently small initial subset $0 \ . \ . \ n - 1$ (written $\square n$, where $\square$ is read "block") of $\mathbb{N}$ (natural numbers). For instance, if a, b, and c are objects, then the tuple denotation

$$a, b, c$$

denotes a function with domain $\square 3$ and mapping

$$(a, b, c)0 = a \qquad (a, b, c)1 = b \qquad (a, b, c)2 = c$$

Note in passing that the range of this function is $\{a, b, c\}$.

The tuple consisting of the single object a is expressed as the image τa of that object under the so-called *injection* operator τ; that is, τa denotes a function with domain $\square 1$ and with mapping $\tau a0 = a$. Clearly $\{\tau a\} = \iota a$. The tuple consisting of no objects has domain $\square 0$ (the empty set) and hence is the empty function ε.

Observe that $(a, b)c =$ if c then b else a, and hence no separate construct for conditionals is necessary. However, in Funmath there are two operators, ? and †, with the joint property:

$$c \ ? \ b \ \dagger \ a = (a, b)c$$

This reduces the need for parentheses in nested conditionals.

3.4 Abstraction

Whereas it is possible to do mathematics without variables, i.e., using constants, tuples, and applications only, the advantages of also having variables at our disposal have been obvious since their first use in mathematical notation. Here variables make their appearance in the following way.

An *abstraction* can be used to denote any function. Its general form is

$x : X \ . \ E$ earliest (but still valid) variant
$x : X \wedge P \ . \ E$ Rooijakkers variant
$E \ | \ x : X \wedge P$ van Thienen variant

where x is a variable or variable tuple (tuple built recursively from variables only), X a type, P a filtering proposition, and E an expression (built itself using the four constructs). The $\wedge P$ part is optional (also in the van Thienen variant) and stems from the notation used by Chandy and Misra [22]. The scope of the binding $x : X$ is local (P and E only).

These notations can be seen as derived from the well-known typed lambda expression [23]

$$\lambda x : X \ . \ E$$

by omitting the λ for convenience (the . or | suffices), and providing the additional option for further restricting the domain by means of the $\wedge P$ part.

All variants denote a function whose domain is the set of all x satisfying $x \in X \wedge P$ (assuming $P = 1$ if P is missing) and whose mapping is defined by:

$$(x : X \wedge P \cdot E)F = (E \text{ in which } F \text{ is properly substituted for } x)$$

A few examples illustrate this:

$$(n : \mathbb{Z} \cdot 2 \cdot n)3 = 6 \qquad\qquad \text{since } E = 2 \cdot n$$
$$double = n : \mathbb{Z} \cdot 2 \cdot n \qquad\qquad \text{by extensionality}$$
$$(n : \mathbb{N} \cdot n^2) = (n : \mathbb{Z} \wedge n \geq 0 \cdot n^2)$$

The following abbreviation exists for the van Thienen variant:

$$x : X \mid P \qquad \text{abbreviates} \qquad x : X \wedge P \cdot x$$

To familiarize oneself with this notation, it is a useful exercise to write the abstractions $a : A \mid b \in B$ and $a \in A \mid b : B$ in unabbreviated form (identifying P and E).

The van Thienen variant and its abbreviation are useful for writing set comprehension in the familiar way, for instance:

$$\{m : \mathbb{N} \mid m < n\} = \square n$$

$$\{2 \cdot m \mid m : \mathbb{Z}\} = \{double\} = \text{the set of even numbers}$$

In conjunction with the choice operator [—], it also yields an interpretation for the earlier (but still valid) Funmath syntax E **where** $x : X$ **with** P, namely:

$$E \text{ \textbf{where} } x : X \text{ \textbf{with} } P \qquad \text{stands for} \qquad [E \mid x : X \wedge P]$$

3.5 Preliminary Convention for Curry-Style Polymorphism

The preliminary Funmath convention for Curry-style polymorphism is:

$$\textbf{poly } b : B \wedge Q \cdot \textbf{def } a : A \textbf{ with } P$$

where A and P may depend on b. This notation was introduced as a temporary convention, while looking for a more elegant solution in the functional spirit of Funmath. Such a solution appears to have been found by van den Beuken, and will be presented by him in a later publication.

4 SOME USEFUL GENERAL-PURPOSE OPERATORS IN FUNMATH

This section introduces various useful operators for describing mathematical domains. Most of these operators yield interesting notational coincidences with the "common" language of mathematics when they are applied to either a *tuple* or to an *abstraction*, and interesting generalizations as well. The unification of lists, tuples, sequences, and functions plays an essential role in this respect, as will be seen from the following design considerations. In this first subsection, we freely use common mathematical symbols such as $\times$ and $\rightarrow$; their Funmath definition is given at a later stage.

4.1 Design Considerations for Funmath Operators

Observe that pairs (tuples) are functions, and $A \times A = \square 2 \rightarrow A$. This means that, in Funmath, dyadic functions with domain $A \times A$ are in fact higher order functions, whose domain is a set of functions with codomain A. Hence, for every commonly used $f : A \times A \rightarrow B$ we can (and often shall) define a more general F, over a "larger" set of functions with codomain A, such that

$$F(a, b) = f(a, b) \quad \text{(or } afb \text{ for an infix operator } -f-)$$

How much "larger" the domain of F will be depends on the properties of f, and on the most useful (not necessarily the highest attainable) degree of generalization. A few representative examples are the following:

f	$\wedge$	$\vee$	$\cup$	$\times$	$\circ$	$=$	$\neq$	$\leq$	$<$	$+$	$\cdot$
F	$\forall$	$\exists$	$\cup$	$\times$	$\bigcirc$	con	inj	asc	inc	Σ	Π

$f = +$ $F = \Sigma$ with $\Sigma\, g$ = sum of all gx as x ranges over $\mathcal{D}g$

$f = \wedge$ $F = \forall$ with $\forall\, g \equiv 0 \notin \{g\}$; similarly $\exists\, g \equiv 1 \in \{g\}$

$f = =$ $F = con$ with $con\, g \equiv \forall\, (x, y) : (\mathcal{D}g)^2 \,.\, gx = gy$

$f = \neq$ $F = inj$ with $inj\, g \equiv \forall\, (x, y) : (\mathcal{D}g)^2 \,.\, x \neq y \equiv gx \neq gy$

Of course, all these operators can be formally defined in Funmath (see later). We call F the *elastic extension* of f. Once F is defined, a definition of the form

$$\textbf{def } -f \ldots = F\, (-, \ldots) \qquad \text{preliminary syntax}$$

may extend f to tuples of size > 2 such that $afbfc = F(a, b, c)$. This new f (no new symbol is needed) is called the *variadic extension* of f. For example,

$$(a + b + c) = \Sigma\, (a, b, c) \qquad (a = b = c) \equiv con\, (a, b, c)$$

$$(a \wedge b \wedge c) \equiv \forall\, (a, b, c) \qquad (a \neq b \neq c) \equiv inj\, (a, b, c)$$

Traditional notational shortcuts now have a uniform basis. When applied to abstractions, we obtain familiar notations as in

$$\Sigma\, (i : \square n \,.\, x^i) = (x^n - 1)/(x - 1)$$

A further design decision in Funmath (which it shares with Veritas and APL) is that $\mathbb{B} = \{0, 1\}$ instead of $\mathbb{B} = \{\textbf{false}, \textbf{true}\}$. Hence, $\mathbb{B} \subseteq \mathbb{N} \subseteq \mathbb{R}$. The motivation is that every useful $b : \mathbb{B}^2 \rightarrow \mathbb{B}$ has useful counterparts $r : \mathbb{R}^2 \rightarrow \mathbb{R}$ or $r : \mathbb{R}^2 \rightarrow \mathbb{B}$ (a relation) satisfying $b = r \upharpoonright \mathbb{B}^2$. Representative examples are

b	$\equiv$	$\Leftarrow$	$\Rightarrow$	$>$	$<$	$\oplus$	$\langle\langle$	$\rangle\rangle$	$\wedge$	$\vee$	B	$\forall$	$\exists$
r	$=$	$\geq$	$\leq$	$>$	$<$	$\oplus$	$\langle\langle$	$\rangle\rangle$	$\sqcap$	$\sqcup$	R	$\sqcap$	$\sqcup$

where $\oplus$ denotes sum modulo 2 [24] and $\langle\langle$ (or $\rangle\rangle$) selects the leftmost (or rightmost) element of a pair. All these operators also have elastic extensions, two of which are shown in the table.

4.2 Operators for Function Types and for Functions

We have already introduced two primitive operators of type $\mathcal{F} \to \mathcal{T}$, namely:

- The domain operator $\mathcal{D}$, with $\mathcal{D}f = $ domain of f
- The range operator $\{—\}$, with $\{f\} = $ range of f.

The following properties of $\{—\}$ illustrate the aforementioned coincidences:

- $\{a, b, c\} = $ the set containing precisely $a, b,$ and c
- $\{E \mid x : X \wedge P\}$ and $\{x : X \mid P\}$ denote set abstraction.

Examples of other useful operators for function types are the function type arrow $\to$, the codomain predicate *cod*, and the codomain definer *Fam* ("family of"):

def $—\to— : \mathcal{F}$ **with** $\to = (A : \mathcal{T}, B : \mathcal{T}) \, . \, \{f : \mathcal{F} \mid \mathcal{D}f = A \wedge \{f\} \subseteq B\}$

def $— \ cod \ — : \mathcal{F} \times \mathcal{T} \to \mathbb{B}$ **with** $f \ cod \ B = \{f\} \subseteq B$

def $Fam : \mathcal{T} \to \mathcal{T}$ **with** $Fam \ B = \{f : \mathcal{F} \mid f \ cod \ B\}$

Observe that $\to \, \in \mathcal{T} \times \mathcal{T} \to \mathcal{T}$, but writing this in the definition would have been circular. An interesting application of these function type operators is to the definitions of the *all* and *some* operators

def $\forall \ : Fam \ \mathbb{B} \to \mathbb{B}$ **with** $(\forall \ f) \equiv 0 \notin \{f\}$

def $\exists \ : Fam \ \mathbb{B} \to \mathbb{B}$ **with** $(\exists \ f) \equiv 1 \in \{f\}$

which again yield some of the aforementioned coincidences:

$\forall \ (a, b, c) = a \wedge b \wedge c$ and $\exists \ (a, b, c) = a \vee b \vee c$
$\forall \ (x : X \, . \, P)$ and $\exists \ (x : X \, . \, P)$ denote quantification as usual

Furthermore, we introduce the *constant function definer* $^{\bullet}$:

def $—^{\bullet}— : \mathcal{U} \times \mathcal{T} \to \mathcal{F}$ **with** $a^{\bullet} A \in A \to \iota a$

and the *function domain restrictor* $\rceil$:

def $— \rceil — : \mathcal{F} \times \mathcal{T} \to \mathcal{F}$ **with** $f \rceil A = x : (\mathcal{D}f \cap A) \, . \, fx$

An important ordering relation on functions is the *subfunction* relation $\sqsubseteq$:

$$\textbf{def } - \sqsubseteq - : \mathcal{F} \times \mathcal{F} \to \mathbb{B} \textbf{ with } (f \sqsubseteq g) = (f = g \upharpoonright \mathcal{D}f)$$

whereas the *function merge* or *assembly* operator & maps a pair of functions to their least upper bound under $\sqsubseteq$, provided it exists:

$$\textbf{def } - \& - : \{(f, g) : \mathcal{F} \times \mathcal{F} \mid \forall x : (\mathcal{D}f \cap \mathcal{D}g) . fx = gx\} \to \mathcal{F} \textbf{ with}$$

$$f \And g = x : (\mathcal{D}f \cup \mathcal{D}g) . (x \in \mathcal{D}f ? fx \dagger gx)$$

The definition of its elastic extension & is left as an exercise.

The *one-point function constructor* $\mapsto$ is defined by

$$\textbf{def } - \mapsto - : \mathcal{U} \times \mathcal{U} \to \mathcal{F} \textbf{ with } (x \mapsto y) \in \iota x \to \iota y$$

The usage of these operators is illustrated by the definition:

$$\textbf{def } \tau : \mathcal{U} \to \mathcal{U}^1 \textbf{ with } \tau a = (0 \mapsto a)$$

and by the property that $(a, b, c) = \&(0 \mapsto a, 1 \mapsto b, 2 \mapsto c)$. It is also the basis for defining the elastic extension Σ of $+$. The defining properties for arguments with finite domain and codomain $\mathbb{C}$ are

$$\Sigma \, \varepsilon = 0$$

$$\Sigma \, (x \mapsto c) = c$$

$$\Sigma \, (f \And g) = \Sigma \, f + \Sigma \, g \text{ provided } \mathcal{D}f \cap \mathcal{D}g = \emptyset$$

Making this into a complete Funmath definition, extending to infinite series, and deriving the familiar properties is left as an exercise.

Often-used operators on functions are composition ($\circ$) and inverse ($^-$). These are defined here in such a way that $f \circ g$ and f^- always exist, although they might be the empty function ε. Auxiliary operators such as the bijective domain ($\mathcal{B}$), bijective range ($\mathcal{R}$), and injectivity (inj) and surjectivity ($surj$) predicates complete the menu:

$$\textbf{def } - \circ - : \mathcal{F}^2 \to \mathcal{F} \textbf{ with } f \circ g = x : \mathcal{D}g \land (gx \in \mathcal{D}f) . f(gx)$$

$$\textbf{def } \mathcal{B} : \mathcal{F} \to \mathcal{T} \textbf{ with } \mathcal{B}f = \{x : \mathcal{D}f \mid \forall y : \mathcal{D}f . fx = fy \equiv x = y\}$$

$$\textbf{def } \mathcal{R} : \mathcal{F} \to \mathcal{F} \to \mathcal{T} \textbf{ with } \mathcal{R}f = \{f \upharpoonright \mathcal{B}f\}$$

$$\textbf{def } -^- : \mathcal{F} \to \mathcal{F} \textbf{ with } f^- \in \mathcal{R}f \to \mathcal{B}f \land f(f^-y) = y$$

$$\textbf{def } inj : \mathcal{F} \to \mathbb{B} \textbf{ with } inj \, f \equiv \mathcal{B}f = \mathcal{D}f$$

$$\textbf{def } - surj - : \mathcal{F} \to \mathcal{T} \to \mathbb{B} \textbf{ with } f \, surj \, B \equiv \{f\} = B$$

We conclude this subsection with some conventions regarding higher order functions. We write $A \to B \to C$ for $A \to (B \to C)$. Given $f : A \to B \to C$, we write fab for $(fa)b$. Infix operators are (whenever doing so is useful) implicitly overloaded with their Curried version in both arguments, that is: given $-f- : A \times B \to C$, then, for any $a : A$ and $b : B$:

$$af \in B \to C \text{ with } (af)b = afb$$

$$fb \in A \to C \text{ with } (fb)a = afb$$

Making this overloading explicit (type $A \leftrightarrow B \to C$) is under consideration.

4.3 The Functional Generalized Cartesian Product

The Funmath Cartesian product operator $\times$ is defined by

def $\times : Fam\ \mathcal{T} \to \mathcal{T}$ **with** $\times F = \{f : \mathcal{D}F \to \cup F \mid \forall\, x : \mathcal{D}f\ .\ fx \in \mathcal{F}x\}$

The idea can be best understood by comparison with function equality:

$$f \in \times F \;\equiv\; \mathcal{D}f = \mathcal{D}F \wedge \forall\, x : \mathcal{D}f\ .\ fx \in Fx$$

$$f = g \;\;\equiv\; \mathcal{D}f = \mathcal{D}g \wedge \forall\, x : \mathcal{D}f\ .\ fx = gx$$

interpreted as follows: Whereas g is an *exact* specification of f, the Cartesian product $\times F$ is an *approximate* specification of f (approximation analogy). The approximation can be as "tight" as desired, since $f = g \equiv f \in \times(\iota \circ g)$.

The following examples illustrate how the particular instances where F is an application, a tuple, or an abstraction coincide with certain traditional notations.

a. *First example:* $F = B \bullet A$. Then clearly $\times F = A \to B$.

b. *Second example:* $F = (A, B)$. Then $\mathcal{D}F = \mathbb{B}$ and $\cup F = A \cup B$. Also, $F0 = A$ and $F1 = B$. Substitution into the definition yields:

$$\times(A, B) = \{f : \mathbb{B} \to A \cup B \mid f0 \in A \wedge f1 \in B\}$$

Obviously, $a \in A \wedge b \in B \equiv (a, b) \in \times(A, B)$. Hence $\times(A, B)$ is the familiar Cartesian product. It is therefore proper to introduce the traditional $\times$ notation by

def — $\times \ldots = \times(—, \ldots)$

Observe that $A \times A \times A = \square 3 \to A$. We write A^n for $\square n \to A$ (arrays of size n). Given the complete definition of the *block* operator $\square$

def $\square : \mathbb{N} \cup \iota\infty \to \mathcal{P}\mathbb{N}$ **with** $\square n = \{m : \mathbb{N} \mid m < n\}$

it is easy to see that $A^\infty = \mathbb{N} \to A$ (infinite sequences).

c. *Third example:* $F = a : A\ .\ B$ (where, of course, B may depend on a). In that case, $\forall\, a : A\ .\ Fa = B$ by definition of abstraction. Hence,

$$\times a : A\ .\ B = \{f : A \to \cup(a : A\ .\ B) \mid \forall\, a : A\ .\ fa \in B\}$$

This is the usual definition of a dependent type [5], which is also used in category theory [25], constructive type theory [26], and so on, where it is denoted by the separate abstraction construct $\Pi a : A \,.\, B$.

We introduce the following convenient abbreviations, which also help to emphasize that a Cartesian product is a set of functions:

$$A \ni a \to B \qquad\qquad \text{for } \times a : A \,.\, B$$

$$A \ni a \to B \ni b \to C \quad \text{for } \times a : A \,.\, (\times b : B \,.\, C) \text{ etc.}$$

where B may depend on a, and C on both a and b. Observe that, in combination with $\ni$, the arrow $\to$ is just notation, and is not compositionally interpretable as the function arrow.

This usage of $\times$ also covers Church-style polymorphism.

d. *Fourth example:* Let $F = \blacksquare$ where

$$\textbf{def } \blacksquare : \mathbb{N} \to \mathscr{P}\mathbb{N} \textbf{ with } \blacksquare n = \{m : \mathbb{N} \mid m \le n\}$$

Clearly, $\mathscr{D}\blacksquare = \mathbb{N}$, $\cup\blacksquare = \mathbb{N}$ and $\forall\, n : \mathbb{N} \,.\, \forall\, m : \mathbb{N}.m \in \blacksquare n \Leftrightarrow m \le n$. Hence,

$$\times\blacksquare = \{f : \mathbb{N} \to \mathbb{N} \mid \forall\, n : \mathbb{N} \,.\, fn \le n\}$$

The operator $\blacksquare$ can be generalized to $\mathbb{R}$, in which case $\times\blacksquare$ constitutes an example of a Cartesian product with an uncountable number of elements.

4.4 Sequences and Their Operators

Sequences are often-used concepts in systems theory, discrete-time signal processing, and computer science. They will also appear in later examples.

The *sequence types* of interest are defined using the following operators:

$$\textbf{def} - \uparrow - : \mathscr{T} \times \mathbb{N} \cup \iota\infty \to \mathscr{T} \textbf{ with } A \uparrow n = \Box n \to A$$

$$\textbf{def} -^{\omega} : \mathscr{T} \to \mathscr{T} \textbf{ with } A^{\omega} = \cup(A \uparrow)$$

$$\textbf{def} -^{*} : \mathscr{T} \to \mathscr{T} \textbf{ with } A^{*} = \cup((A \uparrow) \rceil \mathbb{N}) \quad -A^{*} = \cup n : \mathbb{N} \,.\, A^{n}$$

$$\textbf{def} -^{+} : \mathscr{T} \to \mathscr{T} \textbf{ with } A^{+} = A^{*} \backslash A^{0}$$

As mentioned earlier, we write A^{n} for $A \uparrow n$. Classes of interest are as follows:

Sequences over A: the set A^{ω}
Arrays of length n over A: the set A^{n} ($n \in \mathbb{N}$)
Streams over A: the set A^{∞} (infinite sequences)
Lists over A: the set A^{*} (finite, arbitrary length)
Nonempty lists over A: the set A^{+}.

Clearly, $A^{*} \cup A^{\infty} = A^{\omega}$, $A^{*} \cap A^{\infty} = \emptyset$, $A^{0} \cup A^{+} = A^{*}$, $A^{0} \cap A^{+} = \emptyset$, $A^{0} = \iota\varepsilon$. Of course, in expressions such as A^{*}, A may again be a sequence type, which also yields a generalized notation for matrices.

The *operators over sequences* used in the sequel are as follows. The *length* operator #:

$$\mathbf{def}\ \#:\mathcal{U}^\omega \to \mathbb{N} \cup \iota\infty \text{ with } \mathcal{D}x = \Box(\#x)$$

The *inject* operator τ:

$$\mathbf{def}\ \tau:\mathcal{U} \to \mathcal{U}^1 \text{ with } \tau a0 = a$$

The *concatenation* operator ++ (chaining sequences):

$$\mathbf{def}\ -\!+\!+\!-:(\mathcal{U}^\omega)^2 \ni (x, y) \to \mathcal{U}^{\#x+\#y}$$

$$\mathbf{with}\ (x ++ y)k = (k < \#x)\ ?\ xk \dagger y(k - \#x)$$

An illustrative property in combination with the Cartesian product is the following. Given $A : \mathcal{T}^\omega$ and $B : \mathcal{T}^\omega$, then

$$a \in A \land b \in B \Rightarrow (a ++ b) \in \times(A ++ B)$$

The *cons* (or *prefix*) operator $>-$ and the *snoc* (or *postfix*) operator $-<$:

$$\mathbf{def}\ -\!>\!-\!-:\mathcal{U} \times \mathcal{U}^\omega \ni x \to \mathcal{U}^{\#x+1} \text{ with } a >- x = \tau a ++ x$$

$$\mathbf{def}\ -\!-\!<\!-:\mathcal{U}^\omega \ni x \times \mathcal{U} \to \mathcal{U}^{\#x+1} \text{ with } x -< a = x ++ \tau a$$

The *shift* operator σ:

$$\mathbf{def}\ \sigma \in \mathcal{U}^\omega \backslash \mathcal{U}^0 \ni x \to \mathcal{U}^{\#x-1} \text{ with } \sigma xk = x(k+1)$$

It is easy to prove that these operators are well defined. Useful properties of the concatenation operators are:

$$(x ++ y) ++ z = x ++ (y ++ z) \quad \text{(associativity)}$$

$$x ++ \varepsilon = x \text{ and } \varepsilon ++ x = x \qquad \text{(identity element)}$$

$$\#(x ++ y) = \#x + \#y$$

and, because of the first property, $(a >- x) ++ y = a >- (x ++ y)$. These operators and their properties provide the link between system models where explicit indexing is more helpful (sampling models, signal processing, many-dimensional structures) and where indexing is distracting (event-based models, concurrency theories, certain classes of algorithms). For instance, the theory of lists in the aforementioned Bird-Meertens formalism [14] can be entirely expressed within Funmath with negligible notational differences.

In any proof activity about lists, e.g., of type A^*, recurrent patterns soon make it apparent that many useful functions $f : A^* \to B$ (mapping lists to objects in some other domain B) satisfy

$$\exists\, b : B\ .\ f\varepsilon = b$$

$$\exists\, g : A \to B\ .\ \forall\, a : A\ .\ f(\tau a) = ga$$

$$\exists\, -\$- : B \times B \to B\ .\ \forall\, (x, y) : (A^*)^2\ .\ f(x ++ y) = (fx)\ \$\ (fy)$$

where, in view of the third property, it is convenient to assume that f *surj* B. For obvious reasons, such functions are called *list homomorphisms*. A typical example is the Σ operator. The general definition of Σ was introduced earlier. For lists (in $\mathbb{C}^*$, obviously), it yields the following properties:

$$\Sigma \; \varepsilon = 0$$

$$\Sigma \; (\tau c) = c$$

$$\Sigma \; (x \; {+\!\!+} \; y) = \Sigma \; x + \Sigma \; y$$

which clearly characterize Σ as a list homomorphism.

Useful theorems for reasoning about lists without using explicit indexing are the *list induction theorems*. Induction on the length of a list is one often-used variant. Another useful variant is the following: For any type A and any predicate $P : A^* \to \mathbb{B}$:

$$P\varepsilon \wedge (\forall \, x : A^* \, . \, \forall \, a : A \, . \, Px \Rightarrow P(a >\!- x)) \Rightarrow \forall \, a : A^* \, . \, Px$$

Inductive proofs are convenient when definitions or properties of operators are stated in a recursive fashion. As a matter of style, once certain algebraic properties are established, further theorems can be derived from these properties without requiring induction again.

5 SPECIFICATION AND TRANSFORMATION REASONING USING FUNMATH

5.1 Specification in Funmath

A *specification* is a predicate that must be satisfied by the objects of interest. As a syntactic convenience, a specification Sp with a definition of the form

$$\textbf{def } Sp : X \to \mathbb{B} \textbf{ with } Spx = P$$

may be written as

$$\textbf{spec } Sp \textbf{ for } x : X \textbf{ with } P$$

with the same facilities for implicit quantification as in definitions in the case where X is a function type. Of course, if a unique object x exists that satisfies $x \in X \wedge P$, then the specification can be replaced by

$$\textbf{def } x : X \textbf{ with } P$$

An example is the formal specification of *sorting* for a given type A with total ordering $\leq$. For this purpose, we introduce two auxiliary operators.

- The inventory operator $\$$:

$$\textbf{def} - \$ - : A \times A^* \to \mathbb{N} \textbf{ with } a \; \$ \; x = \Sigma \; i : \mathscr{D}x \, . \, (xi = a)$$

- The *ascending* predicate *asc:*

$$\mathbf{def}\ asc : A^* \to \mathbb{B}\ \mathbf{with}\ asc\,x = \forall\ (i, j) : (\mathcal{D}x)^2\ .\ (i < j \Rightarrow xi \leq xj)$$

Now the formal specification of sorting for $(A, \leq)$ is

$$\mathbf{spec}\ sorting\ \mathbf{for}\ f : A^* \to A^*\ \mathbf{with}\ \$(fx) = \$x \wedge asc(fx)$$

It is an interesting (but nontrivial) exercise to prove that the sorting function is unique, and that hence the specification can be replaced by

$$\mathbf{def}\ sort : A^* \to A^*\ \mathbf{with}\ \$(sort\ x) = \$x \wedge asc(sort\ x)$$

Observe that this definition does not include any design decision. Descriptions in functional *programming* languages always reflect some chosen algorithm (e.g., quicksort, treesort, smoothsort, Batcher sort).

5.2 Transformational Reasoning

Transformational reasoning is a somewhat disciplined form of deductive reasoning in which the successive steps are chained according to the following scheme:

$$E_0\ R_0\ \{\text{justification}_0\}\ E_1$$
$$R_1\ \{\text{justification}_1\}\ E_2, \text{etc.}$$

where the E_i are expressions and the R_i are relational operators $(=, \leq, \equiv, \Rightarrow)$ compatible with the type of the E_i. The justification refers to the application of theorems or axioms to subexpressions of E_i and E_{i+1} to establish that $E_i R_i E_{i+1}$. For instance, assuming that $x \in \mathbb{R}$:

$$fx \leq \{0 \leq x^2\}x^2 + fx$$

Equational reasoning is a particular form of transformational reasoning where the R_i are equivalence relations and will be illustrated in later examples. The intuitive rules under which the more general relations can be used in a transformational chain are being formalized.

6 SOFTWARE EXAMPLE: VERIFICATION OF AN ALGORITHM

6.1 A Sorting Algorithm in Comma

Comma is the executable subset of Funmath. The operators $++$ and $>-$ for lists have known operational interpretations (consistent with their declarative interpretation, of course). If we assume that for the considered $(A, \leq)$ the $\leq$ operator can be realized algorithmically, then the following Funmath definition falls within the Comma subset and hence can also be interpreted as a program. More specifically, it is a form of the *quicksort* algorithm:

def $q : A^* \rightarrow A^*$ **with** $q\varepsilon = \varepsilon; q(a >\!\!- x) = qu ++ (a >\!\!- qv)$ **where** $(u, v) = sax$

def $s : A \rightarrow A^* \rightarrow (A^*)^2$ **with** $sa\varepsilon = \varepsilon; sa(b >\!\!- x) = b \leq a \ ? \ (b >\!\!- u, v)$
where $(u, v) = sax$

Remark: The declarative interpretation of the semicolon is logical conjunction.

6.2 Verification

Verification refers to proving that $q = sort$ in the declarative interpretation. The quicksort algorithm q contains two parts: splitting (s) and recombining ($++$). The specifications contains two conditions, one involving $ and one involving *asc*. In the various theorems of the proof, each of these conditions will be related to each of the parts of the algorithm. This results in four combinations, which determine the structure of the proof. It happens to be advantageous to introduce the following auxiliary relations to unravel *asc*:

def $se : A \times A^* \rightarrow \mathbb{B}$ **with** $asex = \forall i : \mathcal{D}x . a \leq xi$

def $ge : A \times A^* \rightarrow \mathbb{B}$ **with** $agex = \forall i : \mathcal{D}x . a \geq xi$

The reason for this advantage is that *ase* and *age* are list homomorphisms.
    The verification proof is organized as follows:

- Lemma for s (splitting): If $(u, v) = splitax$, then
  a. $\$u \stackrel{\wedge}{+} \$v = \$x$ (L s \$)
  b. $ageu \wedge asev$ (L s *asc*)
- Lemma for $++$ (recombining):
  a. $\$(x ++ y) = \$x \stackrel{\wedge}{+} \$y$
     furthermore $\$\varepsilon = 0 \bullet A$ and $\$(\tau a) = (= a) \rceil A$ (L $++$ \$)
  b. $asc(x ++ (a >\!\!- y)) = ascx \wedge ascy \wedge agex \wedge asey$ (L $++$ *asc*)
- Proposition relating $ and *asc*:
  $\$x = \$y \Rightarrow gex = gey \wedge sex = sey$ (P \$ *asc*)
- Verification theorem (putting everything together):
  a. $\$(qx) = \$x$ (T \$)
  b. $asc(qx)$ (T *asc*)

For easy reference, these statements are labeled mnemonically as follows: L = lemma, T = theorem, followed by the operator/predicate to which it pertains. The auxiliary operator $\wedge$ is a particularization of the function extension that will also be used in the hardware example. It is defined polymorphically by

poly $(A, B, C, X) : \mathcal{T}^4$

def $\stackrel{\wedge}{\,} : (A \times B \rightarrow C) \rightarrow (X \rightarrow A) \times (X \rightarrow B) \rightarrow (X \rightarrow C)$
    with $(x \stackrel{\wedge}{g} y)c = (xc)g(yc)$

Clearly, the first equality in lemma (L ++ $) can also be written $a\ \$\ (x\ ++\ y) = a\ \$\ x + a\ \$\ y$. In fact, the lemma states that (for a given A) the function $, which in view of our convention for infix operators may be considered Curried in both arguments, is itself a list homomorphism. The predicate *asc* is not a list homomorphism, but the related functions *se* and *ge* are.

We illustrate part of the verification by proving T $ using induction over the length of the argument.

Proof:

- Base step: $\$(q\varepsilon) = \{\text{def} . q\}\varepsilon$
- Induction hypothesis: $\forall\ u : A^* \ . \ \#u \leq \#x \Rightarrow \$(qu) = \$u$
- Induction step:

$$\$(q(a\ >-\ x))$$
$$= \{\text{def} . q\}\ \$\ (qu\ ++\ (a\ >-\ qv))\ \textbf{where}\ (u, v) = sax$$
$$= \{\text{def} . >-\}\ \$\ (qu\ ++\ \tau a\ ++\ qv)\ \textbf{where}\ (u, v) = sax$$
$$= \{L\ ++\ \$\}\ \$\ (qu)\ \hat{+}\ (= a)\ \hat{+}\ \$(qv)\ \textbf{where}\ (u, v) = sax$$
$$= \{\text{ind. hyp.}\}\ \$\ u\ \hat{+}\ (= a)\ \hat{+}\ \$v\ \textbf{where}\ (u, v) = sax$$
$$= \{Ls\$\}(= a)\ \hat{+}\ \$x$$
$$= \{L\ ++\ S\}\ \$\ (\tau a\ ++\ x)$$
$$= \{\text{def} >-\}\ \$\ (a\ >-\ x)$$

q. e. d.

7 HARDWARE EXAMPLE: DERIVATION OF A CIRCUIT

7.1 The Reals Hardware Description Subset

Reals is the network description subset of Funmath based on the principle of systems semantics [12,27,28].

The type of a net is described by means of so-called *uncommitted types,* i.e., types that are uninterpreted until meaning is attached to them. This makes it possible to associate various mathematical models with a given system description, for instance structure, static behavior, and several kinds of dynamic behavior. Attaching such mathematical models is done at the language level (for the uncommitted type names and names of atomic, i.e., primitive, systems), not for individual descriptions. This has the advantage that every description expressed in the sublanguage inherits all models defined for the uncommitted types and atomic system names.

The uncommitted types are *base types,* declared as such by the user and jointly constituting an enumeration type $\mathscr{E}$; *composite types,* defined recursively as images of tuples of base types under the Cartesian product operator; and *system types.* For *directional* systems, i.e., where it is advantageous to distinguish between input and output, system types are defined by expressions of the form $A \Rightarrow B$ where A and B are base or composite types and $\Rightarrow$ is the directional system type operator. The operators for adirectional system types are disussed elsewhere [3,4].

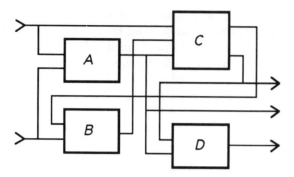

Fig. 1: Schematic representing a structural interpretation

The directional nets themselves are described using the tuple and application constructs. An illustrative example is the following:

def $U : \mathscr{C}$
def $A, B, D : (U^2 \Rightarrow U)^3$
def $C : U^3 \Rightarrow U^2$
def $S : U^2 \Rightarrow U^3$ **with** $Sx = c_1, a, D(c_1, a)$ **where** $a = Ax; c = C(x_0, B(c_0, x_1), a)$

In the *structural interpretation,* a base type, e.g., V in the example, is the type of a net (in electrical systems: a collection of connected points). A composite type (e.g., V^2) is the type of a composite net, and a system type is the type of a system with specified input and output net types. Different base types are used to differentiate between media (e.g., electrical, magnetic, mechanical). System types are illustrated in the example as they are used to characterize the atomic (black-box) systems A, B, C, and D, and also the system S, whose structure is described by an expression. Observe that, in this expression, the system names syntactically occur in "function" positions. The symbols in the "argument" positions denote nets, whose types are easily inferred from the system types and the tupling. They must be seen as "local constants" (names for nets). In the present version of Reals, the following convention is used:

- Every occurrence of given (sub)system name designates a different instantiation of the same (sub)system (*instantiation by occurrence*).
- Every occurrence of a given net name designates the same net (*instantiation by name*).

In the example, for the sake of clarity, capital letters are used for system names and lowercase letters for net names. The structural interpretation of the expression can be represented by the schematic in Fig. 1.

7.2 Some Useful Operators for Behavioral Descriptions

Various *behavioral interpretations* can be attached to the language by interpreting a base type B as a corresponding signal type S (namely, $S = \mathbb{T} \rightarrow V$ where $\mathbb{T}$ is some time domain and V some value domain), and system types as signal processing functions (e.g., $B^n \Rightarrow B^m$ is interpreted as $S^n \to S^m$).

An illustrative example is the subclass of *memoryless systems,* which are usually the processing components in systems with memory. Memoryless systems have the defining property that their signal (or dynamic) behavior is fully defined by their static behavior, i.e., mapping of instantaneous values from input to output. For instance, the (idealized) static behavior of an adder is described by $+$, of type $\mathbb{C} \times \mathbb{C} \to \mathbb{C}$, from which the (idealized) dynamic behavior of type $(\mathbb{T} \to \mathbb{C}) \times (\mathbb{T} \to \mathbb{C}) \to (\mathbb{T} \to \mathbb{C})$ is derived using the $\overset{\wedge}{-}$ operator defined earlier, namely, $(x \overset{\wedge}{+} y)t = xt + yt$ for signals x and y of type $\mathbb{T} \to \mathbb{C}$.

The extension operator $\overset{\wedge}{-}$ was defined for dyadic functions only. We now consider arbitrary adicity. One way of mapping static behaviors to dynamic behaviors would be the operator $\overset{\sim}{-}$ defined by

poly $(A, B, X) : \mathcal{T}^3 \bullet$

def $\overset{\sim}{-} : (A \to B) \to (X \to A) \to (X \to B)$ **with** $\tilde{g}s = g \circ s$
equivalently $\tilde{g}sx = g(sx)$

Given static $g : Vn \to V^m$, clearly $\tilde{g} \in (\mathbb{T} \to V^n) \to (\mathbb{T} \to V^m)$. This simple solution would also cover deeper nestings, e.g., as in $(V^n)^m$, without further ado. Unfortunately, $S^n = (\mathbb{T} \to V)^n$ rather than $\mathbb{T} \to V^n$, and hence $\overset{\sim}{-}$ does not produce functions of the desired type. However, since

$$(\mathbb{T} \to V)^n = \Box n \to \mathbb{T} \to V \quad \text{and} \quad \mathbb{T} \to V^n = \mathbb{T} \to \Box n \to V$$

the required type conversion can be achieved by the transposition operator T (for nesting depth 1) or a simple generalization thereof (for arbitrary nesting depth). The transposition operator T is defined as follows:

poly $(A, B, C) : \mathcal{T}^3 \bullet$

def $T : (A \to B \to C) \to (B \to A \to C)$ **with** $Tfba = fab$

This can be encapsulated in the extension operator by parameterizing the latter with the desired nesting depths in the domain and the codomain of the argument. For nesting depths of at most 1, as in our examples, it is often convenient to provide four variants of the extension operator, defined in the following table:

Operator	Nesting	Type	Mapping
$\overset{-}{-}$	0, 0	$(C \to D) \to (X \to C) \to (X \to D)$	$\overset{-}{g}s = g \circ s$
$\overset{<}{-}$	0, 1	$(A^n \to D) \to (X \to A)^n \to (X \to D)$	$\overset{<}{g}s = g \circ Ts$
$\overset{>}{-}$	1, 0	$(C \to B^m) \to (X \to C) \to (X \to B)^m$	$\overset{>}{g}s = T(g \circ s)$
$\overset{=}{-}$	1, 1	$(A^n \to B^m) \to (X \to A)^n \to (X \to B)^m$	$\overset{=}{g}s = T(g \circ Ts)$

The information i, j in the nesting column indicates nesting depth in the codomain and the domain, respectively, of the argument. The type is polymorphic in the types A, B, C, D, X, and in the exponents m, n, which are of type $\mathbb{N} \cup \{*, \infty, \omega\}$.

An illustrative example is the summing operator Σ. If, for the sake of this illustration, we assume $\Sigma \in \mathbb{C}^* \to \mathbb{C}$, then $\overset{\scriptscriptstyle\leq}{\Sigma} \in (X \to \mathbb{C})^* \to (X \to \mathbb{C})$. This is useful in signal processing applications to describe summation of a collection of signals. More specifically, let $s\_\_ : \square n \to \mathbb{T} \to \mathbb{C}$ be a finite collection of signals (s_i being the ith signal), then the sum signal $f : \mathbb{T} \to \mathbb{C}$ is defined by $f t = \Sigma\, i : \square n\,.\, s_i t$. This expression cannot be translated symbolwise into a Reals expression because the time variable t has no equivalent in Reals (such an equivalent must have a structural interpretation). However, it can be shown that

$$\Sigma\, i : \square n\,.\, s_i t = \overset{\scriptscriptstyle\leq}{\Sigma}\, st$$

and hence $f = \overset{\scriptscriptstyle\leq}{\Sigma}\, s$. The proof is left as an exercise to the reader. *Hint:* first prove the *lambda transposition* lemma: $(x : X\,.\, EF) = T(x : X\,.\, E)F$, provided x is not free in F, using standard lambda calculus.

Now the expression $\overset{\scriptscriptstyle\leq}{\Sigma}\, s$ can be symbolwise translated into Reals as $\Sigma\, s$ with the following correspondence:

- in $\overset{\scriptscriptstyle\leq}{\Sigma}\, s$ we have $\overset{\scriptscriptstyle\leq}{\Sigma} \in (\mathbb{T} \to \mathbb{C})^n \to (\mathbb{T} \to \mathbb{C})$ and $s \in (\mathbb{T} \to \mathbb{C})^n$
- in $\Sigma\, s$ we have $\Sigma \in B^n \Rightarrow B$ and $s \in B^n$ (reusing Σ for convenience)

7.3 Hardware Example: Derivation of a Discrete Function Generation

A *function generator* is a device in electronic instrumentation for generating a time-varying analog signal that is predefined by the user. Its discrete-time equivalent will be called a *discrete function generator*. We show how to derive such a generator for any function $f : \mathbb{N} \to \mathbb{R}$ (i.e., $\mathbb{R}^\infty$) that can be specified by a linear difference equation. The generator must produce the value $f n$ at time instant n.

In general, a derivation is considered complete when an expression D is obtained that can be translated symbolwise into a Reals expression R whose behavioral interpretation is equal to the standard declarative interpretation of D. The derivation of D from the original specification S may only use steps that guarantee no violation of S. Then R (i.e., its behavioral interpretation) will satisfy S. Within these restrictions (which are none other than the laws of mathematics), these steps must achieve two goals:

- elimination of the time variable (which has no meaning in Reals)
- elimination of nonrealizable functionals.

For this example, assume that the function to be realized is specified by the following k'th order linear difference equation:

$$\textbf{def}\; f : \mathbb{R}^\infty \;\textbf{with}\; f n = n < k\; ?\; b n \dagger i : \square k\,.\, a_i (n - k) \cdot f(n - 1 - i)$$

with given initial conditions $b : \mathbb{R}^k$ and given (possibly time-varying) coefficients $a : (\mathbb{R}^\infty)^k$.

The *elimination of the time variable* in the subexpression containing Σ proceeds as follows:

$$\Sigma \, i : \square k \, . \, a_i(n-k) \cdot f(n-1-i)$$
$$= \{\text{arithmetic}\}\Sigma \, i : \square k \, . \, a_i(n-k) \cdot f(n-k+k-1-i)$$
$$= \{\text{def} . \, \sigma^j\}\Sigma \, i : \square k \, . \, a_i(n-k) \cdot \sigma^{k-1-i} f(n-k)$$
$$= \{\text{def} . \, \overset{\wedge}{\_}\}\Sigma \, i : \square k \, . \, (a_i \,^\wedge \sigma^{k-1-i} f)(n-k)$$
$$= \{\text{property}\Sigma\}\overset{\leq}{\Sigma} \, (i : \square k \, . \, a_i \,^\wedge \sigma^{k-1-i} f)(n-k)$$

Hence,

$$fn = \{\text{just derived}\}n < k \, ? \, bn \dagger \Sigma \, (i : \square k \, . \, a_i \,^\wedge \sigma^{k-1-i} f)(n-k)$$
$$= \{\text{def} . \, ++, k = \#b\}(b ++ \overset{\leq}{\Sigma} \, i : \square k \, . \, a_i \,^\wedge \sigma^{k-1-i} f)n$$

and, by η conversion,

$$f = b ++ \overset{\leq}{\Sigma} \, i : \square k \, . \, a_i \,^\wedge \sigma^{k-1-i} f$$

The *elimination of nonrealizable functionals* in this case concerns σ, since this functional models a predictive device: $\sigma \, xn = x(n+1)$, where n represents time. However, every σ can be cancelled by a delay, defined by

$$\textbf{def } D\_\_ : \mathcal{U} \to \mathcal{U}^\omega \ni x \to \mathcal{U}^{\#x+1} \textbf{ with } D_v x = v >- x$$

It is easy to prove that $\Sigma \circ D_v = id$ (cancellation) and that

$$b ++ \, = \bigcirc i : \square k \, . \, D_{bi}$$

where $\bigcirc$ is composition of a list of functions:

$$\textbf{def } \bigcirc : \mathcal{F}^* \to \mathcal{F} \textbf{ with } \bigcirc \varepsilon = id \wedge \bigcirc(f >- x) = f \circ \bigcirc x$$

From these two properties of D (and function composition) we obtain

$$\forall \, j : \square k \, . \, (\sigma^j \circ (b ++)) = \bigcirc i : j \, .. \, (k-1) \, . \, D_{bi})$$

Hence,

$$\forall \, j : \square k \, . \, \sigma^j f = \bigcirc(i : j \, .. \, (k-1) \, . \, D_{bi})(\overset{\leq}{\Sigma} \, i : \square k \, . \, a_i \,^\wedge \sigma^{k-1-i} f)$$

which allows us to rewrite the expression as

$$\textbf{def } f : \mathbb{R}^\infty \textbf{ with } f = g_0 \textbf{ where } g : (\mathbb{R}^\infty)^k$$

$$\textbf{with } g_{k-1} = D_{b(k-1)}(\overset{\leq}{\Sigma} \, i : \square k \, . \, a_i \,^\wedge g_{k-1-i}); g_j = D_{bj} g_{j+1}$$

Since the D_v and all other functionals are realizable, this expression can be translated symbolwise into Reals (where B denotes the base type):

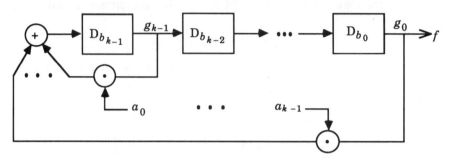

Fig. 2: Schematic of a discrete function generator

$$\textbf{def } f : B \textbf{ with } f = g_0 \textbf{ where } g : B^k$$

$$\textbf{with } g_{k-1} = D_{b(k-1)}(\Sigma\ i : \square k\ .\ a_i g_{k-1-i});\ g_j = D_{bj} g_{j+1}$$

Here we used a straightforward convention for uninterpreted system names, namely, $\Sigma :$ $B^* \Rightarrow B$, $D_\nu : B \Rightarrow B$ and $—\cdot— : B^2 \Rightarrow B$. The structural interpretation of this description is schematically represented in Fig. 2.

7.4 Two Interesting Particular Instances

Interesting particular instances are the Fibonacci generator and the factorial generator with specifications

$$\textbf{def } fib : \mathbb{N}^\infty \textbf{ with } fibn = n < 2\ ?\ (0, 1)n \dagger fib(n-1) + fib(n-2)$$
$$\textbf{def } fac : \mathbb{N}^\infty \textbf{ with } facn = n = 0\ ?\ 1 \dagger n \cdot fac(n-1)$$

and realizations

$$\textbf{def } fib : B \textbf{ with } fib = g_0 \textbf{ where } g : B^2 \textbf{ with } g = D_0 g_1, D_1(g_0 + g_1)$$
$$\textbf{def } fac : B \textbf{ with } fac = g_0 \textbf{ where } g : B^2 \textbf{ with } g = D_1(g_1 \cdot g_0), D_1(sg_1)$$

An interesting detail in the realization of fac is the subsystem s realizing the successor function. It is part of the so-called *time base generator* producing the time-varying coefficient a_0 with mapping $a_0 n = n + 1$.

8 CONCLUSION: RELEVANCE TO HARDWARE/ SOFTWARE CODESIGN

The various examples have demonstrated that the declarative formalism Funmath provides a unified framework for analyzing and designing both hardware and software. We have shown how to express "pure" (behavioral) specification independently of the realization medium, as well as realizations in either medium.

In comparison with codesign formalisms based on programming language concepts, Funmath has the additional notational advantage of close correspondence in both form and content with the common language of mathematics whenever dealing with the typical formulas in applied mathematics, physics, and engineering.

It also has the semantic advantage of having its roots in the analog domain, allowing it to deal with problems in continuous domains. History has shown how hard it is to build analog features into a language as an afterthought.

REFERENCES

[1] R. T. Boute, "Funmath: Towards a General Formalism for System Description in Engineering Applications," in *Advances in Electrical Engineering Software*, P. P. Silvester, Ed., pp. 215–226, Computational Mechanics Publications, Southampton, and Springer-Verlag, Berlin, Aug. 1990.

[2] R. T. Boute, "Declarative Languages—Still a Long Way to Go," in *Computer Hardware Description Languages and Their Applications*, D. Borrione, R. Waxman, Eds., pp. 185–212, North Holland, Amsterdam, April 1991.

[3] M. Seutter, *et al.*, *Glass: A System Description Language and Its Environment, Version 2.0*, Department of Computer Science, University of Nijmegen, June 25, 1991.

[4] R. T. Boute, "ESPRIT Project 881—FORFUN, Formal Description of Digital and Analog Systems by Means of Functional Languages," *ESPRIT '90 Proceedings of the Annual ESPRIT Conference*, pp. 212–226, Kluwer Academic Publishers, Dordrecht, Dec. 1990.

[5] K. Hanna and N. Daeche, "Implementation of the Veritas Design Logic," in *Theorem Provers in Circuit Design*, V. Stavridou, T. Melham, and R. Boute, Eds., pp. 77–84, North Holland, Amsterdam, 1992.

[6] P. Jackson, "Nuprl and Its Use in Circuit Design," in *Theorem Provers in Circuit Design*, V. Stavridou, T. Melham, and R. Boute, Eds., pp. 311–336, North Holland, Amsterdam, 1992.

[7] J. M. Spivey, *The Z Notation—A Reference Manual*, Prentice-Hall, New York, 1989.

[8] D. Turner, "Miranda: A Non-Strict Functional Language with Polymorphic Types," in *Functional Programming Languages and Computer Architecture*, J. P. Jouannaud, Ed., Vol. 201 of *LNCS*, pp. 1–16, Springer-Verlag, Berlin, 1985.

[9] H. B. Curry and R. Feys, *Combinatory Logic*, Vol. 1, North Holland, Amsterdam, 1974.

[10] M. Sheeran, "μFP: A Language for VLSI Design" in *1984 ACM Symposium on LISP and Functional Programming*, pp. 104–112, ACM, New York, 1984.

[11] M. Sheeran, "Describing and Reasoning About Circuits Using Relations," in *Theoretical Foundations of VLSI Design*, K. McEvoy, J Tucker, Eds., pp. 263–298, Cambridge University Press, Cambridge, MA, 1990.

[12] R. Boute, "System Semantics and Formal Circuit Description," *IEEE Trans. Circ. Syst.* CAS-33(12), pp. 1219–1231, Dec. 1986.

[13] J. Backus, "Can Programming Be Liberated from the von Neumann Style?—A Functional Style and Its Algebra of Programs," *Comm. ACM* 21(8), pp. 613–641, Aug. 1978.

[14] L. Meertens, "Algorithmics—Towards Programming as a Mathematical Activity," in *Mathematics and Computer Science,* J. W. De Bakker et al., Eds., CWI Monographs, Vol. 1, pp. 289–334, North Holland, Amsterdam, 1986.

[15] H. P. Barendregt, *The Lambda Calculus, Its Syntax and Semantics,* North-Holland, Amsterdam, 1985.

[16] P. Suppes, *Axiomatic Set Theory,* Dover Publications, New York, 1972.

[17] R. M. Amadio and L. Cardelli, "Subtyping Recursive Types," Rapport Technique No. 133, INRIA, Rocquencourt, 1992.

[18] A. Felty, "Encoding Dependent Types in an Intuitionistic Logic," Rapport de Recherche No. 1521, INRIA, Rocquencourt, 1992.

[19] B. C. Pierce, "Programming with Intersection Types, Union Types and Polymorphism," CMU-CS-91-16, School of Computer Science, Carnegie Mellon University, Feb. 1991.

[20] T. E. Forster, *Set Theory with a Universal Set,* Clarendon Press, Oxford, 1992.

[21] H. B. Curry, *Foundations of Mathematical Logic,* Dover Publications, New York, 1977.

[22] K. M. Chandy and J. Misra, *Parallel Program Design—A Foundation,* Addison-Wesley, Reading, MA, 1988.

[23] J. C. Reynolds, "Towards a Theory of Type Structure," in *Programming Symposium Proceedings,* B. Robinet, *et al.,* Eds., pp. 408–425, Lecture Notes in Computer Science 19, Springer-Verlag, Berlin 1974.

[24] R. T. Boute, "The Euclidean Definition of the Functions Div and Mod," *ACM Trans. Progr. Lang. Syst.,* 14(2), pp. 127–144, April 1992.

[25] B. C. Pierce, *Basic Category Theory for Computer Scientists,* The MIT Press, Cambridge, MA, 1991.

[26] B. Nordström, K. Petersson, and J. M. Smith, *Programming in Martin-Löf's Type Theory: An Introduction,* Clarendon Press, New York, 1990.

[27] R. T. Boute, "Systems Semantics: Principles, Applications and Implementation," *ACM Trans. Prog. Lang. Syst.,* 10(1), pp. 118–155, Jan. 1988.

[28] R. T. Boute, "On the Formal Description of Non-Computational Objects," in *Declarative Systems, Proc. IFIP TC 10/WG 10.1 Workshop on Concepts and Characteristics of Declarative Systems,* G. David, R. T. Boute, B. D. Shriver, Eds., pp. 99–123, North-Holland, Amsterdam, 1990.

CHAPTER 3

(Inter-)Action Refinement
The Easy Way*

Manfred Broy
Institut für Informatik
Technische Universität München
München, Germany

Abstract: We outline and illustrate a formal concept for the specification and refinement of networks of interactive components. We describe systems by modular, functional specification techniques. We distinguish between black-box and glass-box views of interactive system components as well as refinements of their black-box and glass-box views. We identify and discuss several classes of refinements such as *behavior refinement, communication history refinement, interface interaction refinement, state space refinement, distribution refinement,* and others. In particular, we demonstrate how these concepts of refinement and their verification are supported by functional specification techniques leading to a general formal refinement calculus. It can be used as the basis for the development of distributed interactive systems.

1 INTRODUCTION

It is well accepted by now that the development of distributed systems is most adequately carried out by going through a sequence of development phases (often called *levels of abstraction*). Through these phases an envisaged system or system component is described in more and more detail until a sufficiently detailed description or even an efficient implementation of the system is obtained. The individual steps of such a proceeding can be

* This work was supported by the Sonderforschungsbereich 342 "Werkzeuge und Methoden für die Nutzung paralleler Architekturen."

captured by appropriate notions of *refinement*. In a refinement step, parts or aspects of a system description are made more complete or more detailed. Often refinement steps include a considerable restructuring of system descriptions.

Throughout this study we consider interactive system components (sometimes called *open systems*). Interactive systems are connected to the outside world by communication *channels* (often also called *ports*).

For the classification of refinements, we can distinguish between the following views of a system:

- *Black-box view:* In the black-box view of a system component, only its interaction with its environment is described. The black-box view of a system component consists of its *syntactic interface* (input and output channels and the sort of messages for each channel) and its *semantic interface* (sometimes called its *behavior,* that is, the causal relationship between input messages and output messages).
- *Glass-box view:* In the glass-box view details of the internal system structure are described. This includes a description of the internal state space of the system and/or the internal distribution of the system into subsystems. The subsystems may again be described in different levels of detail (in a black-box view or a glass-box view).

Clearly, the black-box view is more abstract. It does not take into account how a system is presented or realized but characterizes its behavior with respect to the surrounding environment. The black-box view is captured by an *interface specification.*

A glass-box description also defines, however more implicitly, a black-box view. Therefore, a black-box view of a system is often given implicitly in terms of a glass-box description. Accordingly we have to distinguish between glass-box descriptions that are just auxiliary constructions for giving a black-box view and glass-box views that describe the actual internal structure (in terms of states or distribution) of the envisaged system realization.

Throughout the specification and development of a distributed system and its components, a variety of aspects need to be described and refined. These aspects include the following:

- *For the black-box view:* The *syntactic* (channels by which system components are connected to the outside world and the sort of messages for each channel) and *semantic interface* (the system's observable behavior).
- *For the glass-box view:* The *internal representation* of the system; the system may be represented by a *state transition system* or by a *distributed system.* In a state transition system, the representation of the states and the state transition function is included. A distributed system consists of a network of subcomponents forming subsystems and the syntactic and semantic properties of these subcomponents (their black-box and perhaps also glass-box views), their internal connections by channels, and the control and data flow within and between the components.

These two views are not independent. The internal structure and the properties of the subcomponents also induce an external behavior. The two complementary views give rise to the notion of correctness. Given an interface description (black-box view) and an internal description (glass-box view) the glass-box view is called *correct* with respect to the black-box view if the properties of the system forming the black-box view are logically implied by the properties of the system expressed by the glass-box view.

Both views include the involved data sorts and computation structures, which in the black-box view describe the sorts of messages and in the glass-box view describes in addition the internal data, actions, and states of the system and its subcomponents.

The behavior of a system may be described by logical formulas in a very abstract, property-oriented way. Since a description of the glass-box view also implicitly includes the description of a behavior, the behavior of a system may be described in terms of a state machine with input and output, or it may be described by a programming language such as notations in a constructive ("algorithmic") way. Also this syntactic form of a system description is a target for refinement steps.

Refinement steps for the black-box and glass-box views are always expressed via a transformation of the syntactic description of the system. Obviously, some of these refinement steps do not change the semantics of a system description, merely the way it is presented.

Based on the preceding classification of system descriptions into levels of abstraction and syntactic description forms, we may distinguish between the following types of refinement:

- *Black-box refinement:* Behavior refinement (leaving the syntactic interface unchanged) and communication history and interface interaction refinement (even changing the syntactic interface such as the number of channels and their sorts).
- *Glass-box refinement:* Refinement of the state space (data structure refinement); distribution (architectural) refinement (refining a component into a network); refinement of subcomponents of a distributed system; and refinement of the interaction between the subcomponents.
- Refinement by rewriting and reformulating the syntactic form of a system specification without changing its meaning.

Although algebraic and functional specification techniques provide a common formal logical framework in which these different concepts of refinement can be captured, different refinement concepts use and need quite different development, specification, and verification styles and formats. For all of the mentioned concepts of refinement, it is helpful to provide an appropriate syntactic and semantic refinement relation that formalizes the syntactic and semantic relationship between the original and the refined system. Since refinement is the decisive concept in system development, obviously the usefulness of a development formalism depends strongly on its flexibility with respect to incorporating refinement notions.

A well-defined formal approach to program refinement is that of *program transformation* [1]. A program transformation can be viewed as a rule for obtaining from a given specification or program a more refined semantically equivalent one provided the rule is applicable. Working just with schematic transformation rules may sometimes be too narrow. Often refinement steps cannot be captured by simple schematic rules but need more elaborate descriptions [2–4].

In the following we study various notions of refinement within a functional axiomatic formalism. We start by defining a functional system model. Then we introduce functional system specification techniques and a number of composition operators such as sequential and parallel composition and feedback. With the help of the composition operators, we can form networks from given components. We use logical implication as the basic notion of refinement for system specifications. More specific forms of refinement are then defined that allow us to change the number of channels and the granularity of the messages of a system component. Finally, refinements of the glass-box views are studied. All notions are demonstrated with the help of a simple running example.

2 SYSTEM MODEL AND SPECIFICATION

In this section we introduce functional models of interactive systems and system components. We define the basic mathematical structures and concepts for the specification of components.

2.1 Basic Structures

In the following, interactive systems are supposed to communicate asynchronously via unbounded first-in/first-out (FIFO) channels. Streams are used to denote histories of communications on channels. Given a set M of messages, a *stream* over M is a finite or infinite sequence of elements from M. By M^* we denote the finite sequences over M; M^* includes the empty stream denoted by $\langle\rangle$.

By M^∞ we denote the infinite streams over the set M; M^∞ can be represented by the total mappings from the natural numbers $\mathbb{N}$ into M. We denote the set of all streams over the set M by M^ω. Formally we have

$$M^\omega =_{\text{def}} M^* \cup M^\infty$$

We introduce a number of functions on streams that are useful in system descriptions.

A classical operation on streams is *concatenation,* which we denote by $^\wedge$. The concatenation is a function that takes two streams (say, s and t) and produces a stream $s^\wedge t$ as the result, starting with the stream s and continuing with the stream t. Formally the concatenation has the following functionality:

$$.^\wedge. : M^\omega \times M^\omega \to M^\omega$$

If the stream s is infinite, then concatenating stream s with a stream t yields stream s again:

$$s \in M^\infty \Rightarrow s^\wedge t = s$$

Concatenation is associative and has the empty stream $\langle\rangle$ as its neutral element:

$$r^\wedge(s^\wedge t) = (r^\wedge s)^\wedge t \qquad \langle\rangle^\wedge s = s = s^\wedge\langle\rangle$$

For any message $m \in M$ we denote by $\langle m \rangle$ the one-element stream consisting of the element m.

On the set M^ω of streams we define a *prefix ordering* $\sqsubseteq$. We write $s \sqsubseteq t$ for streams s and t if s is a *prefix* of t. Formally we have

$$s \sqsubseteq t \quad \text{iff} \quad \exists\, r \in M^\omega \colon s^\wedge r = t$$

The prefix ordering defines a partial ordering on the set M^ω of streams. If $s \sqsubseteq t$, then we also say that s is an *approximation* of t. The set of streams ordered by $\sqsubseteq$ is complete in the sense that every directed set $S \subseteq M^\omega$ of streams has a *least upper bound* denoted by lub S. A nonempty subset S of a partially ordered set is called *directed* if

$$\forall\, x, y \in S \colon \exists\, z \in S \colon x \sqsubseteq z \wedge y \sqsubseteq z$$

With least upper bounds of directed sets of finite streams we may describe infinite streams. Infinite streams are also of interest as (and can also be described by) fixpoints of prefix monotonic functions. The streams associated with feedback loops in interactive systems correspond to such fixpoints.

A *stream processing function* is a function

$$f : M^\omega \to N^\omega$$

that is *prefix monotonic* and *continuous*. The function f is called *prefix monotonic* if for all streams s and t we have

$$s \sqsubseteq t \Rightarrow f.s \sqsubseteq f.t$$

For better readability we often write for the function application $f.x$ instead of $f(x)$. A prefix monotonic function f is called *prefix continuous* if for all directed sets $S \subseteq M^\omega$ of streams we have

$$f.\text{lub}\ S = \text{lub}\{f.s : s \in S\}$$

If a function is prefix continuous, then its results for infinite input can already be determined from its results on all finite approximations of the input.

By $\perp$ we denote the pseudoelement that represents the result of diverging computations. We write $M^\perp M \cup \{\perp\}$. Here we assume that $\perp$ is not an element of M. On $M^\perp$ we define also a simple partial ordering called the *flat ordering* as follows:

$$x \sqsubseteq y \quad \text{iff} \quad x = y \vee x = \perp$$

We use the following functions on streams

$$ft \colon M^\omega \to M^\perp$$

$$rt \colon M^\omega \to M^\omega$$

The function *ft* selects the first element of a nonempty stream. The function *rt* deletes the first element of a nonempty stream.

To keep our notation simple, we extend concatenation $^\wedge$ also to elements of the message set M (treating them like one-element sequences) and to tuples of streams (by concatenating the streams elementwise). For the special element $\perp$ we specify $\perp^\wedge s = \langle\rangle$. This equation reflects the fact that there cannot be any further message on a channel after trying to send a message that is to be generated by a diverging (and therefore never ending) computation.

The properties of the introduced functions can be expressed by the following equations (let $m \in M$, $s \in M^\omega$):

$$ft.\langle\rangle = \perp, \quad rt.\langle\rangle = \langle\rangle, \quad ft(m^\wedge s) = m, \quad rt(m^\wedge s) = s$$

All of the introduced concepts and functions such as the prefix ordering and the concatenation carry over to tuples of streams by pointwise application. Similarly the prefix ordering induces a partial ordering on functions with streams and tuples of streams as range.

We denote the function space of (n, m)-ary prefix continuous stream processing functions by:

$$[(M^\omega)^n \rightarrow (M^\omega)^m]$$

The operations ft and rt are prefix monotonic and continuous, whereas concatenation $^\wedge$ as defined earlier is prefix monotonic and continuous only in its second argument.

2.2 Specification

In functional system modeling as used in the sequel, the observable behaviors of a system component are described by giving a *syntactic interface* consisting of

- a number of input channels with sort information for each channel (specifying the sort of the messages received on each channel),
- a number of output channels with sort information,

and a *semantic interface specification*. More technically, an input (or output) interface is syntactically determined by the number n of channels and by sets M_i, $1 \le i \le n$, of messages for each channel. We write

$$M_i^n$$

to denote the set

$$M_1^\omega \times \cdots \times M_n^\omega$$

By

$$[M_i^n \rightarrow N_i^m]$$

we denote the set of prefix continuous stream processing functions of functionality

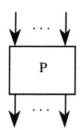

Fig. 1: Graphical representation of component P

$$M_1^\omega \times \cdots \times M_n^\omega \to N_1^\omega \times \cdots \times N_m^\omega$$

The semantic interface (the behavior) of a system component is represented by a set of functions characterized by a predicate

$$P: [M_i^n \to N_i^m] \to \mathbb{B}$$

The predicate P specifies the set of possible behaviors of an interactive component, and it is called a *behavioral* interface specification (Figure 1).

The *behavior* of a deterministic system is represented by a prefix continuous function

$$f \in [M_i^n \to N_i^m]$$

The function f associates with every tuple of input streams $x \in M_i^n$ a tuple of output streams $f.x \in N_i^m$. Nondeterministic systems are described by predicates that characterize a set of functions representing their set of possible behaviors.

We illustrate our specification technique by a simple example.

EXAMPLE: Interactive Queue

An interactive queue is a system that receives a stream of data elements from a given set D and request signals represented by the symbol $¿$. The queue then produces a stream of data in reply. It can be specified by a predicate

$$QU : [M^\omega \to M^\omega] \to \mathbb{B}$$

where the set M of messages is given by

$$M = D \cup \{¿\}$$

The specification QU is given by the following formula:

$$
\boxed{
\begin{array}{l}
QU.f \equiv f \in [M^\omega \to M^\omega] \wedge \forall\, x \in D^*, d \in D, y \in M^\omega: \\[4pt]
\quad f.x = \langle\rangle, \\[2pt]
\quad f(d^\wedge x^\wedge ¿^\wedge y) = d^\wedge f(x^\wedge y)
\end{array}
}
$$

For simplicity, the request signal $¿$ is included also in the sort of the messages in the output stream. This is used later in the further development of the example.

The predicate QU does not characterize a function f uniquely. If the first input is a request signal, then nothing is specified about the interactive queue's behavior. The predicate QU specifies a set of functions.

□

In our setting we do not distinguish between *nondeterminism* (as an operational notion of choices made during a computation) and *underspecification* (as a property of a description allowing several functions to fulfill a specifying predicate). This unifying view of nondeterminism and underspecification is justified by the conception that freedom of choice in a specification (underspecification) can be resolved on the one hand during the design by *design* decisions narrowing (or completely removing) underspecification or on the other hand by nondeterministic choices during *execution* (nondeterminism). One of the strong properties of the current approach is that no distinction between underspecification and nondeterminism (introducing a more operational view) has to be made. (For the difficulties with refinement concepts for more sophisticated concepts of nondeterminism, see [5,6].)

Sets of functions provide a very convenient way for representing the behavior of interactive systems. Sets of functions can be specified by logical formulas. A logical formula that formalizes a property of a function f is generally valid not just for one particular function (as in the case that a specification characterizes f uniquely), but for a set of functions. If this set is empty the specification is called *inconsistent*.

2.3 Forms of Composition

For composing stream processing functions and thereby forming networks, we use the three classical forms of composition, namely, *sequential* and *parallel* composition and *feedback*.

Let $g \in [M_i^n \to N_i^m]$ and $h \in [\bar{M}_i^{n'} \to \bar{N}_i^{m'}]$; we denote the *parallel composition* of g and h by $g \| h$ where

$$g \| h \in [M_i^n \times \bar{M}_i^{n'} \to N_i^m \times \bar{N}_i^{m'}]$$

Parallel composition can be visualized by the diagram given in Figure 2.

For input histories $x \in M_i^n$ and $y \in \bar{M}_i^{n'}$, we define the function obtained by parallel composition of the functions g and h by

$$(g \| h)(x \oplus y) = g(x) \oplus h(y)$$

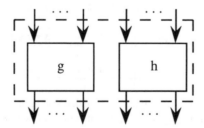

Fig. 2: Parallel composition

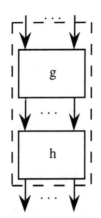
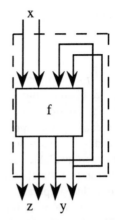

Fig. 3: Sequential composition   **Fig. 4:** Graphical illustration of feedback

where $\oplus$ denotes the concatenation of tuples of streams.

Let the function $g \in [M_i^n \rightarrow N_i^m]$ and the function $h \in [N_i^m \rightarrow \bar{N}_i^{m'}]$ be given; we denote the function obtained by the *sequential composition* of the function g and the function h by $g;h$ where

$$g;h \in [M_i^n \rightarrow \bar{N}_i^{m'}]$$

Sequential composition can be visualized by the diagram given in Figure 3.

For the input history $x \in M_i^n$, we define the function obtained by sequential composition of the functions g and h by

$$(g;h).x = h.g.x$$

We define the feedback operator μ^k for a function $f \in [M_i^n \times K_i^k \rightarrow N_i^m \times K_i^k]$. If we apply the fixed-point operator to a function f, we obtain the function

$$\mu^k f \in [M_i^n \rightarrow N_i^m \times K_i^k]$$

It is the function derived from f by k feedback loops. The feedback operator can be visualized by the diagram given in Figure 4.

For the input history $x \in M_i^n$, we define the function $\mu^k f$ that is obtained by k feedback loops from the function f by

$$(\mu^k f).x = \mathbf{fix}\ \lambda z, y\colon f(x, y)$$

where $z \in N_i^n$ and $y \in K_i^k$. By **fix** we denote the least fixed-point operator. In this equation the fixed-point operator is applied to the function $\lambda z, y\colon f(x, y)$, which for every given value of x denotes a function that does not depend on its parameter z [z is a parameter that does not influence the result of $\lambda z, y\colon f(x, y)$].

In a more readable version, we may specify the μ-operator as follows: We have

$$(z \oplus y) = (\mu^k f).x$$

if $z \oplus y$ is the least solution (fixed-point) of the following equation:

$$(z \oplus y) = f(x \oplus y)$$

Formally $(\mu^k f).x$ denotes a fixed-point relative to x, such that for every given tuple x of streams we obtain a tuple of streams $(z \oplus y)$ by a fixed-point construction.

The least fixed-point concept reflects the characteristics (the causality) of feedback in communications in an appropriate manner. The output of the component with behavior f on its feedback lines is sent back to its own input channels. If further output requires more input than available, no further output is generated. This is properly modeled by the assumption that the chosen fixed-point is the least one.

The introduced operators carry over to specifications in a straightforward way. Let Q and R be specifications of functions with appropriate functionality; we extend the three introduced operators to specifications as follows:

$$(Q\|R).f = \exists\, g, h\colon Q.g \wedge R.h \wedge f = g\|h$$

$$(Q\,;R).f = \exists\, g, h\colon Q.g \wedge R.h \wedge f = g;h$$

$$(\mu^k Q).f = \exists\, g\colon Q.g \wedge f = \mu^k g$$

The composition of specifications is understood as the pointwise composition of the specified functions.

2.4 Networks of Communicating Systems

Informally speaking a distributed system consists of a number of components interacting via channels. Some of these channels may be connected to the system's environment. The channels connected to the system's environment define the system's syntactic interface $[M_i^n \rightarrow N_i^m]$.

The system's *internal syntactic (static) structure* (visible in the glass-box view) of a network is mathematically represented by an expression formed by sequential composition, parallel composition, and feedback from basic components including those for permuting, copying, or deleting their input lines.

As can be seen, all types of finite networks can be represented that way. In addition, infinite networks can be defined by recursive equations for networks.

3 NOTIONS OF REFINEMENT

In this section, we treat several concepts of refinement of interactive systems. There are many related notions of refinement that are useful in system development. We concentrate primarily on behavior refinement, communication history refinement, and interface refinement, but only briefly touch and discuss other types of refinement.

Many different proposals exist for formalizing the notion of refinement. We choose here the most simple and most basic logical notion of refinement of specifications, namely, logical implication: A behavior specification Q is called a *behavior refinement* of the behavior specification P if both P and Q have the same syntactic interface and, if, in addition, we have

$$Q.f \Rightarrow P.f$$

for all functions f. We then write $Q \Rightarrow P$. Accordingly, a behavior refinement never introduces new observable interactions; instead, it restricts the behavior by adding properties. An inconsistent specification is a refinement for every specification with the same syntactic interface. It is, however, not a very useful refinement, since it cannot be refined into an implementation.

We will understand all other classes of refinements considered in the following to be special forms of behavior refinements where Q and P are in a more specific syntactic or semantic relationship.

Concepts of refinement for data structures and their characteristic operations are well known and well understood in the framework of algebraic specification (see, for instance, [7]). In the modeling of distributed interactive systems data structures are used to represent

- the messages passed between the components
- the histories of interactions between components (streams of messages)
- the states of the system.

In all three cases we may use the very general notion of data structure refinement. As demonstrated in the sequel, several concepts of system refinement can be obtained by variations of data structure refinement.

3.1 Refining Black-Box Views: Behavior Refinement

We consider two versions of refinement of the black-box view: refinement of the syntactic interface (by changing the number and the names as well as the sorts of the channels) of a system and refinement of the behavior of a system. If the syntactic interface is refined, then a concept is needed for relating the behaviors of the original and the refined system. This can be done by appropriate mappings (for another approach to refinement, see [8,9]).

3.1.1 Behavior Refinement

A behavior refinement is obtained by sharpening the requirements formalized in the specification. If we have the specifying predicate

$$P: [M_i^n \rightarrow N_i^m] \rightarrow \mathbb{B}$$

a behavior refinement is any predicate

$$\hat{P}: [m_i^n \rightarrow N_i^m] \rightarrow \mathbb{B}$$

where

$$\hat{P} \Rightarrow P$$

(or more precisely $\forall f: \hat{P}.f \Rightarrow P.f$). Of course, a refinement is only practically helpful if $\hat{P}$ (and in consequence P) is consistent; more formally, if we have

$$\exists f: \hat{P}.f$$

From a methodological point of view there are many different reasons for performing a behavior refinement. A typical example is the sharpening of specifications for the inclusion of exceptional cases.

EXAMPLE: Inclusion of Exceptional Cases

In the queue specification QU as shown in the first example, nothing was said about the exceptional case where a request signal $¿$ is received by the queue before a data message arrives. A behavior refinement QU' for the specification QU is simply obtained by adding a requirement for that case.

$$\boxed{\begin{array}{l} QU'.f \equiv f \in [M^{\omega} \to M^{\omega}] \wedge QU.f \wedge \forall \, y \in M^{\omega}: \\ \qquad\qquad f(¿y) = ¿f.y \end{array}}$$

This specification requires that a request signal $¿$ received when the queue is empty is processed by just reproducing the request in the output stream.

$\square$

Often behavior specifications are written in the *assumption/commitment format* (also called *rely/guarantee format*). A simple functional assumption/commitment specification has the following form

$$P.f \equiv \forall \, x: A.x \Rightarrow C(f, x)$$

Here A is called the *input assumption* and C is the *commitment specification*. This simple scheme of specification immediately suggests straightforward concepts of behavior refinement:

- weakening the input assumptions A
- strengthening the commitment specification C.

This is especially useful for refinements to make incompletely specified systems more robust by taking into account exceptional input situations and specifying the required behavior in reaction to these.

3.1.2 Communication History Refinement

In this section we treat refinements that change the syntactic interface of a component, that is, the number of input and output channels as well as their message sorts. These are often refinements between different levels of abstractions. We study refinement steps from an abstract level to a (more) concrete level. Then the behaviors of the

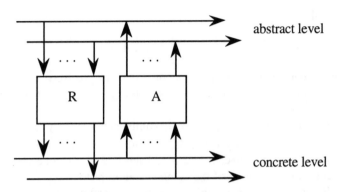

Fig. 5: Communication history refinement

refined component are related to the behaviors of the original component. This can be achieved by translating communication histories for the channels on the abstract level to communication histories for the channels on the concrete level.

In our setting a syntactic interface is given by a set of n (input or output) channels with their corresponding sorts M_i of messages. Communication histories for these channels are given by the elements of the set

$$M_i^n$$

In a communication history refinement a tuple of streams representing a communication history is replaced by another tuple of streams. For doing that we specify a translation. In our framework such a translation is defined by specifications R (*representation specification*) and A (*abstraction specification*) defining translations between the communication histories of the abstract level and the concrete level. This translation leads to commuting diagrams of the form illustrated in Figure 5.

A pair of predicates specifying interactive system components

$$R: [m_i^n \rightarrow \bar{M}_i^{n'}] \rightarrow \mathbb{B} \qquad representation\ specification$$

$$A: [\bar{M}_i^{n'} \rightarrow M_i^n] \rightarrow \mathbb{B} \qquad abstraction\ specification$$

is called a *communication history refinement pair* for the communication histories from M_i^n with representation elements in $\bar{M}_i^{n'}$ if the abstraction specification A and representation specification R are consistent; that is, the formula

$$\exists\ \alpha: A.\alpha \wedge \exists\ \rho: R.\rho$$

holds and for all functions

$$\alpha: [\bar{M}_i^{n'} \rightarrow M_i^n], \qquad \rho: [M_i^n \rightarrow \bar{M}_i^{n'}]$$

we have that

$$A.\alpha \wedge R.\rho \Rightarrow \rho\ ;\alpha = I$$

or, for short,

$$R\,;A = I$$

where I denotes the identity function (or more precisely the predicate that character-izes the identity function). Then A is called the *abstraction specification* and R is the *representation specification*.

By the functions ρ with $R.\rho$ a communication history $x \in M_i^n$ can be rewritten into a communication history $\rho.x \in \bar{M}_i^{n'}$. From $\rho.x$ we can obtain x again by applying any function α with $A.\alpha$ since $x = \alpha.\rho.x$. Therefore, $\rho.x$ can be viewed as a (possibly "less abstract") representation of the communication history x.

In many approaches a relation is used instead of the representation specification R. The specification R is, however, very similar to a relation. Every function ρ with $R.\rho$ represents one choice of representations for the abstract communication histories.

In the sequel we use the following notion for *restricting* a function to a particular subdomain. Given a function

$$f\colon D \to E$$

for $C \subseteq D$ we denote by $f\,|\,C$ that the function f is restricted to arguments from C. Formally, the restriction of the function f to the set C yields the function

$$f\,|\,C\colon C \to E$$

where

$$(f\,|\,C).x = f.x \quad \text{for } x \in C$$

From these definitions, we immediately derive the following properties for communica-tion history refinement pairs A, R:

1. All abstraction functions α with $A.\alpha$ are surjective.
2. A is deterministic on the image of R; that is, all functions α with $A.\alpha$ behave identical on the image of R; formally expressed, defining the image of R by a set $J \subseteq \bar{M}_i^{n'}$, where

$$J = \{\rho.x \in \bar{M}_i^{n'} : x \in M_i^n \wedge R.\rho\}$$

we have for all functions α and α'

$$A.\alpha \wedge A.\alpha' \Rightarrow \alpha\,|\,J = \alpha'\,|\,J$$

3. All functions ρ with $R.\rho$ are injective. More generally, we have for all x and x' and all representation functions ρ and ρ':

$$R.\rho \wedge R.\rho' \wedge \rho.x = \rho'.x' \Rightarrow x = x'$$

Property 1 immediately follows by the surjectivity of I. Property 2 can easily be proved as follows: Assume $A.\alpha$ and $A.\alpha'$; then for $y = \rho.x$ with $x \in M_i^n$, we have

$$\alpha.y = \alpha.\rho.x = x = \alpha'.\rho.x = \alpha'.y$$

Property 3 immediately follows by the injectivity of I.

EXAMPLE: Communication History Refinement

1. A simple example for communication history refinement is multiplexing. In multiplexing by interleaving messages, one channel is used instead of several. We define the representation specification as follows:

$$R1.\rho \equiv \rho \in [\mathbb{N}^\omega \to \mathbb{N}^\omega \times \mathbb{N}^\omega] \wedge \forall\, x \in \mathbb{N}^\omega:$$
$$\rho(x) = (ft.x,\, ft.rt.x)^\wedge \rho(rt.rt.x)$$

We define the abstraction specification as follows:

$$A1.\alpha \equiv \alpha \in [\mathbb{N}^\omega \times \mathbb{N}^\omega \to \mathbb{N}^\omega] \wedge \forall\, x, y \in \mathbb{N}^\omega:$$
$$\alpha(x, y) = (ft.x)^\wedge (ft.y)^\wedge \alpha(rt.x, rt.y)$$

We immediately obtain the following theorem.

Theorem: $(R1; A1) = I$

2. Let the set M of messages be defined as in the earlier example of interactive queues. To allow data from D and request signals to be sent on separated channels, we introduce a synchronizing message $\sqrt{}$. We define the sets of messages:

$$TD = D \cup \{\sqrt{}\}$$
$$TR = \{¿, \sqrt{}\}$$

We define the representation specification as follows:

$$R2.\rho \equiv \rho \in [M^\omega \to (TD^\omega \times TR^\omega)] \wedge \forall\, d \in D, x \in M^\omega:$$
$$\rho(d^\wedge x) = (d^\wedge \sqrt{},\, \sqrt{})^\wedge \rho.x$$
$$\rho(?^\wedge x) = (\sqrt{},\, ¿^\wedge \sqrt{})^\wedge \rho.x$$

We define the abstraction specification as follows:

$$A2.\alpha \equiv \alpha \in [(TD^\omega \times TR^\omega) \to M^\omega] \wedge \forall\, d \in D, y \in TD^\omega, z \in TR^\omega:$$
$$\alpha(\sqrt{}^\wedge y,\, \sqrt{}^\wedge z) = \alpha(y, z)$$
$$\alpha(d^\wedge y,\, \sqrt{}^\wedge z) = d^\wedge \alpha(y, \sqrt{}^\wedge z)$$
$$\alpha(\sqrt{}^\wedge y,\, ?^\wedge z) = ?^\wedge \alpha(\sqrt{}^\wedge y, z)$$

The symbol $\sqrt{}$ is used to separate the data messages and request signals. We immediately obtain the following theorem:

Theorem: $(R2; A2) = I$

$\square$

Let us now briefly look at the specification obtained by the sequential composition $(A; R)$, that is, all functions f such that $(A; R).f$. The set

$$\{f: (A; R).f\}$$

denotes the sheaf of functions that map representations of communication histories onto (in the sense of the abstraction) equivalent representations.

For practical purposes, we are not always interested in a communication history refinement that works correctly on the full set of communication histories. Often we are interested only in correctness for a subset of the considered input space. Let

$$S: M_i^n \rightarrow \mathbb{B}$$

be a predicate that defines a subset of communication histories. It is called a *communication history restriction*. A pair of consistent predicates is called a *communication history refinement pair with respect to the restriction S* if for all tuples of streams $x \in M_i^n$:

$$S.x \wedge A.\alpha \wedge R.\rho \Rightarrow \alpha.\rho.x = x$$

Communication history refinements can be used, in particular, to define refinements of interacting components. This is treated in detail in the following section.

3.1.3 Interface Interaction Refinement

We consider a specification of an interactive component

$$P: [M_i^n \rightarrow N_i^m] \rightarrow \mathbb{B}$$

and predicates

$$R: [M_i^n \rightarrow \bar{M}_i^{n'}] \rightarrow \mathbb{B}$$
$$\hat{P}: [\bar{M}_i^{n'} \rightarrow \bar{N}_i^{m'}] \rightarrow \mathbb{B}$$
$$\bar{A}: [\bar{N}_i^{m'} \rightarrow N_i^m] \rightarrow \mathbb{B}$$

where R is a representation specification (with a corresponding abstraction specification A) and $\bar{A}$ is an abstraction specification (for a representation specification $\bar{R}$); the triple

$$(R, \hat{P}, \bar{A})$$

of predicates is called a *component interface interaction refinement* for the component specification P with representation specification R and abstraction specification $\bar{A}$, if the following condition is fulfilled (also called *U-simulation*):

$$R; \hat{P}; \bar{A} \Rightarrow P \quad U\text{-simulation}$$

This condition is graphically expressed by the commuting diagram given in Figure 6.

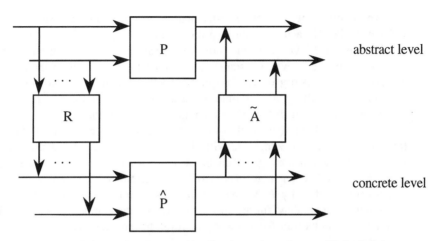

Fig. 6: Commuting diagram of interface interaction refinement (*U-simulation*)

EXAMPLE: Interface Interaction Refinement

1. *Addition:* Using the example of the communication history refinement given earlier, we may refine the following specification:

$$\text{ADD}.f \equiv [(\mathbb{N}^\omega \times \mathbb{N}^\omega) \to \mathbb{N}^\omega] \wedge \forall\, x, y \in \mathbb{N}^\omega:$$
$$f(x, y) = (ft.x + ft.y)^\wedge f(rt.x, rt.y)$$

The refinement is defined by $(R1, \text{ADD}', I)$ where ADD' is specified as follows:

$$\text{ADD}'.f \equiv f \in [\mathbb{N}^\omega \to \mathbb{N}^\omega] \wedge \forall\, x \in \mathbb{N}^\omega:$$
$$f.x = (ft.x + ft.rt.x)^\wedge f(rt.rt.x)$$

We obtain the following theorem

> **Theorem:** $R1 \,;\, \text{ADD}' \,;\, I \Rightarrow \text{ADD}$

2. *Queues:* We specify the predicate QI by a state-oriented specification technique, which is treated more systematically in the following section.

$$QI.f \equiv (f = h.\langle\rangle) \text{ where } h : D^* \to [(TD^\omega \times TR^\omega) \to (TD^\omega \times TR^\omega] \wedge \forall\, q \in D^*, d \in D, y \in TD^\omega, z \in TR^\omega:$$
$$(h.q).(\sqrt{}^\wedge y, \sqrt{}^\wedge z) = (\sqrt{}, \sqrt{})^\wedge (h.q).(y.z)$$
$$(h.q).(d^\wedge y, \sqrt{}^\wedge z) = h(q^\wedge \langle d\rangle).(y.\sqrt{}^\wedge z)$$
$$(h.\langle\rangle).(\sqrt{}^\wedge y, \text{¿}z) = (\langle\rangle, \text{¿})^\wedge (h.q).(\sqrt{}^\wedge y, z)$$
$$(h.d^\wedge q).(\sqrt{}^\wedge y, \text{¿}z) = (d, \langle\rangle)^\wedge (h.q).(\sqrt{}^\wedge y, z)$$

We immediately obtain the following theorem:

> **Theorem:** $R2 \,;\, QI \,;\, A2 \Rightarrow QU'$

□

The component interaction refinement as just introduced basically expresses that we may replace in a refinement step the component specified by P with a component specified by $(R; \hat{P}; \bar{A})$. After this refinement, instead of computing with the component P on the "abstract" level, we transform an input history given on the abstract level by R into an input history on the "concrete" level, compute with the component $\hat{P}$, and transform the result by $\bar{A}$ back onto the abstract level. This form of refinement leads to a behavior refinement of the original component specification P.

There are alternatives to this form of refinement (see also [10]) for a systematic treatment). Instead of computing with the component P on the abstract level, we may translate an input history given on the abstract level by an appropriate representation specification $\hat{R}$ into an input history on the concrete level, where we compute with a component specified by $\hat{P}$. We require that this form of computation be a refinement of the computation obtained for the abstract input with the component specified by P on the abstract level and a transformation of the result to the concrete level by a representation specification $\bar{R}$.

This concept of refinement between levels of abstraction is formalized as follows. Given representation specifications and corresponding abstraction specifications:

$$R: [M_i^n \to \bar{M}_i^{n'}] \to \mathbb{B}, \qquad A : [\bar{M}_i^{n'} \to M_i^n] \to \mathbb{B}$$
$$\bar{R}: [N_i^m \to \bar{N}_i^{m'}] \to \mathbb{B}, \qquad \bar{A} : [\bar{N}_i^{m'} \to N_i^m] \to \mathbb{B}$$

and specifications

$$P: [M_i^n \to N_i^m] \to \mathbb{B}$$
$$\hat{P}: [\bar{M}_i^{n'} \to \bar{N}_i^{m'}] \to \mathbb{B}$$

then $\hat{P}$ is called a *refinement of P under the representation specifications R and* $\bar{R}$ if

$$R; \hat{P} \Rightarrow P; \bar{R}$$

This formula is visualized by the commuting diagram of Figure 7.

Of course, with the help of the abstraction specification $\bar{A}$ for the representation specification $\bar{R}$ we obtain:

$$R; \hat{P}; \bar{A} \Rightarrow P$$

However, even if we work with specifications R and $\bar{R}$ for which abstractions do not exist, refinements of the form

$$R; \hat{P} \Rightarrow P; \bar{R} \qquad \textit{downward simulation}$$

are often useful, because they allow us to relate specifications at different levels of abstraction where the representations of the abstract communication histories are not necessarily unique. Broy [11] shows that the condition

$$R; \hat{P} \Rightarrow P; \bar{R}$$

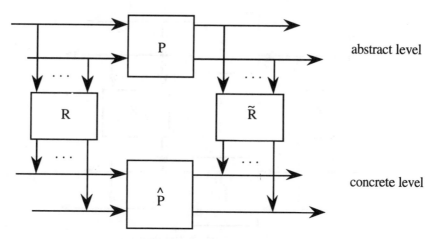

Fig. 7: Downward simulation

can be used as the basic condition for a compositional refinement of networks. A compositional refinement concept allows for the refinement of a network by refinements of its components (for another approach to the composition of specifications, see [12]).

Two further versions of interaction refinement are obtained by the following condition (Figure 8):

$$\hat{P} \, ; \, \tilde{A} \Rightarrow A \, ; \, P \qquad upward\ simulation$$

and by the stronger condition (also called U^{-1} simulation; Figure 9):

$$\hat{P} \Rightarrow A \, ; \, P \, ; \, \tilde{R}$$

By this formula the specification $\hat{P}$ is a behavior refinement of the specification $(A; P; \tilde{R})$. This last version of refinement is the strongest requirement. All other three versions of refinement can be deduced if this refinement formula is valid.

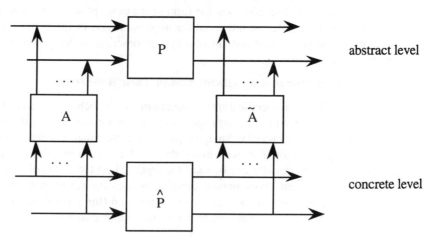

Fig. 8: Upward simulation

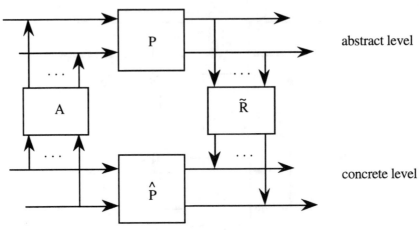

Fig. 9: U^{-1} simulation

The introduced notion of interaction refinement is just a generalization of notions of refinement and implementation as developed in the framework of algebraic specifications (see [7]).

3.2 Refinement of the Glass-Box View

In the glass-box view we are not only interested in the observable behavior of a system but also in its internal structure. In pure behavior specifications, nothing is said about the internal structure of a system. However, if we describe the observable behavior of the system by

- a state-oriented description or
- a network description,

then if we assume a glass-box view the form of the description gives additional information about the representation and about the implementation of the system. Thus, it is the *form* rather than the logical content of a system description that represents the internal structure of a system.

3.2.1 State-Oriented Specifications and Their Refinement

Functional system specification techniques model the behavior of systems in terms of system histories. Nevertheless, such specifications can also be written in a state-oriented style. This is done by choosing an appropriate set State called the *state space*. Then we associate a specification $P.\sigma$ with every state $\sigma \in$ State. In principle, any set State of sufficiently large cardinality can be used for representing the states of a system.

A straightforward state-oriented description uses the set of states to describe the behavior of a component by a state transition function (for simplicity, we treat only the case of a system with one input channel and one output channel)

$$\tau: (\text{State} \times M) \to \mathcal{P}(\text{State} \times N^{\omega})$$

and a set of initial states Init $\subseteq$ State. Here M is the set of input messages and N is the set of output messages. The close relationship to the functional specification concepts can be shown as follows. Each state defines a specifying predicate

$$H: \text{State} \rightarrow ([M^{\omega} \rightarrow N^{\omega}] \rightarrow \mathbb{B})$$

by means of the following formula (we take the most liberal predicate $H.s$ that fulfils the following formula)

$$
\begin{array}{|l|}
\hline
(H.s).f \equiv \forall\ m \in M : \exists\ s' \in \text{State},\ f' \in [M^{\omega} \rightarrow N^{\omega}],\ y \in N^{\omega}: \\
(s', y) \in \tau(s, m) \land \forall\ x \in M^{\omega} : f(m^{\wedge}x) = y^{\wedge}f'(x) \land (H.s').f' \\
\hline
\end{array}
$$

In this way every state is mapped onto a predicate characterizing a set of stream processing functions.

Based on this recursive specification of the predicate H we may obtain a component specification

$$P: [M^{\omega} \rightarrow N^{\omega}] \rightarrow \mathbb{B}$$

from the given state machine description by the following formula:

$$P.f = \exists\ s \in \text{Init}: (H.s).f$$

EXAMPLE: State-Based Description of an Interactive Queue

A state-based description of an interactive queue is given by choosing the state space State by

$$\text{State} = D^*$$

and the specification of the transition function τ for $\sigma \in D^*$, $m \in D$, as follows:

$$
\begin{aligned}
\tau(\sigma, m) &= \{(\sigma^{\wedge}m, \langle\rangle)\} \\
\tau(m^{\wedge}\sigma, \dot{\iota}) &= \{(\sigma, m)\} \\
\tau(\langle\rangle, \dot{\iota}) &= \{(\langle\rangle, \dot{\iota})\}
\end{aligned}
$$

We reformulate the specification QU' to the specification QS based on the state transition function.

$$
\begin{array}{|l|}
\hline
QS.f \equiv (f = h.\langle\rangle)\ \textbf{where}\ h: D^* \rightarrow [M^{\omega} \rightarrow M^{\omega}] \land \forall\ d \in D, q \in D^*, x \in M^{\omega}: \\
\qquad (h.\langle\rangle).(\dot{\iota}^{\wedge}x) = \dot{\iota}^{\wedge}(h.\langle\rangle).x \\
\qquad (h.(d^{\wedge}q)).(\dot{\iota}^{\wedge}x) = d^{\wedge}(h.q).x \\
\qquad (h.q).(d^{\wedge}x) = (h.(q^{\wedge}d)).x \\
\hline
\end{array}
$$

We may notice the uniform patterns of the equations for h. All equations are of the form

$$(h.\sigma).(m^{\wedge}x) = b^{\wedge}(h.\sigma').x$$

where σ denotes the given state and m denotes an input message. By b we denote the output message and by σ' the resulting state. We can also represent the equations for h by the following table:

σ	m	b	σ'
$\langle\rangle$	i	i	$\langle\rangle$
$d^{\wedge}q$	i	d	q
q	d	$\langle\rangle$	$q^{\wedge}d$

It is straightforward to show that $QU' \Leftrightarrow QS$.

□

State-oriented descriptions of system components can be understood as a particular style of functional system specification. State-oriented system specifications are often advocated, since an adequate choice of the state space may lead to a better understanding of the described system behavior. On the other hand, the rather concrete, operational, single-step-oriented nature of state-based specifications can make the reasoning about systems more inconvenient.

The state transition functions as introduced here correspond to so-called I/O automata [13]. For I/O automata a straightforward notion of equivalence (and of refinement) is obtained by observing input and output. This is not true for state transition system models without input and output. This type of machine needs a special notion of equivalence for defining refinements.

For state-oriented system specification, we can also study the notion of state refinement. Technically speaking, a state refinement is given by a function

$$\rho: \text{State} \to \text{State}'$$

such that for all $\sigma \in$ State:

$$(\hat{H}\rho.\sigma).f \Rightarrow (H.\sigma).f$$

A state refinement is considered to be correct if the corresponding component specification is a correct refinement of the given component specification. A state refinement can be used in system development to change the presentation of the states.

In [14] the concept of stuttering is introduced. Roughly speaking, in a state-based approach with this concept, two systems are considered equivalent if they show the same state traces apart from finite repetitions of states. Stuttering is needed for an equivalence relation that is appropriate as a basis for refinements (see also [15]).

3.2.2 Distribution Refinement

The glass-box view of a system can be described with network of components that interact by exchanging messages. In this way, both a black-box view (by abstracting from the network and just considering the external behavior) and a glass-box view (taking the network representation of the system as the description of its distributed realization) are provided.

When the system is represented by a network, of course, further *local* refinements of the subcomponents, their behavior, their interaction, and their states are possible, leading

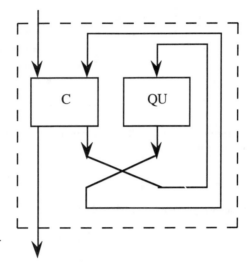

Fig. 10: Graphical representation of the distribution refinement component QU

to refinements of the system. This is due to the fact that in the functional approach the operators (sequential composition, parallel composition, and feedback) are monotonic with respect to refinement: The refinement of a subcomponent always leads to a refinement of the whole system. In this sense the refinement concept is *compositional.* For a proof of the compositionality of interface interaction refinement see [11].

A special case of distribution refinement replaces a state-oriented description of a system component with a network of subsystems that are again described in a state-oriented way, such that the collection of all states of the subcomponents can be understood as a refinement (in the sense of data structure refinement) of the initial state.

Considering the external (observable) behavior (the black-box view), there is no difference between a component that is represented by a single "sequential" program (for instance by a state machine) and a component with its behavior represented by a network of distributed interacting subsystems. However, there is a difference with respect to the glass-box view. Replacing a component specification with a network description is called *distribution refinement.*

EXAMPLE: Distribution Refinement: Queue Again!

We refine the specification QU to a network described by the following recursive equation, which can be understood to be the recursive definition of a predicate and also as the recursive definition of a network:

$$QU = \mu^2((C \| QU);(I \| X))$$

where I is the specification of the identity function, and X permutes its input lines. This formula describes a network that can be graphically represented by Figure 10.

The behavior of C is defined as follows:

$$C.f \equiv (f = h.¿) \text{ where } h: M \to](M^\omega)^2 \to (M^\omega)^2] \land \forall\, m, i \in M, x, z \in M^\omega:$$

$$
\begin{aligned}
(h.m).(i^\wedge x, z) = \ &\textbf{if } i = ¿ \ \land m = ¿ \quad \textbf{then } (¿, \langle\rangle)^\wedge (h.m).(x, z) \\
&[\!] \ i \in D \ \land m = ¿ \quad \textbf{then } (h.i).(x, z) \\
&[\!] \ i = ¿ \ \ \land m \in D \quad \textbf{then } (m, ¿)^\wedge (h.ft.z).(x, rt.z) \\
&[\!] \ i \in D \ \land m \in D \quad \textbf{then } (\langle\rangle, i)^\wedge (h.m).(x, z) \\
&\textbf{fi}
\end{aligned}
$$

In this specification the auxiliary function h is again specified in a state-oriented style, namely, by equations of the form

$$(h.m).(i^\wedge x, z) = b^\wedge (h.m').(x, z')$$

for which we give the following table:

m	i	b	m'	z'
$¿$	$¿$	$(¿, \langle\rangle)$	$¿$	z
$¿$	d'	$(\langle\rangle, \langle\rangle)$	d'	z
d	$¿$	$(d, ¿)$	$ft.z$	$rt.z$
d	d'	$(\langle\rangle, d')$	d	z

□

Distribution refinements are in particular difficult to prove correct, since in general complex forms of feedback have to be dealt with. A correctness proof for the distribution refinement given here can be found in [16].

3.3 Refinement by Reformulation of the Specification

There are many different ways of describing the external (observable) behavior (black-box view) as well as the internal structure (glass-box view) of system components. We may distinguish (among others) roughly the following different forms of behavior descriptions:

- axiomatic, property-oriented descriptions
- state-based descriptions
- recursive predicate descriptions
- assumption/commitment specifications
- network descriptions.

These different ways of describing the behavior of a system component are related with different methods for syntactically expressing refinements, and all of these different methods can be formalized in a straightforward manner in our unifying functional framework.

As discussed in Section 3.2, the form of description sometimes can be understood to give information about the glass-box view of the component. Of course, one may talk more explicitly about the glass-box view in descriptions of the form: "the system consists of particular subcomponents that are connected by particular channels." The more implicit way of describing the glass-box view of a system by a state transition system or a network makes it necessary, however, to distinguish between the following intentions when writing specifications:

- specifications that by their form describe system structures in the sense of the glass-box view
- specifications in terms of state transition systems or distributed systems that are used only for specification purposes and should not be understood as descriptions of the glass-box view.

If a specification is given in terms of a set of axiomatic laws (for instance, in the assumption/commitment format) and later it is reformulated by some recursive equations for the specifying predicate, this does not necessarily say anything about the glass-box view. Even state-oriented specifications may be used—not for implicitly describing a realization in the sense of the glass-box view—but rather as a specification concept. In this case we also speak of *abstract states* [14].

Often a component specification

$$P: [M_i^n \rightarrow N_i^m] \rightarrow \mathbb{B}$$

is described by a recursive equation for the predicate P (see the specification for P derived from a state machine description; for a more comprehensive treatment of recursion for specifications, see [11]):

$$P.f \equiv \exists\, g_1, \ldots, g_k : \tau[g_1, \ldots, g_k] \sqsubseteq f \wedge P.g_1 \wedge \ldots \wedge P.g_k$$

In general, we associate with such a recursive description the weakest predicate that fulfills this equation. For this form of definition we immediately obtain simple concepts of refinement.

Refinement by reformulation has to do with changing or refining the syntactic description of the behavior of an agent. Two particularly interesting representations of the behavior of agents are

- net representations
- constructive representations.

Both representations can be characterized by their particular syntactic forms: a constructive representation of the behavior of an agent

$$Q: [M_i^n \rightarrow N_i^m] \rightarrow \mathbb{B}$$

is of the form

$$Q = G \tag{3.1}$$

where G is an expression formed of interactive component specifications that are again in constructive form (including possibly Q) or given as executable components. Equation (3.1) defines a net representation for Q, if G contains only net forming operations. Again the net representation is called constructive if all the involved interactive component specifications are in constructive form.

4 CONCLUSIONS

This study makes an attempt to classify various forms of refinements of system structures in a formal specification, refinement, and verification framework. It is quite clear that in the development of a large system, numerous refinement steps are needed. During development the system will be described at several levels of abstraction such that more and more refined system versions are obtained.

We did not treat the methodological aspects of refinement at all in this study. A methodology gives advice at which levels of abstraction a system should be described during the development and which refinement steps should be tried in which order. Nevertheless, we claim that all the refinement steps that are needed in a method-oriented system development are covered by the refinement concepts described in this study (see [17]).

A flexible concept of refinement is the key to a formal method for the development of systems and their components. It is one of the decisive questions for the tractability of a specification and development method—the ease with which we can express and verify refinement. In this chapter, we have shown how easily the different refinement concepts can be expressed and verified within the formalism of functional system specification techniques. The compositionality of the introduced concept of refinement is proven in [11]. The correctness of most of the refinements given in this paper have been verified using the LARCH prover [16], which is an interactive verification system based on rewriting.

Appendix A: Full Abstractness

Two specifications characterizing different sets of stream processing functions can, nevertheless, be understood to characterize the same behavior of a component, if the difference between the two sets lies just in some superficial difference that is not observable in computations. To avoid such superficial differences, we may restrict our considerations to so-called *fully abstract* predicates for specifications.

Fully abstract predicates [18] do not present more information about an interface than necessary. A specification P is termed *fully abstract* if

$$(\forall\, x\colon \exists\, g\colon P.g \wedge f.x = g.x \wedge f\,|\,\{z\colon z \sqsubseteq x\} \sqsubseteq g\,|\,\{z\colon z \sqsubseteq x\}) \Rightarrow P.f$$

In a fully abstract specification we do not have any representation of behavioral details in the specification that cannot be observed by appropriately chosen environments (for a justification of this choice, see [18]).

The notion of fully abstract specification results from a concept of observability as induced by the basic operators for composing specifications. These operations are sequential and parallel composition as well as feedback. We introduce a predicate transformer

$$\text{ABS: } [M_i^n \to N_i^m] \to [M_i^n \to N_i^m]$$

mapping every specification $P \in [M_i^n \to N_i^m]$ onto its abstraction

$$(\text{ABS}.P).f \equiv \forall\, x \colon \exists\, g \colon P.g \wedge f.x = g.x \wedge f \,|\, \{z \colon z \sqsubseteq x\} \sqsubseteq g \,|\, \{z \colon z \sqsubseteq x\}$$

For abstract specifications we obtain

$$\text{ABS}.P = P$$

The use of fully abstract specifications has advantages when proving the equivalence of components' behaviors. Of course, our choice of full abstractness is influenced by the operators we consider.

Appendix B: Indefinite Representations

In communication history refinements we have considered representation specifications

$$R \colon [M_i^n \to \bar{M}_i^{n'}] \to \mathbb{B}$$

and abstraction specifications

$$A \colon [\bar{M}_i^{n'} \to M_i^n)] \to \mathbb{B}$$

such that

$$R \,;\, A = I$$

Let us now call such representation specifications and abstraction specifications *definite*, since they associate a unique abstraction with each representation of a communication history. However, there are cases for which a representation specification can allow some loss of information in the sense that some different abstract communication histories $x, x' \in M_i^n$ are represented by the same elements in $\bar{M}_i^{n'}$. This may be appropriate, if not all the information given in x and x' is actually relevant.

A representation specification

$$R \colon [M_i^n \to \bar{M}_i^{n'}] \to \mathbb{B}$$

for which an abstraction specification A with

$$R \,;\, A = I$$

does not exist is called *indefinite* representation specification. Similarly, a specification A is called indefinite abstraction specification if a specification R does not exist such that the preceding equation holds.

Not all interface interaction refinements have to be based on definite representation and abstraction specifications. Interface interaction refinements may also be of the form $(R; \hat{P}; A)$ where R is not a definite representation specification and A is not a definite abstraction specification.

For instance, if the component interface specification P is nondeterministic and not injective, we may take advantage of the nondeterminism contained in P and choose R and A in a more liberal, indefinite way. In particular, the specification R may identify all input histories that cannot lead to distinguishable output in P. The functions ρ with $R.\rho$ need not be injective then. For input histories $x, x' \in M_i^n$ we may allow $\rho.x = \rho.x$, even if $x \neq x'$, provided that

(a) a function p exists with $P.p$ such that $p.x = p.x'$, or more generally
(b) functions p and p' exist with $P.p$ and $P.p'$ such that $p.x = p'.x'$.

Of course, (a) is a special case of (b). Similarly, the abstraction specification A may be nondeterminate, provided the nondeterminism in A corresponds to the nondeterminism in the component specification P.

Along these lines, two aspects lead to more freedom in choosing the representation specification for a given component specification P when looking for an interface interaction refinement $\hat{P}$.

1. If P does not distinguish between certain inputs x and x' (for instance, if for all functions g with $P.g$ we have $g.x = g.x'$), then x and x' do not have to be represented by different elements.
2. If P produces for some input x nondeterministical results $g.x$ and $g'.x$ (let g and g' be functions such that both $P.g$ and $P.g'$ hold), then $g.x$ and $g'.x$ may be represented by the same element in the output of P.

For explaining this more general notion of interaction refinement, we study neutral elements for specifications with respect to sequential composition. Trivially, the identity specification is always neutral, since

$$(P ; I) = (I ; P) = P$$

Given a component specification P specifying a (possibly) nondeterministic behavior, a function f is called *left-neutral* for P if for all functions g:

$$P.g \Rightarrow P(f;g)$$

A left-neutral function does change the behavior of an interactive component just in a way that nondeterministic effects are rearranged. Obviously, the identity function is always left-neutral.

Given a specification P, let $LN(P)$ denote the specification where

$$LN(P).f \equiv \forall g: P.g \Rightarrow P(f;g)$$

Obviously the set $\{f: LN(P).f\}$ is algebraically closed under function composition since the composition of left-neutrals leads to left-neutrals again. Moreover, since

$$I \Rightarrow LN(P)$$

we have

$$P = LN(P)\,;\,P$$

In analogy, a function f is called *right-neutral* for P if for all functions g:

$$P.g \Rightarrow P(g;f)$$

We write $RN(P).f$ as the abbreviation for the specification where

$$RN(P).f \equiv \forall\, g : P.g \Rightarrow P(g;f)$$

In particular, we have

$$P = LN(P)\,;\,P\,;\,RN(P)$$

Now let us come back to the concept of interface interaction refinement $\hat{P}$ for P. Even if for the representation specification $\bar{R}$ a definite abstraction does not exist but just a specification $\bar{A}$ such that

$$\bar{R}\,;\,\bar{A} \Rightarrow RN(P)$$

we obtain from

$$R\,;\,\hat{P} \Rightarrow P\,;\,\bar{R}$$

the deduction

$$
\begin{aligned}
R\,;\,\hat{P}\,;\,\bar{A} &\Rightarrow \\
P\,;\,\bar{R}\,;\,\bar{A} &\Rightarrow \\
P\,;\,RN(P) &\Rightarrow \\
P &
\end{aligned}
$$

So even if $\bar{R}$ is not a definite representation specification, we can use it for interaction refinements of P. However, we cannot use it for interaction refinements of arbitrary specifications with the right syntactic interface as is possible for definite representation specifications.

ACKNOWLEDGMENTS

I thank my colleagues at the TU Munich for stimulating discussions. Frank Dederichs and Ketil Stølen did a careful reading of one version of the manuscript and provided helpful remarks.

REFERENCES

[1] M. Broy, "Algebraic Methods for Program Construction: The Project CIP," SOF-SEM 82; see also P. Pepper, Ed., *Program Transformation and Programming Environments*, NATO ASI Series, Series F: 8, Springer Verlag, Berlin, pp. 199–222, 1984.

[2] C. A. R. Hoare, "Proofs of Correctness of Data Representations," *Acta Info.* 1, pp. 271–281, 1972.

[3] C. B. Jones, "Systematic Program Development Using VDM," Prentice Hall, Englewood Cliffs, NJ, 1986.

[4] T. Nipkow, "Nondeterministic Data Types: Models and Implementations," *Acta Info.* 22, pp. 629–661, 1986.

[5] L. Aceto and M. Hennessy, "Adding Action Refinement to a Finite Process Algebra," in *Proc. ICALP 91,* Lecture Notes in Computer Science 510, pp. 506–519, 1991.

[6] W. Janssen, M. Poel, and J. Zwiers, "Action Systems and Action Refinement in the Development of Parallel Systems—An Algebraic Approach," unpublished manuscript, 1991.

[7] M. Broy, B. Möller, P. Pepper, and M. Wirsing, "Algebraic Implementations Preserve Program Correctness," *Sci. Computer Program.,* 8, pp. 1–19, 1986.

[8] R. J. R. Back, "Refinement Calculus, Part I: Sequential Nondeterministic Programs," REX Workshop, in *Stepwise Refinement of Distributed Systems,* J. W. deBakker, W.-P. deRoever, G. Rozenberg, Eds., Lecture Notes in Computer Science 430, pp. 42–66, 1988.

[9] R. J. R. Back, "Refinement Calculus, Part II: Parallel and Reactive Programs," REX Workshop, in *Stepwise Refinement of Distributed Systems,* J. W. de Bakker, W.-P. de Roever, G. Rozenberg, Eds., Lecture Notes in Computer Science 430, pp. 67–93, 1988.

[10] J. Coenen, W. P. deRoever, and J. Zwiers, "Assertional Data Reification Proofs: Survey and Perspective," Bericht Nr. 9106, Christian-Albrechts-Universität Kiel, Institut für Informatik und praktische Mathematik, Feb. 1991.

[11] M. Broy, "Compositional Refinement of Interactive Systems." SRC Report 89, Digital Systems Research Center, July 1992.

[12] M. Abadi and L. Lamport, "Composing Specifications," SRC Report 66, Digital Systems Research Center, Oct. 1990.

[13] N. Lynch and E. Stark, "A Proof of the Kahn Principle for Input/Output Automata," *Info. Computation,* 82, pp. 81–92, 1989.

[14] L. Lamport, "Specifying Concurrent Program Modules," *ACM Toplas,* 5(2), pp. 190–222, Apr. 1983.

[15] M. Abadi and L. Lamport, "The Existence of Refinement Mappings," SRC Report 29, Digital Systems Research Center, Aug. 1988.

[16] M. Broy, "Experiences with Machine Supported Software and System Specification and Verification: Using the Larch Prover," SRC Report 93, Digital Systems Research Center, 1992.

[17] M. Broy, F. Dederichs, C. Dendorfer, M. Fuchs, T. F. Gritzner, and R. Weber, "The Design of Distributed Systems—An Introduction to Focus," Technische Universität München, Institut für Informatik, Sonderforschungsbereich 342: Methoden und Werkzeuge für die Nutzung paralleler Architekturen TUM-I9202, January 1992.

[18] M. Broy, "Functional Specification of Time Sensitive Communicating Systems," REX Workshop, in *Stepwise Refinement of Distributed Systems*, J. W. de Bakker, W.-P. de Roever, G. Rozenberg, Eds., Lecture Notes in Computer Science 430, pp. 153–179, 1990.

CHAPTER 4

Applying Modeling to Embedded Computer Systems Design

D. Gareth Evans   Derrick Morris
Department of Computation
University of Manchester Institute of Science and Technology (UMIST)
Manchester, United Kingdom

Abstract: A hardware/software codesign method is presented, which makes extensive use of executable modeling techniques to validate the behavior and design of a system under development. This chapter uses a simple computer system engineering lifecycle to identify issues that can be addressed by executable modeling and the requirements for tool support. Models are captured in graphic notation that is based on structured analysis data flow diagrams but which have significant semantic differences. These arise because of the need to model hardware as well as software, and because of the precision required for models to be executed. An example of such a model, that of a digital telephone exchange, is given. The features and architecture of the set of tools that are used to support the capture, execution, analysis, and translation of the models discussed.

1 INTRODUCTION

Three critical steps that need to be taken to produce a successful computer system product are the capture of complete and approved user requirements, the generation of a cost-effective design that satisfies these and possibly other nonfunctional requirements, and the realization of an implementation that conforms to this design. Other significant factors in ensuring the commercial success of the system are completion of the development within budget and on time, and the ease with which its design and implementation can be comprehended by those who may subsequently need to maintain and modify the system. There are probably few practitioners who would dissent from this view, and it is widely accepted that an organized methodology for the specification, analysis, and design of computer systems is a necessary and vital part of the engineering process used in their manufacture. The importance of good documentation throughout the process is also accepted.

Research into methods for achieving some or all of these requirements, particularly with respect to the software in computer systems, is as old as the computer business itself. However, although significant advances have been made during the past three decades, it still remains an important area of computer systems research. This is partly because the "target moves." System size and complexity continue to increase and the tolerance level for error decreases, particularly in safety critical systems [1]. Also, inertia has to be overcome in transferring the "solutions" developed through research into actual production processes used in industry. Examples are not hard to find of 10- to 20-year gaps between the leading edge of research and the practice in industry. The problems responsible for this are manifold but, clearly, in order for new methods to be adopted they must offer very significant proven advantages and possibly lend themselves to evolutionary introduction. Hence, research continues in an attempt to perfect methods and assess their benefits.

With respect to overall system planning and to the software of systems, most of the research to date and the developments that spring from it are concerned with either structured graphical methods, formal methods, or object orientation. The Yourdon [2] and Ward/Mellor [3] structured analysis methods are well-known examples of a graphical approach and VDM [4], Z [5], and functional programming languages [6] typify the formal approach. Object orientation is not as easily separated out since it uses graphical techniques to illustrate the hierarchical structure of objects and the way in which they interact [7], and its main structuring concept (abstract data types [8]) is also a feature of most formal languages. Recently, research has been most strongly focused on the formal and object-oriented methods, although the structured graphical methods have made a bigger breakthrough in industry, and they have also gained new impetus through the arrival of desktop graphics.

Initially, high-level approaches to hardware specification received less attention. This is changing with the adoption of hardware description languages (HDLs), such as VHDL [9]. HDLs aim to provide verification of functionality and performance by simulation, and automatic implementation through synthesis. Also, to augment these textual languages, graphics-based tools have been developed, such as the SES/workbench [10].

It is against this background that the authors have investigated the construction and uses of dynamic models of complete computer systems. The motivation for the work has arisen partly out of their involvement in producing actual systems, and hence having a need, and partly out of the desire to experiment with better methods and tools for doing the job. The tools developed are intended to contribute to most phases of the product life cycle, but they are centered around a working, that is, executable, model of the system. Initially the model provides the means to clarify behavioral objectives; later it supports the exploration of implementation structures and finally it assists in the development and testing of an implementation. Figure 1 shows where the modeling tools might be applied in a conventional waterfall life cycle, although in practice they tend to encourage a more "prototype oriented" life cycle.

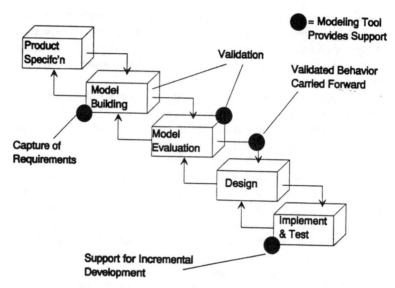

Fig. 1: Possible application of modeling tools in the waterfall life cycle

The main research interest in this work is to understand the ways in which executable models, and tools to manipulate them, can aid the system engineering process. Although a notation for specifying computer system models is presented, it is a means to an end, as are the supporting tools. Hence, an easy implementation path has been devised to provide tools for analyzing, executing, and translating models, which have been captured in a structured analysis [2,3,11] style by a commercial CASE tool. In effect, the notation is an adaptation of structured analysis, in which there are modified semantics for the graphs and a simple procedural language for specifying (or programming) the behavior of primitive processes and data. This modification allows sufficient behavioral detail to be included to make analysis and dynamic evaluation of a captured model possible. Inevitably, the experience generates views on a more ideal graphical basis for dynamic models, but developments of this kind are better carried out on a commercial scale.

This chapter elaborates further on the purpose and method of dynamic modeling of computer systems and the experimental environment in which the research is taking place. It also discusses features of current and projected developments of the modeling tools. The value of dynamic modeling is being investigated by applying the method and tools to actual system developments; hence, some substantial executable models have been constructed. Part of one of these, a PABX, is presented later in order to convey a feeling of what is involved with the practical use of models. Finally, some tentative conclusions are offered that have arisen out of the research to date.

2 MODELING A COMPUTER SYSTEM

For the purpose of this chapter the scope of the term *computer system* should be taken to mean systems involving one or more computers, special-purpose hardware, and embedded software control programs. Embedded systems as defined by Zave [12] fall within the class of systems under consideration as do real-time systems of the kind developed by Ward and Mellor [3]. Distributed control systems involving concurrency and parallelism are particularly relevant to our own interests.

In the context of this work, a *model* represents an operational system displaying the selected features of a proposed system. The model needs to be both computer readable and easy for humans to comprehend when presented on a workstation screen or in hardcopy form. The notation chosen facilitates the top-down decomposition of a system into a network of collaborating processes. This is expressed in diagrams that have rigorously defined semantics, and the bottom-level "primitive" processes are specified (or "programmed") in a textual language. This choice has been made in order to combine the human readability obtained from diagrams with the precision and computer readability that stems from formally defined textual language.

The term *modeling* is used here to mean creation of a model of the type mentioned and its use at most stages of a production life cycle. It obviously includes the capture of the model and its presentation in human-readable form. As indicated in Figure 1, this supports the initial validation of a behavioral proposal, and is in fact achieved by direct use of the CASE tool. The added tools access the data captured by the CASE tool to provide support for exercising, analyzing, and translating the model. These activities are also considered to be part of modeling. Thus modeling completely takes over the role of specification and analysis as traditionally carried out by methods such as structured analysis, but it continues much further into the life cycle. Also, the notation adopted allows the model to include behavioral detail of the digital and analog hardware that is an integral part of the system. Execution of the model allows validation of chosen aspects of behavior and some verification of the design structure. Finally, because the model is normally an architectural model of a proposed implementation and not just a specification, it plays a part in the design, implementation, and testing phases. For example, the model might be used as a test harness for both code modules (or "objects") and simulations of hardware components as outlined later.

In general, all models will represent, in graphical form, the proposed architecture for a system. They will also normally have a natural language statement of the function of each component, so that the operation of the model is comprehensible to humans. A model will also have "programmed" definitions for all the basic (or "primitive") components, which become active in the course of executing it, in order to validate chosen aspects of external behavioral or investigate chosen aspects of internal behavior. For example, the interface to an actual embedded system might take the form of buttons, switches, and displays. A graphical representation of these can be provided with the model so that a user can stimulate action in the model and sample its responses. Any system components involved in these reactions must have their behavior pattern programmed. In a different kind of system, the requirement might be to investigate performance issues pertaining to internal communication channels. Here, some internal components might be programmed to generate statistically valid traffic on these channels, and the responses of all of the components involved in the propagation of this traffic will also need to be programmed. In this case the only output of interest might be a log of system activity.

Detail that is not needed in connection with executing a model, for validation or verification purposes, would not normally be provided. To do so would raise the model to the status of an implementation and greatly increase the effort needed to produce it. However, as mentioned earlier, an important feature of the language for specifying primitive processes allows them to call on the services of conventional software running in the underlying operating system, and it may be possible to achieve a fully operational model for modest additional cost.

For example, straightforward parts of a system can be coded early and used to generate the behavior of the processes that they represent under the control of the model interpreter. In a similar manner, existing code, for example, code that is a component of a previous system, can be reused. Also the behavior of hardware components can be provided by independent simulations. Ideally these "programs" that support the execution of the model would be coded as objects in C++, or in the case of hardware components as simulation models in VHDL or Verilog.

We mentioned that this mechanism for "driving" conventional programs from the dynamic model allows it to be used as a test harness for debugging software components. This is a very useful testing aid for systems that have a significant custom hardware content under development in parallel with the software. Tested software can be delivered early, without it having been provided with access to the actual hardware. The facility becomes even more useful if the software is to be integrated with hardware in the ROM of a large system committed to silicon.

In summary, the case for modeling a system rests on getting the important features right before committing to them in an implementation. Then, these features need to be carried accurately into the implementation stage.

3 MODEL SPECIFICATION

3.1 The Graphical Specification of a Model

As stated earlier, the graphical model is based on data flow diagrams captured by a CASE tool for structured analysis [13]. The term *data flow* goes back to the origin of structured analysis when it was developed as a technique for specifying the flow of application data through a data processing system [11]. Even in more recent extensions of structured analysis, as a means of specifying the behavior of real-time systems [3,14], this aspect lingers. The data flow lines are not normally used for internal control messages and alternative means are provided to describe such traffic.

We have not followed these conventions of data flow diagrams, which date back nearly two decades, because we believe that a more liberal interpretation is beneficial. In fact, for the purpose for which they are used here, data flow diagrams would be better named *message flow diagrams*. Some of the messages will, of course, transport the raw data entering the system and information derived from it. However, others will comprise an interactive dialogue of commands, questions, responses, and answers.

The features of data flow that are exploited provide for the definition of a network of processes (circles), bounded by external sources and sinks (rectangles), interconnected by message paths (arrowed lines), and information stores (two horizontal lines), which enable state information to be retained in the network. A number of examples are shown in the figures given later in this chapter.

An important stylistic point is that, although the information stores can be accessed by several processes, this is avoided wherever possible. The arguments for this policy are concerned with achieving a structure that attenuates some common sources of error and confusion. They are well presented by software engineers on the basis of limiting the extent of knowledge of data structure details by "information hiding" [15], or in object-oriented jargon by "encapsulating" detail [7]. Traditional use of data flow would not normally conform with this policy.

A very important feature of conventional data flow diagrams is retained. This is that a system of interconnected processes is expressed as a hierarchy of diagrams. Thus, the major processes into which a system is decomposed on a first-level diagram are themselves decomposed into subprocesses on lower level diagrams. In a typical design, this hierarchy would be developed to several levels. Hierarchical decomposition also applies to the message flows and information stores. Their names together with a definition of their structure are entered in a data dictionary. This allows a flow on a diagram high up in the hierarchy to be defined as a composite flow having several strands. On lower level diagrams the strands can appear separately instead of as part of a composite flow.

To interpret the semantics of such a hierarchy of diagrams, it is useful to think in terms of the flattened network of primitive processes that arises from substituting for each nonprimitive process the subgraph of that process. A primitive process is one for which no subgraph is given, and its definition is given in textual form as described in the next section. The interpretation of this flattened network is that all the primitive processes operate concurrently, consuming the messages that are flowing as fast they are produced (except where delays are explicitly specified). The message flows consist of discrete packets of information. In general, the effect of consuming a packet is that the process state may be updated, the system state may be updated, and messages may be sent to other processes. (A process state exists in variables that are defined in the body of a primitive process definition, and a system state exists in the information stores shown on the diagrams.)

All reactive computer systems respond to events. Very often events result in state changes. A great deal of research has gone into to considering how these should be expressed [3,14]. However, having decided in this system to treat data flow as a general-purpose message system, we have chosen to use the arrival of messages as event triggers. Thus, in any snapshot of a system, although all the processes are in principle active, most will be busy "waiting" the arrival of a message. This, by mutual agreement, provides the means whereby one process can control another, and no other form of control (such as those use by Ward and Mellor [3] and Hatley and Pirbhai [14]) is used. Sometimes messages have no actual information content, since their sole purpose is to trigger action.

The liberal interpretation of data flow mentioned here means that in most systems the processes that can be categorized as *transform* or *object* processes. The hallmark of a transform process is that it receives *information packets* via incoming flows, applies transformations to them, and then transmits the modified information as packets on outgoing flows. Thus, the transformation processes participate in the propagation of information through a processing network, and they may also update information stores. Hardware processes are very often of this kind.

The key feature of an object process is that it is responsible for a conceptual entity within the system and it provides a protocol, i.e., a set of commands, to manipulate the attributes of the entity. Typically, this kind of process receives a command packet via an incoming message path, it interrogates and possibly updates the object's state, and responds by sending back an information packet. Object processes have flows that may be considered as command/status, request/response, or query/result pairs. To identify the matched pair conveniently and to impose some additional semantics on this type of communication, a distinctive flow line that implies bidirectional communication and explicitly identifies the initiator of the transaction is desirable. Provision for this is made and the resulting flow is referred to as a *channel*. However, a good graphical representation cannot be achieved with the Teamwork CASE tool, therefore we have not attempted to demonstrate channels in this paper. Figure 2 shows an example of an object process in which a channel would replace flows 3 and 4.

So far we have considered only *time-discrete* communication via packets. Information that is constantly available (*time continuous*), even though it may from time to time change its value, also has to be considered. It could be represented as an information store, with one process writing new values and other processes reading whatever is the current value. However, this time-continuous connection is so common, particularly in hardware, that we prefer to use a special notation. For this purpose we use dotted lines, and refer to them as *wires*. Like message flows, they can represent multiple strands on a high-level diagram, which are then shown separately at a lower level. Fortuitously, broken lines are provided by the CASE tool, albeit for a completely different reason.

In summary, a system is represented graphically as a network of processes. As a result of the object-oriented style in which the graphical decomposition is carried out, many of the processes on the higher level diagrams have the qualities of objects, and they are all considered to have concurrent operation. In the jargon of object orientation, the processes are "agents that encapsulate the detail concerned with meeting responsibilities allocated to them," and they get the job done through collaborating with others by means of messages. They do not normally resemble the transformation processes on a typical DeMarco diagram [11]. Decomposition is normally continued, at least until no processes have internal concurrency, i.e., they only have one thread of execution. Processes that represent complex objects, which do not naturally decompose into simpler objects, may be further decomposed into processes corresponding to the functions that are permitted on the object (sometimes called *methods*). These processes may well have shared access to the information stores that provide the object with state. Diagrams at the lowest level of a hierarchy will often display these features.

3.2 The Specification of Primitive Processes

Our research is not committed to any particular style of textual language for primitive process specification. The work to date has concentrated on achieving a flexible implementation model that will support a variety of process specification languages. Hence, the current language is a very simple procedural one. It has sufficed as a means to verify the operation of the overall system, develop the algorithms for effective scheduling of the basic processes, and conduct experiments with dynamic models. Within the language,

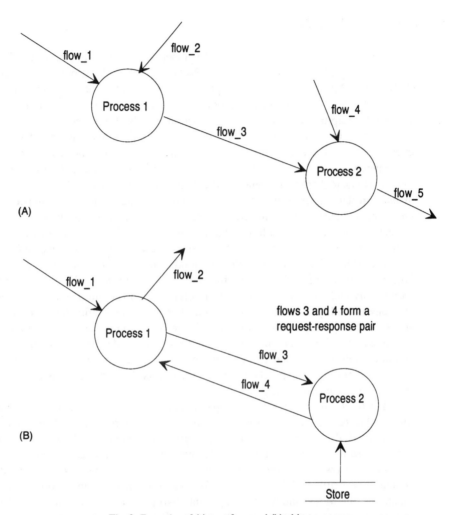

Fig. 2: Examples of (a) transform and (b) object processes

the most significant novelty relates to the kinds of operands, which might be the network information stores, the message flows and time-continuous wire flows graphically connected to the process, and more conventionally local variables. It was the nature of these operands—and their structure and scope implications—that persuaded us not to attempt to use a standard language and compiler. Fortunately, because the language is only used for definition of simple primitives, it needs only minimal features in its statement structure.

The main statement types in the language are an assignment statement, an IF-THEN-ELSE statement, a FOR loop, and a set of built-in functions. These built-in functions provide for timing control relating to both programmed delays and the precise time of consumption and propagation of messages. They also provide some pseudo random number sequences for statistical modeling purposes and the very important call to programs in the underlying operating systems. Finally, they provide access to conventional files so that specific test sequences can be input and behavior details recorded.

4 THE MODELING TOOLS

The current modeling tools have been developed as an enhancement to the Cadre Team-work system [13]. They run on Hewlett Packard 9000 workstations and operate through X-Windows. Multiple windows are provided giving both static and dynamic views of the model. These and the main components of the tool set are summarized in Figure 3. The Model Capture window is entirely determined by the CASE tool, which provides facilities to capture, print, and browse through a model. It also incorporates a procedural interface so that the rest of the software can interrogate the captured model.

Since we intend to explore other graphical capture systems, most of the rest of the tool set is isolated from the detail of the Teamwork model by an Inquiry Interface. This, in fact, presents a simplified view of the model in the form of a flattened network of processes and stores interconnected as described earlier. The way in which the detail of the network is made available through the inquiry interface is generalized so that it can apply to any graphical notation that specifies a network of interconnected objects.

The Model Compiler compiles the model into a set of files that specify both the objects and connection links of the flattened network. In these, the objects are numbered sequentially and the link specifications reference the object numbers, so that the network topology is readily apparent. Also the primitive process specifications are translated into an executable (reverse polish) format. All the other components of the tool set use the Compiled Model as their main specification of the model. However, they may require additional information that pertains to the model hierarchy or additional text items, for example, specifying nonfunctional constraints. This they obtain by using the Inquiry Interface directly but sparingly.

The Model Interpreter, for example, uses the Inquiry Interface only to obtain textual information relating to the externals to the model. There is enough information in the Compiled Model for it to operate the processes and propagate the message traffic without recourse to the Inquiry Interface. Its main task is to produce the correct behavior of a model with respect to time. We stated earlier that the semantics of the model implies concurrent execution of the processes. To model such behavior in a monoprocessor implementation, the Model Interpreter is split into two parts, a process scheduler and a process interpreter. These cannot be described in detail here but, briefly, the process scheduler schedules the processes for interpretive execution against a conceptual simulation clock. In each simulation clock cycle, all processes are given the opportunity to execute their complete process specifications, and any messages they generate are fully propagated. In general, many processes will execute in a given clock cycle, and they may do this more than once if they are the recipients of messages from several sources. Those that do not execute are either suspended due to explicitly specified delays or wait for messages that do not arrive during the clock cycle.

We have found that these methods of suspension permit a simple scheduling algorithm to model time-dependent behavior accurately and provide a way of supporting consistent interprocess communication without having to solve complex flow analysis problems. Note that, at this stage, we are primarily concerned with establishing the logical correctness of stimulus response systems, and not with the propagation and switching delay problems of an actual hardware implementation.

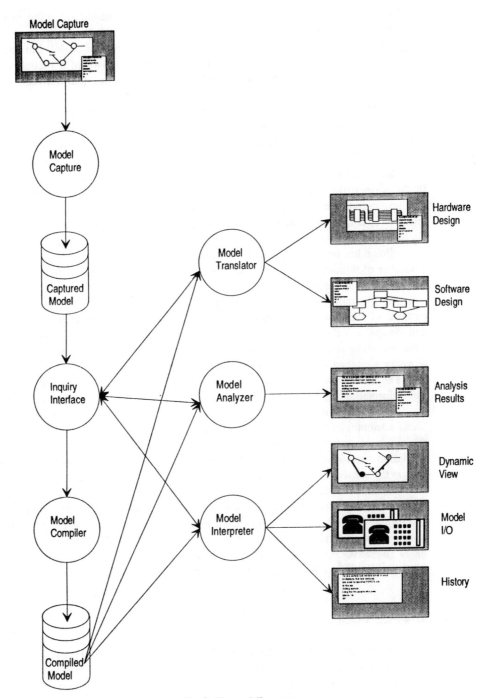

Fig. 3: The modeling system

The Model Interpreter provides three views of the dynamic execution of a model, as depicted in Figure 3. A modeler may use any or all of these views depending on the type of model constructed and the motivation for executing the model. For example, if the motivation is to validate aspects of the functional behavior of a model, it may be sufficient to consider only the model's external interface (i.e., that between the model and its environment).

The Model I/O window provides the means to stimulate a model by providing input. It also allows us to view the model's response. The simulated external environment is model specific, so the achievement of icon representation might require the modeler to write a set of programs in a high-level language. Basically, the modeling of the external environment falls into one of two categories: off-line validation and interactive validation. In the former, the user creates file input data that are supplied to the model and the resulting output is compared with the expected results. In the latter case, a prototype user interface is constructed and the modeler may investigate model behavior interactively by playing a number of "what if" games. For example the PABX telephone exchange model that follows has been validated in this way with an interface that presents the user with a number of windows, each of which contains a set of icons representing the buttons of a telephone and the state of the line.

The Dynamic View window of Figure 3 provides an animated view of a selected partition of the network of processes. This supports the evaluation of the internal structure and design of selected parts of the modeled system. The modeler may view internal behavior at the level of individual model events and actions or may view the subsystem behavior averaged over a number of simulation clock cycles.

The History window is used to examine a historical log of the model's behavior. The information held in the log is model specific and controlled by the modeler.

The Model Analyzer process provides primarily a static analysis of the nonfunctional attributes of the captured model. Metrics are generated both from the analysis of the graphical structure of the model (such as reachability and complexity) and from information specifically captured in the model, such as reliability, timing, and cost. This area is the subject of ongoing research and is not discussed further.

Having produced a model that has satisfactory dynamic and static characteristics, we now want the model detail to be carried forward into subsequent design stages in a controlled, and preferably automated, manner. The Model Translator provides support for translating model subsystems into an HDL (e.g., VHDL) and a software design methodology (e.g., HOOD [16]). Again, this is an area of ongoing research, and a prototype Model to HOOD translation tool has been constructed and is currently being evaluated.

5 AN EXAMPLE MODEL

In this section some diagrams from a model of a PABX telephone exchange are presented. For simplicity, they are organized as if most of the hardware is external to the model. This hardware is assumed to consist of four units. The style of the model is consistent with them being capable of producing interrupts and having control registers mapped into the address space of the processor(s) that operate the system. In reality, these "hardware" units might be implemented using microcontrollers and software, and the model could be extended to incorporate their internal behavior. In fact, this would make it more typical of the type of computer system that we would normally model, but it would introduce too much detail for our purposes here. Thus, for the purpose of this chapter the model is assumed to have a boundary consisting of the four external hardware objects:

> Lines
> Channels
> Digit Receivers
> Trunks,

together with an operator terminal that provides an Operator Services Manager with a command interface for configuring and monitoring usage of the system.

The Line Interface (Lines) automatically detects events on the subscriber lines such as handset lifted (Off_Hook), handset replaced (On_Hook) and Recall button operated. For each such event, we assume a message is sent to the controller that signals the event and provides the associated line number. The modeling system allows these messages to queue, hence there are no crisis time problems.

The Channels provide the means for one subscriber line to be connected to another subscriber line or trunk line, thereby providing a voice connection. The Channels are also capable of generating on demand the necessary audible tones on the connected lines. They also allow a digit receiver to be connected to a line in order to receive dialed information.

Each time a digit is dialed on a connected line, the Digit Receivers will send a message to the controller, giving the digit receiver number and the value of the digit. By retaining state information related to the allocation of digit receivers and channels, the model is able to associate dialed information with calling lines.

Figure 4, is the highest level diagram, the "context" diagram, of the model of the PABX controller. It shows the system boundary just described. To define the context of the system completely, data dictionary entries are required for all the message flows shown in Figure 4. The content of these entries is as follows:

On_Hook, Off_Hook, and Recall	are	line numbers
Trunk_Call_In and Trunk_Cancel	are	trunk line numbers
Set_Up_Channel	is	the set of commands for configuring the channels
Digit	is	a dialed digit + the receiver number
Command	is	the set of commands an operator uses
Response	is	the set of responses to the operator commands

The first-level decomposition of the system into its major subprocesses is shown in Figure 5. Here three processes are shown and they have clear and distinct responsibilities that relate to:

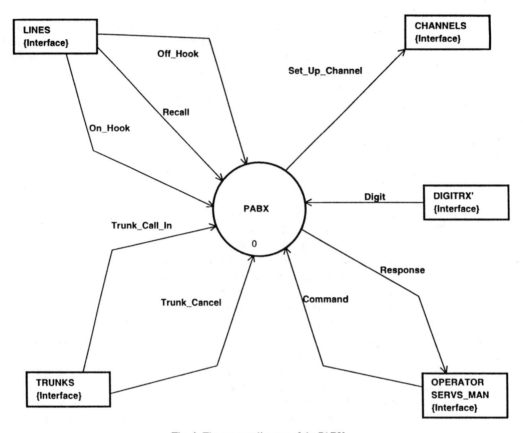

Fig. 4: The context diagram of the PABX

1. management of lines (Line_Manager)
2. organizing calls (Call_Manager) and
3. management of trunk lines (Trunk_Line_Manager).

Rather than giving the definition of each new flow that is introduced on Figure 5, it is more useful, at this stage, to describe the flow of messages that results from the collaboration of the processes in the course of handling a straightforward call from a subscriber *A* to a subscriber *B*. In other words, to conduct a verbal walkthrough.

If both *A* and *B* are local subscribers, the first event of a call is when the line interface Lines notices that *A* has lifted the handset, as a result of which it sends an Off_Hook message to the Line_Manager. The Line_Manager should find the line status to be idle, in which case it will pass the line number in a Dialing_Request message to the Call_Manager. This results in a channel and a digit receiver being allocated and the connection of a dialing tone. All this is achieved by sending appropriate Set_Up_Channel messages to the Channels hardware. Also a Set_Line_State message is sent to the Line_Manager so that it is aware that the status of the line is now "dialing in progress." As each digit is dialed, it will be detected by the Digit Receivers and corresponding Digit messages will

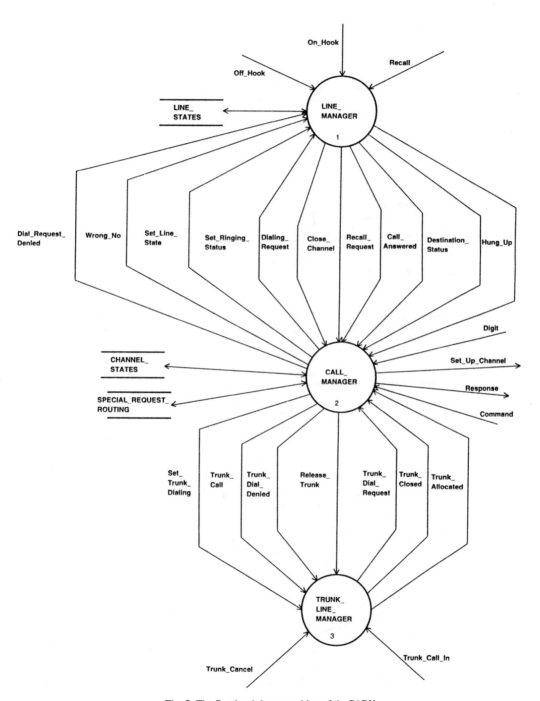

Fig. 5: The first-level decomposition of the PABX

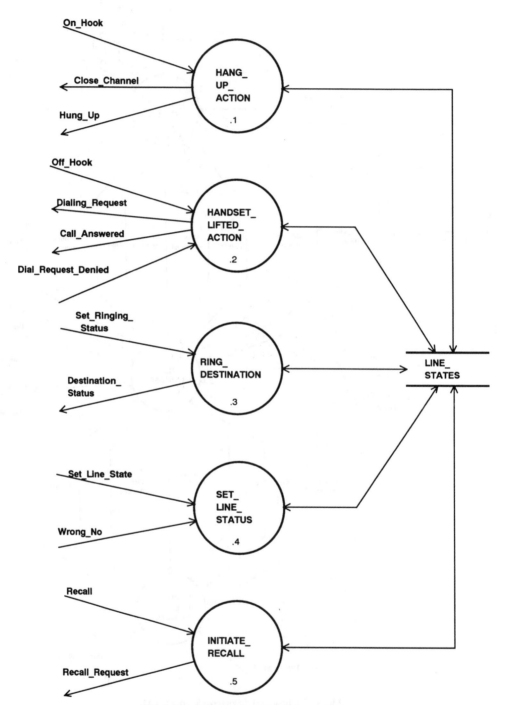

Fig. 6: The decomposition of Line_Manager

be sent to the Call_Manager. The reception of the first digit results in a Set_Up_Channel message to remove the dialing tone from the channel. When the dialed digits constitute a complete valid number, the associated line (*B*) will be connected to the channel allocated to the call and the ringing tone will be connected to the channel. Again these actions are achieved by sending Set_Up_Channel messages. Also a Set_Line_State message is sent to inform the Line_Manager that the line status of line B is "ringing." This ensures that when subscriber *B* lifts the handset, a Call_Answered message rather than a Dialing_Request message is sent to the Call_Manager, and on receipt of this the Call_Manager removes the ringing tone and leaves the voice connection operating.

Two external events are necessary to close the call completely. First one subscriber, say, *A*, will replace the handset. This will cause the Line_Manager to receive an On_Hook message and to send *A*'s line number in a Hung_Up message to the Call_Manager. The Call_Manager responds by disconnecting line *A* from the channel, generating a disconnected tone for *B* and informing the Line_Manager that the new status of line *B* is disconnected. When *B* hangs up, the Line_Manager's response will be to send Close_Channel to the Call_Manager, thereby causing the channel to be released.

Calls that are initiated by trunk lines, or have destinations that are trunk lines, operate in a similar manner to local calls with the state and status of trunk lines being controlled by the Trunk_Line_Manager.

Obviously, much complexity is implied by the message flows shown on Figure 5 that we have not yet discussed. Our purpose has been to demonstrate that verbal walkthroughs can be applied to the main behavioral aspects of a model at quite an early stage. The detail accumulates as a result of refining the process and catering to special cases.

Figure 6 shows a decomposition of the Line_Manager into five subprocesses, based on the delegation of responsibility. These subprocesses are considered simple enough to be treated as primitive processes, and we hope that, as a result of the previous walkthrough, the reader agrees that their functions are clear. However, they all have the need to access the Line_State information, hence they cannot be regarded as encapsulated objects. Some rearrangement of the model might be considered to achieve a better object-oriented structure. We prefer to leave Figure 6 as it is and regard it as a diagram showing the operations (or "methods") available within an object—the Line_Manager. In our opinion, the major problems in this system arise from the need to multiplex central resources and a more abstract approach based on objects such as "calls" and "subscribers" would result in a model that was not a viable architectural model of the system to be built. The price to be paid for this stance is that the relative timings of the messages entering Figure 6 need to be identified and the consequences explored in order to establish the integrity of the shared information.

The decomposition of the Call_Manager is not given here, but it comprises five subprocesses, four of which are treated as primitive and one is further decomposed. Again the decomposition is largely on the basis of delegation (or "divide and conquer"). We cannot claim that the action of all these processes within the Call_Manager is as simple as those discussed, nor could we claim that it would be easy to check their correctness by manual walkthroughs. We can, however, state that all the primitive processes have been programmed and their operation has been verified by execution. Also we would claim that they provide very clear and usable specifications from which an implementation can be efficiently produced. A *structured design* has been produced to substantiate this claim.

The model has actually been provided with an icon interface, which represents the keys of telephone handsets and displays the nature of the audible responses their use produces. By means of this interface, calls are simulated in order to test the switching mechanisms. An implementation of the Operator Services Manager functions has been provided as a separate stand-alone program, and a Verilog model of the Lines hardware has also been proposed.

6 CONCLUSIONS

The main objective of our research is to explore the ways in which the development and use of dynamic models that exhibit the behavior and architecture of computer systems can become an integral part of the system engineering process. Also we are seeking an understanding of the costs and benefits that would result. As a way of making progress with the research, a graphics-based modeling notation has been devised for creating models that are executable, well structured and readable.

Several executable models of systems have been created, and exercised to advantage, by means of a tool set created as an extension of a commercial CASE tool. The costs of making the models have been moderate, which allays intuitive fears that to create an executable model might involve as much work as creating an implementation. Modeling the hardware components to a level that supports the simulation of overall system behavior seems to be particularly economical. Achievement of an overall system model is greatly facilitated by having the high-level behavior specified by diagrams and in a declarative style. Also, the low-level detail for many parts is often not required in the execution of the model. When it is, the ability to connect to actual implementation software for the straightforward but often voluminous parts achieves further economies. Thus we tentatively conclude that dynamic modeling is cost effective. The main benefit perhaps derives from the control that it offers to the technical manager of a product development process.

We must admit, however, that we have found it easy to get started on system models, but difficult to complete useful ones. In fact, we made about five attempts before a satisfactory structure was devised for the PABX model, although we expect that it would now be relatively easy to produce a model of a similar system. Also we draw some consolation from the belief that it would be equally difficult to produce the system without a model—and much more expensive. Furthermore, the opportunity to approach the objective iteratively would be more limited. Guidelines on how to attack the task of making a model from scratch are slowly emerging, and we expect it to get easier. The conventional approach used in structured analysis [2] has not worked well for us. We believe that this is because we have the requirement to model architecture and performance in addition to behavior.

The research is not finished and several aspects require more work. Some of this is directed toward gaining a better understanding of the issues that relate to the application of these kinds of methods in industry. Although we recognize that modeling methods and tools for complete systems are beginning to gain impetus, there is too little information available to support the serious policy decisions that companies would face in adopting them in their mainstream processes. We hope to add to this knowledge as our research progresses by conducting collaborative case studies and re-engineering experiments.

Another line of ongoing research is concerned with the graphical notation. Data flow diagrams have provided a satisfactory start to the work and enabled the techniques for analysis and interpretative execution of graphical specifications to be developed. However, the notation, due to its origins, does not make much provision for behavior inside reactive systems. It is to be expected that a richer and more object-oriented notation would bring additional advantages, hence our plan is to experiment with alternative capture tools at the front end of our system.

The textual language for specifying primitive process behavior is also an area that needs further research. However, it is clearly best if existing compilers and language systems can be used. There are two possibilities for this. Either the mechanism for making calls out of the interpreted process specifications, to conventional programs, can be used, or a different model compiler can be produced that will generate from the captured model an equivalent (say, C++) program rather than data for an interpreter to use. We intend to explore both in connection with various declarative and object-oriented languages and system simulation tools such as the SES/workbench.

Finally there is an aspect of the present graphical notation that has not been discussed in this paper. It concerns the modeling of highly parallel hardware architectures, in which there is substantial repetition of identical elements. Work is continuing on this, along the lines briefly reported elsewhere [17].

ACKNOWLEDGMENTS

The work reported here has involved significant contributions from most of our colleagues in the Systems Engineering Group at UMIST. We would particularly like to mention three former PhD students who pioneered some of the basic ideas—Suning Tang, Samia Kada, and Zakia Hachem—and also Colin Theaker, Peter Green, William Love, and Timothy Frost who are closely involved with us in an ESPRIT project (ESPRIT OMI/DE 6909) that is concerned with deeply embedded systems. We are, of course, very grateful to the European Commission and to the Industrial Partners for the opportunity to participate in such a major project.

REFERENCES

[1] D. L. Parnas, J. Schouwen, and S. P. Kwan, "Evaluation of Safety-Critical Software," *Comm. ACM,* 33(6), pp. 636–648, 1990.

[2] E. Yourdon, *Modern Structured Analysis,* Prentice-Hall, Englewood Cliffs, NJ, 1989.

[3] P. T. Ward and S. J. Mellor, *Introduction and Tools, Structured Development for Real-Time Systems,* Vol. 1, Yourdon Press Computing Series, Englewood Cliffs, NJ, 1985.

[4] C. B. Jones, *Systematic Software Development Using VDM,* Prentice-Hall, Englewood Cliffs, NJ, 1986.

[5] J. M. Spivey, *The Z Notation,* Prentice-Hall, Englewood Cliffs, NJ, 1989.

[6] C. Reade, *Elements of Functional Programming*, Addison Wesley, Reading, MA, 1989.

[7] G. Booch, "Object-Oriented Development," *IEEE Trans. Software Eng.*, 12(2), 1986.

[8] R. S. Turner, "Abstract Data Types," in *The Concise Encyclopaedia of Software Engineering*, D. Morris and B. Tamm, Eds., Pergamon Press, New York, 1992.

[9] D. L. Perry, *VHDL*, McGraw-Hill, New York, 1991.

[10] P. P. Jain, S. Dhinga, and J. C. Browne, "Bringing Top-Down Synthesis into the Real World," *High Performance Syst.*, 10(7), pp. 86–94, July 1989.

[11] T. DeMarco, *Structured Analysis and System Specification*, Yourdon Press, Englewood Cliffs, NJ, 1978.

[12] P. Zave, "The Operational Versus the Conventional Approach to Software Development," *Comm. ACM*, 27(2), 1984.

[13] P. Zave, *HP Teamwork User's Manual*, 3rd ed., Hewlett Packard, 1989.

[14] D. J. Hatley and I. A. Pirbhai, *Strategies for Real-Time System Specification*, Dorset House Publishing, New York, 1987.

[15] D. L. Parnas, "On the Criteria To Be Used in Decomposing Systems into Modules," *Comm. ACM*, 15(12), pp. 1053–1058, Dec. 1972.

[16] P. Robinson, *Object-Oriented Design*, Prentice-Hall, Englewood Cliffs, NJ, 1992.

[17] D. Morris and D. G. Evans, "Modeling Distributed and Parallel Computer Systems," in *Parallel Computing*, North-Holland, Vol. 18, pp. 793–806, 1992.

CHAPTER   5

Toward a Common Model of Software and Hardware Components

Jørgen Staunstrup
Department of Computer Science
Technical University of Denmark
Lyngby, Denmark

Abstract: This paper discusses a common model for describing hardware and software components. Today, many advanced electronic products consist of a mixture of the two types of components. To design such products, it is necessary to coordintae the development of the hardware and software. The paper presents some general requirements for a common model of hardware and software, and some specific elements of a common model taken from the design language Synchronized Transitions.

1 INTRODUCTION

With VLSI technology, it is now possible to construct both powerful general-purpose programmable components (microprocessors) and complex specialized components (application-specific integrated circuits, ASICs). An advanced electronic product typically consists of a mixture of such hardware and software components. Unfortunately, hardware and software are typically designed separately, using different design techniques, different design tools, and by different people. However, interest is growing in developing codesign techniques where hardware and software design are integrated. To describe a codesign, one needs an abstract model that is general enough to cover both hardware and software components and also enables a designer to describe his or her design without making a commitment as to what should be realized as software and what should become hardware. This chapter motivates and introduces such a model of a computation that can be realized in either hardware, software, or a mixture of the two.

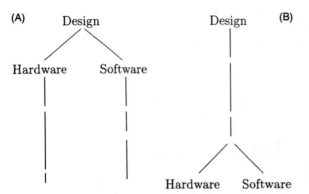

(A) Design   Design   (B)

Hardware   Software

Hardware   Software

Fig. 1: Early binding of hardware and software versus late binding

Figure 1(a) shows the traditional situation in which a product is designed by separating the hardware and software development at a very early phase of the design. If an abstract model covering both hardware and software were available, one could instead do as suggested in Figure 1(b), where a large part of the design is done without binding the components to a particular kind of realization.

Codesign has applications in a wide variety of specialized electronic products, e.g., communications equipment, controllers, and instruments. Consider the following simple example, where codesign could be relevant:

EXAMPLE:

Use pulse width modulation to design a simple regulator for an ac motor. The output of the regulator is three sequences of digital signals, one for each of the three phases needed to control the motor. Each sequence of digital signals consists of pulses that are high values of varying duration. The duration determines the speed of the motor. The input to the regulator is an indication of the desired speed. The motor regulator is shown in Figure 2.

□

The motor regulator design is rather simple and all functions could be realized in a single VLSI chip. However, it can be advantageous to make some parts of the design changeable (programmable), whereas other parts, which are unlikely to change or that are time critical, can be realized as hardware. Hence, this simple example illustrates the need for an integrated design of software for programmable components and special-purpose hardware.

Construction of general-purpose computers is also an example of hardware/software codesign, in which the development of a processor, compilers, and run-time system are integrated. But this must be considered a special case, because of the limited architectural

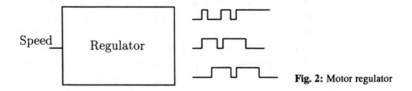

Fig. 2: Motor regulator

variation that has made it possible to perform significant optimizations. The hardware architecture of specialized electronic products exhibits a much greater variation. On the other hand, many such specialized products do not require sophisticated optimizations and are affected by the most important factors of "time to market" and reliability. In this chapter, the emphasis is on codesign for such specialized products.

2 A MODEL FOR CODESIGN

A designer must have a model for a design that allows him or her to scrutinize it, for example, to analyze bottlenecks or inconsistencies in interfaces. The choice of model is a delicate balance between the abstract and the concrete. If the model is too concrete, the designer is constrained by low-level decisions even in the early phases of the design process. On the other hand, if the model is too abstract, it may later become difficult to create an efficient realization. When doing codesign, the model should not favor a particular kind of realization, for example, a software realization.

A close relationship exists between the model and the notation/language/tools used for describing a design. To do codesign, one needs a model and a corresponding language that is abstract enough to allow descriptions of both hardware and software. However, almost all existing models and languages aim at either describing software (programming languages) or circuits (hardware description languages). Both kinds of language aim at describing a *computation,* but they are usually based on very different concepts. Almost all programming languages are based on the von Neumann model, in which a computation is described by a *sequence* of instructions operating on data stored in a memory (see Figure 3). An instruction counter keeps track of which instruction in the sequence to execute next. However, in most circuits many parts operate in parallel; so sequencing is at best an extra obstacle, and in some cases it might even preclude an efficient realization. For a hardware designer, the spatial relationship between different components is a primary concern; therefore, many hardware description languages emphasize structural descriptions where the physical organization of parts is explicitly specified.

Both programming and hardware description languages (HDLs) are used for describing computations, and this is also the main purpose of a codesign language. However, the computation should not be described sequentially or structurally, because that would bias the realization. A model based on fine-grained parallelism is capable of specifying computation without premature binding to a particular realization. It is, therefore, proposed

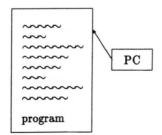

Fig. 3: Sequential program

that a codesign language be based on such a model. The model can describe the functional behavior of the design, and it can be used for various kinds of analysis; for example, identification of bottlenecks and inconsistencies in interfaces. It has been demonstrated that a computation modeled with fine-grained parallelism can be used both to develop software [1,2] and to synthesize circuits [3,4]. In the proposed model, a fine-grained parallel computation is described as a state transition system. The finite state machine is a well-known concept with applications both in hardware and in software design. In principle, a single finite state machine is sufficient. There are, however, pragmatic reasons for factoring a design into a number of state machines, each describing a well-defined part of the design.

Consider again the motor regulator described in the introduction. It can be designed as four parts, one for controlling each of the three phases, and one for calculating the appropriate regulation signals from the inputs. The three parts for the outputs are essentially counters; they are provided with an integer value and generate pulses with a length proportional to this integer. The three counters are three independent concurrent state machines. The state of such state machines is specified by declaring one or more variables, for example:

```
c: INTEGER
out: BOOLEAN
```

describes a state consisting of two variables (called c and out). State changes are described by assigning new values to variables, for example:

$$\ll \ \texttt{c>0} \ \rightarrow \ \texttt{out, c:= true, c−1} \ \gg$$

This describes a state change that can be performed when $c > 0$, and it updates the variables out and c with the new values $true$ and $c − 1$, respectively. A complete design description consists of a number of such state changes, called $transitions$. In the fine-grained parallel model, transitions are concurrent.

The fourth part of the motor regulator, called the $calculator$, computes the integer values needed by the counters. This is also specified as a transition system operating concurrently with the actual counting done in the three counters. So the complete motor regulator is modeled as four simple concurrent state machines.

The motor regulator illustrates the mapping of different state machines to different types of realization. The calculator depends on the application domain, and it may require some experimentation to fine tune it; however, the counters are the same for all applications. Therefore, they are realized in hardware, whereas the calculator is implemented in software executed on a microprocessor connected with the counters. This allows us to make needed adjustments in the calculator yet still achieve a good performance by realizing the counters in hardware, where they can operate simultaneously.

The motor regulator has four components (state machines). In larger designs there are many more, but as the motor regulator shows, these state machines can be realized in either hardware or software.

2.1 Example: A Priority Queue

In this section, the design of a priority queue is described. Even though a priority queue is a simple example, it illustrates the advantages of having an abstract description of a design that can be realized as either hardware, software, or a combination of the two.

A priority queue is a data structure that holds a set of elements from a domain with an ordering relation $<$ so that any two elements can be compared. The two external operations on a priority queue are insertion and removal. New elements can be inserted at any time (unless the queue is full). Removal takes out the *smallest* of the elements currently in the queue. Hence, the design of the priority queue must ensure that when an element is removed, it is indeed the smallest (according to the ordering of the elements).

The interface to the priority queue consists of two registers: an input register *in* and an output register *out* (Figure 4). Let *empty* denote a value that is different from all other values that can be inserted in the queue. An element may be inserted in the queue when the input register is empty. Insertion is performed by assigning an element to *in*. An element may be removed when the output register is full ($out \neq empty$). It is removed by copying the value of the register *out* and assigning the value *empty* to it.

Priority queues have many applications, for example, in event-driven simulators where the priority queue stores all elements scheduled for execution. In this case, the priority is the starting time of the event. The event-driven simulation algorithm always executes the event with the smallest (earliest) starting time, which is supplied by the priority queue. Priority queues are also used in several efficient graph algorithms, e.g., graph traversal. In an event-driven simulator, the operations on a priority queue are often the bottleneck of the algorithm, hence it is important to use an efficient realization of the priority queue. In software, it can be implemented so that the execution time of insertions and removals is proportional to the logarithm of the number of elements stored in the priority queue. However, even with such a realization, the priority queue can be the bottleneck, when the event queues are large and the operations frequent, as is the case in circuit simulators. It can, therefore, be advantageous to realize the priority queue in hardware, which makes the simulator a codesign where most of the simulation algorithm is realized in software, while the time-critical priority queue is realized in hardware. This partitioning is discussed in further detail later, but first the behavior of the priority queue is specified.

Assume that *f* and *l* are two registers similar to *in* and *out* (see Figure 5). Futhermore, it is assumed that there is a number of similar pairs of registers indicated by .... The lower row of registers *out, l*, etc., always holds elements in increasing order, while the upper row *in, f*, etc., holds elements under insertion, traveling from left to right until they find their proper place. When this happens, they are inserted in the bottom row

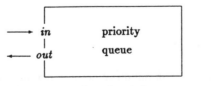

Fig. 4: *In* and *out* registers for priority queue

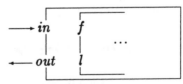

Fig. 5: Priority queue

of registers, if there is an empty register; otherwise, they are exchanged. If the latter is the case, then the element previously stored in the bottom row starts traveling from left to right. So the register *out* always contains the smallest value currently stored in the queue. The behavior explained informally in this paragraph can be defined precisely as a fine-grained concurrent computation:

$$
\begin{aligned}
&\ll \text{ in } < \text{ out} &\to \text{ in, out}:= \text{ out, in } \gg \\
&\ll \text{ out } = \text{ empty } \land \text{ in } \le \text{ f } \land \text{ in } \le \text{ l} &\to \text{ in, out}:= \text{ out, in } \gg \\
&\ll \text{ in } \ne \text{ empty } \land \text{ f } = \text{ empty } \land \text{ in } \ge \text{ out} &\to \text{ in, f}:= \text{ f, in } \gg \\
&\ll \text{ out } = \text{ empty } \land \text{ f } \ge \text{ l } \land \text{ in } \ge \text{ l} &\to \text{ l, out}:= \text{ out, l } \gg
\end{aligned}
$$

This describes four concurrently executing transitions. The first two transitions ensure that *out* always holds the smallest of the four elements: *in, out, f,* and *l.* The third transition moves the element stored in *in* to the right, so that it can find its proper place among the other elements stored in the priority queue. This makes room for a new insertion ($in = empty$) even though the element from *in* may not yet have found its correct place among all the other elements currently in the priority queue. When an element is removed, *out* becomes empty, and the fourth transition removes the second smallest element and places it in *out.* Note the parallel nature of this solution, where many elements can be moving simultaneously.

The priority queue specified here can easily be realized in hardware as well as in software. A hardware realization would have two externally visible registers—*in* and *out*—and a number of internal registers corresponding to *f, l, ...* Furthermore, a number of comparators are needed. The priority queue can also be realized in software. In general, any concurrent computation can be realized sequentially by executing the concurrent operations in some order. The order does not affect the result if the concurrent computation is designed correctly. It may, however, affect the efficiency. Hence, it is simple to obtain a functionally correct software realization, but it can require some effort to make it efficient.

For the priority queue, a combination of software and hardware might be the optimal realization. The traffic is most intense at the head of the queue. Toward the end, there is no traffic unless the queue is almost full. It could, therefore, be advantageous to realize the first registers in hardware and use software to realize the tail. The exact partitioning depends on the application and the speed required.

The priority queue illustrates two important points, one is the use of fine-grained concurrency to specify a computation independently of its realization. The other is the use of combined hardware/software realizations to obtain an optimal trade-off between cost and speed. By giving an abstract description of the computation without commitments to a particular kind of realization, it becomes possible to map the description to hardware, software, or combinations of the two.

2.2 Example: All Pairs Shortest Path

This section presents a solution to an optimization problem, usually known as "all pairs shortest path." As was the case for the priority queue, the design solving the op-

W	a	b	c	d	e	f	g
a		2	8	10			
b			3				
c						4	
d			12			5	
e						16	
f	2	4	12	3			1
g		2			12		

Fig. 6: Example of a cost matrix

timization problem is described as a fine-grained parallel computation, which can be realized both in hardware and in software.

Consider a table of prices for flying between various cities (a cost matrix), called a, b, c, ... (see Figure 6). Absence of an entry in the cost matrix W indicates that there is no direct connection between the corresponding two cities. The cost is assumed to be infinite (or some finite approximation that is larger than all other costs). The cost matrix shows that the price of flying from a to c is 8, and when flying from e to f, it is 16, etc. The table does not give any price of flying from a to f; however, by going through d the price becomes 15. The question is one of whether this is the cheapest way of getting from a to f. Maybe it can be done in a cheaper way by going through d, e, or by making more than one stopover. To answer this question, we need an algorithm that can compute the cheapest way of getting between any pair of cities. The problem is to compute the minimal distances between any pair of nodes, allowing paths going to an arbitrary number of intermediate nodes. Let N denote the number of cities in the cost matrix.

Assume that $d[i, j]$ contains an estimate of the cheapest way of getting between i and j. If there is a city k such that $d[i, k] + d[k, j] < d[i, j]$, it means that a cheaper route between i and j has been found, and hence $d[i, j]$ should be updated.

$$\ll d[i, k] + d[k, j] < d[i, j] \rightarrow d[i, j] := d[i, k] + d[k, j] \gg$$

This update transition is executed repeatedly, whenever $d[i, k] + d[k, j] < d[i, j]$, an improved estimate, is assigned to $d[i, j]$. Similar transitions are updating $d[i, j]$ for all $k : 1 \leq k \leq N$, i.e., all possible intermediate cities. Similarly, all other pairs i, j are updated, which yields a computation where N^3 transitions operate concurrently and repeatedly. Every time $d[i, j]$ is updated, a cheaper route has been found, which may lead to improvements in other routes, etc. All costs in the initial matrix W are positive, which means that sooner or later the design enters a state where no further reductions of the costs can be made, i.e., where

$$\forall i, j, k : d[i, k] + d[k, j] \geq d[i, j]$$

When this assertion holds, $d[i, j]$ contains the minimal costs of getting between any pair of cities. A proof of this is given in [1].

The computation of the cheapest route between all pairs of cities has certain similarities with the priority queue presented earlier. Both are "chaotic computations" in which a number of similar and simple transitions works collectively toward a common goal. The concurrent execution is what makes the computation reach this goal. As pointed out earlier, the description of the all pairs shortest path algorithm is a high-level design where many details, which are important for an efficient realization, are left open. In the case of the priority queue, it is not difficult to see the relationship between the high-level description and a reasonably efficient circuit, but with regard to the all pairs shortest path computation, it is not that simple. In this case, the problem is to find a spatial placing of all the circuit elements that only require local communication. Reference [5] shows how this can be done.

On the other hand, the computation can also be realized by the following program fragment (Warshall's algorithm):

```
FOR i:=1 TO N DO
  FOR j:=1 TO N DO
    FOR k:=1 TO N DO
      IF d[i,k]+d[k,j]<d[i,j] THEN d[i,j]:= d[i,k]+d[k,j]
```

The important point illustrated by both the priority queue and the all pairs shortest path algorithm is the possibility of describing a design without committing oneself to a particular kind of realization. For both examples, it is possible to map the design to either hardware, software, or combinations of the two. So far, the modeling aspects of a codesign language have been stressed, but it is also important that such a language can be used for scrutinizing a design, for example, to be able to do verification, performance analysis, and synthesis. We cannot cover these aspects in this chapter, but they are discussed in [4].

3 INTERFACES

An encapsulation mechanism is an important part of a codesign language, because it enables the designer to partition a design into components that can be considered separately. Such an encapsulation mechanism is found in all programming languages and HDLs, e.g., procedures in Pascal and entities in VHDL. In a codesign language, the encapsulation mechanism must allow the realization of some components by software and others by hardware. Different components must be able to communicate. This communication mechanism is called the interface (see Figure 7). The interface of a component must be independent of how the component is realized. Furthermore, it is important that the interface be modeled in a way that allows efficient realization in both hardware and software. We propose to model the interface of a component by one or more state variables. Communication between components is made by reading and writing the state variables in the interface. A component can also have additional internal state variables, which are hidden from other components.

Different technologies may be used to realize different components, for example, realizing one component in hardware and another in software. The realization of the state variables is different in hardware and software, but the interpretation in the abstract

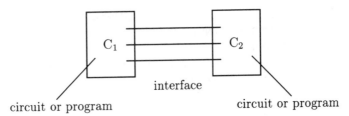

Fig. 7: Interface between two components

model is the same. This possibility of a dual realization is an important attribute of state variables when used to interface hardware and software. Other interface mechanisms, for example, messages as found in CSP [2], may have nicer properties than state variables from a software point of view. However, for codesign it is important that the abstract model of the interface mechanism be mapped efficiently to both hardware and software. If this is not the case, it is easy to lose the performance advantage obtained by realizing some components as special-purpose hardware.

The motor regulator can be used to illustrate how interfaces are specified. The design of the regulator is divided into four components as described in Section 2 (see Figure 8). The interface of each of the three counters is a single state variable of type integer. A component is specified as a cell, and the interface is specified as a parameter list; in this case, it consists of a single parameter: *limit:*

```
CELL counter(limit: INTEGER)
```

Inside the counter, the parameter *limit* is used like any other state variable, e.g., in expressions and assignments. The counter cell has a local state variable *c*, which is used to control the width of the pulses. These are generated from the variable *out*, which is set to *true* for the duration of a pulse; *out* is also a part of the interface, since it must be externally visible. A complete description of the counters interface is shown next. It consists of the integer *limit,* which is the interface to the calculator and of the the interface to the motor, which is a Boolean *out* modeling the digital control signal.

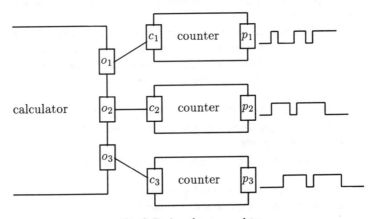

Fig. 8: Design of motor regulator

```
CELL counter(limit: INTEGER; out: BOOLEAN)
STATE c: INTEGER
BEGIN
   ≪ c=0 → out, c:= false, limit ≫
   ≪ c>0 → out, c:= true, c−1 ≫
END
```

In a codesign different cells may be realized in different technologies, for example, by realizing one cell in hardware and another in software. Therefore, it is important that efficient realizations of state variables make up the interfaces in *both* hardware and software. In software, state variables are realized as program variables, i.e., represented in memory. In hardware several alternatives are available depending on the technology; one possibility is to represent state variables with wires connecting the subcircuits using the variables. These wires always contain the current value of the corresponding state variables, and they are connected with the inputs of subcircuits reading them. Similarly, they are connected to the outputs of subcircuits writing them. Associated with each wire is some refresh-mechanism maintaining the current value.

As stressed earlier, this dual view of a state variable is an important advantage of using state variables to interface hardware and software.

4 SYNCHRONIZED TRANSITIONS

The fine-grained parallel model described in this chapter is based on the design language Synchronized Transitions [6], which has been used for developing both hardware and software. The Synchronized Transitions language has many similarities with UNITY [1]. Both describe a computation as a collection of atomic, guarded assignments without any explicit flow of control. In the book on UNITY [1], many examples are given that illustrate how this can be used as a general programming paradigm. Our work on Synchronized Transitions has shown that the same model can be used for the development of application-specific VLSI circuits [4]. At FZI in Karlsruhe, it has been demonstrated that it is possible to partition and map UNITY descriptions automatically into efficient hardware [7,8].

Several prototype tools exist that support design using Synchronized Transitions. These tools are translators that transform descriptions in Synchronized Transitions into various other forms. The three main classes of such translators, helping the designer at different phases of the design, are as follows:

Synthesis: produces circuit descriptions, e.g., netlists or layouts

Verification: produces verification conditions, which can be checked by a mechanical theorem prover

Simulation: produces a C program, which can be executed to simulate the design.

The tools have been used to develop a number of nontrivial circuits, for example, a chip for high-bandwidth interprocessor communication [9], interfacing hardware and software components. A more complete description of Synchronized Transitions is given in [4].

5 CONCLUSIONS

This chapter has sketched a codesign language in which it is possible to describe a computation with no commitments as to what should be realized as software and what should become hardware. Two important aspects of such a language were stressed: one is to model a computation as a fine-grained parallel computation, the other is to model interfaces between different components of a codesign with state variables. The design language Synchronized Transitions is based on these considerations.

ACKNOWLEDGMENTS

The development of Synchronized Transitions is part of a research project on codesign supported by the Danish Technical Research Council. Anders P. Ravn provided valuable insight in the initial development of the Synchronized Transitions notation. Jens Sparsø and Jan Madsen gave many useful comments on an earlier version of this manuscript. Mark Greenstreet's enthusiasm and creativity has been a constant source of inspiration in the development of Synchronized Transitions.

REFERENCES

[1] K. Mani Chandy and Jajadev Misra, *Parallel Program Design: A Foundation,* Addison-Wesley, Reading, MA, 1988.

[2] C. A. R. Hoare, "Communicating Sequential Processes," *Comm. ACM,* 21(8), pp. 666–667, Aug. 1978.

[3] Alain J. Martin, "Compiling Communicating Processes into Delay-Insensitive VLSI Circuits," *Distributed Computing,* 1(4), pp. 226–234, 1986.

[4] Jørgen Staunstrup, *A Formal Approach to Hardware Design,* Kluwer Academic Publishers, New York, 1994.

[5] Jan L. A. van de Snepscheut, "A Derivation of a Distributed Implementation of Warshall's Algorithm, *Sci. Computer Program.,* 7, pp. 55–60, 1986.

[6] Jørgen Staunstrup and Mark R. Greenstreet, "From High-Level Descriptions to VLSI Circuits," *BIT,* 28(3), pp. 620–638, 1988.

[7] Edna Barros and Wolfgang Rosenstiel, "A Clustering Approach to Support Hardware/Software Partitioning," in *Codesign: Computer-Aided Software/Hardware Engineering,* Jerzy Rozenblit and Klaus Buchenrieder, Eds., IEEE Press, New York, 1994.

[8] Edna Barros and Wolfgang Rosenstiel, "A Method for Hardware Software Partitioning," in *Proceedings of COMPEURO 92,* pp. 580–585, 1992.

[9] Mark R. Greenstreet, "Using Synchronized Transitions for Simulation and Timing Verification," in *Proceedings from DCC'92, IFIP Transactions A-5,* Jørgen Staunstrup and Robin Sharp, Eds., pp. 215–236, Elsevier, New York, 1992.

CHAPTER   6

Modeling of Complex Systems Using Hierarchical Petri Nets

Gisbert Dittrich
Fachbereich Informatik,
Universität Dortmund
Dortmund, Germany

Abstract: It is well known that high level nets in connection with channel/agency nets as variations of Petri nets are very well suited for the modeling of concurrent systems. To handle the modeling of large-scale systems it turns out to be appropriate to apply *hierarchically represented nets,* which means to split the whole description of the system into a well-structured set of comprehensive descriptions using nets that are organized in a tree.

We describe *methods* to model functional requirements and designs of large-scale systems by hierarchically represented nets supporting the process of developing the overall description of the system. To support these methods, appropriate tools are neccessary. Our actual version of a prototype of a *tool* consists of an *editor,* which supports graphical representation of hierarchically represented nets in multiple windows, and an integrated *simulator/animator,* which enables the token game according to the firing rules for place/transition nets as well as for some sort of timed, stochastic nets.

Further improvements and enhancements of our tool and gaining experience in modeling with this equipment are currently in progress.

1 INTRODUCTION

This chapter studies representations of systems in the early phases of development; in particular, concurrent systems (at first, we neglect other distinguishing attributes). Here we are especially interested in the modeling of functional requirements (later on in modeling of—for example—performance aspects too) and the embedding of those requirements into a system's design. For these descriptions validation should be possible in order to avoid early and very expensive failures. A system's description is also helpful for the representation of already existing systems so that we can analyze them.

We are interested in intuitive and easy-to-understand descriptions. Therefore, we use a graphically oriented approach, namely, nets. We explain net representations of systems, using Petri nets as a graphical language, especially in a hierarchically represented description. We show that these representations can also be applied to describe big, complex systems regardless of their additional attributes.

We then give an idea of some methods that demonstrate how to apply Petri net descriptions. Since the application of methods strongly depends on tools supporting such an approach, we suggest some tools and tool components that would be useful, and we also describe the functionality of PetriLab, which has been developed at the University of Dortmund. These explanations are followed by a brief section about applications. In closing, we make some final remarks.

The material presented here has undergone evolutionary developed in recent years. Information can be found in [1–5].

2 NET-BASED REPRESENTATIONS

We model our systems by using certain variations of so-called Petri nets. The basic idea in all variations is to model reality by means of bipartite, directed graphs, which may have inscriptions on the nodes and the edges (Figure 1).

One sort of node, called a *transition,* is represented by rectangles and essentially describes active components such as functions. The other type of node, *place,* is represented by circles and describes passive components such as data or conditions. Edges are only permitted between nodes of different sorts. Thus the underlying nets are defined as

> *Definition:* $N = (P, T; F)$ is a **net**
> $: \Leftrightarrow$ P, T are sets , $P \cap T = \emptyset$
> $F \subseteq (P \times T) \cup (T \times P)$ flow relation (see, e.g., [6])

Concrete data are modeled by so-called "tokens," filled in places. Exploiting the inscriptions mentioned earlier according to a so-called "firing rule" leads to a description of a transformation, associated with a transition, that describes a manipulation of the tokens on the adjacent places to the "firing" transition. This may be intuitively understood as dynamic behavior and describes some sort of precise semantics. The models vary widely

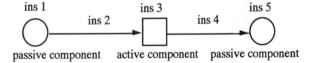

Fig. 1: Basics of Petri nets   passive component   active component   passive component

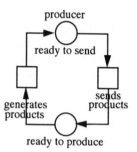

Fig. 2: "Producer" as a condition/event net

with different firing rules. Some important examples are predicate/transition nets, colored Petri nets, place/transition nets, condition/event nets, elementary nets, timed nets, stochastic nets, etc. (see, e.g., [7,8]).

The effect of a firing rule are here explained by examples. As a trivial example let us consider the very well-known rough description of the producer-consumer problem as a condition/event net.

Suppose a producer is able to produce a product and to bring this product to market. He or she may produce the product again and again. This can be modeled on an underlying graphical description as given in Figure 2 in the following manner: Markings will be transformed along a very trivial firing rule, namely, that of condition/event nets: In this case situations are described by putting tokens on places, which represent the holding of some conditions. The firing rule describes in a precise manner the effects of a transition on the adjacent places: A transition is referred to as *activated* if all places directly before the transition are filled with tokens and all places just behind are empty. An activated transition "fires" by removing the tokens from the foregoing and filling the subsequent places simultaneously. In Figure 3 on the left side the situation is shown before firing the transition "producer sends products (to market)"; on the right side it shows the situation after the transition is fired.

Remark: In a medium such as a book, the description of the effect of firing a transition is really cumbersome. Instead, a tool on a computer that can show this effect as an animation of tokens on places is more adequate and very impressive. Later we make some remarks on tools available for this task.

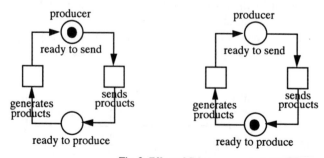

Fig. 3: Effect of firing

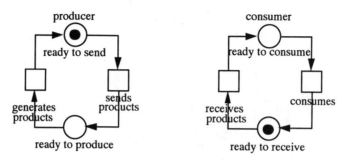

Fig. 4: Producer-consumer uncoupled

In the same manner as a producer, a consumer can be modeled analogously. Thus we describe in Figure 4 a producer and a consumer as uncoupled subsystems. These are able to run concurrently. (It is also possible to model complicated distributed systems in that manner.)

Now we model some sort of coupling between these systems by an additional place called a *store*. Thus, the situation is as follows: The consumer has to wait until the producer has sent a product to the store so that the consumer can receive it. As shown in Figure 5, "producer sends products" must fire before "consumer receives products" is activated.

Modifying the modeling by giving a weight to some arcs and capacities to some places as is done in Figure 6 results in a little bit more complicated description of the producer-consumer problem that uses a description of a so-called place/transition net. Here the firing rule manipulates the tokens according to the inscriptions. Thus, in the

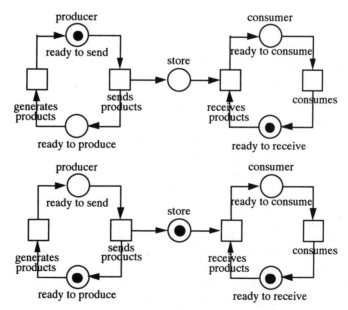

Fig. 5: Firing in producer-consumer connected

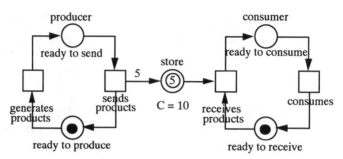

Fig. 6: Producer-consumer modeled as a place/transition net

example of Figure 6, if we start with a marking that is chosen analogously to the one shown in the upper part of Figure 5, the firing of "producer sends products" increases the number of tokens on place "store" by 5, if the capacity condition of "store" will hold. Here it is evident that we have more than one token in one place.

As mentioned earlier, there are other net models like predicate/transition [7] or colored nets (see especially [9]), that might have different sorts of tokens and a much more complicated firing rule. Nevertheless, all of these models possess a precise firing rule, and therefore can be understood as nets with precise semantics. Additionally, let us mention that there are different sorts of stochastic and timed net models too.

In addition, net descriptions exist that have only *praeformal* semantics. They are called *channel/agency* nets according to the following definition:

Definition: CAN $= (P,T; F, A,$ in) is a **channel/agency net**
      $: \Leftrightarrow$ $(P,T; F)$ is a net
           A is a set of (possible) inscriptions
           in: $P \cup T \cup F \to A$ (partial) function (see, e.g., [10])

Praeformal means that it is informal (therefore, without precise semantics) but can be enhanced to a formal description by adding or modifying appropriate descriptions.

3 STRUCTURED NET DESCRIPTIONS

In Figure 7 we show a detailed description of the functionality of a part of our tool "PetriLab"' as a channel/agency net. The goal of showing this description is only to suggest that it is a bad idea to model big, complex system descriptions via flat Petri net representations. Do not try to understand the details represented in Figure 7. This depiction is very incomprehensible and thus neither good to handle nor to explain.

For manipulating big or very big descriptions of systems (e.g., those given in Figure 7) we exploit *abstraction,* which is modeled here by some sort of coarsening. Therefore, we want to break down the description given by one big net into a set of comprehensible nets, which is structured in a hierarchy. On the other hand, the development of a description should be done by generating directly a well-structured set of subsystems. For that we will use refinement extensively.

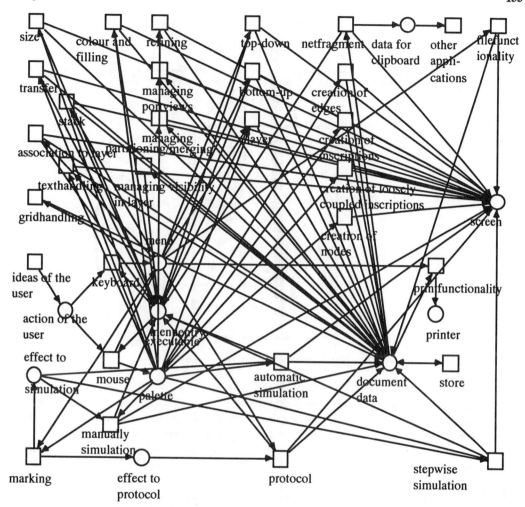

Fig. 7: A flat modeling of a part of "PetriLab"

To illustrate the idea of refinement in this context let's use only a very rough description of the intended "program PetriLab" and its connection to the environment, as shown in Figure 8 (denoted as "Tool PetriLab" in the following). Here only data dependencies are modeled.

By refinement we can describe what should be in the nodes "program PetriLab" and "outputs" and how the connections between them and to the additional environment should be refined. Thus we now get a more detailed description of the system shown in the lower part of Figure 9. The information given in the entire Figure 9 can be described

Fig. 8: "Program PetriLab" within environment

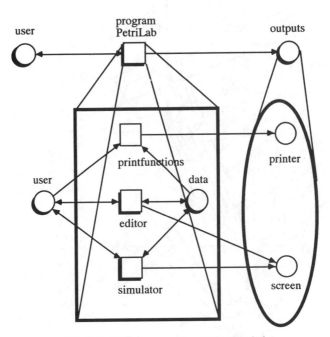

Fig. 9: Relation: coarse versus refined description

by a root diagram (for the example displayed in Figure 8) and a new diagram for each real refinement of a node if we admit some redundancy. Redundancy is expressed by repeated representation of adjacent nodes of a refined node as so-called ports. This can be seen in Figure 10, where "user" and "outputs" occur as ports (visualized by a different representation) in that diagram that represents the refinement of the node "program PetriLab."

If refinements are available for nodes, which occur as ports, different views on the ports are possible, as shown, e.g., for "program PetriLab" in Figure 11. These are examples of diagrams, which reveal views on refinements of nodes in a hierarchical representation of parts of the information described in Figure 7. In Figure 12 in the Hierarchy tree window an overview of the set of all existing diagrams is displayed. Besides the

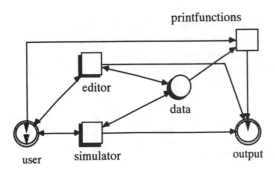

Fig. 10: "Program PetriLab"

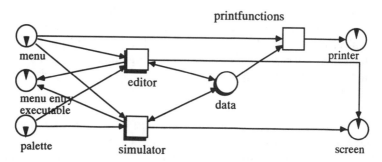

Fig. 11: "Program PetriLab" with refined ports

node "Tool PetriLab" on the top left, which represents the coarsest description of our system (Figure 8), each node represents a diagram of a refined node. For example, in the diagram of "Tool PetriLab" the nodes "user," "program PetriLab," and "outputs" occur. Each of these nodes has a further refinement, which is visualized by shadows under the nodes. Therefore, the representations of these nodes with refinements are displayed directly on the right side of the node "Tool PetriLab" in Figure 12. "Program PetriLab" (see Figure 10) has nodes "editor," "simulator," and "data," which again possess refinement diagrams. The representations of the latter nodes occur directly on the right side of "program PetriLab" in Figure 12. Thus, we have got refinements in refinements. In this sense: Refinement can be iterated! The full description of the hierarchy tree of refinement nodes is displayed in Figure 12.

Thus, we hope we have made plausible how to present the same information for one flat description such as that in Figure 7 in a hierarchically structured manner. This approach includes the main idea for a definition of a hierarchical Petri net.

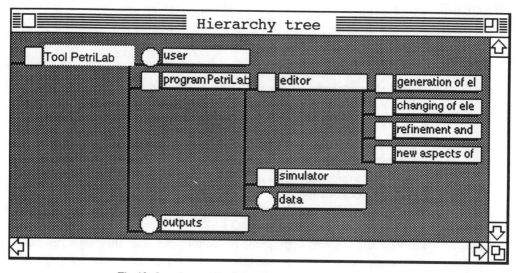

Fig. 12: Overview on all existing diagrams, hierarchically structured

Remark: A formal definition of a hierarchical Petri net (HPN), mirroring this intention of HPN as suggested earlier, is available in [11]. Because of the need for some technical means, this definition is omitted here. Some of the first ideas about how to extend these concepts of hierarchization to high-level Petri nets with precise semantics can be found, e.g., in [12]. An approach to hierarchically organized colored Petri nets is documented, e.g., in [9].

To exploit this concept in reality, we must have a concept of modularity in this context. The main idea can be gained by isolating a subtree of a hierarchical net as a building block. The connections of the root of that subtree to other nodes in the hierarchical net yield an interface in a canonical manner. This leads to the concept of a building block (with parameters) in this context. This approach corresponds roughly to the modeling of procedures or of data types in programming languages, depending of whether the root of the subtree is a transition or place. Thus "good" building blocks can be classified as it is done in other languages. For example, "small" interfaces lead to loosely coupled systems, built from building blocks.

Remark: The first ideas regarding building blocks can be found in [13]. A formal definition of the concept and of its binding into a "main tree" is given in [11].

The application of this concept can be manyfold: It enables a modularized description of a complex hierarchical net, thus leading to a design, developed from a given description of requirements (top-down development). On the other hand, a design can be given by gluing different building blocks together to a complex hierarchical net. Thereby, manyfold insertion of a building block in different instances is possible (bottom-up development).

4 METHODS

Let's make some suggestions on how to generate system descriptions as applied to Petri nets:

- First of all, we need a proposal on how to develop the (especially) functional requirements of a system mainly top-down from scratch up to a design:
  - Start with one (maybe very rough) channel/agency net.
  - Subsequently build a net hierarchy by refinements. Do not bother to change, enhance, or reduce your description.
  - Enrich with informations up to the point at which the leaf diagrams in the hierarchy tree can be expressed with precise semantics. (For example, performance attributes such as durations of activities can be modeled by times associated to transitions (using, e.g., timed nets).)
  - (Eventually) identify appropriate building blocks, thus inducing a design.
  - To validate your document, simulate and/or analyze it (or parts, building blocks, or subsystems of it).

- Now decide which subsystem will be hardware or software or something else.
- Then go into subsequent phases of development (e.g., rapid prototyping).

As appropriate alternatives to this method we have the following:

- *Bottom-up:* This essentially (as already mentioned above) means build a complex new system by gluing existing building blocks together.
- *"Yo-yo":* A mixture of both the top-down and bottom-up approaches are possible.

5 TOOLS AND TOOL COMPONENTS

Experience has shown that these methods will only be accepted if good support by an appropriate tool is available.

What sort of tool is required?

We are interested in validated Petri net documents represented as hierarchically structured nets. Therefore, we should be able to model as shown in Figures 10, 11, and 12.

Possible components of a tool that could be used to solve this task are displayed in Figure 14. First of all we need a comfortable *editor* to create and update such documents. To validate structured sets of nets, appropriate tool components would be helpful such as a *simulator/animator* used to play the token game (and to visualize it) if the document is specified as sufficiently complete, and (eventually) an analyzer to check for some properties, for which theory is available. (Please take notice of the fact that we have represented the refinements of the nodes "Petri net tools" and "PN documents" of Figure 13 simultaneously.) Some rough ideas of further tools for exploiting the validated PN descriptions can be represented as follows.

Figure 15 sketches the idea that up to that point a system description using hierarchically represented nets is possible regardless of the further development of parts or subsystems as hardware or software or, e.g., a mechanical component. Therefore, HPNs in our opinion represent an appropriate unified system description language. At that point an extraction of subparts/building blocks/subsystems from the whole system description as a HPN should be carried out, probably supported by a component that in Figure 15 is called a "decider." These HPN descriptions of subsystems then have to be further developed by specialized components according to the decision made by the decider. In this sense in our opinion HPNs are useful for hardware/software codesign.

What about available tools to solve the tasks mentioned here?

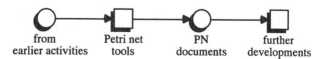

from   Petri net   PN   further
earlier activities   tools   documents   developments

Fig. 13: A Petri net tool in its environment

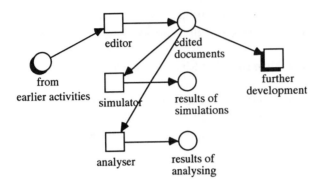

Fig. 14: Components of a Petri net tool

There are many tools available for editing, validating, and analyzing different variations of hierarchically represented Petri nets. For public available tools in this context, refer to [14].

What about our work on such tools up to now?

We only have contributed to HPN tools. Our main tool is "PetriLab," which comprises an editor for hierarchically represented channel/agency nets and an integrated simulator for some sort of interpreted Petri nets with precise semantics. Thus the play of the token game is possible under appropriate circumstances. The concept of a building block is not supported up to now. For example, the modeling of the functional requirements of the kernel of PetriLab was done in PetriLab.

Figure 16 displays a screen shot of the editor of this program at work. The program's editor supports:

- graphical representation in color
- multiple windows
- comfortable drawing by using a grid

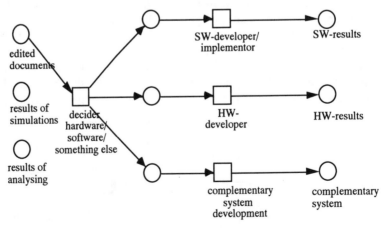

Fig. 15: (Essentially) refinement of "further developments" from Figure 13

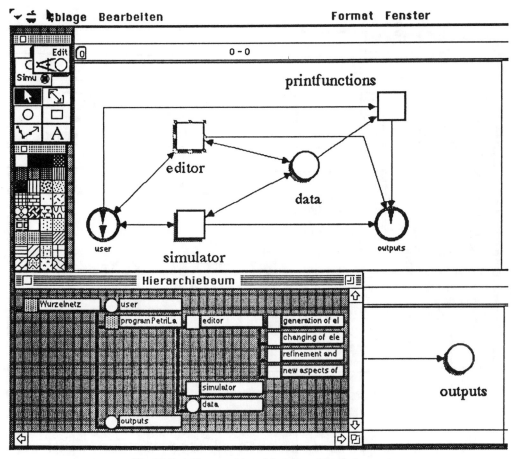

Fig. 16: Part of a screen shot of the editor of PetriLab at work

- multiple layers per diagram (with this feature we are enabled to make an appropriate modeling of the different views of the, for example, producer-consumer problem in one diagram)
- refinement of both sorts of nodes (even if they are adjacent)
- visualizing of the local environment of nodes as ports
- temporary inconsistencies are allowed
- reusability of components (using copy-paste up to now).

Toggled to simulation (refer to the upper left corner in Figure 16 and the lower left corner in Figure 17) it supports simulation, which means playing the token game for place/transition nets and some sort of timed and stochastic nets, especially:

- inserting tokens into places
- firing according to the rule for either place/transition or timed, stochastic nets: manually, automatically, with different velocities

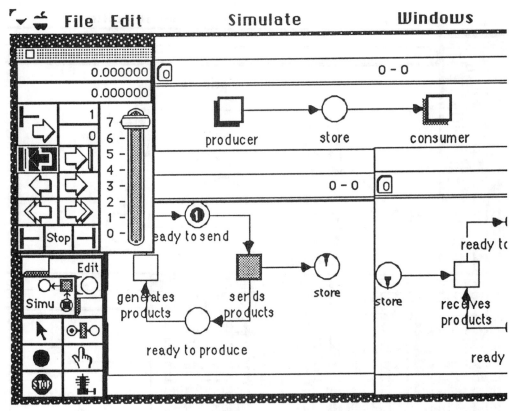

Fig. 17: Part of a screen shot of producer-consumer before firing "sends products"

- place/transition net descriptions including the following features: multiple tokens in one place, capacity of places, and natural numbers as weights of arcs
- timed, stochastic net descriptions including the following features: modeling the duration of time of firing of a transition: deterministic (0 possible) or exponentially distributed, and solution of conflicts according to predefined probabilities
- setting of stop conditions
- comfortable recording.

PetriLab is available (for our personal purposes only) as a prototype on an Apple Macintosh developed with MPW using Object Pascal and MacApp [15,16]. Previous versions of different parts of this program are described in [17–20]. Associated work is described in [21–24].

Figures 17 and 18 show the situation before and after, respectively, firing of the enabled transition "sends products" in a hierarchically modeled version of a trivial producer-consumer situation analog to that described in Figure 5.

Additionally we have developed the first stand-alone prototype of an analyzer that nowadays is not in use. This analyzer is developed for nonhierarchically represented place/transition nets without graphical representation and supports analyzing:

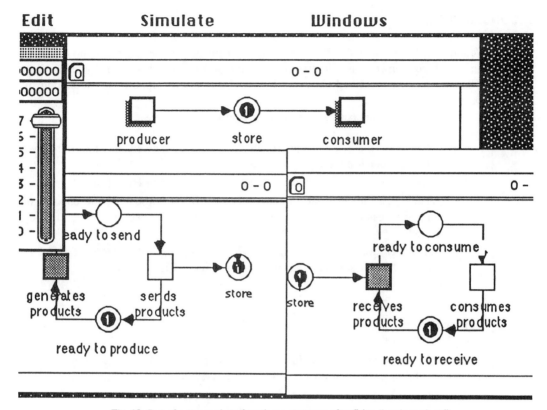

Fig. 18: Part of a screen shot of producer-consumer after firing "sends products"

- P, T invariants, deadlocks, traps
- some reachability aspects (by covering graphs).

A prototype (for our purposes only) is available on Atari, developed in Modula 2 [25].

6 APPLICATIONS

What about modeling of systems with the approach sketched in this paper? As emphasized earlier, acceptance of this proposed approach is only possible if comfortable tools for support are available. Despite this fact, early proposals to model with some sort of hierarchically represented Petri nets without such tools are given in, e.g., [26–28]. Early contributions to methods on how to model with HPNs can be found in, e.g., [26,29,30] and especially in [13,31,32]. Modelings using our tools are sketched in [3,4]. In the citated literature HPNs are applied to describe pure hardware as well as pure software systems in the early phases of development. Thus we are convinced that HPNs are well suited to this purpose. Some of the first examples that exploited HPNs for hardware/software codesign are introduced in [33].

7 CONCLUSIONS

We have tried to show that certain variations of Petri nets are very well suited to model functional requirements and the main part of design for complex systems by using them as hierarchically represented nets, and how we are able to support such modeling by appropriate tools.

Our projects in this context for the near future are as follows:

- Checking our methodogical approach with our up-to-now existing tool in that we will model much more complex systems.
- Reimplement the existing tool using the clear concept of HPH from [11].
- Enhance this tool in some directions especially by introducing the concept of building blocks in order to be able to support structured design and a bottom-up method.
- Add further tools for transforming of HPN descriptions into a programming language or HDL description, as suggested in Figure 15.

ACKNOWLEDGMENTS

Thanks to K. Tochtermann for reading the manuscript and making suggestions for improvements and to C. Rubach for creating a Tech version.

REFERENCES

[1] G. Dittrich, "Specifications with Nets," in *Computer Aided Systems Theory—EURO-CAST '89,* F. Pichler, R. Moreno-Diaz, Eds., LNCS Vol. 410, pp. 111–124, Springer Verlag, Berlin, 1990.

[2] G. Dittrich, "Tools for Modelling with Petri-Net Like Nets," in *Computer Aided Systems Theory–EUROCAST '89,* F. Pichler, R. Moreno-Diaz, Eds., LNCS Vol. 410, pp. 191–199, Springer Verlag, Berlin, 1990.

[3] G. Dittrich, "Modelling of Large Scale Systems by Hierarchical Nets," in *Proc. 8th Intl. Congress of Cybernetics and Systems,* New York, 1990.

[4] G. Dittrich, "Modellieren mit und Simulieren von hierarchischen Petri-Netzen," in *Fortschritte in der Simulationstechnik,* F. Breitenecker et al., Eds., Band 1, pp. 203–207, Vieweg Verlag, 1990.

[5] G. Dittrich, "Modellierung komplexer Systeme mit hierarchischen Netzen," *Proc. of 3. Fachtagung Entwurf komplexer Automatisierungssysteme,* TU Braunschweig, pp. 265–288, 1993.

[6] W. Brauer, Ed., *Net Theory and Applications,* LNCS Vol. 84, Springer Verlag, Berlin, 1980.

[7] W. Brauer, W. Reisig, and G. Rozenberg, Eds., *Petri Nets: Central Models and Their Properties,* LNCS Vol. 254, Springer Verlag, Berlin, 1987.

[8]   W. Brauer, W. Reisig, and G. Rozenberg, Eds., *Petri Nets: Applications and Relationships to Other Models of Concurrency,* LNCS Vol. 255, Springer Verlag, Berlin, 1987.

[9]   K. Jensen, K., *Coloured Petri Nets,* EATCS Monographs on TCS, Springer Verlag, Berlin, 1992.

[10] G. Dittrich, G., "Petrinetze," Spezialvorlesung WS 84/85, Interne Berichte der Abteilung Informatik, Universität Dortmund, 1985.

[11] R. Fehling, "Hierarchische Petrinetze," Verlag Dr. Kovač, Hamburg, 1992.

[12] A. Rüping, "Beiträge zur Methodik hierarchischer Petrinetze, Ein Konzept für eine hierarchiebezogene Modellierung mit interpretierten Netzen auf der Basis von Netzmorphismen," Diplomarbeit am FB Informatik, Universität Dortmund, 1988.

[13] A. Leufke, and D. Wolberg, "Bausteine für Petri-Netze—Konzept und Einsatz," Diplomarbeit am FB Informatik, Universität Dortmund, 1989.

[14] O. Herzog, W. Reisig, and R. Valk, Eds., "Special Volume: Petri Net Tools Overview 92," *Petri Net Newsletters* 41, published by Gesellschaft für Informatik, SIG on Petri Nets and Related System Models, Apr. 1992.

[15] A. Brodda, and P. Buttler, "PetriLab," Diplomarbeit am FB Informatik, Universität Dortmund, 1990.

[16] T. Gers, "PetriLab—STTI, ein Simulator für stochastische und zeitbehaftete Petrinetze," Diplomarbeit am FB Informatik, Universität Dortmund, 1990.

[17] G. Dittrich, and G. Szwillus, Eds., "PETE—Ein Petrinetz-Editor," Abschlussbericht der Projektgruppe PETE, Interne Berichte des FB Informatik, Dortmund, 1987.

[18] B. Evertz-Jägers, "Objektorientierte Entwicklung eines Editors zur Erstellung hierarchischer K/I-Netze," Diplomarbeit am FB Informatik, Universität Dortmund, 1988.

[19] G. Dittrich and B. Evertz-Jägers, "Der Kanal-Instanz-Netz Editor KINED," Forschungsbericht No. 308 des Fachbereichs Informatik, Universität Dortmund, 1989.

[20] G. Dittrich, and R. Fehling, R., Eds., "Endbericht der Projektgruppe PetSi," Interne Berichte des FB Informatik der UniDo, Dortmund, 1989.

[21] M. Schmenner, "Entwurf und Implementierung eines Programms zur Überprüfung der syntaktischen Korrektheit von Beschriftungen verschiedener PN-Typen," Diplomarbeit am FB Informatik, Universität Dortmund, 1987.

[22] F. Buschmann, "PETENET-ein multi-user-fähiger Petrinetzeditor für hierarchische Petrinetze," Diplomarbeit am FB Informatik, Universität Dortmund, 1989.

[23] M. Pickers, "MOVE," Diplomarbeit am FB Informatik, Universität Dortmund, 1991.

[24] K. Durand, "Ein Beitrag zur Simulation neuronaler Netze mit Hilfe von Petri-Netzen," Diplomarbeit am FB Informatik, Universität Dortmund, 1992.

[25] D. Fabian, "Ein Tool zur Analyse von Petrinetzen," speziell S/T-Netzen, Diplomarbeit am FB Informatik, Universität Dortmund, 1987.

[26] W. Reisig, *Systementwurf mit Petrinetzen,* Springer Verlag, Berlin, 1985.

[27] G. Dittrich, and G. Eising, Eds., "Software für Materialflusssysteme," Abschlussbericht der Projektgruppe SOMAT, Interne Berichte des FB Informatik, Universität Dortmund, 1986.

[28] H. Aigner, "RAPPS—Rapid Prototyper für formale Petrinetz-Spezifikationen," Diplomarbeit am FB Informatik, Universität Dortmund, 1987.

[29] A. Maryniak, "Petri-Netze: Allgemeine Begriffsklärung und anwendungsorientierte Einführung in die Modellierung," Diplomarbeit am FB Informatik, Universität Dortmund, 1988.

[30] R. Viethen, "Petri-Netze: Methodikansätze und anwendungsorientierte Einführung in die Modellierung," Diplomarbeit am FB Informatik, Universität Dortmund, 1988.

[31] M. Reck, "Von informellen zu formalen Spezifikationen durch Petri-Netze und Abstrakte Datentypen," Diplomarbeit am FB Informatik, Universität Dortmund, 1988.

[32] M. Reck, *Methoden und Beschreibungsmittel für die Programmentwicklung,* Forkel Verlag, Wiesbaden, 1991.

[33] C. Ohsendoth-Haase, "Zur Spezifikation eingebetteter mikroelektronischer Systeme: Ein kundenorientiertes Phasen-Modell und die Generierung verwertbarer VHDL-Beschreibungen," Dissertation, Dortmund, 1992.

CHAPTER 7

SOLAR: An Intermediate Format for System-Level Modeling and Synthesis

A. A. Jerraya   K. O'Brien

System Level Synthesis Group

TIMA/INPG

Grenoble Cedex, France

Abstract: This chapter presents SOLAR, a design representation for system-level concepts. The main motivation behind the development of SOLAR is to link CASE tools and integrated circuit computer-aided design tools, thereby allowing mixed hardware/software codesign.

The SOLAR system model is designed to accommodate the main concepts handled by system-level specification languages that are relevant to synthesis. The goal is to use this representation for the design and synthesis of complex, control-flow dominated hardware systems. To achieve these goals, SOLAR supports high-level concepts within several description styles (structure and behavior) and several description levels ranging from the software system level to the register transfer level.

An example of a hardware/software codesign environment built around SOLAR is described. The environment allows the combination of a system-level design language and a hardware design language. We show that the use of system-level specification reduces the volume of information handled by a factor of almost 50.

1 INTRODUCTION

Several projects currently in progress (StateCharts [1], SpecCharts and BIF at Irvine [2,3], SIF and MV at BNR and INPG [4,5], work at Eindhoven [6], SDW at Italtel [7], ADL at Siemens [8]) are all trying to bridge the gap between the system level of specification and existing logic and behavioral synthesis tools.

1.1 Motivations

According to Bourbon [9], most application-specific integrated circuits (ASICs) work first time according to their logic specification. This performance is due to the acceptance and extensive use of register-transfer level synthesis systems in industry. Unfortunately, about 50% of these ASICs are reworked because they fail when inserted into their environment. Most of the failures are due to specification errors, communication problems, and electrical defects related to board implementation. It is probable that most of these failures could be avoided if circuit design were integrated with system design.

Two kinds of solution are being explored today in the field of system-level design automation. The first tries to bring VLSI design and synthesis tools to a higher level by developing high-level and behavioral synthesis tools. The second uses existing CASE tools for VLSI system design. In our system, the two solutions are combined. As we shall see, an efficient design methodology starting from a true system-level specification should also include a high-level or behavioral design step. On the other hand, high-level synthesis by itself is not the solution for VLSI design in the 1990s.

The main motivation behind this work is the development of SOLAR, a design representation aimed at linking CASE tools and integrated circuit (IC) computer-aided design (CAD) tools, thereby allowing the design and synthesis of mixed hardware/software systems.

1.2 Objectives

This chapter presents SOLAR [10,11], a design representation for high-level concepts in control-flow dominated system synthesis. The goal is to use this representation for the design of complex, control-flow dominated hardware systems. To achieve these goals SOLAR supports high-level concepts such as hierarchical and interacting finite state machines (FSMs) and high-level communication.

The objectives of SOLAR are twofold. First, a basic data structure needs to be identified that will allow all of the aforementioned requirements to be accommodated. Second, system-level synthesis tools need to be developed, including partitioning and communication synthesis. These tools will produce a set of interconnected FSMs that may feed existing silicon compilers.

1.3 SOLAR: Bridging the Gap Between CASE Tools and IC CAD Tools

SOLAR is composed of a data representation model and a textual language. Although human readable, SOLAR is not intended to be a new specification language. Such languages already exist. For example, the behavior of the hardware may be more easily described in a dedicated hardware description language (HDL) such as VHDL [12], UDL/I [13], or SILAGE [14]. On the other hand, system software specifications can be readily represented in existing languages, such as ESTELLE [15], LOTOS [16] and SDL [17] for communication protocols, CSP [18] and OCCAM for concurrent systems,

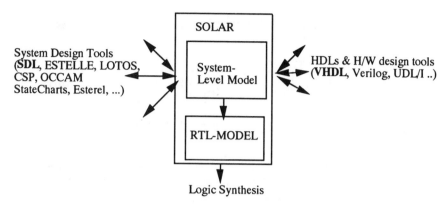

Fig. 1: The SOLAR environment

ESTEREL [19] and StateCharts [20] for real-time systems, and so on. What SOLAR provides is an intermediate, unifying format for several such languages, which allows mixed hardware/software designs to be represented in a form suitable for their eventual synthesis. Figure 1 shows a framework example where such a representation may be useful.

The SOLAR system model is designed to accommodate the main concepts handled by system-level specification languages (SDL, CSP, StateCharts, etc.) that are relevant to synthesis. Of course, some restrictions on the permissible input will apply in order to have predictable and coherent results. This includes only allowing subsets of the description languages to be used.

The definition of SOLAR is based on several exploratory projects (MV [4] and SIF [5]) carried out at Bell-Northern Research (BNR) Laboratories in Canada.

The next section presents the main concepts involved in system-level synthesis and gives examples of existing models used for their representation. Section 3 gives an outline of SOLAR's basic concepts. These are elaborated in Section 4. Section 5 presents the COSMOS synthesis environment where various tools that use SOLAR are described. These tools perform both system-level and behavioral-level synthesis. Finally, Sections 6 and 7 draw some conclusions and give some indications of future objectives.

2 SYSTEM-LEVEL DESIGN, SPECIFICATION AND SYNTHESIS

In this chapter, Lamport's definition of the word *system* is adopted: "a system is anything that interacts with its environment in a discrete (digital) fashion across a well-defined boundary" [21]. Of course, this definition may apply just as well to a complete computer network as to a C routine.

Figure 2 shows an example of a system composed of computer, a multimeter, and a robot that communicates through a protocol XX (e.g., IEEE488). A typical application for this system is an environment in which the computer commands the robot (e.g., to open or close a valve) according to the measurements taken by the digital multimeter

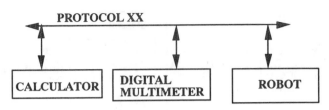

Fig. 2: System example

(e.g., temperature). The realization of such a system involves the design of interfaces for the robot, the computer, and the multimeter. These interfaces may be software, hardware, or mixed hardware/software subsystems (e.g., microprogrammed components).

In an ideal world, the design of such a system would start from a unique system specification given in one language. The validation of this specification would be done in a single environment. The top level of such a specification may be composed of three subsystems that communicate through a channel (Figure 3). This abstract specification is used for the next steps of the design which might include:

- hardware/software partitioning
- software design
- hardware design

In the real world, separate tools and methodologies are used for the design and specification of hardware and software. One of the reasons for this is the fact that hardware design tools are still based on low-level specifications that are not powerful enough to describe complex systems.

2.1 Previous Work

Even if several commercial tools already exist [22] for what is known as *system-level design automation,* we are still far from true automatic system-level design and synthesis. In fact, as shown in Figure 4(a), most commercial tools are simple translators that start from a system-level specification and produce a specification in a language such as VHDL that may feed existing register-transfer level (RTL) synthesis systems. With such a translation scheme, one has to restrict the system-level specification language to a

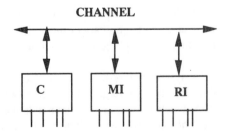

Fig. 3: Possible specification of system of Figure 2

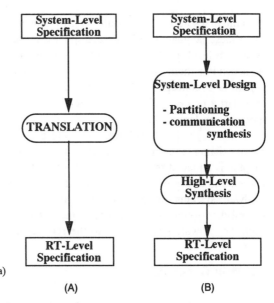

Fig. 4: Linking system-level and RT-level: (a) translation scheme and (b) synthesis steps

subset that matches the model accepted by existing RTL synthesis systems. We can easily see that with such a scheme, system-level facilities are used as simple capture facilities for existing RTL synthesis tools. In other words, system-level specification tools are used in order to describe the design at the RT level.

A true system-level design automation methodology will include several other design steps apart from a simple translation. Figure 4(b) shows the main steps needed in order to transform a system-level specification into an RT-level one. These include a system-level design and synthesis step that will perform system partitioning and communication synthesis. The result of the system-level synthesis step is a description composed of a set of interconnected processes. A high-level synthesis step is then needed in order to partition each process into a set of interconnected RT-level blocks. This last step includes scheduling and allocation. Such a methodology makes use of several description levels and formats (see Section 5).

Each of these steps refines the input specification, producing a lower level, equivalent description. Experiments have shown the each refinement increases the volume of information by a factor of 7 (see Sections 5.1 and 5.5).

As stated earlier, several projects currently in progress are trying to bridge the gap between system-level specification and existing VLSI design automation tools. To allow for mixed hardware/software codesign, each of these projects explores one of four ways:

1. Use a system specification language such as SDL, ESTELLE, LOTOS, State-Charts, ESTEREL, CSP, etc.

2. Use an HDL such as VHDL, VERILOG, or UDL/I.

3. Create a new system-level specification language such as SpecCharts [2].

4. Use an intermediate form such as BIF [3] or SIF [5] that allows efficient handling of system-level concepts and accurately mirrors hardware.

With the first solution, one would have to reinvent most hardware design environments and adapt these languages to hardware specification. As it turns out, some concepts handled by system-level specification languages cannot be efficiently mapped onto hardware. With the second method, one would be faced with the limitation of HDLs for supporting some system-level concepts such as communication through channels and process control (stop or restart a process). The third solution is attractive, but is there room for a yet another specification language?

Finally, the fourth solution seems to be the most promising, since it maximizes the use of existing tools and methodologies. SOLAR, the intermediate format presented in this chapter, is aimed at the representation of control-driven specifications at the system level. The goal is to use this representation for the design of complex, control-flow dominated hardware systems. To achieve these goals, SOLAR supports high-level concepts within several description styles (structure and behavior) and several description levels ranging from the software system level to the register transfer level.

2.2 Main Concepts

Several system-level description languages exist. Regardless of the syntax of these languages, which may be graphical or textual, most of them are based on a few basic concepts. The four main concepts are hierarchy, concurrency, communication, and synchronization. Most of these concepts are also used by HDLs, but with a different meaning. For instance, on the hardware side, hierarchy is used for specifying structural or procedural configurations, whereas at the system level, hierarchy implies process hierarchy with underlying process control techniques. For communication and synchronization, the gap between software and hardware is even larger. In fact, at the system level, communication is achieved through the use of high-level constructs (variable sharing, message passing). In most HDLs, communication can only be made through ports and signals.

No existing HDL, in our experience, provides all the required facilities for the specification of the four concepts just listed. Some HDLs such as HSL-FX [23] and UDL/I have tried to provide restricted facilities for process control, but none provides facilities for high-level communication and exception specification (reset, initialization, emergency situations, etc.). HardwareC [24] provides nice facilities for communication specification, but it provides only restricted facilities for the specification of process control. VHDL '93 also supports shared variables for interprocess communication. However, no new facilities are given for the specification of process control. The lack of these concepts makes most HDLs verbose when used to describe complex controllers.

Most of the paradigms listed are handled by system-level description languages oriented toward protocols (SDL, ESTELLE, LOTOS etc.), real-time systems (StateCharts, ESTEREL), and parallel programming (CSP, OCCAM).

2.3 Models and Languages

Several models may be used to analyze and verify such languages. These include the trace theory (based on Turing machines), Petri nets, the single FSM model, and extended FSM models. The most popular model is the extended FSM. All of these models provide

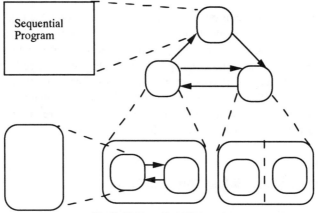

Fig. 5: The extended FSM model

a formal analysis of descriptions. They may be classified according to their modeling power, analytical power, and clarity power [25]. The extended FSM model seems to be a good trade-off. Besides, the manipulation of this model is the easiest to automate.

Figure 5 shows a hierarchical system modeled by a set of communicating FSMs. Here we use Harel's notation [20]. Each box represents an FSM. Dashed lines extending from boxes imply a subhierarchy. Unbroken arrows imply transitions between FSMs. A dashed line between two FSMs denotes that these two execute concurrently. This representation is an extension of the classical state diagram with two concepts, hierarchy and parallelism. In this diagram a state may be one of the following:

- a leaf state
- a set of sequenced states
- a set of parallel states

This representation can model most of the control-driven specification languages listed earlier. In fact, the differences between all these languages is the way they organize the following:

- the leaf state
- the transition between states and hierarchical states
- the interaction between states
- The facilities for the specification of unstructured control

3 SOLAR: BASIC CONCEPTS

SOLAR was designed to support several abstraction levels ranging from the system level to the RT level. It is based on the extended FSM model. The principal building block of SOLAR is called the *StateTable*. It allows the specification of hierarchical and communicating FSMs. In addition, three structures have been added in order to allow modular specification and to facilitate interprocess communication. The *DesignUnit* construct is introduced to allow the structuring of a system description into a set of interacting subsystems. The *ChannelUnit* concept allows the high-level specification of communication between any number of concurrent subsystems. The *FunctionalUnit* concept allows the high-level specification of shared operators between sequenced FSMs. These three concepts are also based on the extended FSM model. They are introduced in order to simplify the analysis and synthesis of SOLAR specifications.

3.1 Hierarchical FSMs: The StateTable

The basic construct in SOLAR is the StateTable. A SOLAR StateTable consists of a (possibly empty) set of declarations and an unlimited combination of states (single FSMs) and StateTables. All of these are capable of being executed sequentially, concurrently, or both. Transitions between states are not level restricted. In other words, transitions may traverse hierarchical boundaries. Such transitions are known as *global transitions*. This is an important concept in control-flow dominated systems. A transition must be permitted between any two FSMs, regardless of their positions in the hierarchy.

3.2 System Hierarchy: The DesignUnit

The DesignUnit construct allows the structuring of a system description into a set of interacting subsystems. Each subsystem interacts with the external world through a well-defined boundary. It is the only way for the specification of communicating systems in SOLAR.

Inter-DesignUnit communication is achieved in one of two ways. First, through the classic port concept where single wires send data in one or two directions, and second through communication channels that allow the designer to specify schemes of varying degrees of complexity.

Figure 6 shows a system-level representation containing four DesignUnits. Each DesignUnit can contain one or more StateTables, describing its internal behavior. In addition, a DesignUnit may itself be hierarchical (DU0 of Figure 6) containing other DesignUnits.

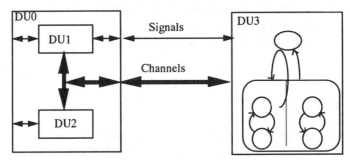

Fig. 6: The SOLAR DesignUnit

The overall behavior of the system is thus distributed among the DesignUnits. The structure of a DesignUnit is discussed in more detail in Section 4.

3.3 Communication: The ChannelUnit

The SOLAR ChannelUnit model [26] mixes the principles of monitors and message passing. It is known as the Remote Procedure Call (RPC) model [27,28]. The ChannelUnit allows communication between any number of processes.

The use of an RPC-based methodology gives us the flexibility to model most communication schemes, and at the same time provides us with the possibility of clear and efficient semantics. Monitors [29] were initially developed to control access to a resource by encapuslating both the resource and the operations that manipulate it. These operations are normally procedure-like constructs and can be invoked as such by concurrent processes sharing the resource. Thus, the implementation of the resource is completely independent of the processes that access it.

A channel consists of many individual connections that not only act as a transport mechanism for the communicated data but also provide a handshaking interface to ensure both the synchronization and the avoidance of access conflicts. We can view such a channel as a shared resource. Access to the channel is governed by a fixed set of procedures known as *methods*. Once access to the channel has been achieved, communication can proceed in any predefined way (serial/parallel transfer, synchronous/asynchronous message passing, and so on).

Figure 7 shows the channel model in SOLAR. This diagram shows n processes communicating over a common channel. These processes are represented by DesignUnits in SOLAR. The channel model consists of a controller, which stores the resource's current state, a set of interconnect signals, and an interface that encapsulates I/O ports and a set of methods, which are the only means of accessing the resource. The methods and the ports constitute the visible part of the channel. Methods can be accessed by any appropriately connected DesignUnit. The controller is a private function, inaccessible to the sharing DesignUnits but it does interact with the methods via the interconnect signals to provide synchronization and to ensure mutual exclusion.

Note that the communication scheme's description is completely isolated, meaning that the designer can ignore its implementation details when using it and ignore how it is to be used when implementing it. The methodology used also implies that the possibility exists of providing the designer with a wide range of communication schemes from which he or she can choose the one most suitable to the particular application [26].

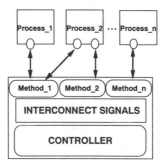

Fig. 7: The SOLAR ChannelUnit

3.4 Mixing Behavior and Structure: The FunctionalUnit

FunctionalUnits are introduced in order to allow for the mixing of behavior and structure. They allow the use of existing functions in a behavioral specification. A FunctionalUnit is SOLAR's equivalent of a multifunction unit. It can be called from within a behavioral description in order to perform a given operation. It can accept and return parameters. In terms of hardware, it allows us to create partial designs that can easily be introduced into new systems [30,31]. Figure 8 shows how a FunctionalUnit can be specified and invoked.

A FunctionalUnit is an entity capable of performing several operations. A set of standard FunctionalUnits is provided by the system (adders, multipliers, ALUs, etc.). New, customized functional units may be introduced by the user. These may be large complex blocks such as cache memories, I/O units, and so on.

A FunctionalUnit specification [Fig. 8(a)] is composed of an interface and a set of operations (or procedures) that may be performed by the FunctionalUnit. Each operation specifies the execution details of a command of the FunctionalUnit. This may be a complex StateTable. The operations of a FunctionalUnit cannot execute in parallel. Thus, a FunctionalUnit cannot be shared by parallel processes.

The operations may be invoked from the user's description [Fig. 8(b)]. This is a generalization of the notion of operators (logic and arithmetic operators) used in behavioral specifications. The interface specifies the parameters of the FunctionalUnit.

A synthesis system can contain a library of FunctionalUnits. The library description contains the FunctionalUnit's behavior and other pertinent information. The designer in-

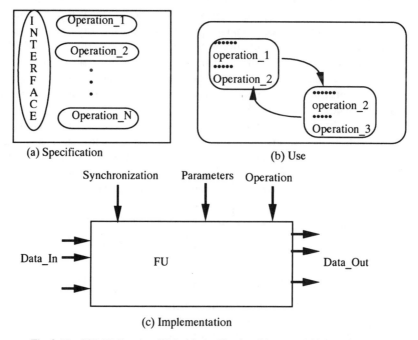

Fig. 8: The SOLAR FunctionalUnit: (a) specification, (b) use, and (c) implementation

vokes a FunctionalUnit through a simple calling syntax. FunctionalUnits can be of any degree of complexity and can themselves contain FunctionalUnits.

3.5 Views and ViewTypes

The objective of SOLAR is to provide an intermediate format for the representation of mixed hardware/software systems in a manner that is suitable for synthesis. Translations to SOLAR are made from high-level, task-specific languages. Thus, a given system may be specified in many languages and at different levels before being unified under SOLAR. To avoid complicating the simple descriptions while at the same time providing all of the necessary infrastructure for system-level concepts, SOLAR is divided into three levels. These are the system level, the behavioral level, and the register-transfer level. Of course, the register-transfer level is a subset of the behavioral level, which is, in turn, a subset of the structural level.

To enable a DesignUnit to be used as both a behavioral and structural entity, the concept of views was introduced. Two different views are allowed in a SOLAR file: behavior and structure. For each view, several ViewTypes are allowed. Figure 9 shows this hierarchy of views and ViewTypes.

A structural View specifies a system as a hierarchy of subsystems interacting through well-defined boundaries. In the case of an *interconnected system* ViewType, the interaction is performed through physical signals. This kind of ViewType is similar to the classical netlist. In the case of a *communicating system* ViewType, channels may be used for interaction between subsystems.

A behavioral view specifies a system as a set of communicating processes. The ViewType is fixed according to the organization of these processes. The *register-transfer level* specifies a process at the clock cycle level. Each transition of the StateTable takes exactly one basic cycle to execute. The *process level* specifies a single process system that can execute operations. An operation may need several basic cycles to execute. The process may include a hierarchy of sequenced FSMs (or processes). In the case of a hierarchy of sequential processes, this ViewType is equivalent to the organization of routines in a monitor: Only one process can execute at a given time. At this level, global transitions and exceptions may be specified. The *communicating process* ViewType level specifies a collection of hierarchical, parallel, and interacting processes. Only this level allows true parallelism.

A view has two main components: an interface and contents. The interface includes the declaration of the ports and the accesses (see next section) that will connect the DesignUnit to the external world. For the lowest level of description, the interface may

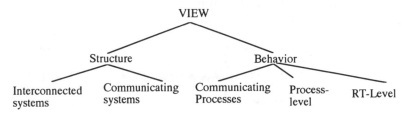

Fig. 9: SOLAR views and ViewTypes

include the specification of physical synchronization signals, such as clocks and resets. Variables can be declared at all behavioral levels of SOLAR and have scoping rules similar to EDIF. They can be used for interprocess communication.

4 SOLAR THROUGH A SYSTEM-LEVEL SPECIFICATION EXAMPLE

This section introduces in an informal way the syntax and the execution model of SOLAR. This introduction is done through a communicating system example.

SOLAR is an EDIF-like textual intermediate format that can also represent system-level concepts. Several EDIF constructs and conventions are used. For example, the SOLAR netlist is identical to the EDIF one. This was chosen for ease of parsing and, along with an object-oriented database implementation, allows the language to be easily extended.

4.1 SOLAR Structure

Figure 10 shows a simple system that contains two blocks, a host and a server, specified at the communicating system level. The blocks are interconnected via a single channel. In other words, the system is specified as a collection of communicating units. At this stage, we only know that we have two processes that communicate somehow.

Figure 11 shows the organization of the SOLAR file corresponding to the representation of Figure 10. All SOLAR descriptions must start with the keyword SOLAR (preceded by an open bracket). This is followed by the name of the description. The SOLAR description of Figure 11 consists of a single DesignUnit of view *structure*. This DesignUnit contains instantiations of the principal blocks of Figure 10 and the means by which they are interconnected. The interface contains the system's interface with the outside world (in this case, two port declarations). The two instances refer to other DesignUnits representing the *host* and *server* blocks. These are described elsewhere in the system. In this example, each instance contains a PortInstance and an AccessInstance. A PortInstance is a simple port connection, whereas an AccessInstance is a channel interface. The netlist identifies what ports and channels are connected.

4.2 DesignUnit Specification

A DesignUnit specification is composed of a name and a set of views. Each view specifies the DesignUnit function at a given level. In the example, only one view is given for each DesignUnit. The DesignUnits *host* and *server* are specified as a *process level* ViewType. The *host-server* DesignUnit is specified as a *communicating system* ViewType.

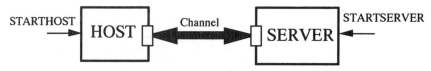

Fig. 10: Communicating system example

```
(SOLAR request-manager
  (DESIGNUNIT host_server
    (VIEW structure
      (VIEWTYPE "communicatingsystems")
      (INTERFACE
        (PORT startsend (DIRECTION IN) (BIT))
        (PORT startrecv (DIRECTION IN) (BIT))
      )
      (CONTENTS
        (INSTANCE host
          (VIEWREF behavior host)
          (PORTINSTANCE restart)
          (ACCESSINSTANCE dataout)
        )
        (INSTANCE server
          (VIEWREF behavior server)
          (PORTINSTANCE restart)
          (ACCESSINSTANCE datain)
        )
        (NET startsend
          (JOINED    (PORTREF startsend)
                     (PORTREF restart (INSTANCEREF host))))
        (NET startrecv
          (JOINED    (PORTREF startrecv)
                     (PORTREF restart (INSTANCEREF server))))
        (NET datain
          (JOINED    (ACCESSREF datain    (INSTANCEREF server))
                     (ACCESSREF dataout   (INSTANCEREF host))))
      )
    )
  )
)
```

Fig. 11: Example of communicating system specification

Figure 12 gives the full specification of the DesignUnit *host*. This DesignUnit has a view of type *behavior,* which implies a communicating process organization. The host function is restricted to sending messages to the *server* across the channel.

A DesignUnit interface includes the declaration of the ports and the accesses that will connect a DesignUnit to the outside world. A port can be of any predefined type. It also possesses a direction that can either be In, Out, or InOut. An access is used by a DesignUnit to make a connection to a channel. An access must specify a unique name as well as the name and the view of the channel with which it wants to communicate. The interface of the DesignUnit of Figure 12 contains both a port and an access declaration. The ViewRef clause of the access statement indicates which ChannelUnit and which view are to be used.

The unique view in Figure 12 is composed of a ViewType construct (line 3), an interface (lines 4–6) and a contents (lines 7–29). The function of the DesignUnit is specified by the contents. It is composed of two declaration clauses (a variable and a constant) and a StateTable.

The StateTable is the most important construct in SOLAR (see also Section 4.4). A StateTable specification contains a set of states and some specific attributes such as a default entry state, a reset state, and so on. The StateList clause (line 11) gives the names of all the states defined in the StateTable. A StateTable may contain states that are themselves StateTables. Each leaf state contains a set of actions that will be executed when the state is activated. These may include port and variable assignment statements as well as state transition specifications.

The StateTable may also contain GlobalActions that are used for transition clustering and exception specification. A GlobalAction is used to specify a set of conditions that will cause a transition from within a hierarchical FSM, *regardless of its internal state,* to another single state. For example, in the host StateTable (lines 13–15), if the signal *restart = '1',* the next state will be restart. Using classical state diagrams, this would require three transitions.

SOLAR also supports unstructured control statements such as Exit and NextState. The NextState statement allows the specification of transitions from any FSM to any other FSM in a SOLAR description. In the case of the StateTable *host,* only local transitions are used.

Some other statements are used in this specification. Besides the common statements such as ASSIGN, IF-THEN-ELSE, and WAIT, there is the CUCALL statement that is used to execute a method of one channel. For instance, the CUCALL statement in State *send* (lines 24–25) calls the method *put* of the channel accessed through the access *dataout.* The call is made with the parameter *counter,* which is assigned to the formal parameter *request* defined in the referenced method. After communication synthesis, CU-CALLs reduce to standard procedure calls.

4.3 ChannelUnit Specification

The channel in SOLAR allows communication between any number of processes. It is composed of an interface, a set of methods that define the protocol to access the channel, and a controller.

```
1    (DESIGNUNIT host
2      (VIEW behavior
3        (VIEWTYPE "ProcessLevel")
4        (INTERFACE
5          (PORT restart (DIRECTION IN) (BIT))
6          (ACCESS dataout (VIEWREF behavior request-manager)))
7        (CONTENTS
8          (VARIABLE counter (INTEGER 0))
9          (CONSTANT maxcount (INTEGER 100))
10         (STATETABLE host
11           (STATELIST idle restart send)
12           (ENTRYSTATE idle)
13           (GLOBALACTION
14             (IF (== restart 1) (THEN (NEXTSTATE restart)))
15           )
16           (STATE idle
17             (NEXTSTATE idle))
18           (STATE restart
19             (ASSIGN counter 0)
20             (CUCALL init dataout)
21             (NEXTSTATE send)
22           )
23           (STATE SEND
24             (CUCALL put dataout
25               (PARAMETERASSIGN request counter))
26             (ASSIGN counter (+ 1 counter))
27             (IF (>= counter maxcount)
28               (THEN (NEXTSTATE idle))
29               (ELSE (NEXTSTATE send)))))))))
```

Fig. 12: Host DesignUnit: full specification

159

A ChannelUnit interface contains not only the individual ports that constitute the I/O of the channel, but also the methods used by the communicating processes to access the ports. A method consists of a set of parameters and a hierarchical FSM (StateTable) that represents its behavior. Methods define half of the handshaking required to access a channel. The other half is located in the controller. An interface for a ChannelUnit that may be used as a communication medium between the *host* and *server* of Figure 10 is shown in Figure 13.

The contents section contains the controller behavior (see Figure 14). In other words, it performs the handshaking with the different methods and also updates the internal state of the channel. The controller may be seen as a resolution function that may be a complex process. It is a generalization of the resolution function of VHDL, which is stateless (a combinatorial process).

4.4 Hierarchical StateTable Specification

Hierarchical StateTables are used to specify communicating processes. A StateTable represents a (possibly communicating) process or FSM. It is hierarchical, possessing the capability of including simple, flat states or other StateTables. The basic elements of a StateTable are as follows:

```
(STATETABLE stname
        (VARIABLE ...)
        (CONSTANT ...)
        (STATELIST ...)
        (ENTRYSTATE ...)
        (DEFAULTNEXTSTATE ...)
        (RESETSTATE ...)
        (GLOBALACTION ...)
        (STATE...)
)
```

Variables and constants can be of any predefined type and can also be indexed. A variable is declared by specifying its name, its type and an optional initial value:

```
(VARIABLE data (INTEGER 0))
```

Arrays require the keyword "(ARRAY" as well as the size. The statement

```
(VARIABLE (ARRAY breq 3) (BIT))
```

declares a 3-bit bit_vector with members breq(0) through to breq(2), breq(0) being the most significant bit. When used, for example, in assignments, individual elements of an array are accessed through the use of the "(MEMBER'" keyword. Thus the following two statements are equivalent:

```
(CHANNELUNIT REQUEST MANAGER
  (VIEW BEHAVIOR (VIEWTYPE "COMMUNICATINGPROCESS")
    (INTERFACE

      (PORT REQIN (DIRECTION IN) (BIT))
      (PORT REQACK (DIRECTION OUT) (BIT))
      (PORT DATAIN (DIRECTION IN) (INTEGER))
      (PORT RESTART (DIRECTION IN) (BIT))
      (PORT RDY (DIRECTION IN) (BIT))
      (PORT B_FULL (DIRECTION OUT) (BIT))
      (PORT INQUIRE (DIRECTION OUT) (BIT))
      (PORT INQACK (DIRECTION IN) (BIT))
      (PORT DATAOUT (DIRECTION OUT) (INTEGER))
      (METHOD INIT

        (STATETABLE INIT (STATELIST INIT)
          (STATE INIT
            (ASSIGN RESTART '1'))))
      (METHOD PUT (PARAMETER REQUEST (INTEGER))
        (STATETABLE PUT (STATELIST PUT)
          (STATE PUT
            (IF (== B_FULL '1') (THEN (WAIT (UNTIL (== B_FULL '0'))))
              (ELSE (ASSIGN REQIN '1')
                (ASSIGN DATAIN REQUEST)))
            (WAIT (UNTIL (== REQACK '1')))
            (ASSIGN REQIN '0'))))
      (METHOD GET (PARAMETER REQUEST (INTEGER))
        (STATETABLE REQUEST (STATELIST REQ)
          (STATE REQ
            (IF (== RDY '1') (THEN (WAIT (UNTIL (== RDY '0'))))
              (ELSE (ASSIGN INQUIRE '1')
                (ASSIGN DATAIN REQUEST)))
            (WAIT (UNTIL (== INQACK '1')))
            (ASSIGN INQUIRE '0'))))

      (CONTENTS .....)

)
)
```

Fig. 13: Example of channel specification in SOLAR

161

```
(CHANNELUNIT REQUEST_MANAGER
  (VIEW BEHAVIOR
    (INTERFACE ...)
    (CONTENTS
      (CONSTANT BUF_SIZE (INTEGER 0))
      (VARIABLE (ARRAY BUFFER BUF_SIZE) (INTEGER 0 0 0 0 0 0 0 0))
      (VARIABLE BUFFIN (INTEGER 1))
      (VARIABLE BUFFOUT (INTEGER 1))
      (STATETABLE REQUEST_M
        (STATELIST INIT SEND_RECV)
        (ENTRYSTATE INIT)
        (STATE INIT
          (ASSIGN BUFFIN '1')
          (ASSIGN BUFFOUT '1')
          (NEXTSTATE SEND_RECV))
        (STATE SEND_RECV
          (PARACTION
            (GLOBALACTION
              (IF (== RESTART '1') (THEN (NEXTSTATE INIT))))
            (STATETABLE RECV
              (STATELIST WAIT_REQ BUF_FULL)
              (STATE WAIT_REQ
                (WAIT (UNTIL (== REQIN '1')))
                (ASSIGN (MEMBER BUFFER BUFFIN) DATAIN)
                (ASSIGN REQACK '1')
                (IF (== (+ 1 (MOD BUFFIN BUF_SIZE)) BUFFOUT)
                  (THEN (NEXTSTATE BUF_FULL))
                  (ELSE (ASSIGN BUFFIN
                         (+ 1 (MOD BUFFIN BUF_SIZE)))
                        (NEXTSTATE WAIT_REQ))))
```

```
(STATE BUF_FULL
    (ASSIGN B_FULL '1')
    (WAIT (UNTIL (!=(+ 1
                     (MOD BUFFIN BUF_SIZE)) BUFFOUT)))

    (ASSIGN B_FULL '0')
    (NEXTSTATE WAIT_REQ)))
(STATE SEND
    (ASSIGN INQUIRE '0')
    (IF (== BUFFIN BUFFOUT)
        (THEN (WAIT (UNTIL (!=BUFFIN BUFFOUT)))))
    (ASSIGN INQUIRE '1')
    (WAIT (UNTIL (== RDY '1')))
    (ASSIGN DATOUT (MEMBER BUFFER BUFFOUT))
    (ASSIGN INQACK '1')
    (ASSIGN BUFFOUT (+ 1 (MOD BUFFOUT BUF_SIZE)))
    (NEXTSTATE SEND))))))
```

Fig. 14: Example of hierarchical StateTables

```
breq(1) := '0';      and      (ASSIGN (MEMBER 1 breq)'0')
```

A SOLAR state can be defined as the triple

$$State ::== (A, T, C)$$

where A is a set of actions to be executed, T is a set of transitions that can be taken from the current state, and C is a set of conditions that determine which transition will be taken. This set of conditions includes global exceptions as well as internal tests.

An action can be a simple expression, a set of expressions to be executed in parallel or series, or a hierarchical declaration. A simple expression can either be an assignment, a branch statement, or a procedure call. An assignment has the form:

```
(ASSIGN valnameref expr)
```

where *valnameref* is a variable and *expr* is a mathematical expression. More complex operations can be used by using specific FunctionalUnits to execute them, passing the operators as parameters. Call statements pass control to a FunctionalUnit (FUCALL) or invoke a communication process (CUCALL).

Control flow within a State may be intrastate, interstate, or a call. The first type concerns the classic flow-of-control constructs such as IF, CASE, WHILE, EXIT, and WAIT. This type of construct passes control to other statements within the same state.

The set of transitions is determined by the NextState statements within a state and the global transitions that affect the state. The NextState construct allows a transition to another state anywhere in the hierarchy. In addition to the aforementioned control-flow statements, a StateTable allows the use of more powerful constructs for changing states such as the GlobalAction statement.

Figure 14 details the contents of the channel of Figure 10. The controller is a hierarchical FSM composed of two sequenced components: the state *init* and the state *send_recv*. The state *init* resets the buffer and transfers the control to *send_recv*. The state *send_recv* is composed of two parallel components; *send,* which is in charge of sending the requests to the *server,* and *recv,* which receives requests from the *host* and queues them in the buffer. The state *recv* is composed of two sequential FSMs, *wait_req* and *buf_ful*. The first accepts all requests. The state *buf_ful* is activated when the buffer is full. Transitions between FSMs are specified through the NextState primitive. The GlobalAction specifies a restart exception.

5 USING SOLAR FOR SYNTHESIS

This section introduces COSMOS, a hardware/software codesign environment based on SOLAR. COSMOS is intended to fill the gap between system-level tools and existing synthesis tools.

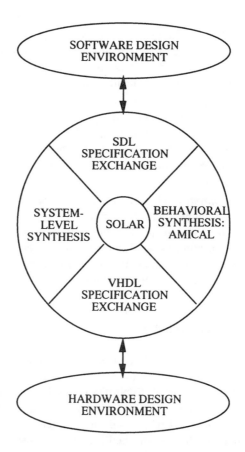

Fig. 15: The COSMOS environment

The COSMOS environment is presented in Figure 15. COSMOS uses SOLAR as a unified synthesis intermediate form for supporting several description levels. Currently, COSMOS is based on SDL (standard CCITT) for the system side and VHDL (standard IEEE) for the hardware side.

The framework supports several description levels ranging from RTL to system level. Each level can be compiled in one of three ways. The first produces a hardware model (VHDL) that may be used within a hardware design environment. The second method makes use of a synthesis tool that produces a lower level model in the synthesis intermediate form. The third way produces a software model that can be used for the validation of the implementation within a software environment.

COSMOS is thus connected to two kinds of environments: a software system design environment and a hardware design environment. It includes system-level synthesis tools for communication synthesis and partitioning, as well as behavioral synthesis tools for architectural synthesis. A mixed hardware/software system codesign may follow one of three approaches:

1. *System approach:* The full design is specified and verified at the software side. After a hardware/software partitioning step, the hardware parts are translated

into SOLAR. The synthesis tools may be used for hardware partitioning and high-level synthesis. The final step produces a VHDL specification at the RT-level that may feed existing silicon compilers. This approach may be used for the specification and validation of the full system within the software environment.

2. *Circuit approach:* The full design is specified and verified at the hardware side. After a hardware/software partitioning step, the software parts are translated into SOLAR. The final step produces a software specification. This approach may be used for the specification and validation of the full system within the hardware environment.

3. *Mixed approach:* The software parts are specified and validated within the software environment and the hardware parts are specified and validated within the hardware environment. The full system may be validated in the software side (after translating the hardware parts into software specifications). To validate the full system within the hardware environment, the software parts should be translated into hardware specifications.

5.1 System-Level Modeling

The objective of SOLAR is to allow a designer to describe different parts of a system using specialized languages, and to unify these blocks in a common format that is suited to synthesis. At the system level, COSMOS is interfaced to other system design automation tools through SDL. SDL is an FDT (formal description technique) standardized by the CCITT. SDL is, like SOLAR, based on an extended FSM model. The main concepts handled by SDL are the system, the block, the process, and the channel.

Table 1 shows the correspondence between SDL and SOLAR concepts. The translation of most SDL concepts into SOLAR, with the exception of communication concepts, is fairly straightforward.

The translation of the SDL communication concepts (Channel and SignalRoute) leads to a re-organization of the description. In SDL, communication is based on message passing. Processes communicate through SignalRoutes. Channels are used to group all the communication between blocks. The communication methodology used by SOLAR allows such systems to be modeled.

TABLE 1: Correspondance between SDL and SOLAR

SDL	SOLAR
Block, System	DesignUnit
Channel, SignalRoute	Distributed among processes
Process	DesignUnit + ChannelUnit
Service, Procedure	StateTable
State	State

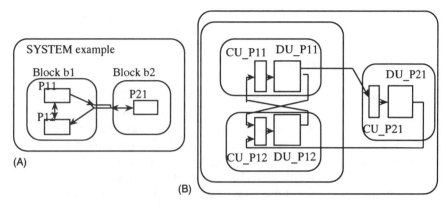

Fig. 16: Modeling the SDL channel in SOLAR: (a) SDL model and (b) SOLAR model

This scheme is summarized in Figure 16. Figure 16(a) shows a system example. It is composed of two communicating blocks. Block b1 contains two processes (P11, P12) that communicate with P21, a process that belongs to block b2. The translation of this system into SOLAR will produce the structure shown in Figure 16(b). Each process is translated into a DesignUnit composed of a hierarchical FSM and a ChannelUnit. This translation assumes that the transmission does not introduce delays.

SOLAR models tend to be somewhat longer than their SDL counterparts. Table 2 shows a summary of the number of lines of code required for three examples, a simple algorithm for storing telephone numbers, a send-and-wait communication protocol, and a telephone answering machine that can be operated remotely. We can see from Table 2 that the SOLAR code resulting from the automatic translation [32] is about six times the size of the initial SDL code. Only part of this extra size is due to the Lisp-like nature of SOLAR producing extra parentheses, etc. In terms of character size, SOLAR programs are more than seven times bigger than the original SDL code. This extra code is cause for some concern, however, because it could lead to inefficient designs.

One of the main reasons for this difference in code size is the SDL communication scheme. This was modeled through a SOLAR channel construct that explicitly describes the SDL communication scheme. In SDL, first-in/first-out quenes (FIFOs) are implicitly included in each process, and all signals, no matter what their type, are automatically stored in this FIFO. In addition, the ordering of messages in the queues can be explicitly controlled. It has already been pointed out [33] that this type of communication scheme is not very efficient in terms of hardware. Thus, because of the high cost of communication,

TABLE 2: Comparison of SDL and SOLAR Program Sizes

Example	Code SDL	Code SOLAR
Telephone number store	35	179
Send-and-wait protocol	54	333
Remote answering machine	150	645

it would be more efficient, from a hardware point of view, to have larger initial SDL processes and less interprocess communication.

5.2 System-Level Synthesis

Once a system-level model has been obtained in SOLAR, we can begin synthesizing the design. Different synthesis techniques are applied to different levels of the model. For example, at the system level we still have a hierarchical set of communicating FSMs. This model is unacceptable to most behavioral synthesis tools. System-level synthesis involves distributing the communication among the processes and identifying single processes that can be handled at the behavioral level. This latter task involves expanding and partitioning the processes, thereby eliminating system-level constructs such as parallelism, hierarchy, and global transitions.

Figure 17 shows the principle of system-level synthesis. The topmost block is a State-Chart-like representation of a hierarchical system. System-level synthesis may be defined as the partitioning of such a description into a set of interconnected processes, with the overall control distributed among the processes. This is shown at the bottom of Figure 17. Each of the processes is independent of all others and may be treated individually by synthesis tools.

The two main tasks carried out during system-level synthesis are partitioning and communication synthesis.

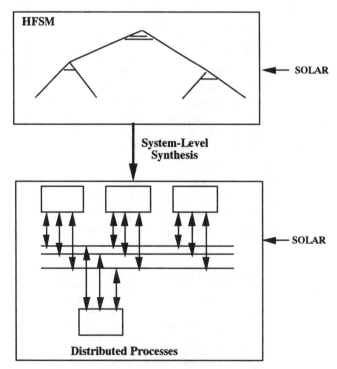

Fig. 17: System-level synthesis in COSMOS

5.3 Partitioning

Partitioning at a higher level is essential in order to obtain efficient designs. Much of the research into partitioning has thus far concentrated on lower levels where the system has already been specified at the RT level. The literature provides a good classification and references to these methods [34–36]. Partitioning in COSMOS [37] focuses on another form of partitioning that operates on a higher level of abstraction—that of the communicating process level. There are many advantages to performing partitioning at this level. First and most obviously, there will be a reduction in the subsequent hardware required to implement the design, because the hardware used will be shared among exclusive operations. Another advantage is that scheduling can now be applied concurrently to each partition, thereby reducing behavioral synthesis complexity.

Partitioning starts with a set of hierarchical and communicating processes described in SOLAR, as shown in Figure 17. It caters to both area and performance considerations simultaneously. Associated with each process are various cost functions that are dependent on different features of the processes such as data-path operators, control operations, I/O operations, shared variables, states, and so on. Once each of the cost functions has been established, the system can start to find the best clustering combination for the design. The main operations performed by the partitioning algorithm are as follows:

Split: This operation transforms two sequential machines into two parallel machines. This is achieved through the introduction of idle states and extra control signals. This operation will reduce the overall size of the machine.

Merge: The Merge operation fuses two sequential processes into a single process with the objective of being able to share resources among exclusive operations.

Move: This operation allows us to transfer a process from one part of the tree to another. This operation would normally be a transitory step before performing one of the other operations.

Cut: The operation Cut transforms a set of parallel processes into a set of interconnected processes. Parallel processes that share variables will be assigned communication channels that contain protocols governing access to these variables.

5.4 Communication Synthesis

The goal of this work is to transform a system containing a set of communicating processes into a set of interconnected processes that interact across standard buses [26].

The two inputs to the communication synthesis algorithm are a graph representing the partitioned system and a library of ChannelUnits. The graph may contain many different communication channels, each implementing a different protocol. The communication synthesis algorithm chooses the most suitable ChannelUnit from the library (based on certain criteria such as protocol, implementation technology of the communicating DesignUnit, user-imposed constraints, etc.) and "binds" it to the corresponding channel in the graph. CUCALLs in the DesignUnits are replaced with a local calls to a copy of the appropriate method and the corresponding handshake signals. The local calls will be translated based on the DesignUnit's implementation technology. For example, if the DesignUnit is to be implemented entirely in software, the call will in fact be a system call, making use of existing communication mechanisms.

5.5 Behavioral-Level Synthesis Based on VHDL

A path exists within the COSMOS environment that allows SOLAR to be translated to a VHDL at the behavioral and RT levels [38]. This VHDL subset is quite comprehensive, accepting almost all sequential statements.

AMICAL [30,31] is an interactive architectural synthesis system based on VHDL. It starts with a behavioral specification given in VHDL and generates a structural description that may feed existing silicon compilers acting at the logic and RT levels. It is expected that the use of AMICAL will reduce the complexity of the design by an order of magnitude.

Synthesis starts with two kinds of information. These are the behavioral description and an external library of functional units (FUs). The external library of FUs may include standard execution units (adders, multipliers, ALUs, etc.) as well as more complex units defined by the designer. These can be large complex blocks such as cache memories, I/O units, etc. After behavioral synthesis, an RTL description in SOLAR is produced for logic-level synthesis tools. Figure 18 summarizes the AMICAL design flow.

The screen dump shown in Figure 19 gives a flavor of the AMICAL environment at work. The right window shows a VHDL description of the GCD algorithm, taken from the High-Level Synthesis Workshop benchmark suite. The upper left window contains the StateTable produced by the scheduler [39]. The middle left window shows the resulting data path produced by the allocation step. The bottom window provides information about the command in progress.

One of the main strengths of AMICAL is its ability to maintain the coherence between the information in the three main windows, i.e., the different aspects of the design. Interactively, the user may ask for the correspondence between the controller and the data path. In Figure 19, we have asked for information about an operation (highlighted)

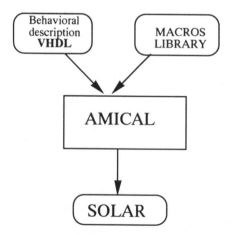

Fig. 18: AMICAL design flow

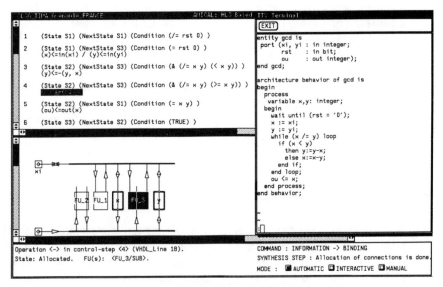

Fig. 19: The AMICAL behavioral synthesis environment

in control step 4 and the system has highlighted the resources of the data path used for the execution of this operation (middle left window). In the bottom window, more information is given about the FU that executes the operation and the VHDL line number where the operation is described. Thus, the user knows that the operation selected comes from line 18 in the VHDL description, that the operation is bound to (FU#3), which corresponds to an instance of the FU (SUB).

The RTL models produced by AMICAL tend to be somewhat longer than their behavioral counterparts. Table 3 shows a summary of the number of lines of code required for four examples, a simple algorithm for computing the GCD of two integers, a Bubble-Sort algorithm, a simplified telephone answering machine, and a memory management unit.

The first column of Table 3 shows the initial VHDL code size. The second column is an equivalent SOLAR description at the behavioral level and after the initial input has been scheduled. The reason for the sometimes large difference in code size between the two behavioral-level descriptions is due to the fact that the scheduler performs some code transformations such as in-line procedure expansion. The third column presents the size of the SOLAR equivalent description as generated by AMICAL after allocation has been performed.

TABLE 3: Comparison of VHDL, SOLAR Program Sizes

Example	Code VHDL	SOLAR Behavior	SOLAR RTL
GCD	42	102	826
BubbleSort	61	206	1569
Simplified answering machine	151	563	3504
MMU	739	3504	17754

We can see from Table 3 that the RTL SOLAR code resulting from AMICAL is about seven times the size of the behavioral SOLAR code. Note that the RTL code does not include the description of the components (functional units, registers, etc.). The corresponding VHDL description at the RT level tends to be of the same size as the SOLAR RTL description.

From Tables 2 and 3, we can expect that a system-level representation will be approximately 50 times smaller than its RTL equivalent. This fact is verified for the answering machine example. For the other examples, the size of the description tends to increase by a factor of 7 when going from one level to the next lower level.

6 STATUS AND FUTURE WORK

A first version of the SOLAR representation has been implemented in an object-oriented environment. The present system provides a framework for building a data representation starting from a SOLAR file and vice versa. Several examples have been described in SOLAR in order to identify the strengths and weaknesses of the underlying concepts. These examples have shown that the model is able to handle efficiently hierarchical FSMs and high-level communication schemes.

However, some extensions to the SOLAR representation are required. The most urgent modification is the introduction of explicit timing specifications. A TimeOut construct will be introduced based on similar concepts used in StateCharts and SDL. Experiments with system-level synthesis using SOLAR has shown that the representation of an FSM as a transition table could be more efficient. In some cases, this representation inherently includes scheduling information and is therefore more suited to algorithms that require scheduled descriptions, such as merging parallel FSMs (see Section 5.3) and resource allocation in behavioral synthesis.

Among the design approaches listed in Section 5, the present realization is mainly geared toward the circuit approach. The existing tools favor the passage from the software specification to the hardware implementation. To handle the system and mixed approaches, several new developments are still needed. These include SOLAR to SDL translation tools and an improved version of the VHDL to SOLAR translator.

7 CONCLUSIONS

We have presented SOLAR, an intermediate representation designed for the synthesis of mixed hardware/software designs at the system level. SOLAR uses an EDIF-like syntax to model systems as a set of communicating FSMs. In addition, SOLAR possesses the following properties:

- It provides a means whereby a designer can specify parts of a design in specific languages. These blocks can subsequently be unified in a common intermediate form that is geared toward synthesis.

- It allows designs to be validated through existing simulation environments. This is achieved by providing translation mechanisms from all levels of SOLAR to VHDL and, in the near future, from SOLAR to SDL.

An example of a hardware/software codesign environment built around SOLAR has been described. The environment allows the combination of a system-level design language (SDL) and a hardware design language (VHDL). It has been shown that this type of environment dramatically reduces the volume of the specification handled (by a factor of almost 50).

REFERENCES

[1] R. A. Tierney, "Modelling Complex Systems," *VLSI System Design,* May 1988.

[2] F. Vahid and S. Narayan et al., "SpecCharts: A Language For System-Level Synthesis," *Proc. CHDL'91,* pp. 145–154, IFIP, Apr. 1991.

[3] N. D. Dutt et al., "A User Interface for VHDL Behavioural Modeling," *Proc. CHDL'91,* Marseille, France, pp. 375–393, IFIP, Apr. 1991.

[4] A. Jerraya, P. Paulin, and S. Curry, "Meta VHDL for High-Level Controller Modelling and Synthesis," *Proc. VLSI'91,* Edinburgh, Scotland, Aug. 1991.

[5] P. G. Paulin and A. Jerraya, "SIF: A Synthesis Interchange Format," *5th Intl. Workshop on High-Level Synthesis,* Germany, March 1991.

[6] M. P. J. Stevens and F. P. M. Budzelar, "System Level VLSI Design," *Microprocessing Microprogramming,* 30, pp. 321–330, 1990.

[7] S. Antoniazzi and M. Mastretti, "An Interactive Environment for Hardware/Software System Design at the Specification Level," *Microprocessing Microprogramming,* 30, pp. 545–554, 1990.

[8] U. Wienkop, "Behavioral Circuit Description on the System Level," *Microprocessing Microprogramming,* 30, pp. 561–566, 1990.

[9] Bruce Bourbon, "On System Level Design," *Comp. Des.,* pp. 19–21, Dec. 1990.

[10] A. Jerraya, K. O'Brien, I. Park, and B. Courtois, "Towards System-Level Modeling And Synthesis," *Proc. VLSI'92,* India, Feb. 1992.

[11] A. Jerraya, K. O'Brien, and T. BenIsmail, "Linking System Design Tools and Hardware Design Tools," *Proc CHDL'93,* Ottawa, Canada, pp. 331–338, Apr. 1993.

[12] "VHDL Language Reference Manual," Standard 1076/B, IEEE, June 1987.

[13] "UDL/I Language Reference Manual," Draft Version 1.0b4, Japan Electronic Industry Dev. Ass., October 1990.

[14] P. N. Hilfinger, "A High-Level Language and Silicon Compiler for Digital Signal Processing," *Proc. IEEE Custom Integrated Circuits Conf.,* Portland, OR, May 1985.

[15] International Standards Organization, ESTELLE (Formal Description Technique Based on an Extended State Transition Model)," ISO/DIS 9074, 1987.

[16] International Standards Organization, "LOTOS: A Formal Description Technique Based on the Temporal Ordering of Observational Behavior, ISO, IS 8807, Feb. 1989.

[17] R. Saracco and P. A. J. Tilanus, "CCITT SDL: An Overview of the Language and Its Applications," *Comp. Networks ISDN Syst. Special Issue,* 13(2), 1987.

[18] C. Hoare, "Communicating Sequential Processes," *Comm. ACM,* 21(8), pp. 666–677, Aug. 1978.

[19] G. Berry and L. Cosserat, "The Esterel Synchronous Programming Language and Its Mathematical Semantics," Technical Report, Ecole Nat. Superieure de Mines de Paris, 1984.

[20] D. Harel et al., "Statecharts: A Working Environment for the Development of Complex Reactive Systems," *IEEE Trans. Software Eng.,* 16(4), pp. 231–274, Apr. 1990.

[21] L. Lamport, "A Simple Approach to Specifying Concurrent Systems," *Comm. ACM,* 32(1), pp. 32–45, Jan. 1989.

[22] R. Goering, "Emerging Tools and High-Level Design," *Elec. Eng. Times,* pp. 42–44, Aug. 10, 1992.

[23] T. Hoshino, O. Karatsu, and T. Nakashima, "HSL-FX: A Unified Language for VLSI Design," *Proc. CHDL85,* Northholland Publ., pp. 321–336, Aug. 1985.

[24] D. C. Ku and G. DeMicheli, "Hardware C: A Language For Hardware Design," Technical Report, CSL-TR-88-362, Computer Systems Lab, Stanford University 1988.

[25] G. J. Holzmann, *Design and Validation of Computer Protocols,* Prentice-Hall, Englewood Cliffs, NJ, 1991.

[26] K. O'Brien, T. BenIsmail, and A. A. Jerraya," A Flexible Communication Modelling Paradigm for System-Level Synthesis," *Intl Workshop on Hardware-Software Co-Design,* Cambridge, MA, Oct. 1993.

[27] G. R. Andrews, *Concurrent Programming: Principles and Practice,* Benjamin/Cummings, San Francisco, 1991.

[28] A. D. Birrell and B. J. Nelson, "Implementing Remote Procedure Calls," *ACM Trans. Comp. Syst.,* 2(1), pp. 39–59, Feb. 1984.

[29] C. Hoare, "Monitors: An Operating System Structuring Concept," *Comm. ACM,* 17(10), pp. 549–557, Oct. 1974.

[30] I. Park, K. O'Brien, and A. A. Jerraya, "AMICAL: Architectural Synthesis Based on VHDL," *IFIP Trans. A-22, Synthesis for Control-Dominated Circuits,* G. Saucier and J. Trilhe, Eds., North-Holland, Amsterdam, 1993.

[31] K. O'Brien, I. Park, A. A. Jerraya, and B. Courtois, "Synthesis for Control-Flow-Dominated Machines," in *Application-Driven Architecture Synthesis,* F. Catthoor and L. Svensson, Eds., Kluwer Academic Publishers, Boston, 1993.

[32] M. Romdhani, "Compilation Du Langage SDL En Vue D'Une Réalisation Matérielle," Internal Report, INPG/TIM3, June 1992.

[33] W. Glunz and G.Venzl, "Hardware Design Using CASE Tools," *Proc. VLSI'91,* Edinburgh, Scotland, 1991.

[34] K. Kuçukçakar and A. Parker, "CHOP: A Constraint-Driven System-Level Partitioner," *Proc. 28th DAC,* pp. 514–519, 1991.

[35] E. Dirkes-Lagnese, "Architectural Partitioning for System-Level Design of Integrated Circuits," Research Report CMUCAD-89-27, Carnegie-Mellon University, Mar. 1989.

[36] F. Vahid "A Survey of Behavioral-Level Partitioning Systems," TR #91-71, University of California, Irvine, Oct. 30, 1991.

[37] T. BenIsmail, K. O'Brien, and A. A. Jerraya, "Interactive System-Level Partitioning with PARTIF," European Design and Test Conference, Paris, France, Feb. 1994.

[38] T. Abbassi and S. BenAtallah, "Modelisation Multiniveaux De Systèmes VLSI Dans Le Langage VHDL," Internal Report, INPG/TIM3, June 1992.

[39] K. O'Brien, M. Rahmouni, and A. A. Jerraya, "A VHDL-Based Scheduling Algorithm for Control-Flow Dominated Circuits," *6th Intl. Workshop on High-Level Synthesis,* Laguna Beach, CA, Nov. 1992.

CHAPTER 8

A Hierarchical View
of Time

P. Gillard
Department of Computer Science
Memorial University of Newfoundland
St. John's, Canada

K. C. Posch
Institute for Applied Information Processing
and Communications Technology
Graz University of Technology
Graz, Austria

Abstract: Modeling and simulation tools for large-scale systems typically employ event queues as a model for time. This paper discusses two conceptual expansions of event queues. One is characterized by a totally local view of time with respect to individual structured modules; the other uses a two-dimensional data structure, which behaves like an event queue with respect to one dimension only. A design example is sketched that shows the user's view of the concurrent modeling system using these data structures. Because hardware and software may be described in the same environment, simulation of mixed hardware/software systems is possible. A gradual transition from a software model to hardware model allows for delayed implementation decisions.

1 INTRODUCTION

Hierarchy and structure have been considered to be among the most important design guidelines for complex digital circuits. As a result of this, structured design concepts such as modularity, regularity, and locality have evolved and also introduced methods that became necessary in order to match complex problems to their solutions in VLSI technology [1]. A structural view has been used extensively in the context of the geomet-

---

A short version of this paper has been published in the *Proceedings of the 34th Midwest Symposium on Circuits and Systems,* Monterey, California, 1991.

rical domain, the topological domain, and the functional domain. This paper emphasizes a hierarchically structured view of the time domain.

One of the more common ways to model the time behavior of a system is through the use of an event queue, lining up all predicted future changes of the system under consideration in a one-dimensional data structure. Simulation of the system is accomplished by working through this *global* queue and changing the state of the system variables accordingly. "Real" systems, in contrast, typically consist of modules that have primarily *local* dependencies.

Instead of employing a global conglomerate of events as a model for time, a highly structured view of time, or events in time, is proposed here. Between the two extreme models for time, global and local, one can span a range of possibilities with regard to efficiency of modeling. This chapter discusses two examples out of this range. Section 4 discusses a totally local view of time, and Section 5 introduces a multidimensional quasi event queue. Both proposed simulation methods work with the same circuit description method outlined in Section 2 and used in the example in Section 6.

A major ingredient of this work is the object-oriented paradigm. This style of programming simplifies the design and implementation of the experimental solutions to the modeling techniques substantially. In fact, according to [2] object-oriented programming can be employed as a basic method for all kinds of CAD related problems. The system described in [3] exemplifies the use of object-oriented programming for the design and modeling of hardware systems.

The language C++ [4] seems to be a good candidate for serving as a hardware modeling language, in much the same sense as VHDL [5,6]. In addition, it has the benefits of (1) being a general computer language able to describe any kind of processes and (2) already being known by a broad community. The ease of extension of the language through the use of abstract data types, inheritance, and polymorphism allowed the authors to develop prototypes implementing the ideas described here. But why would one introduce another hardware description language (HDL) at all? The answer to this is strongly influenced by the design methodology used. VHDL has come to be known as a good specification language. But when design is understood as a process of finding and crafting solutions to problems, VHDL does not seem to be the right medium for this task in many problem domains. For finding new solutions at system level, or at the algorithmic level, typically a variety of languages and methodologies is needed. A VHDL specification may be part of the product of this high-level design work [7].

Section 6 sketches a design example where a concurrent modeling system that uses the techniques described in Sections 2 through 5 is employed as a modeling tool. This system is written in C++ and may be linked as a library of classes to the code written by the user. With this library, classes are available in order to model all typical elements arising in hardware systems. Names and semantics of these elements stay close to their counterparts in VHDL in order to adhere to an established standard.

The designer models solutions to a problem in C++. He or she may structure the model guided by decisions arising from a hardware/software partitioning of the solution. The concurrent behavior may be executed and thus simulated. With some restrictions, a mixed software/hardware model may be simulated. In contrast to the hardware description philosophy of making a clean cut between hardware and software, the methodology here fosters a combined modeling platform for hardware and software. Although strong emphasis is put on the benefits of this methodology, is should be clear that the designer must be aware of a variety of nasty traps arising from this methodology.

2 DEFINITION OF TERMS

The terms used in this chapter follow roughly their meaning in VHDL, although they are simplified for the sake of clarity. A hierarchical model of a concurrent system is an Entity. Entities contain structural information that again is defined in terms of Entities interconnected through Connectors. Functional Entities are the leaf nodes of the tree representing the hierarchy (see Figure 1).

   Ports and Signals are derived from Connectors. Ports define the interface of Entities. Ports can be passage points for any data type, and be of kind In, Out, InOut, or Buffer. Signals are a means of communication between Entities. Signals carry their history and their predicted future values. Again, as in the case of Ports, they can be defined for all kinds of data types. Connectors can have several sources, their Drivers. This allows for the modeling of typical hardware structures such as tristate busses and open collector busses. A Resolution Function resolves the actual value of the Connector as a function of

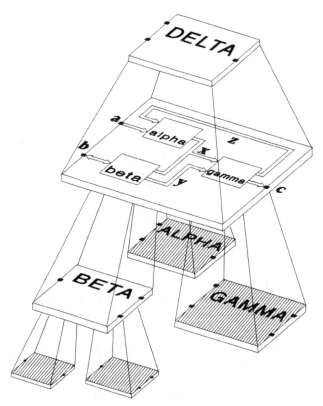

Fig. 1: An example of a hierarchical model

```
class ALPHA : public ENTITY {
// Interface:
        InPort        <double>      a;
        InPort        <BIT>         b;
        OutPort    <double>      c;
// variables:
        GENERIC time_type   delay;
public:
        ALPHA (CONNECTOR<double>& a_formal,
               CONNECTOR<BIT>&     b_formal,
               CONNECTOR<double>& c_formal,
               time_type del )
             : a( a_formal ),
               b( b_formal ),
               c( c_formal ),
               delay( del )
        { }

        void BEHAVIOR() {
            if ( b == TRUE )
                 c.INERTIAL( (b*b), delay );
        }
};
```

Fig. 2: Definition of function Entity ALPHA in C++

its Drivers. A (possibly empty) set of Transactions is associated with each Driver. Transactions consist of a data pair, time and value, representing predicted future changes of the Driver. Entities are a means to implement hierarchy. If one flattened this hierarchy, only functional Entities and their interconnecting communication channels become visible. A functional Entity contains a function with name Behavior, which specifies its behavior. Whenever activated Ports of an Entity change their value, i.e., have an event, Behavior gets evaluated. Figure 2 shows a specification of the Entity ALPHA in a C++-like way. Figure 3 shows the specification of Entity DELTA. An instance of DELTA is declared in function main( ). This implies an implicit call to the simulator, which simulates this Entity until either no further events occur or until interruption from outside takes place.

3 THE SIMULATION CYCLE

The key to simulate parallel systems on sequential machines has been the use of an event queue. Items of this queue have a time stamp and represent (possible) changes of the system and/or a things-to-do-list in simulated time. They are ordered with respect to their time stamp. Predicted future changes are inserted at the appropriate place in the event queue. These queue items consist of a time stamp and either a reference to the changing

```
class DELTA : public ENTITY {
// Interface:
        InPort    <double>      a;
        InOutPort <Vector<BIT> > b;
        OutPort   <double>      c;
// Signals:
        SIGNAL <double>      x;
        SIGNAL <Vector<BIT> > y;
        SIGNAL <BIT>         z;
// Structural and functional Entities:
        BETA  beta;
        ALPHA alpha;
        GAMMA gamma;
public:
        DELTA (CONNECTOR<double>&        a_formal,
             CONNECTOR<Vector>BIT> >& b_formal,
             CONNECTOR<BIT>&          c_formal)
           : a( a_formal ) b( b_formal ), c( c_formal ),
             x( BUS, TristateResolutionFunction ),
             y( initial_value ),
             gamma( x, y, z, c_formal ),
             beta ( b_formal, x, y ),
             alpha( z, a_formal, x )
        { isRootEntity(); }
};

main() {
        SIGNAL <double>      r;
        SIGNAL <Vector<BIT> > s;
        SIGNAL <double>       t;
        DELTA delta( r, s, t );
}
```

Fig. 3: Definition of structural Entity DELTA in C++

element (i.e., Connector), and its predicted value, or a reference to a structural Entity to be evaluated. Simulating the system along the time dimension is done by dequeueing the sequence of items from the end of the queue with the smaller time stamps. Each item produces a possible change of the system's state. The evaluation of a structural Entity affected by a Connector's change produces new (and often different) predictions for future changes of Connectors, which are inserted in the way described previously. Figure 4 illustrates the basic simulation cycle.

Event-driven simulators have been broadly available for the design of digital systems for many years. Software implementations often employ the event queue as a global data structure; in this way, every simulatable submodule of the system had access to it.

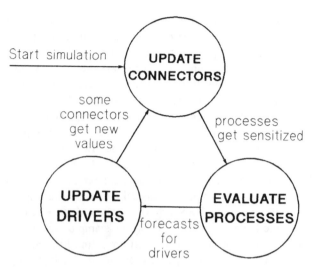

Fig. 4: The basic simulation cycle

In contrast, this chapter proposes to deemphasize this prominent role of the event queue. Actually, from the user's point of view, the function of the individual modules and their structural interconnection is most important. In fact, one could make the argument that the event queue is a minor implementation detail, and thus should be hidden in the internal implementation of the simulator. This perspective is even more natural when considering an object-oriented approach. Every module of a particular system is an entity of some abstract data type. The behavior, or the structure of its component subentities, is defined somewhere else in the system. In the next two sections, we discuss two alternative approaches. In the first, every submodule has access to its own local queue; thus, it is also responsible for the management of its own enqueueing and dequeueing. Simulated time is local to each unit. The second approach is in a sense less radical; here the queue is hidden as a local data structure common to all submodules. It is not visible nor directly accessible to the user.

4 LOCAL QUEUES

The totally local view of time associates an event queue with each module; time "passes" at different rates in each module, depending only on when the inputs to the module itself change. This model is *locally* event driven; modules send messages (i.e., produce outputs) to the inputs of other modules. These messages contain both the time and state information required for evaluation of the next state of the module. Inputs to a module are queued until a full set of inputs is available to permit a correct evaluation of the output from the module at a later time. Since the modules may get inputs from other modules corresponding to their states at different times, the modules may all be in different *time states;* there is no global view of time. This approach is effective for an object-oriented view of simulation, since no global information is required; communication is achieved entirely through the messages sent between modules.

This leads to a *natural* partition of the system being simulated into two classes: *components* and *connectors*. The components are individual Entities that may be constructed from other components, or functional Entities, which have their behavior described directly in the C++ language. They correspond roughly to the physical components in a digital system. The *connectors* are used to interconnect the components. They roughly correspond to wires in a digital system. Outputs from one component are transmitted to the inputs of other components through the connectors. The connectors have associated queues, which contain outputs generated by one component but not yet consumed by other components. Everything used to describe the system to be simulated is derived from one (or both) of these base classes.

In its purely local form, each component has an event queue for each input ("hidden" in the connector to that input). Transactions in the event queue are maintained in strict order of increasing time. *Time-consistent* values are taken from the queue and consumed. The local time is then updated to min(time stamp of active inputs), and outputs are generated with appropriate time stamps. If an output has changed, connected modules are evaluated in a similar way, in, say, a depth-first manner. Evaluation of outputs is *data driven*, a module has the opportunity to generate outputs *when one of its inputs changes*.

In its "pure" form, this model places several constraints on the components. They should not "free run," e.g., a free-running oscillator is not permitted. Outputs should be produced in increasing order of time; an earlier output should not be generated before a later output. For example, if two paths in a model produce a single output, where each path is associated with a different delay, the function should discriminate locally between the two possibilities. The function must ensure that the output from the slow path is not overwritten by a value from the fast path before the output leaves the module. Components should not produce outputs conditionally; output values cannot be overwritten; e.g., a retriggerable one-shot should be explicitly modeled, using feedback. These conditions can generally be readily accommodated in practice. They arise directly from the locality of the model. This extreme locality, however, makes this model potentially useful for a distributed simulator.

In practice, the "pure" form of the model may require an inordinately large number of local queues, particularly where the fanout from modules is high. This can be alleviated by sharing the local queues among all of its fanout inputs. Deleting transactions is slightly more complex, since a transaction can now only be deleted when it has been consumed by all the fanout modules. Effectively, the local queues are associated with module outputs.

5 HIDDEN QUEUE

The basic idea for the hidden queue can be summarized in the following way: For simulation, the very same global event queue as described in Section 3 is used, but it is hidden as a Static data member of all objects participating in the simulation. This upside-down view arises naturally with the use of an object-oriented language. The example given here is based on C++, where user-defined data types are called Classes. Classes are a means to encapsulate data and functions operating on these data. Inheritance allows us to build a hierarchy of classes. In this way, one can model the two main relationships between

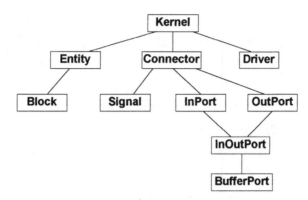

Fig. 5: Hierarchy of classes

different concepts perceived by humans: concept A *is-kind-of* concept B, and concept A *consists-of* concept B. One also could talk about *Is*-relations and *Has*-relations. Figure 5 shows a tree representing a simplified hierarchy of classes used by the authors. Entities, Connectors, and Drivers inherit all properties of a common base class Kernel, which is a container class for the common event queue. In C++, rights to use inherited data or functions are controlled through the keywords Private, Protected, and Public.

The user who models a system by means of defining classes inherited from Entities never comes in touch with the low-level functions managing the queue. He or she probably does not even know about it, because he or she might not even have access to the implementation of the simulation kernel. All the user has to know is how to specify a delayed assignment of a new value to some Connector (see the examples in Figures 2 and 3).

When an instance of a class is declared in C++, an implicit call is made to a function with the same name as the class. These functions are called *Constructors* and are typically used to initialize the data structure of the class. Constructors can be used in an elegant way when modeling concurrent systems. By the very nature of concurrent systems, they start to live at declaration time; this typically means actions and reactions to the surrounding environment. So why not use the Constructor to do the job of bringing it to "life"? The main program then just has to declare one instance of the class to be simulated, no further function calls are necessary. Figure 3 shows the function Main( ) and its simple content. Although one might argue that this little side effect is of minor importance, it expresses the power of the object-oriented paradigm in a nutshell.

The hidden queue management also gains efficiency by using an object-oriented approach. The most important operation on an event queue in a simulation system is to update future predictions for a particular Connector. This can be implemented through insertions and deletions in a linked list. Because insertions and deletions of Transactions are local to a Connector, it does not make sense to keep track of them in a not-so-local event queue. This problem maps directly to multiple inheritance, which is an element of C++. Transactions inherit all features of a linked list element, and as such can be inserted and deleted from the list representing future predictions for a given Connector.

At the same time, Transactions also inherit properties from a class SetItem, and as such can be added to or removed from a particular instance of class Set. It is through

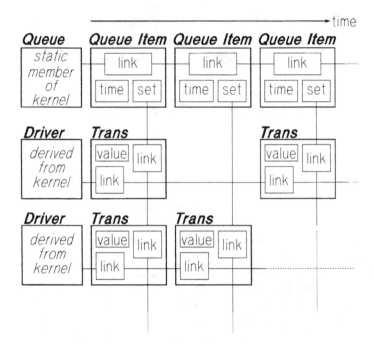

Fig. 6: Transactions and queue items

the nature of Sets that Transactions are traced through simulated time. These Sets are the only event queue items. Insertions and deletions of Transactions are done in both dimensions of this data structure "automatically." Using a 2-D structure makes deletions and insertions of Transactions efficient. Figure 6 gives a sample view of this 2-D data structure. Deletion of a Transaction can only be done after reading its value. Deletions consume no searching time; the implicitly called *Destructor* function takes care of closing the hole in the data structure. Insertion of a new Transaction takes no search time in the horizontal direction, because the insertion point is given from the prior deletion phase. To insert the vertical links properly, searching is not always necessary. In many cases, the previously deleted Transaction has the same time stamp as its successor, so a pointer to the correct queue item is simply handed over. In other cases, the insertion point is found in the vicinity of the previously deleted Transaction. Because of the 2-D organization, the queue does not grow extensively in the horizontal direction.

6 EXAMPLE

Prototypes of concurrent modeling environments using the local queue described in Section 4 and the hidden queue described in Section 5 have been implemented. Each can serve as an extension of the C++ language. The hidden queue was used as a kernel for multilevel description and simulation of hardware-like concurrent systems. An example based on this C++ library containing a set of classes for describing and simulating concurrent behavior is given here. The example sketches the design flow from an initial model toward a multichip implementation of the problem. The underlying design methodology is influenced by the rapid prototyping methodology [8] and makes use of many iterated design cycles, where models gradually migrate from an initial functional sketch toward a target description, which is influenced by the technology used for a particular module.

The example is taken from the cryptographic domain where modulo exponentiation of extremely long integers is used quite often, e.g., in the RSA algorithm [9]. The major design issue in this example is the gain of speed. Due to limited speed, the RSA algorithm has not been used extensively so far. The method that serves as the background for the example here allows speeds in the range of 1 Mbit/sec.

A parallel implementation of the problem $a^b(\bmod\ c)$ may be achieved through the use of residue number systems (RNSs), where carry propagation does not exist at all, and thus multiplication can be done in constant time [10]. According to Knuth [11], exponentiation can be done through iterated squaring and multiplying. Obviously, this problem can easily be prototyped by using unlimited precision types, which are typically available as C++ classes [12]. The design might start with a simple implementation using unlimited precision types, which is called step 1 here:

```
class INT {                    // see reference [12]
        double* values;        // pointer to array of values
        // ....
        INT();                 // constructor
        // overload operators for multiplication and
        // modulo reduction:
        friend INT& operator* (INT& a, INT& b);
        friend INT& operator% (INT& a, INT& b);
};

int main() {
        // ...
        INT x, y, z, m;
        // ....
        x = y * z % m;
        // ....
}
```

In RNS, all digits of a number are computed modulo some base b_i. All bases must be relatively prime. Addition, subtraction, and multiplication in RNS can be done by adding, subtracting, or multiplying digit by digit, respectively. According to the object-oriented paradigm, specification and implementation of some data type are independent. The long integer arithmetic from the preceeding step 1 above is therefore implemented with an underlying RNS. In C++, this means that class INT (representing the integer type with unlimited precision) contains other classes, each representing one digit of the residue number. The b_i of the RNS are stored as a static data member of an RNS digit.

```
class RNS_DIGIT {
     static double* base;         // pointer to common base
     // ....
     RNS_DIGIT(int value, int bas);// constructor

     // overload operators +, -, and *:
     // .....
};

class INT {
     RNS_DIGIT* digits;        // pointer to array of digits
     INT();                    // constructor
     // ....
     friend INT& operator* (INT& a, INT& b);
     // ....
};
```

Because each RNS digit can operate isolated from all others, a multichip hardware system tends to be a favorable candidate as target implementation. Each processing element is in charge of some digit. When considering the operations division, and modulo reduction, things become a bit more complicated. As shown in [13], these operations introduce communication between all processing elements. Depending on the type of communication network, division and modulo reduction need order of $\log(n)$ time, or linear order of time, with n being the number of processing elements. Assuming a bus network, processing elements can basically be modeled in the following way (step 3):

```
enum op_code { setup, input, output, reset, add, sub, mult,
               ... };

class RNS_DIGIT : public ENTITY
{
// interface:
     InOutPort<double> data_bus;
     InPort<op_code>    instruction;
     // ....
// local variables:
     double result, a, b, base;
     // ....
// constructor:
     RNS_DIGIT(CONNECTOR<double> data_bus_formal,
               CONNECTOR<op_code> instr_formal,
               // .....)
       : data_bus (data_bus_formal),
         instruction (instr_formal),
         // ....
         { }
```

```
// behavior:
    void BEHAVIOR() {
        switch(instruction) {
            CASE setup: base = INERTIAL(data_bus);
            CASE input: a    = INERTIAL(data_bus);
            // ....
            CASE add:    result = (a+b) % base;
            // ....
        }
    }
};
```

A module, RNS_DIGIT, is derived from class ENTITY. In this way, RNS_DIGIT inherits all properties necessary to be simulated concurrently. Its interface consists (at least) of bidirectional access to the data bus connecting all processing elements, and an input port for issuing instructions to the processing element. No information about the real coding of these ports is yet specified. Its behavior is defined in the function BEHAVIOR( ). When an instance of class RNS_DIGIT is created, its Constructor function is called, which connects all ports with other Connectors, which may be Signals or Ports of some type.

An RNS system needs an instance of class RNS_DIGIT per digit. With the code sketched next a structural description of the system is given by introducing an array of RNS_DIGITS (step 4):

```
class RNS_SYSTEM : public ENTITY
{
// interface:
    // ......

// contents:
    RNS_DIGIT* array_pointer;   // pointer to array of digits
    CONTROL_PROCESSOR proc;     // instantiation

// constructor:
    RNS_SYSTEM( ..... );
};
```

The functional description of class RNS_DIGIT may serve as a specification for real implementation in hardware. A proper hardware description may be approached through several steps leading to more and more implementation-specific details. Layers of description are introduced whenever the designer decides to do so. Assuming a standard cell design, this goes on until the level of the elements of a standard cell library is reached. As an example, the possible functional implementation of a two-input-multiplexer is sketched next:

```
class MUX2 : public ENTITY
{
// Interface:
      InPort<BIT>  i1;
      InPort<BIT>  i0;
      InPort<BIT>  sel;
      OutPort<BIT> q;
      GENERIC time_type del;
// Constructor:
      MUX2 ( CONNECTOR<BIT>& i1_f,   CONNECTOR<BIT>& i0_f,
             CONNECTOR<BIT>& sel_f, CONNECTOR<BIT>& q_f,
             time_type d )
       : i1  (i1_f,  SENSED),
         i0  (i0_f,  SENSED),
         sel (sel_f, SENSED),
         q   (q_f),
         del (d)
       { }
// functional behavior:
      void BEHAVIOR() {
            if (sel) q.INERTIAL(i1, del);
            else     q.INERTIAL(i0, del);
      }
};
```

If some part of the system, e.g., the CONTROL_PROCESSOR in the code section shown here, will be implemented in software, a functional model for the global function is sufficient. Difficulties arise when endless loops are to be modeled. These loops need to be broken and restarted from outside, in order to allow the underlying "concurrent operating system" (so to speak) to gain command, and do whatever has to be done according to the entries in the event queue.

7 CONCLUSIONS

The simulation of concurrent systems is relatively easy to achieve through the use of C++. This chapter discusses two possibilities for managing the event queues needed for this task. As an example, how to use C++ enhanced with a set of library classes for modeling concurrent behavior, hardware description in the style of VHDL has been shown. It has been argued that C++ can serve as a modeling environment for mixed hardware/software systems. Design alternatives, whether some module in a larger system should be implemented in hardware or software, can be studied and simulated in a common environment. In this sense, the notion of hardware/software codesign is appropriate.

Currently, the library has most VHDL features implemented. Among the major not yet implemented features are multiple Wait statements in a process, and the Generate statement. This almost one-to-one match makes it easy to rewrite concurrent portions of C++ code in VHDL.

REFERENCES

[1] N. Weste and K. Eshraghian, *Principles of CMOS VLSI Design, A Systems Perspective,* Addison-Wesley, Reading, MA, 1986.

[2] W. H. Wolf, "Object-Oriented Programming for CAD," *IEEE Des. Test,* pp. 35–42, Mar. 1991.

[3] A. Kumar et al., "IDEAS: A Tool for VLSI CAD," *IEEE Des. Test,* pp. 50–57, Oct. 1989.

[4] B. Stroustrup, *The C++ Programming Language,* 2nd ed., Addison-Wesley, Reading, MA, 1991.

[5] "IEEE Standard VHDL Language Reference Manual," IEEE Std 1076-1987, IEEE-CS Press, Los Alamitos, CA, Mar. 1988.

[6] R. Lipsett, C. F. Schaefer, and C. Ussery, *VHDL, Hardware Description and Design,* Kluwer Academic Publishers, Boston, 1989.

[7] K. C. Posch, "CHDL++: A C++ Based VHDL-like Hardware Description Language," submitted for publication.

[8] M. Mullin, *Rapid Prototyping for Object-Oriented Systems,* Addison-Wesley, Reading, MA, 1990.

[9] R. L. Rivest, A. Shamir, and L. Adleman, "A Method for Obtaining Digital Signatures and Public-Key Cryptosystems," *Comm. ACM,* pp. 120–126, 1978.

[10] K. C. Posch and R. Posch, "Base Extension Using Convolution Sum in Residue Number Systems," *Computing 50,* pp. 93–104, Springer, 1993.

[11] D. E. Knuth, *The Art of Computer Programming,* Vol. 2, Addison-Wesley, Reading, MA, 1969.

[12] T. Hansen, *The C++ Answer Book,* Addison-Wesley, Reading, MA, 1988.

[13] K. C. Posch and R. Posch, "Residue Number Systems: A Key to Fast RSA Encryption," *Proc. Fourth IEEE Symp. Parallel Distributed Processing,* Arlington, Tex., Dec. 1992.

CHAPTER 9

An Approach to the Timing Verification of VHDL Descriptions

Djamel Boussebha   Norbert Giambiasi
L.E.R.I.—Laboratoire d'Edutes et de Recherche en Informatique
Nimes, France

Abstract: This chapter presents an approach for verifying the temporal scheduling of behavioral models of VHDL. The aim is to verify that a behavioral description satisfies its behavioral specifications described in a formalism based on reified temporal logics and on a notion of physical activity.

1 INTRODUCTION

The verification techniques for hardware descriptions are one of the most pressing problems in VLSI design. This is because most designers use a hardware description language (HDL) such as VHDL (VHSIC Hardware Description Language) to verify the correctness of a hardware description at the first stage of the design.

Two basic approaches are used to verify a description of a hardware system: simulation and formal verification. Whereas simulation compares results, proofs of correctness consist of proving that the description meets its rigorous specifications as defined beforehand by the designer. The advantage of formal verification over simulation is that it is an exhaustive method. In the last few years, researchers have studied and developed formal verification techniques [1]. Many theoretical models have been proposed: algebraic models [2], axiomatic models [3], denotational models using recursive expressions [4], predicate logic [5], higher order logic [6], and various forms of temporal logic [7].

In this chapter, we propose a formal verification technique that consists of verifying the temporal behavior of a VHDL description [8]. We are especially interested in the behavioral subset of VHDL defined in [9].

A VHDL behavioral description can be written in a declarative way by a set of concurrent processes that execute in an undetermined order. Each process is described in a procedural way: it is characterized by a control flow and a data flow. The data flow corresponds to the objects handled in the description and the actions that manipulate these objects. The control flow corresponds to the sequence of actions organized according to the control structures (sequential, parallel, iterative, and selective). We are interested here in the control part. Our first aim is thus to verify that the temporal sequencing of these actions respects the sequencing defined by the behavioral specifications. A subsequent aim is to prove that the temporal order of execution of the processes explicited by a declarative description satisfies the order defined by the behavioral specifications.

The main problems of temporal verification are as follows: (1) How can the behavioral specification be expressed? (2) How can a temporal sub-behavior be obtained from the VHDL descriptions? (3) How can the extracted sub-behavior be compared with the specification?

Verification requires the definition of a formal model, including the expression of the primitives of the VHDL language in terms of the formal model. In our approach, we have used temporal reified logics as a formalism for expressing the behavioral specifications. This formalism expresses a notion of physical activity that has been formally defined for the VHDL actions that represent a real circuit phenomenon (signal and variable assignments, wait statements). It also represents the timing constraints between the actions explicitly defined by a procedural description and between the processes in a declarative description.

The behavioral extraction mechanism differs from one description to another. For a procedural description, to facilitate this operation, we have defined an internal model that highlights the separation and interaction between the control and data flows. The control flow in which we are interested is modeled into a timed and interpreted Petri net.

On the other hand, in the case of a declarative description, the extraction strategy is inspired from the planning model with temporal components [10]. The basic idea is to consider the set of processes as tasks and the VHDL description as the global scheme of the planner (representing the timing scheduling of the execution of a set of interindependent tasks). The verification process consists of simply verifying whether or not this scheme is correct. Next, we have developed a demonstrator that allows us to show whether the obtained sub-behaviors and the behavioral specifications are consistent.

The organization of the paper is as follows: in Section 2, we present an overview of the system and the different units of which it is composed. The definition of the behavioral specifications and the specification formalism we have defined are described in Section 3. Section 4 presents a more detailed discussion of the verification process. Examples are presented to illustrate each step of the verification. Finally, conclusions, experimental results, and future directions are addressed in Sections 5 and 6.

2 SYSTEM OVERVIEW

In this section, we describe the major components of our system as depicted in Fig. 1. The *compiler* compiles the behavioral specifications (expressed in an adequate formalism) into temporal structures, which are much simpler to manipulate (time lattice and tables). The

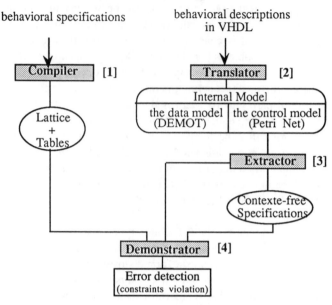

Fig. 1: System organization

role of this preprocessing is done to make the work of the demonstration mechanism easier and to verify the coherence of the behavioral specifications. The job of the *translator* is to translate the VHDL descriptions (procedural) into an internal model, which highlights the separation and interaction between the control and data flows. The control flow is modeled into a timed and interpreted Petri net.

Major tasks of the *extractor* are the following:

1. Prove the validity of the execution paths on the Petri graph, and then determine the timing constraints (temporal sub-behaviors) between actions for each path.

2. Extract directly from a declarative description all possible timing constraints between processes.

The *demonstrator* verifies whether these timing constraints satisfy the constraints defined by the behavioral specifications.

The details of each operation of the system are discussed in Section 4. We first give a very brief introduction to the reified temporal logic and then present a very brief overview of Shoham's logic. With the help of a simple example, we review how the behavioral specifications can be represented using this logic.

3 BEHAVIORAL SPECIFICATIONS

Many approaches have been proposed to better understand and represent time. We have chosen a symbolic representation of time in the form of reified logic. This logic manipulates pairs:

```
<logic assertion: q, temporal qualification of q: t>
```

Such a representation allows us to separate clearly the nontemporal logic component from the temporal component. Thus, the reasoning can be separated into two axes: one nontemporal (use of classic theorem demonstrators) and the other temporal (use of a temporal relations handler).

By using such logic, we can distinguish between two different formalisms of time: *high-level time* [11,12] and *low-level time* [13]. The first concerns the causal aspect and all the phenomena involved with time. The goal is to formalize temporal reasoning. Studies resulting from this formalism can be divided into two main trends: one using point algebra [14] and the other interval algebra [15,16].

The low-level approach is more descriptive and often involves the building of a time map manager. The goal is to manage such a graph: Modifying it so that its interpretation corresponds as much as possible to the real world it is supposed to describe. Allen's [16] work constitutes the best known example of this formalism. Interval algebra is more expressive than point algebra [10]. However, one of the major drawbacks of this model is that the verification of the consistency of a graph is an NP-complete problem [17]. Point algebra has a major advantage at the lower level: The complete management of the temporal relations is achieved in a polynomial time [17]. This advantage can also be obtained by means of restricted interval algebra, which is strictly equivalent to the point algebra [18] .

These various reasons have led us to choose Shoham's logic [11] as the basis of the representation because it manipulates intervals as well as points. We will thus use restricted and point algebra to make the expression of the temporal constraints easier. However, at the lower level, the intervals are translated into time points, which will be processed by the time map manager. With regard to managing the temporal graph, Ghallab's approach [10,19] has been chosen. This choice is justified by the efficiency and good performance of the approach in managing the temporal graph, including both symbolic and numeric temporal relations.

We now present a survey of the characteristics of Shoham's logic. Ghallab's work is described in the next sections.

3.1 Shoham's Logic

We use Shoham's work as a basis. Shoham's logic defines in quite a general way a temporal proposition by the formula: True (t, p), which means that proposition p is true at t [point or interval defined by a pair of points: $I = (\text{start}(I), \text{end}(I))$]. Syntax and semantics have been precisely defined in [11]. Furthermore, inheritance properties, which concern temporal propositions on intervals and points according to the relations that exist between them, have been given.

We need to express intervals and time points, together with their relationships.

- Qualitative relations between two intervals: before ($<$), meet (m), overlap (o), start (s), during (d), finish (f), equal ($=$), and their inverses [after ($>$), is-met-by (mi), etc.; see [15]] (Fig. 2).

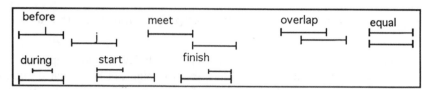

Fig. 2: Primitive relations between intervals

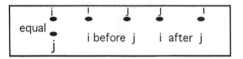

Fig. 3: Simple time point relations

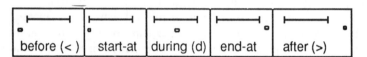

Fig. 4: Relations between an interval and a time point

- Qualitative relations between two time points or extremities of interval: before ($<$), after ($>$), and equal ($=$) (Fig. 3).
- Qualitative relations between an interval and a time point are before, after, during, start-at, end-at. Other relations can be expressed by combining those above; for example (Fig. 4):

    (start-before a T) is equivalent to (or (during a T) (end-at a T) (before a T))

From this logic, we have formally defined two notions: the concept of physical activity for each timing statement of VHDL, which models a physical reality in a circuit (signal and variable assignments and wait statements), and the temporal entities of *event* and *fact*. An event determines a change of state corresponding to the instantaneous transition, which will be temporally localized by a time point; for example, the immediate change of the value of a variable assigment.

Definition 1: A temporal proposition True(t, p) is an event $e(t, p)$ if and only if:

$$(\exists\, t', t'')/[(t' < t < t'') \wedge (\forall\, t1 \in [t', t[) \;\rightarrow\; \text{True}((t', t1), \neg p)) \wedge ((\forall\, t2 \in\,]t, t''])$$
$$\rightarrow \text{True}((t, t2), p))]$$

EXAMPLE:

The way in which the variable assignment $V := \text{`0'}$; immediately takes the new value shown at time point t (corresponds to an event) is illustrated by Fig. 5.

□

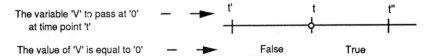

Fig. 5: Example of an event

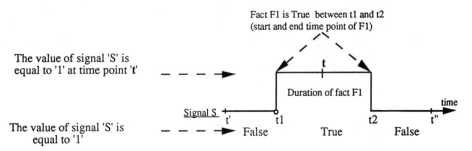

Fig. 6: Example of a fact

A fact represents an event with a duration, and it will be localized by an interval $]t1, t2]$. It is considered as True during this interval if and only if it is False outside the interval. One example of this is the pulse signal (see the following example).

Definition 2: A fact $F((t1, t2), p)$ is a temporal proposition $\text{True}((t1, t2), p)$ if and only if:

$$(\forall\, t \in\,]t1, t2] \,/\, \text{True}(t, p)) => (\exists\, t', t'') \,/\, :$$

- $((t' < t1) \wedge (\forall\, t'1 \in [t', t1[) \rightarrow \text{True}(t'1\neg p)); \wedge$
- $((t2 < t'') \wedge (\forall\, t''1 \in [t2, t''[) \rightarrow \text{True}(t''1\neg, p)$

EXAMPLE:

The way in which a signal assignment $S <=$ '1' after 3 ns; changes value from its initial value to the future value '1' during the interval $]t1, t2]$ (corresponds to a fact) is illustrated by Fig. 6.

□

3.2 Concept of Physical Activity

The concept of physical activity is defined as the waiting time for a time period to elapse or an event to occur. In the next section, we give a precise definition of an activity for each statement modeling a physical phenomenon. We illustrate how we formalize this concept in the case of a signal assignment using an example. We refer the reader interested in this work to [20] for more details.

3.2.1 Signal Assignments Activity

In VHDL, there are two types of delay in signal assignment statements, inertial and transport delay. Shown here are two examples:

$$X <= Y \text{ after 3 ns;} \qquad \text{inertial delay}$$

$$X <= \text{transport } Y \text{ after 3 ns;} \qquad \text{transport delay}$$

The first assignment statement implies inertial delay; that is, the signal propagation will only take place if and only if an input persists at a given level for 3 ns. Thus, in the preceding example, changes in Y (event) will affect X only if they stay at the new level for 3 ns or more (otherwise it is cancelled). In the second case, where a transport delay is specified, all changes on Y will propagate to X regardless of how long the changes stay at the new level.

The physical activity of a signal assignment statement is directly linked to event occurrence on the input signal:

Definition 3: A signal assignment statement is active if and only if an event occurs on the input signal.

The duration of this activity in the case of a transport model is defined as *the time necessary for the value of a signal to change,* e.g., the specified delay (transport delay).

The physical activity of the inertial model is modeled in the same way if any event occurs on the value of the input signal during the given delay. Otherwise, only the new event is projected to occur at time delay; hence, the old event is lost and so on.

To formalize this physical activity, we have defined a temporal representation based on the concepts defined previously (Section 3.1). A physical activity takes place during a time span that has a constrained length (duration). Their effects should be located with respect to this interval. Some effects hold from the beginning of physical activity, others during it or when the physical activities end. As an example of formalization, we illustrate how we represent a transport model. We refer the reader who is interested in the formalization of the other physical activities to [20,21].

EXAMPLE:

The physical activity of a transport model is temporally qualified by a time interval I over which it holds. This interval I represents the time span during which the signal occurs. This event is true after interval I because any other event during I will not be taken into account. Consequently, the duration of the physical activity of a signal of the transport type is equal to a given delay. Such a physical activity is defined by:

$$\text{Sig-Transp}(I, S) \Leftrightarrow (<\text{Signal}>, <\text{delay}> \wedge (\exists t)e(t, <\text{input-signal}>)$$

$$\wedge \ (t \text{ end-at } I) \wedge \text{duration}(I, \text{delay}))$$

The *duration* predicate gives the width (equal to delay) of the fact f. For example, consider the following process:

```
Signal A, B : integer := 0
P1 process
      begin
            A <= transport '1' after 4 ns;
            B <= transport '2' after 2 ns;
            wait ckl;
      end process P1;
```

The specification of signal assignment to A is illustrated by the following diagram:

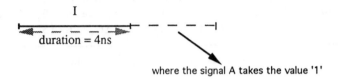

where the signal A takes the value '1'

☐

3.2.2 Variable Assignment Activity

A variable in VHDL immediately takes on the value assigned to it. Consequently, a variable assignment defines an instantaneous physical activity.

3.2.3 Wait Activity

The wait statement activates or suspends the execution of a process. Its syntax is:

wait on <sensitivity-list> until <condition> for <time-out>;

Its semantic is as follows: suspends a process until a signal in the sensitivity-list changes, at which time the condition is evaluated. If it is true, the process resumes. The time-out clause sets a maximum wait time for the process to be suspended; when the wait time expires, the process is reactivated.

The physical activity of a wait statement is defined between the instant the wait time starts and the instant the wait time ends. This corresponds to the given wait time or the time needed to obtain simultaneously an event on a signal of the sensitivity list and the verified conditions [20,21].

3.2.4 Process Activity

In VHDL, a process statement defines a specific behavior to be performed when there is an event in the signals of this sensitivity list (i.e., in the sensitivity list of the implicit or explicit wait statement). This behavior is defined by the sequentially ordered execution statement in the process.

A process that is being executed is said to be *active;* it is said to be *suspended* when it executes a wait statement. In our context, the physical actvity of a process is equal to

```
WHENEVER interrupt at I0
  IF   run'stable at i1, stop = '0' at i2, iowait = '0' at i3,
       not clk'stable at i4, not execute at i5.
    FACT I0 end-at i1, i1 = i2.
    DO affect fetch at I1 [0 δ], affect execute at I2 [0 δ],
       affect interrupt at I3 [0 δ].
       ACTION   I1 = I2, I3 = I1, I2 = I3.
  IF   run at i6
    FACT ().
    DO proc state at I4 [0  δ], proc sysckl at I5 [0 500],
       proc state at I6 [0  δ], proc interrupt-proc at I7 [0 200].
       ACTION   I4 start I7, I6 start I5, I4 < I5, I0 meet I4,
                I0 meet I7, I5 start-at i6, [S(I5) - E(I7)] < 300.
```

Fig. 7: An example of a behavioral specification

the union of the physical activities of the statements of which the process is composed [20,21].

3.3 Behavioral Specification Formalism

Specifications define the intended temporal behavior of a VHDL description. A specification program is a set of behavioral rules. Each rule defines one or several temporal behaviors. Each of these behaviors describes a list of physical activities to be undertaken if certain events or facts take place. The definition of a specification has two parts: One defines the conditions needed to trigger the physical activities and the constraints on these conditions, the other defines the implied physical activities and the temporal constraints between them. We have a description that is based essentially on the concepts defined previously: the events and the facts.

Such specifications are described in Figure 7 which defines a behavioral rule describing the state movement of a processor model (called MARK2) that constitutes a component of a computer system [22]. The **<whenever>** field defines the conditions necessary (represented respectively in the form of events or facts) to activate the part **<Do>**, describing the set of physical activities of either the signal or variable assignments or the wait statement. The word *at* specifies the association of a condition or an activity with the temporal objects I (a time point or an interval).

The **<fact>** and **<action>** fields define, respectively, the temporal constraints between conditions and constraints between activities. The temporal constraints can be expressed in two ways: symbolic constraints ($I_1 > I_2$); and numeric constraints [$-10 <$ start$(I) -$ end$(J) < 5$].

The notation [*tmin tmax*] allows the duration of a condition or of an activity duration to be defined by two numbers (limits). The rule (Fig. 7) specifies the following behavioral:

- When an event occurs on the signal value *interrupt*, the following conditions are tested: (run'stable $= T$), (stop $= 0$), (iowait $= 0$), (not ckl'stable), (not execute).

According to their values, the following behaviors are possible:

- If these conditions are verified, then at the same moment, the signal assignments *interrupt, fetch,* and *execute* are triggered, each has a duration of activity equal to a "δ" ns (a value of time that is infinitesimally small but greater than zero).
- Otherwise, if an event occurs on the signal *run* then at the same moment, the processes *interrupt-proc* and *state* are triggered. Afterward the process *state* and the *sysckl* are triggered in such a way that the activity of the process *interrupt-proc* ends before the activity of the process *sysckl* begins, and that between their activities no more than 300 ns should elapse. The durations of activity of the processes *interrupt-proc, sysckl,* and *state* are 200, 500, and δ ns, respectively.

3.4 The Compiler

The compilation is based on an original approach [10,19], that we briefly describe. This approach proposes an efficient algorithm that does not use the classic technique of propagation constraints; rather it searches for paths in a time lattice, where the nodes represent the time points of the problem and the arcs express the relationship between these points.

The complexity of the access and updating operations is linear according to the size of the lattice. If the addition of a relation causes an inconsistency, the system can easily find the cause. Thus, thanks to this time map manager (called *IxTeT:* Indexed Time Table), the temporal constraints such as they are defined in the parts **<fact>** and **<action>** of the description of the specifications are translated into a time lattice. For example, the constraints of the previous description (Fig. 7) are visualized by the structure shown in Fig. 8.

Two tables, which will integrate the set of conditions and activities used, the time points (organized according to the partial order as defined by the time lattice) in which

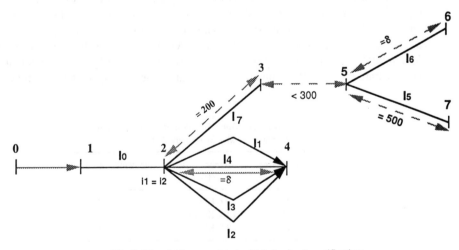

Fig. 8: Time lattice associated with behavioral specifications

Condition Table	0	1	2	4	3	5	6	7
interrupt		<p	>					
run'stable			<>					
stop = 0			<>					
execute								
iowait = 0								
not clk'stable								
not execute								
run					<p>			

Activity Table	0	1	2	4	3	5	6	7
affect interrupt (false)			<7	>				
affect fetch (false)			<7	>				
affect execute (false)			<7	>				
proc state			<1	>		<1	>	
proc sysckl			<1		>			
proc interrupt-proc						<4		>

Fig. 9: Tables associated with time lattice

they intervene (beginning and end), and a link indicating the cause of their insertion, correspond to this time lattice. From these tables, we have all the information concerning an event: all of its transitions to different values, timing bounds between transitions, the sequencing of transitions over time, the timing relations that exist between events, the time points where they occur, and the causality link between events. Figure 9 shows the content of the two tables associated with the lattice in Fig. 8.

The symbol < indicates the beginning of an event, whereas the symbol > indicates its end. The number marked near the symbols < and > is the causality relation. The symbol <> indicates instantaneous events.

The two structures of Fig. 9 have been implemented in the Common Lisp language on a SUN4 workstation. Table 1 shows the algorithmic efficiency of the compiler. It gives an idea of the CPU times necessary [column (C)] to compare two time points and to insert a relation in a lattice of a given size [column (A)]. It also shows the memory requirements [column (B)] for storing a lattice of a given size [column (A)]. The experimental results demonstrate that the algorithms used are linear in memory space and run time.

TABLE 1: Run Times and Memory Space Required for Three Conventionally Sized Time Lattices

Lattice Size (A)	Memory Size (B)	Run Times (millisec) (C)	
500	0.6 Kbytes	10	(1.7)
1000	1.4 Kbytes	25	(1.45)
2000	3.2 Kbytes	30	(1.9)

4 VERIFICATION PROCESS

This section describes in detail the main tasks of the modules (see Fig. 1): translator, extractor, and demonstrator, which constitute the basic components of the verification procedure. We divide this section into two subsections. The first describes the strategy used for the extraction of the timing constraints from the procedural and declarative descriptions of VHDL. The second subsection shows how the temporal demonstration is made. Each phase in the verification process is argued through example.

4.1 Principle Behind Extraction for a Procedural Description

The model we wish to verify in a temporal way is written in the VHDL behavioral subset [8]. We use an internal model, which was developed in order to constitute the general model. Many applications are linked to it [23]: behavioral test, testability measures, symbolic simulation, etc. This internal model highlights, on the one hand, the sequential and concurrent aspects and, on the other hand, the separation and interaction between the data and control flows [23]. The control flow is modeled by a timed and interpreted Petri net and the data flow by a graph structure based on the concepts of a hierarchical multiview model [24]. In our verification problem, we are only interested in the control model.

A data model action is associated with each Petri net transition. Actions with explicit delay (signal assignments, wait statements) are associated with timed transitions. Their transition life is considered to be equal to the delay value. It should be pointed out that the places indicate only the network state at the present time. Indeed, to clarify the verification process, we take an example of the behavioral description (Fig. 10), which supposedly implements the state movement of the processor MARK2 (see [22]). This description constitutes the device (or implementation) to be verified with the behavioral specifications. Therefore, the description of the process *state* involved in the description of Fig. 10 is translated by the timed and interpreted Petri net of Fig. 11, in which O_i corresponds to the statements of the VHDL description. This translation is composed of a simple concatenation of the conditional, sequential, and concurrent subnets [23]. For example, the first two subnets (O2,O4) represent two conditional structures *IF* of the VHDL description and the second the concurrence of the signals (O6 and O7), (O9 and O10), and (O12 and O13).

The former concepts, which define the internal model, can be represented as a result of an object-oriented environment ORL [25] , implemented in Common Lisp. The transformation software of a behavioral description in VHDL into a set of objects of the ORL involves two phases: The first consists only of analyzing the description and transcribing it into lists, by using the VHDL compiler defined in [8].

The second phase consists of generating the objects from the format obtained by compilation. It is carried out by using the object-oriented language ORL. Basic elements of the data and control graphs are represented as generic prototypes in ORL.

In Table 2, we give the results in terms of numbers of objects and memory space for a benchmark of procedural behavioral descriptions written in VHDL.

```vhdl
architecture  BEHAVIOR  of MARK2   is

signal  OWAIT,OWAITI,RUN : BIT;
signal  STOP,INTA,INTE,INTEI : BIT;
signal  INTRET, PCI: ADDR;
signal  CLK,FETCH   : BOOLEAN;
EXECUTE,INTERRUPT : BOOLEAN;
begin
  SYSCLK : process
  begin
    wait CLK,RUN;
    if (RUN) then
      CLK <= transport not CLK after 500ns;
    end if;
  end process SYSCLK;

INTERRUPT_PROC : process
begin
  wait on INTERRUPT;
  INTEI <= '0'; INTRET  <= PC;
  INTA <= '1' after 50ns; IOWAITI  <= '1';
  wait for 150ns; PCI <= VDAD(DATA);
  INTA <= '0' after 50ns; IOWAITI  <= '0';
end process INTERRUPT_PROC;
```

```
STATE : process
begin
    wait CKL, RUN, IOWAIT, STOP, EXECUTE, INTERRUPT;
    if (not RUN'STABLE) and (RUN = '1') then                              O1
        INTERRUPT <= true;                                                O2
    elseif    (RUN'STABLE and (STOP = '0') and (IOWAIT = '0')     O3      O4
                              and not CKL'STABLE     then
        if (EXECUTE and (INTE = '0' or INT = '0') or INTERRUPT)           O5
        then FETCH <= true; else                                         O6
                 FETCH <= false;                                         O7
        endif;
        if FETCH                                                         O8
        then EXECUTE <= true; else                                       O9
                 EXECUTE <= false;                                       O10
        endif;
        if (EXECUTE and (INT = '1' and INTE = '1') then                  O11
             INTERRUPT <= true  else                                     O12
             INTERRUPT <= false;                                         O13
        endif;
    endif;
end process  STATE.
```

Fig. 10: Example of a VHDL description

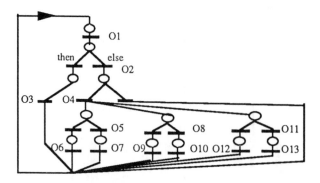

Fig. 11: Petri net associated with process *state*

4.2 The Extractor

On the control model previously defined, the behavioral extraction involves the classic problem of the search for paths in a graph. Indeed, the specifications express the conditions in which certain temporal relations should exist. These conditions define a path or a subgraph of symbolic execution on the control model.

The extraction problem is divided into two phases:

1. Search for the execution path(s) in the graph (paths of which the decision-type nodes are specified in the conditions table) and calculate their durations.
2. Stress the timing relations, which can link the various actions of an execution path. For example, on the Petri graph that models the process *state* (Fig. 11), the given specification expresses the conditions that validate only the path:

$$c_{v1} = \{O1\ O2\ O4\ (O5\ O7,\ O8\ O10,\ O11\ O13)\}$$

The duration of a path is calculated according to the action types of which the path is composed [20,21]. In our example, the execution path c_{v1} contains only the signal-type actions. Its duration is defined by:

$$\text{duration}_{1j}(c_{v1}) = \text{Max}_{i \in [1...j]} d(xi); \text{ e.g. :}$$

$$\text{duration}(c_{v1}) = \text{Max}_{i \in [1...3]} [d(O7, O10, O13)] = \delta \text{ ns}$$

TABLE 2: Objects and Memory Space Required for
Four Conventional Procedural Descriptions

VHDL Procedural Descriptions	Objects/Memory Space
Traffic light controllers	15/26 Kbytes
Simple ALU	103/57 Kbytes
Multiplixor (8E et 2S)	32/35 Kbytes
Comparator (4Bits)	53/50 Kbytes
ROM 1024 (256*4)	36/40 Kbytes

If we consider each node of an execution path as a time interval (or a time point) during which the action holds, then by using the bases defined in Section 3, we can easily represent the temporal relations between the actions. For example, the temporal relation that links actions O7 and O10 is a relation-type start-at because the two actions begin at the same moment, are executed in parallel, and are of the same duration.

To summarize, we obtain the following sub-behavior:

$$\text{Sub-Beh1} = \{I7 = I10, I10 = I13, \text{duration}(I7) = \text{duration}(I10)$$

$$= \text{duration}(I13) = \delta\text{ns}\}$$

The set of these constraints constitutes the temporal sub-behaviors that will be compared with the behavioral specifications.

4.3 Principles Behind Extraction for a Declarative Description

The methodology that we use here is inspired from artificial intelligence techniques and, in particular, the planning with temporal components [10]. Indeed, our approach establishes a comparison and, by referring to the planning, we can perfectly imagine the processes as a set of tasks representing the scheme of plans and the VHDL description as the global scheme of the planner (representing the temporal scheduling of the execution of the set of tasks).

If we pose our problem at the same level as the planning, we notice that our aims are different. The aim of the planning consists of anticipating the evolution of the world according to tasks carried out to attain one (or several) goal(s) fixed at the outset. Whereas in our case we have the scheduling of the tasks (VHDL description), our main aim is simply to verify from the behavioral specifications that this scheduling is correct. To do this, we have defined for each process the specifications that allow us to describe a process independently of all considerations of the context.

Context-Free Specifications

Context-free specifications contain the following:

- The set of conditions that establish the exact context in which the process must be activated
- The set of signals affected by the execution paths when the process is activated, including their explicit delays
- The set of execution paths of the process, with their durations.

Figure 12 shows an example of the context-free specifications of the three processes *sysckl, interrupt-proc,* and *state,* involved in the behavioral description of Fig. 10. Once these specifications are defined, we can extract the temporal constraints between the processes. Indeed, from the conditions and signals affected, we can know the time point at which the process starts its activation. Thanks to execution paths and their durations, we can know the time point where it finishes.

```
(describe-cfspecif (interrupt-proc)
    (Timecond (interrupt))
    (signals (intei [0 δ]) (intret [0 δ]) (inta [0 50]) (iowaiti [0 δ])
             (pci [0 δ]) (iowaiti [0 δ])))
    (paths (cv2 [0 200])))

(describe-cfspecif (state)
    (Timecond (ckl) (run) (stop) (iowait) (execute)
             (fetch) (interrupt))
    (signals (interrupt [0 δ]) (fetch [0 δ])
             (execute [0 δ])))
    (paths (cv1 [0 δ])))

(describe-cfspecif (sysckl)
    (Timecond (ckl) (run))
    (signals (ckl [0 500]))
    (paths (cv3 [0 500])))
```

Fig. 12: Context-free specifications associated with the process *state, interrupt-proc,* and *sysckl.*

For example, consider the context-free specifications of Fig. 12. The field *signals* of the process *state* indicates that at time point δ, an event on the signal *interrupt* will take place, which affects the two processes *interrupt-proc* and *state*. Consequently, the two processes are activated at the same moment and their durations of activity are, respectively, 200 and d ns (equal to the duration of their execution paths). Thus, the temporal relation between the two processes is a start-type relation.

To represent the temporal relation between the processes, we suppose that each process corresponds to a symbolic interval over which its activity holds. A similar process of reasoning is applied to other processes, and we finally obtain:

$$\text{sub-beh2} = \{(\text{Ist start Iin}), (\text{Ist start Isy}) \text{ and } (\text{Iin} < \text{Isy}) \ (\text{duration(state)} = \delta \text{ns})$$

$$(\text{duration(interrupt-proc)} = 200\text{ns}) \ (\text{duration(sysckl)} = 500\text{ns})\}$$

The diagram below sums up the temporal scheduling of the three processes where ($t = 0$) represents the initialization phase of the process. This diagram represents a cycle of execution that is repeated each time.

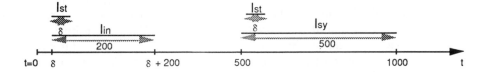

4.4 Demonstrator

The demonstration problem involves the following two steps:

1. Verify if the activities expressed by an execution path belong to the activities table.
2. Verify that the temporal structure of this path is compatible with the one defined in the time lattice. This means verifying the compatibility of the numerical and symbolic constraints, e.g.,

$$\forall \ (I_1, P_1) \in \text{path}, \forall \ (I_2, P_2) \in \text{path} \backslash (I_1 R I_2)$$

$$\exists \ (I_{\text{sp1}}, P_{\text{sp1}}, (I_{\text{sp2}}, P_{\text{sp2}}) \in (\text{lattice} + \text{tables}) \backslash (P_{\text{sp1}} \equiv P_1) \wedge (P_{\text{sp2}} \equiv P_2)$$

$$\wedge \ (I_{\text{sp1}} R I_{\text{sp2}}) \wedge (\text{duration}(I_i) = \text{duration}(I_{\text{spi}}))$$

where R belongs to the set of relations of the restricted algebra of intervals or point algebra.

These two properties describe the existence of a temporal path in the Petri graph that is identical to a behavioral specification. We have illustrated this property in the example of the behavioral specifications defined in Fig. 7 and the timing constraints obtained in Section 4.2 (sub-beh1).

The actions O7, O10 and O13 in the path c_{v1} correspond well to those defined in the activities table (Fig. 9). The symbolic and numerical constraints expressed in the sub-behavior (sub-beh1) are satisfied by the time lattice. For example, if we take two temporal propositions—($I7$, fetch) and ($I10$, execute)—such that ($I7$ **equals** $I10$), we find the same propositions (fetch and execute) linked by the same temporal relation *equal* in the activities table.

The duration-type numerical constraints made explicit by the actions O7, O10, and O13 are also correct: duration($IO7$) = duration(fetch) = δ ns. We will use the same step in the case of the sub-behavior (sub-beh2).

To summarize, we can conclude that the temporal scheduling of actions and the timing order of execution of the processes involved in the behavioral description of Fig. 10 meet the behavioral specifications defined in Section 3.1.

5 IMPLEMENTATION AND RESULTS

This approach has been implemented in Common Lisp using the object representation language ORL [25] to support object-oriented programming. The system runs under Common Lisp V4.0 on a SUN 4 workstation 360 running Unix. It consists of approximately 1500 lines of Common Lisp code and requires about 3.5 MBytes of main memory. The system is in beta test and shows good performances. Table 3 shows the results obtained on several VHDL descriptions. These results concern only the procedural part. Table 3 shows the evolution of the running time for the three modules: The extractor, translator, and demonstrator according to the benchmark VHDL descriptions. Observe that the verification time is linearly dependent on the number of actions of a behavioral description (low-level complexity). The final CPU times in the last column indicate that the algorithm is fast enough to be of practical use. These reasonable times we have obtained are essentially linked to good performances of the compiler (see Table 1) because the comparison operation (timing constraints) is the basic principle of the demonstrator.

Comparison of Our Approach to Other Verifiers

Our approach provides a new specification model of timing behavior, which allows for the specification of complicated temporal relationships between VHDL actions and the modeling of the more complex concepts defined by the VHDL model (transport and inertial delays, wait time, event, etc.). As a result, timing constraints not expressible under

TABLE 3: Run Times (in sec) for Four Conventional Procedural Behavioral Descriptions

Behavioral Rules	VHDL Description	Control Graph Size	Translator	Extractor	Demonstrator	Global Time
1	Traffic light controller	12	1.5	2.0	1.2	4.7
4	ALU	95	4.8	5.5	4.4	14.7
2	Multiplexor	25	2.0	2.8	1.8	6.6
3	Comparator	34	2.8	3.5	2.5	8.8
3	ROM 1024	27	2.3	3.2	2.0	7.5

other specification models [3,6,7,26] are expressible under our behavioral specification formalism.

Most of the formal timing verification methods use tools (a state graph, event driven simulation techniques, etc.) to capture the complete behavior of the implemented design. These tools contain information about signal timing and transitions for every possible combination of input signals. The main disadvantage of these methods is that they are either of an incomplete verification methodology, or that the size of tools used is exponential in the size of the design and thus the verification process tends to be time consuming. Some limitations of the tools used prevent the verification of certain temporal properties, thus involving verification of a limited number of timing behaviors and a limited applicability of these approaches to small-sized hardware systems.

Our verification methodology is based on a simple time representation, which uses efficient tools (IxTeT plus methods of artificial intelligence) for managing the temporal information (see [10,19]).

Although we have used a structure of a graph (Demot and Petri net) for modeling the behavior of a VHDL description (procedural), to speed the verification time considerably, we have divided the complex problem of the verification into three well-defined and less complex subproblems: The first concerns the verification of the declarative part, the second the control part, and the last the data part. Our main aim was to finded a good trade-off between the completeness of the verification methodology and the efficiency (space and CPU times).

Our system provides a much more efficient way to verify a description for medium and complex hardware systems.

6 CONCLUSIONS

The work that has been presented in this paper has allowed a technique of formal verification to be developed, enabling us to specify and to verify the timing behaviors of the behavioral models of VHDL. We first defined a behavioral specification formalism based on Shoham's logic, which permits the behavioral specifications to be described as a set of facts or events temporally linked. From this formalism, we then established a verification procedure, which starts by extracting the temporal sub-behaviors (a set of timing constraints) from given VHDL descriptions and then gives them to the temporal demonstrator to prove whether they respect the behavioral specifications or no.

In its current state, the system does not allow for the temporal verification of the data flow. This is the next task to undertake in order to complete this study.

REFERENCES

[1] M. Yoelli, *Formal Verification of Hardware Design,* Computer Society Press Tutorial, Los Alamitos, CA 1992.

[2] S. Leinwaid and T. Lanmdan, *A Proposal for Automated Design Verification of Digital Systems,* The Weizmann Institute of Science, Rehovot, Israel.

[3] C. Brown, "Automatic Verification of Sequential Circuits Using Temporal Logic,"
     Technical Report CMU-CS-85-100, Department of Computer Science, Carnegie-
     Mellon University.

[4] G. J. Mine and M. Pezze, "Typed CIRCAL: A High Level Framework for Hardware
     Verification," *IFIP Conference,* Glasgow, Scotland, July 1988, pp. 115-135.

[5] H. G. Barrow, "Verify: A Program for Proving Correctness of Digital Hardware
     Design," *Artificial Intell.,* 24, pp. 437–491, 19??.

[6] M. Gordon, "HOL: A Proof Generating System for Higher-Order Logic," in *VLSI
     Specification, Verification and Synthesis,* Kluwer Academic Publishers, Boston, 1988.

[7] G. V. Bochmann, "Hardware Specification with Temporal Logic: An Example,"
     IEEE Trans. Comput., pp. 223–231, March 1982.

[8] "IEEE Standard VHDL Language Reference Manual," IEEE Standard 1076, 1989.

[9] G. N. Nurie and P. J. Menchini, "VHDL Model Portability," *High Performance Syst.,*
     pp. 76–85, July 1989.

[10] M. Ghallab and A. Mounir-Alaoui, "The Indexed Time Table Approach for Planning
     and Actions," presented at NASA Conference on Space Telerobotics, Jan. 31–Feb.
     2, 1989, Pasadena, CA.

[11] Y. Shoham, "Temporal Logics in AI: Semantical and Ontological Considerations,"
     Artificial Intell., 33, pp. 89–104, 1987.

[12] R. Kowalski and M. J. Sergot, " A Logic-Based Calculus of Events," *New Generation
     Computing,* 4, pp. 67–95, 1986.

[13] J. F. Rit, "Modélisation et Propagation des Contraintes Temporelles pour la Plani-
     fications," Thèse de l'INP Grenoble, 1988.

[14] D. McDermott, "A Temporal Logic for Reasoning About Processes and Plans," *Cog-
     nitive Sci.,* 6, pp. 101–105, 1982.

[15] J. F. Allen, "An Interval-Based Representation of Temporal Knowledge," *Proc. 7th
     IJCAI,* pp. 221–226, 1981.

[16] J. F. Allen, "Maintaining Knowledge About Temporal Intervals," *Comm. ACM,* 2(11),
     pp. 832–843, Nov. 1983.

[17] M. Vlain and H. Kaut, "Constraint Propagation Algorithms for Temporal Reason-
     ing," *Proc. AAAI,* pp. 337–382, Aug. 1986.

[18] T. Granier, "Contribution à l'Etude du Temps Objectif dans le Raisonnment," Rap-
     port LIFIA RR 716-I-73, Grenoble, 1988.

[19] M. Ghallab and A. Mounir-Alaoui, "Managing Efficiently Temporal Relations Through
     Indexed Spanningtrees," *Proc. 11th IJCAI,* pp. 1297–1303, 1989.

[20] D. Boussebha, N. Giambiasi, and J. Magnier, "Temporal Verification of Behavioral
     Descriptions in VHDL," *Proc. EURO Design Automation Conference,* September
     1992, Hamburg Germany, pp. 692–698.

[21] D. Boussebha, "Verification temporelle de descriptions comportementales écrites en
     VHDL," Thése de l'université de Montpellier II, 1993.

[22] R. Armstrong, *Chip-Level Modeling With VHDL,* Prentice Hall, Englewood Cliffs,
     NJ, 1989.

[23] N. Giambiasi, J. F. Santucci, and G. Dray, "A Methodology to Reduce the Computational Cost of Behavioral Test Pattern Generation," presented at Design Automation Conference, June 1992, California.

[24] M. Oussalah, N. Giambiasi, and J. F. Santucci, "Expert System Based on Multi-View Multi-Level Models Approach for Test Pattern Generation," in *Knowledge-Based System Diagnosis, Supervision and Control,* S. G. Tzafestas, Ed., Plenum, New York, 1989.

[25] N. Giambiasi, M. Oussalah, and L. Torres, "ORL, Clean Semantics of Multiple Inheritance," presented at *EUUG* Spring 1990, Munich.

[26] D. Doukas, A. Andras, and S. Lapaugh, "Clover: A Timing Contraints Verification System," presented at 28th Design Automation Conference, 1989, Princeton University.

CHAPTER 10

Design-Flow Graph Partitioning for Formal Hardware/Software Codesign

R. B. Hughes   G. Musgrave
Abstract Hardware Limited
Brunel University
Uxbridge, Middlesex, United Kingdom

Abstract: This chapter examines the application of mathematically rigorous formal techniques to the manipulation of flow graphs used in the design partitioning essential for hardware/software codesign. The LAMBDA[1] system, based on HOL, is used to provide a strong formal basis to the definition, manipulation, and use of such graphs in high-level specification, design, and testing.

1 iNTRODUCTION

1.1 Background

Codesign is of increasing concern. In fact, systems to enable a unified approach to complete systems design, encompassing both the mechanical aspects as well as those of electronic hardware and software will be required. One has only to think of a disk drive as an example of a current device that contains all three of these "system" components. Such a device cannot, at present, be designed in a uniform way with current CAD systems. The approach presented here addresses the hardware/software *codesign* problem (it is important to note that we are only addressing the area of *digital systems*) by using a CAD tool based on a *formal logic* core. This allows us to tackle the problem at the highest

---

[1] Logic And Mathematics Behind Design Automation.

level of systems abstraction while maintaining *high integrity* in both the partitioning and in the final design owing to the current design state being transformed by proof.

Formal methods have already been successfully used [1,2] in a variety of complex case studies. In tackling real-world formal design, the integration of user-interaction and automated synthesis must be considered, as it has been before [3]. In addition, however, we require a system in which high-level specification (including features such as user-defined data types and recursively defined functions), and refinement of both data and timing are supported. The LAMBDA/DIALOG design assistant [4] is a system that implements and extends these ideas and by providing VHDL output it can interface with many other, lower level *High-level synthesis* tools [5]. With such useful generic capabilities it can also be used for software engineering design [6,7].

Real-world systems need to contain both hardware and software. Such systems are extremely complex, and partitioning them into software or hardware components is something of an art. Maintaining system integrity through such partitioning is almost impossible. Systems engineers should be able to compose alternative partitionings to minimize silicon area, latency, hardware use, etc. Currently, it is extremely difficult for an engineer to be able to examine these alternatives in a common design environment owing to the large data set and the amount of time that would be involved. Proof of implementation correctness is just one of the criteria used to satisfy the end customer that the product meets its informal requirements; others include animation of the specification and simulation. The time spent in these activities greatly affects the development cost of the product and also reduces the competitive lead that may be present. As a result, modern industry tends to stick to one tried and tested development strategy rather than examine different alternatives. This has been quite cost effective in the past since the systems in question have been quite regular in structure, and a particular design strategy for a particular type of system has evolved over time. In systems developed using such evolved strategies, it is known at the outset which parts of the system will, at the end of the design phase, be implemented by which tools, i.e., the designer knows, in advance, which particular tools are going to be used for implementing different parts of the system, namely, silicon compilers, logic synthesizers, C compilers, EPROM programmers, etc. Increasing complexity in the requirements for modern systems means that the previously used approach is now under considerable strain. To decide how to partition the system in advance is no longer possible for complex systems that might use FPGAs and/or ASICs. Techniques for using such new components will evolve if the requirements for different systems are similar in nature but this is less likely to be the case in the future than it was in the past. Complexity of modern systems requirements leads increasingly to these requirements being diverse. Such diversity and the need for a reduced "time to market" give little time for the evolution of "tried and tested" design methodologies. The additional concerns of high-integrity systems in safety-critical applications add extra burdens to the design task. Clearly, there is a need for new methods and techniques to be applied to systems engineering activities.

In systems engineering there is a need for high-level reasoning aids to help in the actual design process, at the system level, before any decision of partitioning has taken place. By reasoning about the total attributes of the system a better balanced decision process can be embarked upon. This is equally applicable to partitioning that may occur within the hardware level, not just at the hardware/software level, i.e., architectural partitioning.

Many different types of system exist, but in the systems considered here it is only those with digital hardware that are of concern and only synchronous operations are considered. This is a limitation, necessary initially to cope with the immense problems of codesign. To develop software correctly, in terms of a proof, it is necessary to know formally the hardware on which it is running. If tools are provided to allow an increasing degree of *reasoning* about design partitioning, it is possible that software will play an ever increasing role in the construction of such systems. One explanation for this is that hardware is very costly to design and even more costly to produce in silicon. It is therefore likely that a limited set of different hardware architectures will be formally specified and used, with as much of the reconfiguration as possible being done by altering the software that runs on the hardware. By this means, the cost of the system can be kept to a minimum. The need for formal reasoning tools is even more apparent when one considers the range of different types of systems that exists: algebraic and functional systems; model-based systems, which may be specified in terms of states; and process-based systems exhibiting tasks, behaviors, and congruence. Different languages are required for each of these system classes. Previous work in software design [8] focused only on formal verification and synthesis of functional languages, which are well suited to the first class of system. Proof systems and tools for reasoning are also required for set-theoretic and object-oriented languages, used to describe the second class of system, and for concurrent languages needed for our third system class.

System-level design, in its more generic sense, requires the design of software within a system to be considered an integral part of the overall system. This is especially important for safety-critical design work, because trade-offs in one direction imply changes to another area, which might affect overall system performance. This means that, in the end, communications between the hardware and software partitions of the system must be closely examined for correctness since a partitioned system relies on communications between its parts occurring in the right manner in order to perform as envisaged. Thus, the ability to design formally the entire system, bearing in mind various architectural limitations, in a sound logical framework, is considered to be very important.

1.2 Why Formal Methods?

In order to validate the operation of a system to ensure that it meets a user's requirements, it is necessary to examine the operation of the system in a variety of ways. One approach is to test the system. Testing is not possible in general since the number of states that need to be tested in many systems makes an exhaustive test unfeasible; also, some of the states of the system may be unreachable unless the system was designed with testability in mind. The major disadvantage of this, at the design stage, is that it is necessary to implement parts of the system in order to test it. Another approach, which may be carried out at the specification level, or at the level of an intermediate design, is *simulation*. Simulation can be applied to both hardware and software, and involves placing values in a model of the system to be implemented to see how it will perform. Although simulation is certainly better than "breadboarding," it suffers from the same problems as that of testing, in that how does one know that all aspects of the system have been simulated. Is such an exhaustive simulation even possible? Simulations are model dependent.

Such problems with simulation are apparent with current systems; future systems will be even more complex and the demands on high-integrity systems even more stringent. Simulation of systems, sometimes known as *animation* in the software field, is clearly not the best means of checking that a design meets its requirements. One solution to this problem, addressed in this chapter, is to use a mathematical proof. Mathematical proofs can be used to verify the system formally, to ensure that its implementation satisfies its specification and remove the need for simulation since the implementation is then guaranteed to be correct. Additionally, if one composes a system, via formal synthesis, from its specification using a mathematical proof then there is also no need to simulate the system; the system will be guaranteed correct by construction. Managing such mathematical proofs does, however, cause other problems, which are briefly discussed in the following sections.

In this paper we present a formal approach to the issue of using *design-flow graphs* (encompassing both data and control flow) and their partitioning. Partitioning of these graphs is important if the designer is to be able to implement the design, part in software and part in hardware, in a flexible manner. *Design partitioning* [9,10] is also important when implementation in different architectures is considered. We consider that our formal approach to the problem of high-level systems design allows the designer flexibility in exploring the *design space* while ensuring that the design always *satisfies the specification*. Better systems-level solutions can be achieved through the judicious use of codesign. By having a possible trade-off between the hardware and software costs, one can choose how to implement the solution. The generic approach suggested allows interpretation of the *program blocks* of the solution as either items of software that must be executed within a certain time frame by a separate processor or by specialized hardware items. This affords the designer greater flexibility in using formal methods in the overall design of complex systems.

Partitioning is the term used to describe a hierarchy of differing operations. At the system level, the term *partitioning* can be used to indicate the partitioning of the design into software and hardware components. It can also be used to describe the architectural partitioning which takes place within the hardware itself. The ability to examine different partitionings, all of that are guaranteed to be behaviorally correct by design, is an area of key interest at present. State-of-the-art systems that can cope with such multiple-level partitioning, to allow the designer to freely explore the design space, are in great need and are becoming reality. The following sections describe some of the pertinent details of the logic used in the theorem proving core and introduce the concept of *design-flow graphs* and the primitive restructuring operations that are essential for future, high-level, computer-assisted design optimizations via graph partitioning.

2 FORMALIZATION

Like most theorem provers, LAMBDA can make use of equational reasoning to rewrite design requirements into an equivalent, but simpler form. It also supports tactical and inductive proof. In addition, it uses unification, which permits synthesis—the addition of new components in order to achieve a design. The system was designed to be used by engineers rather than logicians, so the user interface is an important element of the

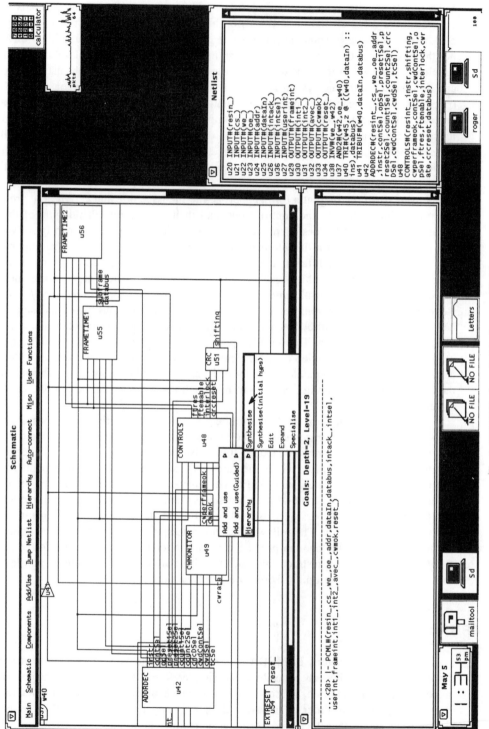

Fig. 1: DIALOG schematic interface—motif style

toolset. A window interface, called DIALOG (see Fig. 1), allows the user to interact with the theorem prover using a schematic editor.

Our theorem prover represents a design state as a logical *rule*. Because the system allows only valid rules to be created, only correct designs can be produced. The system creates new rules/designs by transforming old ones. Thus at the start of any design/proof, we need a logically valid rule; this is often a tautology. As the design progresses, this will be transformed to:

```
IF      current_design + further_work   ACHIEVES task_n
AND     ...
AND     current_design + further_work   ACHIEVES task_1
THEN    current_design + further_work   ACHIEVES specification
```

and finally—*If I have this complete implementation and have an external environment then I have implemented this specification.*

```
completed_design + external_environment   ACHIEVES specification
```

Here the external environment will typically be information about how and when inputs and outputs are supplied.

Thus, to start a new design, we need to start with a tautological form of rule solely containing details of the specification—*If I can implement this specification then I can implement this specification....* The proof system ensures that the design at each and every stage is correct *with respect to* the given specification.

The formal specification of the tasks to be achieved is thus a very important part of the design process. This usually involves converting an imprecise set of requirements in a natural language into a formal (unambiguous) statement of the goals to be achieved. Note that no one (whether using formal methods or not) can avoid the problems that will occur if a system is incorrectly specified. Higher order unification, as used in ISABELLE [11], allows our specifications to include parameters (e.g., latency) whose values are determined during the course of the design.

The specification is written in a logical specification language based on the functional programming language ML [12] together with various logical connectives. This has the advantage that functional specifications can be read into an ML compiler to create ML functions and, hence, be animated.

3 HARDWARE SYNTHESIS IN LAMBDA

A *component* (as well as a *specification*) is modeled as a relation between its input and output signals. The relation describes which combinations of inputs and outputs are possible, thus describing the effect of the component on its environment. Note that since the relation is between *signals,* not just the values of those signals at a particular time, we are not restricted to dealing with purely combinational devices—we can relate an output signal to the value of an input signal at any previous time.

For example, INVDELSPEC specifies a circuit whose output is the inverse of its input, delayed by one cycle:

INV and DELAY components

```
val INVDELSPEC#(i : bool signal,        val INVDELIMP#(i : bool signal,
                o : bool signal) =                     o : bool signal) =
  forall t : time.                        forall t : time.
    o (t + 1) == not (i t);                 exists w. INV#(i,w) /\ DELAY#(w,o);
```

Internal wires are "hidden" using existential quantification, as used in the implementation above. The rule[2] representing the implementation of this specification is:

$$\overline{\text{INV\#1(i,w), DELAY\#1(w,o)}} \vdash \text{INVDELSPEC\#1(i,o)}$$

This is a *theorem* of the formal logic, which states that we can use an INV and a DELAY, appropriately connected, to implement INVDELSPEC.

Implementation of INVDELSPEC

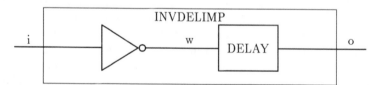

Limitations of the Hardware Model

The DIALOG hardware model is very simple:

- Two-valued (for Booleans)
- Synchronous
- One implicit clock (usually)
- Time modeled as natural number.

We can use the hardware model to prove, owing to the fact that a *false hypothesis implies anything,* that each of the following circuits also meets the INVDELSPEC specification:

---

[2] In the logic, ACHIEVES is represented by "⊢"; IF, THEN, and AND are assumed.

```
val BADCIRC1#(i,o) =
   exists w. PWR#(w) /\ GND#(w)              (* outputs connected together *)
```

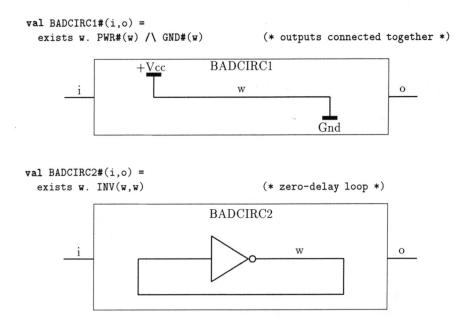

```
val BADCIRC2#(i,o) =
   exists w. INV(w,w)                        (* zero-delay loop *)
```

This is clearly ridiculous—real hardware does not behave like this. What has gone wrong? The problem is that we assume that the relation between the ports of a component, specified by its definition, always holds; in both of the above circuits this is not the case.

Design Rules

How can we avoid this problem? First, the problem only occurs for design errors—well-behaved circuits do not suffer the same problems. Thus, our solution is to keep the model simple, but disallow "paradoxical" circuits. This also avoids the computational expense of a more sophisticated model.

Keeping our existing hardware model, we impose some extra constraints on how circuit descriptions may be constructed. We achieve this by identifying each port of a component as either an input port or an output port; only an output port is allowed to affect the value on a wire.

The DIALOG description of a component is the LAMBDA description plus:

- Modality (input or output) of each port
- List of zero-delay paths through component.

DIALOG enforces design rules to ensure that the naïve, underlying hardware model remains valid:

- Outputs must not be connected.
- No zero-delay loops are allowed.

The first design rule is remarkably effective; although (at the switch level) wires are actually bidirectional devices, the vast majority of them are used to pass information in one direction only. Our design rule checker, implemented as part of DIALOG, will throw out any attempt to construct circuits violating either of the above rules.

4 SOFTWARE SYNTHESIS IN LAMBDA

It would take many pages to explain all of the intricate details of the logic used to allow a truly complete understanding of an approach to software synthesis, owing primarily to the definitions of some of the various algorithms and the notation involved together with a fuller description of functional programming in ML. However, to provide a quick, albeit slightly mathematical, insight into the material a suitably simple example, using rule forms illustrated with the hardware synthesis use of LAMBDA, is given.

The LAMBDA system can be used for verification quite easily, the extension to synthesis for software is to use a two-ended list of hypotheses, which is represented in the following by Δ. The reason behind the use of a two-ended list will become apparent in the explanation of the technique to be used to allow unification to assist in the synthesis of a design. An explanation of how this method may be used to synthesize software from a specification is then given.

If one makes the unification that takes place when applying a rule more general, by making the hypotheses list Δ flexible, then terms may be added to the hypotheses list of the conclusion that enable the substitutions required by the unification to be carried out. For example, suppose one has the rule:

$$\frac{\text{FRED}, \Delta' \;\vdash \text{SOME}}{\text{BILL}, \Delta' \;\vdash \text{THING}}$$

which one wishes to apply to the current rule representing the design state:

$$\frac{\text{MARY}, \Delta \;\vdash \text{THING}}{\text{MARY}, \Delta \;\vdash \text{THING}}$$

where Δ is flexible at both ends; i.e., terms may be added before the Δ and after the Δ in order to satisfy the substitutions required by unification. The rule can be applied if one first moves MARY, in the top rule, to the other end of the Δ list so as to obtain the top rule:

$$\frac{\Delta, \text{MARY} \;\vdash \text{THING}}{\text{MARY}, \Delta \;\vdash \text{THING}}$$

Now, the premise of the above rule unifies with the conclusion of the rule we wish to apply resulting in the new top rule:

$$\frac{\text{FRED}, \Delta, \text{MARY} \;\vdash \text{SOME}}{\text{MARY}, \text{BILL}, \Delta \;\vdash \text{THING}}$$

This would not have been possible without being able to add terms to both ends of the Δ list. By having a two-ended list it is possible to unify with both the MARY hypothesis and the BILL hypothesis. This allows synthesis to be considered quite easily.

For synthesis of something from a specification one would apply the above technique with a tautological form of rule containing the specification as the assertion of the conclusion. By applying various rules to the flexible form of a two-ended Δ list, one can introduce terms into the conclusion that represent essential software components required to implement the specification. When the premise is ultimately reduced to truth, the conclusion would contain the implementation of the specification as terms in the Δ list. If the premise cannot be reduced to truth, then it would mean that the implementation would only be valid provided certain constraints, contained in the premise, are met. This is a paraphrasing of the approach used for the hardware synthesis.

The steps required to synthesize a piece of code to test some property are frequently trivial and would not be a good example of synthesis, since the specification of the function to do the test would be directly executable as ML code. Hence, the example, although simple, illustrates a specification that is *not* directly executable as ML code.

The example addresses the development of code to achieve the synthesis of a function to sort a list of numbers into a descending sequence, i.e., a reverse sorted list. This is particularly simple, but illustrates most clearly the concepts involved. Firstly, in order to apply the techniques illustrated in the first section, it is necessary to define the existing functions in terms of *software components,* which are defined as abbreviations. For example,

$$\text{val QSORT\#(in,out)} = \forall \text{ t. out t} == \text{qsort (in t)}$$

One would normally like to extend the above with existential quantification on n to allow the qsort routine to take some time to calculate its result, as follows:

$$\text{val QSORT\#(in,out)} = \exists \text{ n. } \forall \text{ t. out (t + n)} == \text{qsort (in t)}$$

This is especially true for any real-world implementation, be it hardware or software. Rules about the abbreviations, owing to the similarity with the ML code, are quite easy to prove and must be made before synthesis can proceed.

If one now starts with an abbreviation of the software component required, defined in terms of its properties, and uses this as the basis of the tautological rule started with, then unfolding of the abbreviation would lead to a rule of the form:

$$\frac{\Delta \quad \vdash \text{ inorder (reverse (out t))} \wedge \text{isPerm(out t, in t)}}{\Delta \quad \vdash \text{ REVSORT\#(in, out)}}$$

The reverse requirement can be met by the REVERSE component. Thus it would be possible to have, after some manipulation, the following intermediary rule in which a REVERSE component has been added. For simplicity, some of the additional connection conditions required are not shown.

$$\frac{\Delta \quad \vdash \text{ inorder (w t)} \wedge \text{isPerm(out t, in t)}}{\Delta, \text{REVERSE\#(w,out)} \quad \vdash \text{REVSORT\#(in, out)}}$$

The inorder requirement can be met by either the ISORT, MSORT, or the QSORT component. [These components are for the insertion, merge, and quicksort algorithms, respectively.] Such components will also allow the permutation part of the assertion to be achieved. The choice of which component to use is up to the designer. The following shows a simplified rule state after the ISORT component has been added:

$$\overline{\text{REVERSE\#(w,out), } \Delta, \text{ ISORT\#(in,w)} \quad \vdash \text{REVSORT\#(in, out)}}$$

As a result, a REVSORT component has been constructed by formal transformational synthesis from some existing components, the choice of specific components being done interactively by the user. The format used above is quite in line with the techniques used for the formal synthesis of hardware and one can envisage a future system in which design-flow graphs may be used to encompass both hardware and software design in a coherent way.

Higher order resolution may also be used to let the user perform synthesis in a different way. The approach used is to allow the user to specify the properties of some arbitrary function f, which he or she wishes to synthesize and then, by letting f become flexible, allow resolution to perform the substitutions required for the synthesis to take place. For example, a similar proof to that used previously could start with a rule of the form:

$$\frac{\Delta \quad \vdash \text{out t} == f\ (\text{in t}) \wedge \text{inorder(reverse(out t))}}{\Delta \quad \vdash \text{out t} == f\ (\text{in t}) \wedge \text{inorder(reverse(out t))}}$$

Here, f is applied to some input to generate the output, which must have the properties required. This can be trivially simplified to the following rule form, from which synthesis, after flexing of the f variable, can proceed.

$$\frac{\Delta \quad \vdash \text{inorder(reverse(f (in t)))}}{\Delta \quad \vdash \text{out t} == f\ (\text{in t}) \wedge \text{inorder(reverse(out t))}}$$

Application of the reverse reflexive rules and rules relevant to inorder (isort will be chosen again here to aid comparison with the previous example) can lead to the following rule:

$$\overline{\Delta \quad \vdash \text{out t} == \text{reverse(isort (in t))} \wedge \text{inorder(reverse(out t))}}$$

We can see that f has been functionally synthesized from the specification.

This technique, although mathematically interesting, is not compatible with the concept of software components introduced earlier. It is included to show the flexibility inherent in the paradigm presented.

5 LINKING IT TOGETHER—GRAPH RESTRUCTURING

5.1 Background

Flow graphs, especially data-flow graphs, are currently used mainly by computer scientists to describe different systems. Unfortunately, they are not used in a formal manner, but are, in the main, used to represent pictorially different system partitionings, where *system* is usually a set of computer programs. Formalizing this work is made more difficult owing to the fact that, unlike signal flow graphs, there is no single universal definition of a DFG. Despite this, such flow graphs have been used by Kung [13] for real-world designs. Frequently one can think of DFG as a data-flow graph (e.g., the DeMarco [14] style); one then needs a separate control flow graph to supply the control to the actual hardware used to implement the system. However, we introduce the more general concept of a *design-flow graph*, which encompasses both data and control, so that both aspects can be studied without losing track of the other. By retaining the control flow information, test pattern generation is made more easily achievable; we will not discuss test pattern generation here, but it is of interest in various collaborative research projects. Frequently, one needs to restructure the data-flow graph to be able to optimize it for a particular implementation or to investigate some particular set of properties. Restructuring is used to:

- Obtain appropriate partitioning.
- Reduce complexity.
- Present particular system aspects.
- Aid function allocation.

Recently, attempts [15] have been made to try to formalize the operations that take place when a DFG is restructured.

Primitive restructuring operations are considered to be:

- Grouping—folding and merging
- Expanding—unfolding and splitting
- Translation—raising and lowering.

5.2 Formalization

Description of Operations

It is important to clarify, in natural language terms, what we mean by *folding* and *merging*. This is perhaps best achieved by describing the operations in terms of their nearest *inverse* (Fig. 2).

In the fold/unfold style of operation, a group of nodes is selected to form a new node composed of the subnodes previously selected. Because no information is lost in this process, an unfold operation will return the user to the same state of DFG as before. Note that the designer will be two steps further on in the design, but at the same state as before when a fold is immediately followed by an unfold. Figure 3 illustrates the effect of the merging and splitting of nodes. We can see that the effect of a merge is to combine the effects of two composite nodes, i.e., nodes that have been formed from previous folding operations into a composite node in which the previous nodal definitions are removed, leaving only the subnodes in the design. We need to emphasize that the resulting node has *exactly the same functional behavior* as a node formed by a folding, namely, the nodes formed by the fold and merge operations are *functionally equivalent*. The only difference between the composite nodes formed in each case is in the internal structure of the nodes.

It is also important to realize that the merge operation does not eliminate duplicate nodes. Such elimination is thought possible when no implementation has been carried

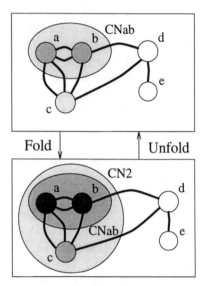

Fig. 2: Folding and unfolding

out since it is then only a matter of comparing the functional specifications of the nodes involved. However, the elimination of an equivalent node after implementation would require that the circuit be split up in such a way as to allow rescheduling to take place. This is a much more difficult operation.

Finally, in the primitive restructuring operations essential for partitioning, the raising and lowering of nodes has been considered (Fig. 4). In the DIALOG system, the operations are limited, at present, to movement across one level of hierarchy only.

These operations will only come into their own when they are used in conjunction with equivalence testing operations and rescheduling of the design so as to permit the

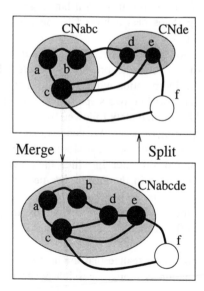

Fig. 3: Merging and splitting

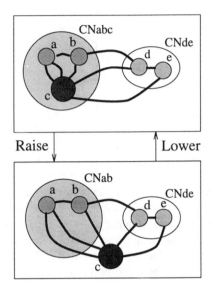

Fig. 4: Raising and lowering

designer to make implementation decisions for the design. In this, the reuse of existing components, where these may be hierarchical in nature, associated scheduling and multiplexing with delays is a key requirement of the designers. Despite the NP-completeness of many of the problems *in the general case,* it is hoped to provide *specialized* solutions to *specific* problems within this domain.

6 SCHEDULING OF FLOW GRAPHS

A flow graph, in its simplest sense, may be thought of as a connection of nodes that performs some calculation connected to other nodes by means of arcs. There may be delays present on these. If the node has no associated delay then the representation is really that of a signal flow graph (SFG). In an SFG, the computational delay associated with a node can be represented by an initial labeling of all the output arcs of the node. To be able to process the data, the inputs to the nodes must occur at the same time, i.e., the computations from some of the nodes must be delayed until all sources of input to a node are available. This is called *scheduling* or *balancing* of the flow graph. In the

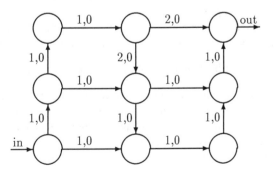

Fig. 5: Simple SFG—before scheduling

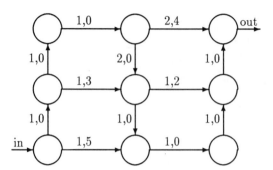

Fig. 6: Simple SFG—after scheduling

example that follows all but one of the nodes have been given an initial latency of 1, the exception having a latency of 2. In the scheduling process, delays are added to the arcs so as to correctly balance the graph. Naturally, the minimum delay possible is the best one to use but it is, in general, not unique and several minimal solutions may exist. The scheduling of a such a graph (see Fig. 5) is illustrated in Fig. 6.

Note that, on examination of the solution, the overall latency of the graph is 9 and that this is the same for any path through the graph. The words *any path* in the previous statement only have meaning for *acyclic* flow graphs.

These operations have been implemented in the DIALOG interface to the LAMBDA system and the preceding scheduling was achieved using the scheduling algorithms available within the existing LAMBDA system. We do not describe the details of the algorithms used here owing to a lack of space. We represent the nodes of the graph as *abbreviations* in the LAMBDA logic, where the specification of an SFG graph is a purely topological description.

7 HIGHER ORDER OPERATIONS

Operations to help provide computer assistance, e.g., higher order graph manipulations for ascertaining optimality according to the design requirements specified by the user, require *nodal equivalence* to be defined in a realistic manner. If the definition is too strict, it will not be possible to substitute an alternative set of nodes. One definition that has been examined is some form of *finest equivalence,* where "finest" is taken to mean an equivalence operation that makes the fewest things equivalent would be necessary. That is, the extension of an equivalence over node and edge labels to an equivalence over nodes and edges.

Given, a node equivalence $=n=$, and a set of successor functions A, a new equivalence $==$ over nodes could be defined as the *finest* equivalence satisfying:

$$\forall \text{ a in A and nodes x and y} : x == y \Rightarrow x =n= y \text{ and } a(x) == a(y)$$

This idea of equivalence states that two nodes are deemed equivalent if they are both *internally* equivalent and connected in the same way to equivalent neighbors. This is stronger than the idea of behavioral equivalence used in our partitioning work, in which the equivalence is restricted to the internal behavior of the nodes. Equivalence is required for the development of algorithms to compute subgraph isomorphism.

An alternative, weaker, definition of equivalence was to say that a node $\mathfrak{N}$ could be added to an equivalence class $\mathfrak{C}$ if it is "internally" equivalent to the nodes already in the class (i.e., it has an equivalent transfer function AND there is a path, not longer than some number m, from node $\mathfrak{N}$ to a node already in $\mathfrak{C}$). It was felt that nodes belonging to the same class would probably be closely placed on silicon, favoring a reconfiguration in the case of faults.

The existing design-flow restructuring operations together with an appropriate definition of nodal equivalence will allow for the future development of some higher order operations to tackle more complex design issues at a very high level of abstraction.

Operations that are likely to be needed, in addition to the essential restructuring operations, are

- Recognition of behaviorally equivalent nodes
- Timing manipulation e.g., trade-off design complexity versus speed
- Elimination of redundant nodes
- Selection and grouping operations to form redundant nodes
- Automation of some recognition operations
- Computer-assisted *optimal* node formation where *optimality* is dynamically defined by the user.

The last two operations are likely to be somewhat advanced and will require a good practical knowledge of how to apply the earlier operations. These levels of operation will be essential in the development of highly generic CAD systems for complete high-integrity system level partitioning and design.

8 CONCLUSIONS

Increasing demands for high-integrity, safety-critical complex systems to satisfy different procurement standards is driving engineers toward formal methods of ensuring system properties. To verify formally an already implemented system, whether one considers the hardware or the software aspects, a formal model of the implementation must be constructed in addition to the formal specification. A mathematical proof then needs to be carried out to ensure that the implementation satisfies the specification. In his thesis, Hughes [8] points out that the same amount of mathematical effort could be used to actually synthesize the correct design directly from the specification, with verification only being used for proofs of new components—these being either hardware or software "components." The formal approach is certainly applicable to problems of scale; current users of LAMBDA have been working with, e.g., the ARINC error encoder chip, at 30,000 gates, various other avionics ASICS of the order of 150,000 gates, and, as systems get more complex, customers are now using LAMBDA to handle codesign problems. In fact, some of the pure hardware designs have been successfully redesigned to give greater configurability by embedding many of the functions in software. Formal hardware/software codesign is in its infancy, but industries that have geared up to address it are already beginning to reap the benefits despite the problem of getting their system designers to think genuinely at the systems level.

The basic problems lie in the fact that there is a large knowledge gap between practicing systems engineers and the mathematical knowledge necessary for manipulating a proof of the sort required for the verification and/or synthesis of complex systems. As such, formal methods have tended to only be of interest to logicians and not to practicing designers, whether they are from the software or hardware field. The gap between their knowledge and the level of mathematics required to handle formal methods is far too wide. There is considerable difficulty in attempting to give sufficient mathematical training to the whole of the engineering community so that they have adequate knowledge to be able to apply these methods. Some of the difficulties lie in persuading people that it is a good idea to learn, but the predominant factor lies in the sheer size of the knowledge gap that is present—the mathematics required is just too far removed from the training and experiences of systems designers. Equally, the design knowledge of the engineer is far removed from the mathematics of the logician.

Thus, in order for the systems engineer to be able to use formal methods in practice, some means of simplifying the mathematics is required so as to minimize the amount of specialized training required. The design-flow graph approach suggested in thus chapter helps address this problem. Using these techniques it is possible for the engineer to examine different aspects of the system and to develop different design solutions, which are all correct, to ascertain which one is optimal. Such high-level reasoning necessitates the use of formal methods and by bridging the knowledge gap it is possible for the engineer to manipulate the design in ways that are familiar to him, the difficulties of the mathematical proof being hidden.

Long-term goals that will greatly assist in the development of *sound systems design* approaches based on *formal design partitioning* are the provision of automated nodal recognition and computer-assisted "optimization," i.e., minimization of a user-defined cost-function. The work is still at an early stage, but the interface between the related work of Politecnico di Milano and Brunel University and our formal methods will be the key to a sound, yet usable, step in the development of design partitioning tools for total systems design encompassing both hardware and software. Our methods retain the information necessary for *design for testability,* because it is important, despite behaviorally correct design, to test the physical device for possible manufacturing defects but yet allow extremely high levels of abstraction, even to the purely topological level, if so desired.

REFERENCES

[1] R. B. Hughes, M. D. Francis, S. P. Finn, and G. Musgrave, "Formal Tools for Tri-State Design in Busses," in *Proc. 1992 Int. Workshop on the HOL Theorem Prover and Its Applications,* Leuven, Belgium, September 1992.

[2] E. Mayger and M. Fourman, "Integration of Formal Methods with System Design," in *VLSI 91,* A. Halaas and P. B. Denyer, Eds., Edinburgh, Scotland, August 1991.

[3] N. D. Dutt, T. Hadley, and D. D. Gajski, "An Intermediate Representation for Behavioral Synthesis," in *Proc. 27th ACM/IEEE Design Automation Conference,* IEEE, pp. 14–19, 1990.

[4] *The LAMBDA System—Complete Reference Set, v. 4.1,* Abstract Hardware Limited, Brunel University, Uxbridge, Middlesex, UK, 1991.

[5] A. Stoll and P. Duzy, "High-Level Synthesis from VHDL with Exact Timing Constraints," in *Proc. 29th ACM/IEEE Design Automation Conference,* pp. 188–193, IEEE, 1992.

[6] R. B. Hughes, "Automatic Software Verification and Synthesis," in *Proc. 2nd Int. Conf. on Software Engineering for Real-Time Systems,* pp. 219–223, Institution of Electrical Engineers, Sep. 1989.

[7] R. B. Hughes and R. M. Zimmer, "Automated Interactive Verification of Functional Programming Languages," in *The Unified Computation Laboratory,* C. M. I. Rattray and R. G. Clark, Eds., pp. 411–423, Oxford University Press, 1992.

[8] R. B. Hughes, "Automated Interactive Software Verification and Synthesis," PhD Thesis, Department of Electrical Engineering and Electronics, Brunel University, Uxbridge, Middlesex, UK, July 1992.

[9] A. Antola and F. Distante, "DFG: A Graph Based Approach for Algorithmic Flow Driven Architecture Synthesis," in *Proc. EUROMICRO 91,* Vienna, Austria, September 1991.

[10] P. R. Chang and C. S. G. Lee, "A Decomposition Approach for Balancing Large Scale Acyclic Data Flow Graphs, *IEEE TOC,* 39(1), Jan. 1990.

[11] L. Paulson, "Natural Deduction Proof as Higher-Order Resolution," *Logic Programming,* 3, pp. 237–258, 1987.

[12] R. Milner, M. Tofte, and R. Harper, *The Definition of ML,* The MIT Press, Cambridge, MA, 1990.

[13] S. Y. Kung, *VLSI Array Processors.* Prentice-Hall, Englewood Cliffs, NJ, 1988.

[14] T. DeMarco, *Structured Analysis and System Specification,* Prentice Hall, Englewood Cliffs, NJ, 1979.

[15] M. Chan and C. Chung, "Restructuring Operations for Data-Flow Diagrams," *Software Eng. J.,* 6(6), pp. 181–195, July 1991.

CHAPTER 11

A Clustering Approach to Support Hardware/Software Partitioning

Edna Barros
Departamento de Informatica
Cidade Universitaria
Recife, Brazil

Wolfgang Rosenstiel
University of Tübingen
Tübingen, Germany

Abstract: In this chapter, we present a clustering approach to supporting hardware/software codesign. The clustering algorithm is part of a system for hardware/software partitioning that has been developed in our research group.

1 INTRODUCTION

The advances of integration technology have made it feasible to design a complex system on a single chip containing, for example, a microprocessor, a memory, and some ASICs. Furthermore, the circuits to be synthesized have become more complex. Joint design of hardware and software is necessary to exploit these technological possibilities.

A method for hardware/software (HW/SW) partitioning has been developed in our research group [1]. Our partitioning approach is based on a problem specification in UNITY [2], which permits the description of a problem in a very high level of abstraction considering only aspects of the logical problem structure, including asynchronous and synchronous behavior, nondeterminism, etc. A short introduction to UNITY is presented in Section 2.

High-level abstraction supports hardware/software partitioning, especially by supporting the analysis of different implementation alternatives for different parts of the description, as well as for the various partitioning possibilities for the description.

This work was supported by the research center in Karlsruhe-Germany FZI, and by the Brazilian Research Council CNPq.

In our clustering approach we make use of this flexibility through a previous classification of assignments according to their parallelism, data dependencies, mutual exclusion, etc. After an overview of our partitioning approach, given in Section 3, the classification mechanism is presented in Section 5. The main idea of our clustering approach is the partitioning of a set of assignments into a set of clusters according to their classification and according to the improvement of performance and resource allocation. The clustering algorithm is presented in Section 6.

2 A (VERY) SHORT INTRODUCTION TO UNITY

UNITY is a method for specifying parallel computations composed of a program notation and a proof system [2]. Here we concentrate our attention only on the program notation. The language is based on *state transitions* where the state of a program is represented by values of variables and state transitions are achieved by modifying them through assignments. The executable part of a UNITY program consists of a list of statements.[1] In the following, we give a list of all possible kinds of statements.

- *Enumerated assignment:* The general form of an enumerated assignment is given by

$$x_1, \ldots, x_n := e_{11}, \ldots, e_{1n} \text{ if } b_1$$
$$\sim$$
$$\sim e_{m1}, \ldots, e_{mn} \text{ if } b_m$$

  Depending on the Boolean expressions in the conditions $b_1, \ldots b_m$, the expressions on the right-hand side are evaluated and assigned synchronously to the variables on the left-hand side. If more than one Boolean condition evaluates to true, the corresponding expressions must evaluate to the same values.
- *Parallel assignment:* The syntax of the parallel assignment is $A_1 \| \ldots \| A_n$. When executing a parallel assignment, all right-hand sides are evaluated in parallel and assigned synchronously to the corresponding left-hand sides. Every possible assignment (enumerated, parallel, quantified) may be a component A_i of a parallel assignment.
- *Quantified assignment:* A quantified assignment is a special form of a parallel assignment. The syntax is $\langle \|i_1, \ldots, i_n : b(i_1, \ldots, i_n) :: A \rangle$. Here $b(\ldots)$ represents a Boolean function, which defines a predicate on the bound variables $i_1, \ldots, i_n$; the body A may be any possible assignment. An instance of $i_1, \ldots, i_n$ is a vector of their values that satisfies b. Execution is done by executing the body for every instance of bound variables in parallel. The predicate b may depend on values of program variables, which may change their values during run time.

---

[1] Here only the assign section of a UNITY program is of interest. The initial section may be seen as defining values, which are downloaded to the processors at the beginning of the execution. The always section is expanded into the assign section. This is described in [3].

- *Quantified statement list:* A further construct in UNITY is the quantified statement list, whose syntax is given by $\langle \Box i_1, \ldots, i_n : b(i_1, \ldots, i_n) :: S \rangle$. Here $b(i_1, \ldots, i_n)$ also represents a Boolean function as already described. But there is a major difference to the function b in a quantified assignment: The number of instances of the bound variables in a quantified statement list must not vary during run time. The body S represents a single statement or a list of statements. A quantified statement list is only a shorthand notation for a list of statements $S_1 \Box \ldots \Box S_k$, i.e., for every instance of the bound variables a single statement may be statically created.

A UNITY program is executed as follows. A statement from the assign section is nondeterministically selected and executed. After that, the next one is selected and executed, and so on. This execution algorithm has to obey the so-called *fairness* rule: every statement is executed infinitely often. A program may be seen as terminated if a fixed point is reached, i.e., execution of any statement does not alter the program state.

In UNITY there is no concept of control flow, and only the synchronous and asynchronous behaviors of a problem are specified, i.e., set of operations occurring at the same time and the operations occurring at distinct time points. In other words, UNITY specifies only what must be done, not where, when, or how it must be done.

3 THE METHOD FOR HARDWARE/SOFTWARE PARTITIONING: AN OVERVIEW

Partitioning a problem specification in parts that are adequate for hardware implementation or in parts exhibiting features for software implementation can be seen as the mapping of the problem specification on to a target architecture composed of software components (as, for example, DSP or RISC processors) and of hardware components, like ASIC or FPGAs, as shown in Fig. 1.

This mapping can be accomplished according to distinct criteria. In our work, we have considered the following set of criteria:

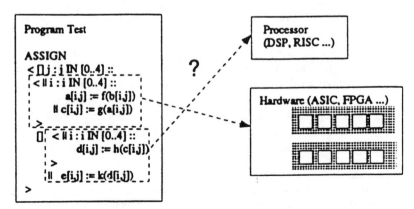

Fig. 1: Partitioning as a mapping problem

- Partitioning should improve the performance.
- Advantage should be taken of the reusability of hardware structures.
- The design constraints such as area, number of pins, and time must be fulfilled.

The first criterion refers to the profitability of the intrinsic parallelism of a synchronous behavior, and to the improvement of parallelism by implementing asynchronous statements as a pipeline. Of course, the overhead introduced by the communication protocol must be analyzed against the parallelism gain obtained by the pipeline.

The criterion reusability of hardware analyzes the possibility for implementing parts of the program exhibiting a similar behavior by using the same functional unit. With regard to this criterion, the designer may decide between a large and fast or small and slow circuit at a high level of abstraction.

Finally, design constraints such as area, number of pins, and time must be fulfilled for each part realized in hardware, as well as for the whole circuit.

The first two criteria can be investigated if the description language provides flexibility for analyzing different implementation alternatives. As mentioned in the previous section, UNITY supports the description of a problem at a very high level of abstraction with regard to its synchrony and asynchrony, as well as to its nondeterministic behavior. Due to these features we have chosen UNITY as our specification language.

Furthermore, UNITY is based on a single logic that permits formal verification. Although this feature of UNITY is not exploited in our work, this is a very rich and important field of research, particularly in the design of complex problems, where the verification by simulation is impracticable (or impossible).

3.1 Related Research

HW/SW partitioning is not a new problem. Although some research work in the 1970s addressed this problem [4], not much progress has appeared in recent years. Recently, with the advances in the integration technologies and with the development of tools for high-level synthesis, the development of approaches supporting HW/SW codesign has becoming more and more important, leading to an increase of research in this area.

An approach for designing embedded ASICs was described by Juntunen et al. [5], where the problem to be synthesized is described in RT-SA/SD, but the HW/SW partitioning has to be done manually.

Another approach has been developed by Gupta [6]. Here a hardware implementation of a specification in Hardware-C is supposed initially. The partitioning between hardware and software proceeds by shifting some kinds of constructs (delay independent constructs) to be implemented in software. The partitioning is analyzed according to the timing constraints given by the user.

Furthermore, the partitioning of behavioral descriptions for architectural synthesis of multichips has been investigated by a number of different researchers. APARTY [7] evaluates different partitions of a DAG description of the problem according to their data dependencies, control steps, and the performed operations. Others perform partitioning considering only a subset of such criteria.

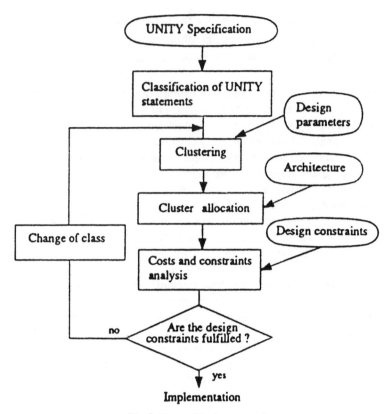

Fig. 2: The partitioning approach

Our work also uses clustering techniques, but the criteria guiding our clustering processes are different from the criteria used in the mentioned approaches. Starting from a specification at a high level of abstraction, where the intrinsic parallelism of the problem is described, we associate a set of implementation possibilities with each part of the problem with regard to its parallelism. After that, we partition a description according to the similarity among implementation alternatives and to the data dependencies. A mechanism for delivering the set of implementation alternatives associated with a description seems to be very useful for guiding hardware/software codesign, because the various implementation alternatives can be analyzed resulting in different partitioning possibilities.

3.2 The Partitioning Approach: An Overview

The main idea of our approach is illustrated in the block diagram shown in Fig. 2. First, the set of possible implementation alternatives is generated for each UNITY assignment. This phase has been called *classification of UNITY elements* and is explained in Section 5. The different implementation possibilities for an assignment have been defined as a set of class values, each of them corresponding to a distinct implementation alternative.

Taking a particular class value, i.e., a particular implementation alternative, as reference, the program is partitioned into a set of clusters. The clustering algorithm is essentially based on the improvement of performance and on the similarity among implementation alternatives. It is presented in Section 6.

The generated clusters are allocated, after that, into the target architecture, and the implementation costs are calculated. These costs are analyzed according to the design constraints. If the constraints are not fulfilled, the current classification of some elements may be changed, and the steps of clustering, allocation, and analysis are performed again, i.e., another implementation alternative will be analyzed. The whole process can be repeated until the constraints are fulfilled. As will be seen later, the designer may choose the default classification, which corresponds to the faster implementation alternative, or may choose a slower alternative for some elements if the constraints are not fulfilled.

4 EXPLAINING BY AN EXAMPLE

All phases of our clustering approach are explained by means of a common example—the design of a multivariable controller. Processes being controlled by a set of interrelated variables occur in a lot of real applications [8].

Our example is a classical multivariable process depicted in Fig. 3. A detailed description of this example can be found in [9]. The control of such a system can be made by the set of PIDs shown in Fig. 4. Decoupling the variables gives the equation for each PID controller in the frequency domain as listed in Fig. 4. More information about decoupling techniques can be found in [9].

The description of the behavior of a PID controller in the time domain is given by the following equation:

$$y(t) = y(t-1) + d_0 x_d(t) + d_1 x_d(t-1) + d_2(t-2)$$

with the constants

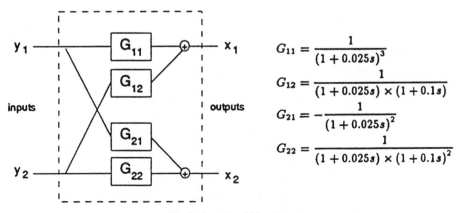

$$G_{11} = \frac{1}{(1+0.025s)^3}$$

$$G_{12} = \frac{1}{(1+0.025s) \times (1+0.1s)}$$

$$G_{21} = -\frac{1}{(1+0.025s)^2}$$

$$G_{22} = \frac{1}{(1+0.025s) \times (1+0.1s)^2}$$

Fig. 3: A multivariable process

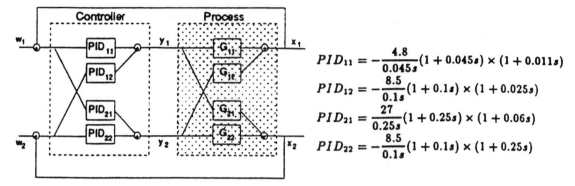

$$PID_{11} = -\frac{4.8}{0.045s}(1 + 0.045s) \times (1 + 0.011s)$$

$$PID_{12} = -\frac{8.5}{0.1s}(1 + 0.1s) \times (1 + 0.025s)$$

$$PID_{21} = \frac{27}{0.25s}(1 + 0.25s) \times (1 + 0.06s)$$

$$PID_{22} = -\frac{8.5}{0.1s}(1 + 0.1s) \times (1 + 0.25s)$$

Fig. 4: A multivariable controller

$$d_0 = k_p\left[1 + \left(\frac{t_a \times k_i}{k_p}\right) + \left(\frac{k_d}{t_a \times k_p}\right)\right], \qquad d_1 = k_p\left[-1 - \left(2\frac{k_d}{t_a \times k_p}\right)\right],$$

$$\text{and} \qquad d_2 = \frac{k_d}{t_a}$$

A UNITY description of the multivariable controller can be seen in Fig. 5.

5 CHOOSING AN IMPLEMENTATION ALTERNATIVE

Due to the high abstraction level of a problem description in UNITY, where the specification is composed of parts exhibiting distinct degrees of parallelism, we can implement it regarding different implementation alternatives by varying the parallelism grain or by sharing the same functional unit among parts.

The various possibilities associated with a problem description can be better visualized in Fig. 6, where the possible alternatives of some parts of the description, presented in the previous section, are depicted.

Consider, first, the quantified assignment containing the assignment e_7 in Fig. 6. The quantification is a set of synchronous assignments, one for each instance of the bound variables. The synchrony of the assignments means that all assignments occur at the same time. It does not dictate, however, how these should be performed, but establishes only the data dependencies inside the quantification.

By varying the degree of parallelism when performing the assignments above we can have different implementation alternatives, as shown in Fig. 6. The first alternative denotes an implementation completely sequential where the set of assignments are executed sequentially inside a loop for each value of i and j. The second alternative comprises an implementation partially parallel where the assignments are performed sequentially for the variable j and in parallel for the variable i. The third alternative comprises an implementation completely parallel where four functional units run in parallel, each of them performing the assignment for one value of i and j.

The designer may, furthermore, share the same functional unit among some parts of the description. This possibility can be seen in Fig. 6, where the two mutually exclusive

---

Program MultiController
Declare ...
Always
$\quad ta = 0.5 \quad ti = 0.1$

$\quad d0[1, 1] = kp[1, 1]\left(1 + \dfrac{ki[1, 1]}{kp[1, 1]}\right) + \left(\dfrac{kd[1, 1]}{[ta \times kp[1, 1]]}\right) \cdots$

$\quad d1[1, 1] = kp[1, 1]\left(-1 - 2 \times \dfrac{kd[1, 1]}{ta \times kp[1, 1]}\right) \cdots$

$\quad d2[1, 1] = \dfrac{kd[1, 1]}{ta} \cdots$

Assign
$\quad\quad t, cnt := t + 0.1, cnt + 0.1 \quad IF\ cnt < ta$ $\hfill (e_1)$
$\quad\quad\quad\quad \sim t + 0.1, ti \quad IF\ cnt = ta$ $\hfill (e_2)$
$\quad \|\ << \|n : nIN[0, 2] ::$
$\quad\quad \|x_d[n, 3] := x + d[n, 3] \quad IF\ cnt \neq ta$ $\hfill (e_3)$
$\quad\quad\quad\quad \sim w - x[n] \quad IF\ cnt = ta$ $\hfill (e_4)$
$\quad\quad \|\ << \|i : i\ IN\ [1, 2]\ with\ cnt = ta ::$
$\quad\quad\quad\quad x_d[n, i] := x_d[n, i + 1]$ $\hfill (e_5)$
$\quad\quad\quad >>$
$\quad\quad >>$
$\Box\ << \|i, j : i\ IN\ [1, 2]\ and\ j\ IN\ [1, 2]\ with\ cnt = ti ::$
$\quad\quad p[i, j, 3] := p[i, j, 2] + d0[i, j]x_d[j, 3] + d1[i, j]x_d[j, 2] + d2[i, j]x_d[j, 1]$ $\hfill (e_6)$
$\quad \|\ << \|k : k\ IN\ [1, 2] ::$
$\quad\quad\quad p[i, j, k] := p[i, j, k + 1]$ $\hfill (e_7)$
$\quad\quad >>$
$\quad >>$
$\|\ << \|n : n\ IN\ [1, 2]\ with\ cnt = ti + 0.1 ::$
$\quad\quad y[n] := p[n, 1, 3] + p[n, 2, 3]$ $\hfill (e_8)$
$\quad >>$
End

Fig. 5: Program UNITY

assignments e_1 and e_2 share the same functional unit. In the second alternative shown in the same figure, the assignments e_1 and e_2 are running on distinct functional units. This alternative can be very advantageous since it can lead to a performance improvement by evaluating the conditions of both assignments in parallel.

The analysis of some implementation alternatives involves first the determination of all possible implementation alternatives associated with each part of the problem description. This will be presented in the next section. After that, the current implementation alternative must be chosen by the designer or must be established by the system, as it will be explained in Section 5.2. Also in Section 5.2, we present how some design parameters controlling the allocation to the CPU, and the sharing of resources among asynchronous statements, should be set by the designer.

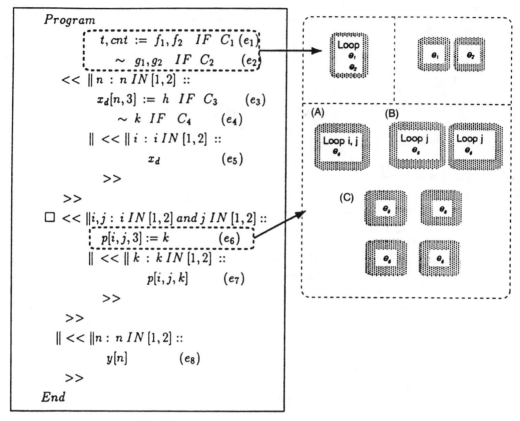

Fig. 6: Example of possible implementation alternatives

5.1 Determining Different Implementation Alternatives for UNITY Elements

This phase can also be called *element characterization* or *type analysis*, since each element is characterized by a set of implementation alternatives or a type is assigned to each element. The type consists of all possibilities for implementing the element. An *element* constitutes our partitioning unit and is given by an enumerated assignment, each assignment inside a mutually exclusive or each element in the body of a quantified assignment.

5.1.1 Features of UNITY Elements

With regard to the high level of abstraction exhibited by a UNITY specification and to the criteria for partitioning a problem in hardware and software, the following features of a UNITY specification should be analyzed in order to support hardware/software partitioning:

- Data dependency among asynchronous elements
- Parallelism

- Mutual exclusion
- Multiplicity.

The analysis of data dependencies among asynchronous elements supports the discovery of situations where a pipelining implementation can be applied. The implementation of asynchronous elements as a pipeline can improve performance. Discovering situations suitable for a pipelining implementation can dictate, furthermore, which parts of the problem should be implemented in hardware and which in software in order to guarantee a balanced workload. If a pipelining implementation is not possible, the sharing of the same functional unit among asynchronous elements can lead to a decrease of area without a time penalty. This can lead to a better trade-off between area and delay.

When analyzing the parallelism exhibited by each part of the specification, we can distinguish two kinds of parallelism: inside a parallel assignment and inside a quantified assignment. Analyzing these two kinds of parallelism separately is very helpful because it permits the analysis of the various alternatives that exploit all possibilities of parallelism.

For each kind of parallelism, the data dependencies among parallel elements are analyzed. Data dependencies, in this case, represent additional synchronization costs, when the related elements are implemented separately. Some synchronization is needed in order to assure that the elements are executed properly.

A third feature to be considered is the occurrence of mutually exclusive assignments. Elements belonging to mutually exclusive assignments can have their conditions evaluated in parallel since only one condition may be true. Exploiting this feature can improve the performance.

Finally, we must consider the multiplicity of an element. By *multiplicity* we mean the degree of parallelism exhibited by the element. In UNITY we can have simple or multiple assignments. Detecting the occurrence of multiple assignments can guide the hardware/software partitioning process, since multiple assignments can be considered good candidates to be implemented in a superscalar RISC processor, i.e., in software.

5.1.2 Characterizing Distinct Implementation Alternatives

The goals of the characterization phase are twofold:

- To detect the mentioned features of each element such as data dependency, parallelism, mutual exclusion, and multiplicity.
- To represent the set of implementation alternatives for each element considering the features above.

In order to achieve these goals we have defined a mechanism for type analysis that is given by the quadruple $C = (O, A, V, f)$ where O is the set of UNITY elements, A the set of attributes to be analyzed for each element, and V the set of attribute values. Each attribute value is given by a set of class values. Each class value represents a particular implementation alternative. The set of values for an attribute k, $k \in V$ is given by V_k, where $V_k \subset V$.

The set of characterization functions is given by f. For the attribute k, $k \in V$ the characterization function is given by $f_k : O \rightarrow V_k$, where $f_k \subset f$. This function assigns a set of class values to each element with regard to the attribute k.

TABLE 1: Subvalues Set for the Attribute Asynchronous Relationship

Class Values	Description
client/sequential	The element consumes (reads) variables produced (written) by other asynchronous element(s).
server/sequential	The element produces (writes) variables to be consumed (read) by other asynchronous element(s).
clientserver/sequential	The element produces (writes) variables for other asynchronous element(s) and consumes (reads) variables produced (written) by other asynchronous element(s).
independent/sequential	There is no data dependency between the elements and all other asynchronous elements.
sequential	There is only one statement or only one quantification of statements. Asynchronous relationship does not exist.

In the case of p attributes, each element is characterized by the attribute vector given by

$$f(e) = \begin{bmatrix} f_1(e) \\ f_2(e) \\ \cdots \\ f_p(e) \end{bmatrix} \tag{1}$$

The set of n objects is characterized by the matrix $n \times p$ given by

$$V = [f_k(e)]_{n,p} = \begin{bmatrix} f_1(e_1) & f_2(e_1) & \cdots & f_p(e_1) \\ f_2(e_2) & f_2(e_2) & \cdots & f_p(e_2) \\ \cdots & \cdots & \cdots & \cdots \\ f_1(e_n) & f_2(e_n) & \cdots & f_p(e_n) \end{bmatrix} \tag{2}$$

Each row corresponds to the measurements of all attributes for a given element and each column, the values of one attribute for all elements.

Taking into account all criteria mentioned previously, we have defined five attributes to be analyzed in the characterization phase:

- Asynchronous Relationship (AR)
- Synchronism Inside Parallel Assignment (SIPA)
- Synchronism Inside Quantified Assignment (SIQA)
- Mutual Exclusion (ME)
- Multiplicity (Mp)

An informal description of all attributes is given next. A formal description of the characterization functions can be found in [10].

ASYNCHRONOUS RELATIONSHIP—AR. This attribute investigates data dependencies among asynchronous elements, i.e., among elements belonging to distinct asynchronous statements. Depending on the kind of dependency, this attribute is set with one of the set of class values listed in Table 1.

The first class value (default value) represents a pipelining or parallel implementation of the element with respect to other asynchronous elements. The second class value is a

TABLE 2: Subvalues Set for the Attribute Synchronism Inside Parallel Assignment

Class Values	Description
client/sequential	The element consumes (reads) one or more variables that are produced (written) by other synchronous element(s) belonging to the same parallel assignment.
server/sequential	The element produces (writes) one or more variables that are at the same time consumed (read) by other synchronous element(s) belonging to the same parallel assignment.
clientserver/sequential	The element produces (writes) and/or consumes (reads) one or more variables that are consumed (read) and/or produced (written) for other synchronous element(s) belonging to the same parallel assignment.
independent/sequential	The set of common variables consumed and/or produced by the element with respect to all other elements belonging to the parallel assignment is empty.
notype	The element does not belong to any parallel assignment.

sequential implementation of them. For a UNITY program containing a single statement the value of this attribute is always equal to sequential.

As mentioned previously, investigating data dependencies among asynchronous elements is very helpful in the partitioning process since we can cluster asynchronous data dependent elements separately for a later analysis about their implementation as a pipeline.

SYNCHRONISM INSIDE PARALLEL ASSIGNMENT—SIPA.   The purpose of this attribute is to investigate the data dependencies among elements belonging to the same parallel assignment. A data dependency here means that there is one or more common variables being consumed and/or produced by two or more elements. According to the possible kinds of dependencies, a related set of class values is assigned to this attribute by the characterization function, as depicted in Table 2. The first class value is considered a default and denotes a parallel implementation. The second one can be chosen by the designer if he or she wants to analyze a sequential implementation.

As mentioned, the SIPA attribute permits us to investigate whether synchronous elements belonging to the same parallel assignment use and/or consume common variables. This kind of information is very useful in the clustering process since the separation of synchronous elements producing and/or consuming common variables can lead to an increase of communications cost. A synchronization protocol is needed, in this case, for guaranteeing that the synchronous statements are performed properly, i.e., any common variable may be written only after it was read for all other synchronous statements.

SYNCHRONISM INSIDE QUANTIFIED ASSIGNMENT—SIQA.   The objectives of this attribute are twofold:

- To detect the occurrence of a quantified assignment and to list all possible implementation alternatives for this kind of assignment by varying its degree of parallelism.
- To investigate the data dependencies[2] among assignments belonging to the body of a quantified assignment.

---

[2] Here the data dependencies have the same meaning as in the case of a parallel assignment. They denote that the set of common used and defined variables among parallel assignments is not empty.

According to the size of the body (i.e., only one assignment or more than one assignment), and to the kind of data dependencies an element can have, one of the set of class values shown in Table 3 is assigned to this attribute.

The first class value (default value) denotes a parallel implementation of the quantification; i.e., for each index a processing unit is allocated for each element belonging to the quantification. The second class value is a family of class values, each of them representing an implementation alternative with a particular degree of parallelism. A quantified assignment can be serialized at the assignment level and/or at the quantification level. In the first case, all statements are performed sequentially using the same hardware structure that is repeated for each instance of the bounds variables. In the second case, the related assignments are performed in parallel, each of them as a sequential loop implementing the quantification.

In order to support the representation of all possible cases, a list of flags is appended to each class value belonging to a pipe family. For each index of the quantification there are two flags, *Assignment* and *Quantification*. The first flag states the serialization at the assignment level. The value *true* means a serial implementation, whereas the value *false* denotes a parallel one. The second flag establishes a sequential implementation at the quantification level. When this flag is *true,* the quantification is implemented sequentially, otherwise it is implemented in parallel. These two kinds of serializations can be combined, providing a lot of flexibility for the designer for analyzing different implementation possibilities with distinct degrees of parallelism.

The analysis of the attribute *SIQA* is very helpful in supporting hardware/software partitioning. The detection of data dependencies among elements belonging to the same quantified assignment can lead to a decrease of the synchronization costs by putting such elements in the same cluster. Furthermore, the flexibility for analyzing implementation alternatives with different degrees of parallelism supports the reusability of hardware structures since parts of a quantification or quantifications exhibiting the same degree of parallelism and behavior can be allocated in the same functional unit. This feature can lead to an optimal trade-off between area and delay.

MUTUAL EXCLUSION—ME. With this attribute we attempt to detect mutual exclusions between elements. Discovering such situations can lead to an improvement of performance, since the conditions of all elements belonging to the same mutually exclusive assignment can be evaluated in parallel. Furthermore, the designer has the flexibility for choosing between a parallel or a sequential evaluation of mutually exclusive conditions. This flexibility can support the finding of a good area/time trade-off by evaluating in parallel time-consuming conditions and sequential conditions, which are not too time consuming.

The attribute *Mutual Exclusion* can have one of the following set of values listed in Table 4.

MULTIPLICITY—Mp. The purpose of this attribute is to distinguish simple enumerated assignments from multiple ones. This kind of analysis can be very helpful to HW/SW partitioning since it permits the detection of elements that are suitable for implementation in a superscalar processor, namely, some multiple assignments.

A multiple assignment is composed of two or more assignments that are performed in parallel. Usually, these assignments are not very complex, and are given by some

TABLE 3: Subvalues Set for the Attribute Synchronism Inside Quantified Assignment

Class Values	Description
vector/*pipeline*_{list of bound vars}/*sequential*	The element is the unique element belonging to a quantified assignment.
clientvector/*clientpipe*_{list of bound vars}/*sequential*	The element belongs to a quantified assignment composed of more than one element, and it consumes (reads) one or more variables that are produced (written) by other element(s) belonging to the body of the same quantified assignment.
servervector/*serverpipe*_{list of bound vars}/*sequential*	The element belongs to a quantified assignment of those bodies consisting of more assignments, and it produces (writes) one or more variables that are consumed(read) by other element(s) belonging to the same quantified assignment.
clientservervector/*clientserverpipe*_{list of bound vars}/*sequential*	The element of a quantified assignment composed of more than one assignment produces (writes) and/or consumes (reads) one or more variables that are consumed (read) and/or produced (written) for the other element(s) belonging to the same quantified assignment.
independentvector/*independentpipe*_{list of bound vars}/*sequential*	The set of common variables consumed and/or produced by the element belonging to a quantified assignment composed of more than one assignment with respect to all other elements belonging to the same body is empty.
notype	The element does not belong to any quantified assignment.

TABLE 4: Set of Subvalues for the Attribute Mutual Exclusion

Class Values	Description
mutual/sequential	The element belongs to a mutually exclusive enumerated assignment and constitutes the first part of this.
exclusive/sequential	The element belongs to a mutually exclusive enumerate assignment and does not constitute the first assignment.
notype	The element does not belong to any mutually exclusive assignment.

arithmetic expressions under a common condition (see Fig. 6). Such assignments are very suitable for implementation into a superscalar processor since the evaluation of the right-hand side and the condition can be made in a single clock cycle.

Detecting this kind of statement and allocating it in a superscalar processor, i.e., in the RISC processor, can improve the performance without additional cost on area, thereby permitting good resource utilization.

The possible values for the attribute of *complexity* for a UNITY element are given in Table 5.

This attribute also permits the designer to analyze the implementation of multiple enumerated assignments, sequentially providing more flexibility in analyzing different implementation alternatives with distinct degrees of parallelism. The implementation possibilities for our example depicted in Figure 6 are listed in Table 6.

5.2 Choosing a Particular Implementation Alternative and Setting Design Parameters

As mentioned in Section 3, the partitioning process is guided by some parameters, which must be set by the user. These parameters include the following:

- *CPUAllocationWay* and *CPUCandidate:* Some elements may be allocated in the control unit, our software component, before the clustering process is carried out.

   The allocation of an element e_i in the CU can be made automatically or can be guided by the user. In the first case, elements exhibiting features for a software implementation are allocated automatically. In the second case, the user can decide which elements may be considered as *CU candidates* and which not.

   If one element should be allocated this is marked as a *CU candidate*. The reader must observe that several elements can be marked as *CU candidate*, but not all elements will be necessarily allocated in the control unit.

   The main features of an element to be considered as a *CU candidate* are its degree of parallelism, its multiplicity, and its area and delay.

TABLE 5: Set of Subvalues for the Attribute Multiplicity

Class Values	Description
simple	The element belongs to a simple enumerated assignment.
multiple/sequential	The element belongs to a multiple enumerated assignment.

TABLE 6: The Implementation Alternatives for Our Example

Elements	AR	SIPA	SIQA	ME	Mp
e_1	*server/ sequential*	*server/ sequential*	—	*mutual/ sequential*	*multiple/ sequential*
e_2	*server/ sequential*	*server/ sequential*	—	*exclusive/ sequential*	*multiple/ sequential*
e_3	*server/ sequential*	*client/ sequential*	*servervector/ serverpipe/ sequential*	*mutual/ sequential*	*simple*
e_4	*server/ sequential*	*client/ sequential*	*servervector/ serverpipe/ sequential*	*exclusive/ sequential*	*simple*
e_5	*server/ sequential*	*client/ sequential*	*clientvector/ clientpipe/ sequential*	—	*simple*
e_6	*client/ sequential*	*server/ sequential*	*servervector/ serverpipe/ sequential*	—	*simple*
e_6					
e_7	*client/ sequential*	*independent/ sequential*	*clientservervector/ clientserverpipe/ sequential*	—	*simple*
e_8	*client/ sequential*	*client/ sequential*	*vector/ pipeline/ sequential*	—	*simple*

The first parameter is a variable specifying whether the CPU allocation should be made during the clustering process or not. In a positive case, how to specify the elements to be allocated in the CPU, automatically or manually. In the second case, the flag *CPUCandidate* must be set by the designer for each element suitable for a CPU allocation.

- *ClassChange, ModifiedAttribute and NewClass:* Set of variables controlling the establishment of the current implementation alternative to be taken as reference in the clustering process.

The current implementation alternative taken as reference in the partitioning process may be determined by the user or may be a default alternative, established automatically. The default values are alternatives exhibiting the highest degree of parallelism, which generate the fastest implementation.

6 THE CLUSTERING ALGORITHM

In order to guide the clustering algorithm, a set of criteria has been defined, which are listed next. These can be seen as a refinement of the general criteria for hardware/software partitioning mentioned in Section 3:

- Similarity among assignments
- Data dependency

- Improvement of parallelism
- Minimization of additional costs.[2a]

The similarity among assignments measures the similarity among kinds of assignments and among their implementation alternatives, i.e., their current implementation alternative. With this criterion, we can keep together elements being performed on the same functional unit, for example. In order establish a similarity scale among the distinct kinds of assignments and among the distinct implementation alternatives, we have defined a metric, which is defined in Section 6.1.

The data dependencies among elements is another important criterion. The occurrence of a data dependency exhibits distinct effects depending on the kind of assignment. In the case of two synchronous elements, a data dependency among them means that the elements should be made close to each other. For two asynchronous elements, however, a data dependency among them means the elements need to be kept separate.

The improvement of parallelism analyzes the possibility to use the concept of a pipelining when implementing asynchronous elements. Using the pipelining concept, however, is associated with additional costs, particularly communications costs. With the criterion of minimization of additional costs, we investigate the obtained pipeline speedup.

In order to group elements according to these criteria, our partitioning approach uses a unique multistage clustering technique. Multistage clustering is based on an established clustering algorithm and has been used for data path design and architectural partitioning [7].

An overview of the various stages of our clustering algorithm can be seen in Fig. 7. In the first stage, the clustering tree is built according to the similarity among assignments. In Section 6.1, the measurement of the similarity among elements regarding their implementation alternatives is described in detail. After the similarity has been measured, the cluster tree is built by using a hierarchical clustering algorithm [11]. The cost function guiding the placement of the cut line at the clustering tree is given in Section 6.2.

In the second stage, the clustering tree is built by considering basically the effectiveness of a pipelining implementation. The closeness function measuring the distance among elements according to the possibility of their implementation as a pipeline is given in Section 6.3. The placement of the cut line has been guided by the cost function presented in Section 6.4.

6.1 Building the Cluster Tree at Stage One: Measuring the Similarity Among Implementation Alternatives

In the first phase of the clustering algorithm, the elements are clustered according to the similarity among their implementation alternatives. For this purpose, a distance matrix including the closeness value for each pair of elements according to their similarity has been generated. The definition of a distance function measuring the closeness between

---

[2a] Additional costs include communication and synchonization costs. In a new version of this work the minimization of area and delay is also considered in the clustering process [10].

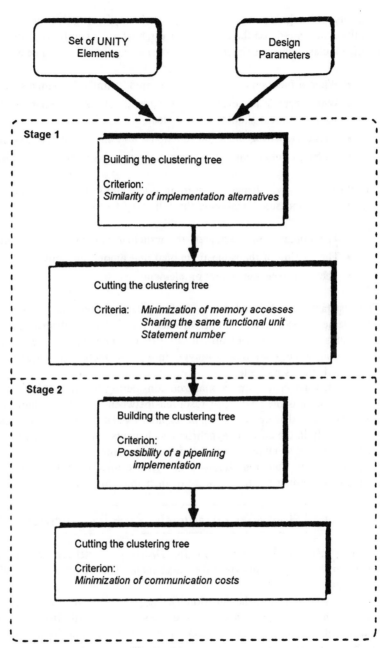

Fig. 7: Our clustering approach

elements with regard to the similarity of their implementation alternatives supposes the definition of a metric on the class values establishing a similarity scale among them. The metric on class values has been defined considering the following heuristics as guidelines:

- When a functional unit has been shared, "similar"[3] elements should be close.
- When there is no reusability of hardware structures, elements belonging to the same statement should be very close.
- Elements sharing the same functional unit should be kept together.
- Elements belonging to the same quantified assignment should be close.

The closeness of two elements according to the similarity of their implementation alternatives can be measured analyzing the following factors:

- The similarity of the degree of parallelism exhibited by the elements
- The sharing of the same functional unit among elements
- The data dependency among elements.

The first factor can be analyzed considering how similar the assignment types[4] are for both elements. Moreover, the current class value of each attribute must be considered. The analysis of the similarity among forms of assignments can be easily done considering the set of attributes classified as notype. In the next section, a function that measures this similarity factor is presented.

The second factor can be analyzed considering the current class value for each attribute, as well as the sharing of resources between the related elements. As mentioned previously, this sharing can be made explicit by the classification or can be performed automatically in the case of asynchronous elements exhibiting a "similar" degree of parallelism and not suitable for a pipelining implementation.

The distance function $D_{\text{similarity}}(e_1, e_2)$ measures the distance between the elements e_1 and e_2 according to the similarity of their implementation alternative.

$$D_{\text{similarity}}(e_1, e_2) = D_{\text{form}}(e_1, e_2) + D_{\text{attribute}}(e_1, e_2) \quad (3)$$

The first factor in Eq. (3), the function $D_{\text{form}}(e_1, e_2)$ delivers the closeness value with regard to the assignment type of each element. This function is explained in the next paragraph.

The second factor, the function $D_{\text{attribute}}(e_1, e_2)$ gives the distance value between the elements e_1 and e_2 concerning the class value for all attributes whose class value is different from *notype*. The consideration of only such attribute is due to the fact that attributes classified as *notype* have been already regarded in the function $D_{\text{form}}(e_1, e_2)$.

---

[3] In the first heuristic, with "similar elements" we mean elements belonging to the same kind or to analogous kinds of assignments.

[4] With "assignment type of an element" we refer to whether the element is an enumerate assignment, or pertains to a mutually exclusive or quantified assignment, or is part of a quantified statement list.

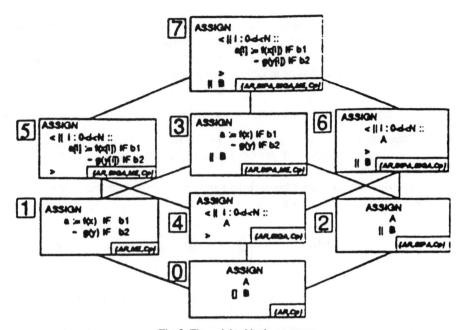

Fig. 8: The weighted lattice structure

The function $D_{\text{attribute}}(e_1, e_2)$ is given by Eq. (4), where $D_k(e_1, e_2)$ denotes a function that measures the distance between two elements e_1 and e_2 concerning the attribute k:

$$D_{\text{attribute}}(e_1, e_2) = \sum_{\substack{k \in \text{AR,SIPA,SIQA,ME,Mp} \\ \text{class value of } k \neq \text{notype}}} D_k(e_1, e_2) \qquad (4)$$

For reasons of space limitation, only the distance function regarding the attribute *asynchronous relationship* is presented in this work. The distance functions for others attributes are based on the same concept and can be found in [10].

6.1.1 Measuring the Similarity of Elements Concerning Their Assignment Type

The statement form of an element has been represented by the set of its attributes whose class value is different of *notype*. This feature is considered as an attribute or characteristic of the element, here, called a *statement form.*

Due to the subset relationship among forms of statements, they have been organized as a lattice structure that denotes a suitable representation for this kind of data [12]. The lattice structure has been represented by a graph where each node denotes an attribute value and an edge, the maximum subset relationship among two nodes.

The lattice representing the values for the attribute Statement Form is depicted in Fig. 8. Each node represented as a rectangle includes the corresponding statement form given as a short UNITY description. Furthermore, the set of valid attributes for each form can be seen in the right corner.

In general, the closeness between objects whose attribute k exhibits features of a lattice can be established using a lattice oriented scale function $f_{\text{scale}K} : A_k \rightarrow R$.

Considering the heuristics mentioned in Section 6.1, the scale of similarity among forms of statements has been defined according to the following order among statements forms:

assignment > mutual exclusive assign. > parallel assign. > quantified assign.

According to this order, as well as to the rule for a lattice [12], the scale function $f_{\text{scaleFORM}} : V_{\text{FORM}} \rightarrow R$ has been defined, resulting in the weighted lattice structure depicted in Fig. 8.

The distance among two objects i and j regarding an attribute k structured as a lattice is given, in general, by Eq. (5):

$$d_k(i, j) = \min \left\{ \sum_{\mu=1}^{h} |f_{\text{scale}K}(a_{s_{\mu=1}k}) - f_{\text{scale}K}(a_{s_\mu k})| : \right.$$

$$\left. (a_{s_0 k}, \ldots, a_{s_h k}) \text{ is set of edges between } a_{ik} \text{ and } a_{jk} \right\} \tag{5}$$

The sequence of edges with minimum distance value is given by $(a_{ik}, a_{ik} \cup a_{jk}, a_{jk})$ or by $(a_{ik}, a_{ik} \cap a_{jk}, a jk)$. The distance function can be, in this case, simplified, and is given by Eq. (6) [12]:

$$d_k(i, j) = | f_{\text{scale}K}(a_{ik} \cup a_{jk}) - f_{\text{scale}K}(a_{ik} \cap a_{jk}| \tag{6}$$

where a_{ik} a_{ik} are the attribute values for the objects I and j, respectively [10].

The distance function D_{form} between elements with regard to their assignment forms is given by Eq. (7). The function $d_{\text{form}}(e_1, e_2)$ results in closeness values, according to the distance function for a lattice, given by Eq. (6). This kind of closeness is only considered when there is no sharing of resources. In this case, constant values are added for each attribute whose class value is different of *notype*. Distinct constant values have been considered in order to guarantee a smaller closeness value for elements belonging to the same statement.

$D_{\text{form}}(e_i, e_j) =$

$$\begin{cases} d_{\text{form}}(e_i, e_j) + \displaystyle\sum_{k=notype^5} ctemax & \text{if (not SharingHW}^6(e_i, e_j) \wedge \text{SN}^7(e_i) \neq \text{SN}(e_j)) \\ d_{\text{form}}(e_i, e_j) + \displaystyle\sum_{k=notype} ctedist & \text{if (not SharingHW}(e_i, e_j) \wedge \text{SN}(e_i) = \text{SN}(e_j)) \\ 0 & \text{if SharingHW}(e_i, e_j) \end{cases} \tag{7}$$

---

[5] For all attribute $k \in \{AR, SIPA, SIQA, ME, Mp\}$ so that $f_K(e_i)$ or $f_K(e_2) = notype$.

[6] SharingHW(e_1, e_2) returns true if both elements are sharing the same functional unit.

[7] SN(e_1) yields the statement number of an element.

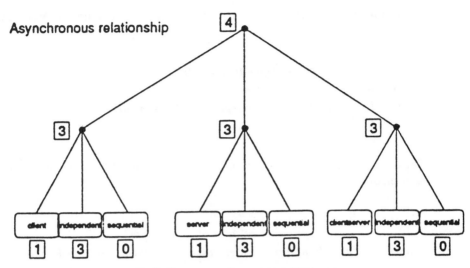

Fig. 9: The corresponding weighted AR hierarchy

In the case of resource sharing, the sum of a constant value for each nonvalid attribute is returning, guaranteeing a smaller closeness value for elements sharing the same resource.

6.1.2 Measuring the Similarity Between Elements Regarding the Attribute: *Asynchronous Relationship*—AR

The aim in analyzing the set of UNITY elements with regard to this attribute is to investigate the data dependencies among asynchronous elements for supporting the improvement of performance by using the pipeline concept.
In order to analyze the feasibility of a pipelining implementation, asynchronous elements should be kept separate in the clustering process. For this purpose we have defined some heuristics guiding the definition of the metric on class values and the distance function:

- Assignments sharing the same functional unit must be kept together, i.e., should be made very close.
- Asynchronous data-dependent elements running on distinct functional units should be kept separated.

According to these heuristics we can observe that some class values can be considered nearer to some than to others. This feature of class values has been captured in the distance function organizing the class values as a quasihierarchical structure, as shown in Fig. 9.

Structuring the values of an attribute as a hierarchy or a quasihierarchy denotes a well-known approach in the numerical taxonomy [12]. In this case, more similar values are grouped to form a subgroup. This subgroup is identified by a *generic* class. Some generic classes can be grouped again, building another generic class and so on. This process is repeated until only one generic class is obtained.

For the attribute asynchronous relationship we have the following Meta classes and their related class values:

- $AR_{1.1} = \{client, independent, sequential\}$
- $AR_{1.2} = \{server, independent, sequential\}$
- $AR_{1.3} = \{clientserver, independent, sequential\}$
- $AR_{2.1} = \{AR_{1.1}, AR_{1.2}, AR_{1.3}\}$

The extended set of distinct class values for the attribute AR including the generic classes is given by

$$C^*_{AR} =$$

$$\{client, server, clientserver, independent, sequential, AR_{1.1}, AR_{1.2}, AR_{1.3}, AR_{2.1}\}$$

In general, elements of a hierarchy on an extended set of values for the attribute k, A^*_k, must satisfy the following relationship:

$$\forall\ a_{ik}, a_{jk} \in A^*_k :$$

$$a_{ik} \underset{\neq}{\subseteq} a_{jk} \Leftrightarrow \begin{cases} a_{jk} \in a_{ik} \\ a_{ik} \supset a_{jk} \end{cases} \tag{8}$$

where a_{ik} and a_{jk} are the attribute values for the elements i and j, respectively.

A metric on the set A^*_k can be defined by a scale function $f_{\text{scale}K} : A^*_k \to R$ assigning a scale value to each node of the hierarchy. This function must satisfy the following rule for a hierarchy or quasihierarchy:

$$f_{\text{scale}K} : A^*_k \to R_+ ::$$

$$\forall\ a_{ik}, a_{jk} \in A^*_k : a_{ik} \underset{\neq}{\subseteq} a_{jk} \Rightarrow f_K(a_{ik}) \leq f_K(a_{jk}) \tag{9}$$

The distance function between objects i and j regarding the attribute k is given by:

$$d_k(i, j) = \begin{cases} \min\{f_{\text{scale}K}(a_{hk}) : \forall\ a_{hk} \in A_k \text{ with } a_{ik}, a_{jk} \subset a_{hk} & \text{if } a_{ik} \neq a_{jk} \\ f_{\text{scale}K}(a_{ik}) & \text{if } a_{ik} = a_{jk} \end{cases} \tag{10}$$

Coming back to the quasihierarchical structure for the attribute asynchronous relationship, it is necessary to define some rules among the distance between class values, so that the heuristics defined previously remain valid. Consider $d_{\text{classAR}}(c_i, c_j)$ as being the distance between two class values. The quasihierarchy must be weighted, so that the function d_{classAR} can satisfy the following rules:

- $\forall v_i \in V_{AR} \vee v_i \in \{client, server, clientserver\}$:
  $d_{classAR}(v_i, sequential) \leq d_{classAR}(v_i, independent)$
- $\forall v_1, v_2 \in V_{AR} \vee v_1, v_2 \in \{client, server, clientserver\}$ with $v_1 \neq v_2$:
  $d_{classAR}(v_1, independent) < d_{classAR}(v_1, v_2)$
- $\forall v_1 \in V_{AR} \vee v_1 \in \{sequential\} : d_{classAR}(v_1, v_1) = 0$
- $\forall v_1, v_2 \in V_{AR} \vee v_1 \in \{independent, clientserver\} \vee v_2 \in \{client, server\}$:
  $d_{classAR}(v_1, v_1) < d_{classAR}(v_2, v_2) \neq 0$

These rules can be fulfilled weighting each node of the quasihierarchy as depicted in Fig. 9.

This weighting function guarantees the maximum distance for two class values representing a data dependency. Furthermore, class values representing the use of a common functional unit are the closest class values.

Satisfying such rules does not guarantee, however, that the mentioned heuristics are preserved. We must make sure that the elements being analyzed are indeed data dependent and asynchronous.

The function measuring the distance between two elements with respect the attribute asynchronous relationship is given as

$$D_{AR}(e_1, e_2) =$$

$$\begin{cases} ctedist & \text{if } SN(e_1) = SN(e_2) \wedge \text{not } ME(e_1, e_2)) \vee \\ & (ME(e_1, e_2) \wedge SharingHW(e_1, e_2)) \\ 0 & \text{if } (ME(e_1, e_2) \wedge \text{not } SharingHW(e_1, e_2)) \\ d_{hierarchyAR}(e_1, e_2) \times f_{correction}(e_1, e_2) & \text{if } SN(e_1) \neq SN(e_2) \end{cases}$$

$$(11)$$

The distance function analyzes, first, whether the elements being analyzed are asynchronous or not. This is done by investigating whether the statement numbers of the elements, given by the function $SN(e)$, are equal or not. In the case of asynchronous elements, i.e., elements belonging to distinct statements, the distance is given multiplying two factors. The first factor $d_{hierarchyAR}$ measures the distance of two class values according to the quasihierarchical structure shown in Fig. 9. The second factor $f_{correctionAR}$ investigates the data dependency among elements, correcting the distance value according to the case.

The distance of two elements according to the hierarchical organization of their classification for the attribute asynchronous relationship is given in Eq. (12). The value AR_i denotes a generic class of the attribute asynchronous relationship and C_{AR}^*, its extended set of class values. The function $CurClass_{AR}$ delivers the current classification of the element e_1 with respect to the attribute asynchronous relationship, the function $f_{scaleAR}$ assigns a weight for each class value according to the hierarchical structure presented in Fig. 9.

TABLE 7: The Current Implementation Alternative

Elements	AR	SIPA	SIQA	ME	Mp
e_1	*server*	*server*	—	*sequential*	*multiple*
e_2	*server*	*server*	—	*sequential*	*multiple*
e_3	*server*	*client*	*servervector*	*mutual*	*simple*
e_4	*server*	*client*	*servervector*	*exclusive*	*simple*
e_5	*server*	*client*	*clientvector*	—	*simple*
e_6	*client*	*server*	*clientservervector*	—	*simple*
e_7	*client*	*independent*	*clientservervector*	—	*simple*
e_8	*independent*	*client*	*vector*	—	*simple*

$$d_{\text{hierarchyAR}}(e_1, e_2) = \begin{cases} \min\{f_{\text{scaleAR}}(\text{AR}_i): & \text{if } \text{CurClass}_{\text{AR}}(e_1) \neq \text{CurClass}_{\text{AR}}(e_2) \\ \quad \forall \ \text{AR}_i \in C^*_{\text{AR}} \text{ with} \\ \quad \text{CurClass}_{\text{AR}}(e_1), \\ \quad \text{CurClass}_{\text{AR}}(e_2) \subsetneq \text{AR}_i\} \\ f_{\text{scaleAR}}(\text{CurClass}_{\text{AR}}(e_1)) & \text{if } \text{CurClass}_{\text{AR}}(e_1) = \text{CurClass}_{\text{AR}}(e_2) \end{cases}$$

$$(12)$$

The function $f_{\text{correctionAR}}$ investigates the data dependency between elements. This factor is given by Eq. (13). The function DataDep returns the data dependency between two elements, resulting in *nodep* if there is no dependency and the kind of dependency, otherwise.

$$f_{\text{correctionAR}}(e_1, e_2) = \begin{cases} 1 & \text{if}(\text{SN}(e_1) \neq \text{SN}(e_2)) \wedge (\text{DataDep}(e_1, e_2) \neq nodep) \\ 0.5 & \text{if}(\text{SN}(e_1) \neq \text{SN}(e_2)) \wedge (\text{DataDep}(e_1, e_2) = nodep) \end{cases}$$

$$(13)$$

In the case of synchronous elements and mutually exclusive elements the distance is given by a constant value. For elements that are classified in order to share the same functional unit, the distance function returns *zero*.

Considering the current alternative listed in Table 7, the closeness measurement for our example calculated according to Eq. (3) is given in Fig. 10. The corresponding clustering tree is also shown in Fig. 10.

6.2 Cutting the Clustering Tree at Stage One

Once the clustering tree has been built, the cut line must be placed at some level of the clustering tree in order to generate a set of clusters. Each subtree below the cut line denotes a cluster. Placing the cut line at some level can improve the quality of the generated clusters regarding some criteria, and can provide a check for the clustering itself [10].

The judgment of generated clusters can be made according to some partitioning criteria. In this stage the following set of criteria has been considered when cutting the clustering tree:

	e_1	e_2	e_3	e_4	e_5	e_6	e_7	e_8
e_1	0	6	29.5	29.5	33.5	36	33.5	33.5
e_2		0	29.5	29.5	33.5	36	36	33.5
e_3			0	3	21.5	25	23	17.5
e_4				0	21.5	25	23	17.5
e_5					0	24	22	21.5
e_6						0	20.3	21.5
e_7							0	24
e_8								0

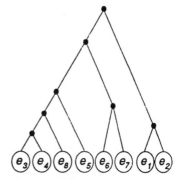

Fig. 10: Resulting closeness measurements and clustering tree

- Asynchrony of the elements inside a cluster
- Resource sharing and allocation
- Minimization of memory accesses.

With the first criterion, it has been investigated for situations where all generated clusters, at some level of the clustering tree, contain only elements that might not be implemented in pipelining. Such elements include elements belonging to the same statement or elements belonging to distinct statements but sharing the same functional unit. Elements that might be implemented as pipelining must belong to distinct clusters. This permits the performance improvement obtained with the pipelining to be measured in the next clustering stage.

Another important criterion to be considered when cutting the clustering tree is the resource allocation and sharing. As mentioned previously, the designer may set some design parameters allowing a preallocation of some elements to the CPU. Considering this allocation, we need to investigate, at each level, the occurrence of *CPU elements* in the generated clusters. Elements allocated to the CPU must be kept in the distinct clusters from ones that are not allocated to the CPU. Furthermore, elements sharing the same functional unit should be kept in the same cluster.

Finally, the number of memory accesses must be considered at each level.

The cutting algorithm, in this stage, tries to minimize the cost function by searching the cluster tree from the bottom up. The cost function f_{cut1} for level h is given by:

$$f_{\text{cut1}}(h) = f_{\text{AsynchronyAtStage1}}(h) \times f_{\text{CPUAllocationAtStage1}}(h) \times f_{\text{MemoryAccesses}}(h) \quad (14)$$

The first factor in Eq. (14) is a function investigating for all subtrees at level h the occurrence of asynchronous elements. According to Eq. (15) the function $f_{\text{AsynchronyAtStage1}}(h)$ analyzes, first, the statement number of all elements for all subtrees at level h. If at least one subtree exists that contains asynchronous elements, the sharing of common resources among such elements must be investigated. Asynchronous elements sharing the same functional unit might belong to the same cluster, whereas asynchronous elements running on distinct units must be kept in distinct clusters.

$$f_{\text{AsynchronyAtStage1}}(h) = \begin{cases} \infty & \text{if } \exists \text{ subtree } c_k \text{ at level } h: \\ & \quad \exists e_i, e_j c_k : (SN(e_i) \neq SN(e_j)) \wedge \text{not SharingHW}(e_i, e_j) \\ 1 & \text{if } \forall \text{ subtree } c_k \text{ at level } h : \\ & \quad \forall e_i, e_j c_k : (SN(e_i) = SN(e_j)) \vee \\ & \quad (SN(e_i) \neq SN(e_j)) \wedge \text{SharingHW}(e_i, e_j) \end{cases}$$

$$\tag{15}$$

In order to ensure that asynchronous elements running on distinct units are kept on different clusters, the function $f_{\text{AsynchronyAtStage1}}$ returns the value *infinity* if at least one subtree at level h exhibits this feature.

The second factor, the function $f_{\text{CPUAllocationAtStage1}}$ searches for subtrees at the level h which include both kind of elements, ones that have been allocated to the CPU and others that have not been allocated to the CPU. According to Eq. (16), which describes this function, the occurrence of at least one subtree at the level h including these two kind of elements makes the function $f_{\text{CPUAllocationAtStage1}}$ return the value *infinity*. The function f_{cut1} returns, also, *infinity* meaning that the cut line should be placed at a level below than level h.

$$f_{\text{CPUAllocationAtStage1}}(h) =$$

$$\begin{cases} \infty & \text{if } \exists \text{ subtree } c_i \text{ at level } h : \\ & \quad \exists e_j, e_k c_i : \text{CPUAllocation}_{\text{Elm}}(e_j) \neq \text{CPUAllocation}_{\text{Elm}}(e_k) \\ 1 & \text{if } \forall \text{ subtree } c_i \text{ at level } h : \\ & \quad \forall e_j, e_k c_i : \text{CPUAllocation}_{\text{Elm}}(e_j) = \text{CPUAllocation}_{\text{Elm}}(e_k) \end{cases}$$

$$\tag{16}$$

In Eq. (16), the function $\text{CPUAllocation}_{\text{Elm}}(e_i)$ analyzes whether the element has been allocated to the CPU or not; returns *true* in the first case and *false* otherwise. Its definition can be found in [10].

Finally, the third factor, the function $f_{\text{MemoryAccesses}}$ returns the number of memory accesses performed at the level h, which is given by the sum of reading and writing accesses as shown in the following equation:

$$\text{MemoryAccesses}(h) = \sum_{\forall c_k \in h} \text{Write}_{\text{Tree}}(c_k) + \text{Read}_{\text{Tree}}(c_k) \tag{17}$$

The placement of the cut line for our example is depicted in Fig. 11. Six clusters have been generated, one including the elements e_3 and e_4, another one including the elements e_1 and e_2 and four clusters including each of them and one of the other elements. The level where the cut line has been placed denotes a place where the function f_{cut1} results in the minimum value. At one level above, the function results in *infinity* since the elements e_3, e_4, and e_8 belong to distinct statements.

6.3 Building the Clustering Tree at Stage Two: Measuring the Distance Among Clusters

The main goal here is to generate a new set of clusters by analyzing the effectiveness of a pipelining implementation.

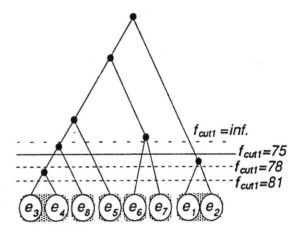

Fig. 11: Resulting closeness measurements and clustering tree

When building the clustering tree, the closeness among the objects, in this case clusters, must be measured first. To achieve the goal mentioned previously, as well as to guarantee the clustering of elements sharing the same functional unit, the following heuristics have been used when defining the distance function:

- Asynchronous clusters with data dependency, i.e., the elements belonging to the two clusters are asynchronous and there is a data dependency among them, should be kept farther from each other than asynchronous clusters, which are data independent.
- Synchronous clusters with data dependency should be considered nearer in comparison with synchronous ones that are data independent.
- Clusters allocated to the CPU should be kept farther from clusters that have not been allocated to the CPU.

The first heuristic supports the analysis of the parallelism improvement obtained when employing pipelining. According to this heuristic, asynchronous clusters that are data dependent should be kept separated. This separation of asynchronous clusters makes it easy to perform a cost analysis when cutting the clustering tree.

The second heuristic tries to improve the number of memory accesses. As mentioned in Section 5, keeping together synchronous clusters that are data dependent can lead to a minimization of memory accesses, as well as of synchronization costs. This heuristic must also be used at this stage in order to guarantee that synchronous elements, allocated to distinct clusters in the first stage, can be grouped again.

Finally, the third heuristic considers the allocation of some clusters to the CPU. Such clusters must be maintained so far as possible from other clusters running on other functional units than the CPU, since such clusters must build a cluster separately.

Considering all heuristics mentioned, the function to measure the distance between two clusters c_1 and c_2, $D_{\text{pipelining}}$ has been defined. This function is given by Eq. (18):

$$D_{\text{pipelining}}(c_1, c_2) = f_{\text{synchrony\&DataDependency}}(c_1, c_2) \times f_{\text{CPUAllocationCluster}}(c_1, c_2) \quad (18)$$

The first factor, the function $f_{\text{Synchrony\&DataDependency}}$ analyzes the data dependency among clusters, as well as their synchrony or asynchrony. This function is given by Eq. (19) and results in the maximum distance value for asynchronous clusters with data dependency and the minimum one for synchronous clusters that are data dependent.

$$f_{\text{Synchrony\&DataDependency}}(c_i, c_j) = \begin{cases} 0.25 & \text{if } (\text{SameStatementNumber}(c_i, c_j)) \wedge \\ & \quad (\text{ThereIsDataDependency}(c_i, c_j)) \\[4pt] 0.5 & \text{if } (\text{SameStatementNumber}(c_i, c_j)) \wedge \\ & \quad \text{not } (\text{ThereIsDataDependency}(c_i, c_j)) \\[4pt] 0.75 & \text{if not } (\text{SameStatementNumber}(c_i, c_j)) \wedge \\ & \quad \text{not } (\text{ThereIsDataDependency})(c_i, c_j)) \\[4pt] 1.0 & \text{if not } (\text{SameStatementNumber}(c_i, c_j)) \wedge \\ & \quad \text{ThereIsDataDependency}(c_i, c_j)) \end{cases}$$

$$(19)$$

The function $\text{SameStatementNumber}(c_i, c_j)$ investigates whether all elements enclosed in the cluster c_i belong to the same statement as all elements of the cluster c_j, resulting *true* in the case of a common statement. In this case, the clusters c_i and c_j are said to be *synchronous clusters,* otherwise they are considered to be *asynchronous clusters*.

The data dependency between clusters c_i and c_j has been analyzed by the function $\text{ThereIsDataDependency}(c_i, c_j)$. This function returns *true* if there is at least one pair of elements (e_i, e_j) with $e_i c_i$ and $e_j c_j$, that is data dependent. In this case, the clusters c_i and c_j are also called *data dependent clusters*.

The third factor, the function $f_{\text{CPUAllocationCluster}}(c_i, c_j)$ investigates the CPU allocation of all elements in the cluster c_i all elements in the cluster c_j:

$$f_{\text{CPUAllocationCluster}}(c_i, c_j) =$$

$$\begin{cases} 0.25 & \text{if } \forall\, e_i \in c_i, e_j \in c_j : \text{CPUAllocation}_{\text{Elm}}(e_i) = \text{CPUAllocation}_{\text{Elm}}(e_j) \\[4pt] 1 & \text{if } \exists\, e_i \in c_i, e_j \in c_j : \text{CPUAllocation}_{\text{Elm}}(e_i) \neq \text{CPUAllocation}_{\text{Elm}}(e_j) \end{cases}$$

$$(20)$$

The resulting closeness measurement and the corresponding clustering tree at stage two for our example are depicted in Fig. 12. The six clusters generated in the first stage denote the objects to be clustered in the this stage (see Fig. 11).

According to the values depicted in the proximity matrix we can see that elements belonging to the same statement are kept nearer, whereas elements corresponding to distinct statements are kept farther. In our example, the cluster containing the elements e_3 and e_4 is nearer to the cluster including the element e_5 than to the cluster containing the element e_7 or element e_6. The elements e_6, e_8 and e_7 are also kept together. Due to its allocation to the CPU, the cluster including the elements e_1 and e_2 is kept farthest from all others clusters.

6.4 Cutting the Clustering Tree at Stage 2

The placement of the cut line at stage two has been guided, basically, by two main criteria: the effectiveness of a pipelining implementation and the allocation of some elements to the CPU.

The cutting algorithm at this stage searches the cluster tree from the top down and computes the function $f_{\text{cut2}}(h)$ for each level h in the clustering tree. The level yielding a minimum value for the function f_{cut2} denotes the position where the cut line should be placed.

The function $f_{\text{cut2}}(h)$ considers both criteria mentioned above for each level h of the cluster tree as it can be seen in Eq. (21):

$$f_{\text{cut2}}(h) = f_{\text{Pipeline}}(h) \times f_{\text{AsynchronyAtStage2}}(h) \tag{21}$$

The first factor, the function $f_{\text{Pipeline}}(h)$ investigates whether there are two or more sub-trees able to be implemented as pipelining, at this level. In this case, the ratio between the computation costs at level h and one level above is returned, which measures the effectiveness of the pipelining implementation.

To measure the computation cost associated with some level h in the clustering tree the function $\text{Cost}(h)$ has been defined. The calculation of the costs inside a clustering tree is based on a cost model, which can be found in [10].

When no pipelining implementation is possible at the this level, the occurrence of elements able to be implemented as pipelining has been investigated at one level below. In the case of a pipelining possibility at one level below, the function $f_{\text{Pipeline}}(h)$ returns a constant value, forcing the search to be made at this level. Otherwise, the occurrence of CPU elements is investigated for all subtrees at level h:

$f_{\text{Pipelining}}(h) =$

$$
\begin{cases}
cte & \text{if } \nexists \text{ subtree } c_i, c_j \text{ at level } h : \text{Pipelining}_{\text{Tree}}(c_1, c_j) \wedge \\
& \quad \exists \text{ subtree } c_k \text{ at level } h : \\
& \qquad \exists \, e_{ik}, e_{jk} \in c_k : \text{Pipelining}(e_{ik}, e_{jk}) \\[2ex]
f_{\text{CPUAllocationAtStage2}}(k) & \text{if } \nexists \text{ subtree } c_i, c_j \text{ at level } h : \text{Pipelining}_{\text{Tree}}(c_i, c_j) \wedge \\
& \quad \nexists \text{ subtree } c_k \text{ at level } h : \\
& \qquad \exists \, e_{ik}, e_{jk} \in c_k : \text{Pipelining}(e_{ik}, e_{jk}) \\[2ex]
\dfrac{\text{Cost}(k)}{\text{Cost}(k+1)} & \text{if } \exists \text{ subtree } c_i, c_j \text{ at level } h : \text{Pipelining}_{\text{Tree}}(c_i, c_j)
\end{cases}
\tag{22}
$$

The function $f_{\text{CPUAllocationAtStage2}}(h)$ investigates whether there is some subtree at level h, including elements allocated to the CPU and elements running on other functional units. This function is given by Eq. (23). According to this equation this function returns zero if there is no subtree at this level h including both kinds of elements, "CPU" elements and "not CPU" elements. Otherwise this function returns a constant value. This feature of the function $f_{\text{CPUAllocationAtStage2}}(h)$ ensures the greatest value for the function f_{cut2} at the level h if there is some subtree containing "CPU" and "not CPU" elements, meaning the continuation of the search at levels below.

	e_1/e_2	e_3/e_4	e_5	e_6	e_7	e_8
e_1/e_2	0	0.255	0.25	1	1	0.75
e_3/e_4		0	0.062	0.25	0.187	0.187
e_5			0	0.25	0.25	0.25
e_6				0	0.062	0.25
e_7					0	0.25
e_8						0

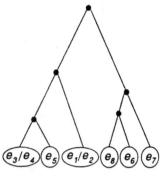

Fig. 12: Resulting closeness measurements and clustering tree

$$f_{\text{CPUallocationAtStage2}}(h) = \begin{cases} 1 & \text{if } (\forall \text{ subtree } c_i, c_j \text{ at level } h : \text{with } c_i \neq \text{leaf} : \\ & \quad \text{CPUAllocation}_{\text{Tree}}(c_i) = \text{CPUAllocation}_{\text{Tree}}(c_j)) \lor \\ & \quad (\nexists \text{ subtree } c_i \text{ at level } h \text{ with } c_i \neq \text{leaf}) \\ cte & \text{if } \exists \text{ subtree } c_i, c_j \text{ at level } h \text{ with } c_i \neq \text{leaf} : \\ & \quad \text{CPUAllocation}_{\text{Tree}}(c_i) \neq \text{CPUAllocation}_{\text{Tree}}(c_j) \end{cases}$$

(23)

The second factor, the function $f_{\text{AsynchronyAtStage2}}(h)$, analyzes the degree of parallelism exhibited by asynchronous elements. As shown in Eq. (24), this function returns a constant value when asynchronous elements might not share the same functional unit, or there is some subtree at the level h including elements exhibiting distinct degree of parallelism. This result forces such elements to be kept in distinct clusters. In the case where all subtrees at the level h either include only elements belonging to the same statement, or its asynchronous elements exhibit the same degree of parallelism and, furthermore, the sharing of resources among them has been set as automatic, the function returns *one* transferring the decision at this level to the function $f_{\text{Pipeline}}(h)$:

$f_{\text{AsynchronyAtStage2}}(h) =$

$$\begin{cases} cte & \text{if } (\text{not AutomaticSharingHW} \land \\ & \quad (\exists \text{ subtree } c_i \text{ at level } h : \\ & \quad\quad \exists e_i, e_j \in c_i : \text{SN}(e_i) \neq \text{SN}(e_j))) \\ & (\text{AutomaticSharingHW} \land \\ & \quad (\exists \text{ subtree } c_i \text{ at level } h : \\ & \quad\quad \exists e_i, e_j \in c_i : \text{SN}(e_i \neq \text{SN}(e_j) \land \text{Dgr}(e_i) \neq \text{Dgr}(e_j))) \\ 1 & \text{if AutomaticSharingHW} \land \\ & \quad (\forall \text{ subtrees } c_i \text{ at level } h : \\ & \quad\quad (\forall e_i, e_j \in c_i \text{ with SN}(e_i) \neq \text{SN}(e_j) : \text{Dgr}(e_i) = \text{Dgr}(e_j))) \lor \\ & \quad \forall \text{ subtrees } c_i \text{ at level } h : \\ & \quad\quad (\forall e_i, e_j \in c_i : \text{SN}(e_i) = \text{SN}(e_j)) \end{cases}$$

(24)

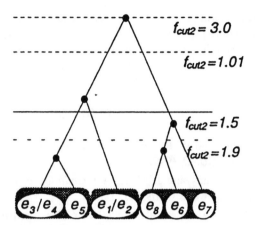

Fig. 13: Resulting clusters at stage two

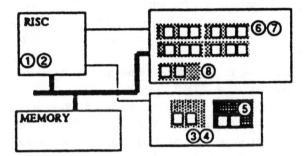

Fig. 14: Resulting allocation

The placement of the cut line at stage two for our example can be visualized in Fig. 13. Figure 14 illustrates the allocation of the clusters in the target architecture. In this work we use a partially predefined target architecture [10].

The cutting process of the cluster tree at stage two yields a set of three clusters. One cluster to be allocated into the CPU (software cluster) including the elements e_1 and e_2. The other two clusters, each of them running on a separated units, denote hardware clusters. One of them includes the elements e_3, e_4, and e_5 and the other one contains the elements e_6, e_7, and e_8.

7 CONCLUSION

We have presented an approach for clustering a problem specification that supports the partitioning in hardware and software. The presented approach is essentially based on the classification into sets of implementation alternatives, and it supports different partitioning possibilities. Additionally this flexibility permits reuse of the same hardware structure.

After the classification, our clustering approach is performed on a higher level of abstraction than other clustering approaches [7]. Here, the assignments are clustered according to the corresponding *type*, where the type of an assignment considers the diverse kinds of parallelism, as well as data dependency.

The clustering approach was implemented using the UNITY compiler developed by GMD/Karlsruhe [3] in MODULA 2. For further work, we might consider the inclusion of a third phase in the clustering process, where the use of common transparent variables among statements is considered.

REFERENCES

[1] E. Barros and W. Rosenstiel, "A Method to Hardware/Software Partitioning." *Proc. of COMPEURO 1992.*

[2] K. M. Chandy and J. Misra, *A Foundation of Parallel Programs Design,* Prentice Hall, Englewood Cliffs, NJ, 1988.

[3] F. Bieler, "An Interpreter for UNITY," Research report, GMD Karlsruhe, 1988.

[4] G. Estrin, "A Methodology for Design of Digital Systems Supported by SARA at Age One," presented at National Computer Conference, 1978.

[5] T. Juntunen *et al., Real Time Structured Analysis in System Level Design of Embedded ASICs, Microprogramming and Microprocessing,* North Holland, Amsterdam, 1988.

[6] R. Gupta and G. De Micheli, "System-level Synthesis Using Re-programmable Components," *Proc. EDAC,* 1992.

[7] E. D. Lagnese, "Architectural Partitioning for System Level Design," in *Proc. 26th Design Automation Conference,* ACM/IEEE, June 1989.

[8] O. Föllinger, *Regelungstechnik,* Hüthig, 1985 (in German).

[9] H. Schwarz, "Vorschläge zur Elimination von Kopplungen in Mehrfachregelkreisen," *Regelunstechnik, 9,* pp. 454–459, 505–510, 1961.

[10] E. Barros, "Hardware Software Partitioning using UNITY." Doctoral Dissertation, University of Tübingen, July 1993.

[11] A. Jain and R. Dubes, *Algorithms for Clustering Data,* Prentice Hall, Englewood Cliffs, NJ, 1988.

[12] O. Opitz, *Numerische Taxonomie,* Gustav Fischer Verlag-Stuttgart, 1980 (in German).

CHAPTER 12

Implementation-Independent Descriptions Using an Object-Oriented Approach

John Forrest
Department of Computation
University of Manchester Institute of Science and Technology (UMIST)
Manchester, United Kingdom

Abstract: Descriptions consisting of connected modules are common for both software and hardware. Description languages are usually strongly typed, and require that the types of connected ports or parameters agree. An implication of this is that the module interfaces must be identified at a very early stage. This chapter describes why this creates problems for the hardware design process, in particular, and reduces flexibility when making hardware/software trade-offs. An alternative strategy is also described: allowing connections between ports based on different protocols and data types, provided methods for their interfacing are known. Finally, an implementation of some of the proposals based on C++ is shown.

1 INTRODUCTION

This chapter is concerned with the implementation of integrated systems, consisting of digital hardware and related software components to be run on a processor. This scenario basically corresponds to that of embedded systems, such as intelligent controllers. It is not intended to cover the development of whole processors, where the instruction set is also to be implemented. Although these may seem similar, the synthesis tools used to implement a new processor are known to require different characteristics than those used to implement the required algorithms, and thus a line has been drawn in order to simplify the problem at hand.

The primary consideration here is the description of systems in such a manner that different parts of the system can be implemented in hardware or software as appropriate. This requires not only an initial, implementation-independent description, but also links to the associated design routes—not least so that the functionality of the whole system can be examined before the hardware is completed.

The general aspects of software and hardware design routes are discussed, identifying their main overlaps and differences, carrying onto what the concept of joint hardware/software descriptions actually means. The characteristics of a general notation for supporting such design are discussed, with particular regard to the requirements of hardware designs, along with how this might be implemented using C++. The background of the research group is touched on, because it has had a strong influence on the approaches taken.

2 HARDWARE AND SOFTWARE DESIGN TECHNIQUES

To derive the required attributes of joint descriptions, we need to examine the basis of separate software and hardware design routes—to look for key characteristics and, where possible, similarities.

Digital hardware design tends to follow the key concept of *abstraction levels.* Each abstraction level represents a hardware module at a given level of description. The levels are really points on a spectrum, but a typical set includes System, where the basic I/O features and functions of the system are defined; Behavioral, where the algorithms used are described; Register-transfer (RTL), where parallel register-function connections are used; Logical, using Boolean equations; and Structural, as a network of existing logical blocks. There are others, such as State Machines (FSM) that do not fall well into any category, and Switch and Transistor, which are not associated with design but with simulation accuracy. It is important to realize that abstraction levels of a given module are not really descriptions of different systems, but descriptions of the same system at different levels of complexity. Having said that, there is a one-to-many relationship between higher and lower levels of abstraction—for example, an algorithmic behavioral description can be mapped onto many RTL networks. Note that although descriptions will typically involve separate performance and functional components, this chapter is fundamentally concerned with behavioral specifications.

Following an essentially top-down style, lower levels are synthesized from higher levels. This synthesis may be (semi-)automatic or, as is traditional, performed by engineers. A key notion is that both the input and output descriptions to this process are preserved—that is, the higher levels of abstraction are not treated as working designs, to be discarded. The higher levels are used, with multilevel simulation, to improve simulation efficiency, and can also be used for subsequent redesign. The abstraction level of the initial design will be colored by a number of factors: It needs to be abstract enough so that the initial design work can be undertaken by only a few people, which is largely determined by the complexity of the eventual problem; but, higher abstraction levels are, by definition, more implementation independent and thus useful when the technologies to be used have yet to be determined.

Software design styles are, in many ways, more varied. On one side, much software is still initially designed using reports in "formal" English, and then encoded in a high-level language. On the other hand there are many CASE tools that provide for higher level descriptions and automatic software production. The ideal behind the latter is to provide a direct route from the CASE description to executable binaries—although this will usually be via the generation and subsequent compilation of high-level code, which should be invisible. However, CASE techniques are usually far from complete in this respect—in the applications area under investigation, most CASE tools just cover the control aspects of systems, and require data actions to be described using an underlying high-level language.

From this description it may appear that software and hardware design routes are very similar. However, this is by no means the case. First, it should be noted that the concepts of control and data parts do not coincide with the terms used in hardware design. It is better to think of software control as being "strategic," whereas hardware control must also encompass the equivalent of micro-instructions—that is, hardware is more detailed. Furthermore, the abstraction levels in software do not directly relate to those used with hardware: Practically the lowest level used with software is algorithmic, in a language such as C, whereas this is a high level on the hardware scale. Much of the reasoning behind this is the level of automation used: Compilers are used almost exclusively in software, with machine instructions rarely noticed. In any case, the relationship between high-level languages and the underlying machine is close. Furthermore, the efficiency of compilers is very good, which means that automatic translation has few drawbacks, and descriptions rarely need to consider the architecture of the machine—the exceptions being a few parts of the program corresponding to the operating system, which are not normally written afresh for each application, and multiprocessing systems, especially those based on message passing. Even here, high-level programming is commonly used, but the descriptions need to be in terms of separate processes—although some compilers will now produce parallel implementations from a sequential source on shared memory systems. Descriptions in terms of separate processes will be implementation independent, because they can be mapped onto most, if not all, single- or multiple-processor architectures—even though, as with hardware, the most efficient implementations will often be dependent on particular parallel topologies.

This scenario needs to be contrasted with hardware: Not only is automatic synthesis significantly poorer than manual design, especially at higher levels, but the description needs to contain many more implementation-dependent descriptions. The reasoning for this is that the basic architecture is generated—software is usually mapped to an existing one—and thus the permutations are much higher. This is not to say that implementation-independent hardware description is not possible in high-level languages, but that they are not really covered by the level of source used by current synthesis tools. As described later, the technique must be to support descriptions more akin to those used with software. However, in order to promote efficient implementations, it must also link to manual design routes.

A further difference between hardware and software design is in testing the derived design. The tradition with software is to produce an implementation and then to test it, although usually testing each module with a test harness. More recently, many CASE tools provide the ability to "exercise" the described higher level models, often with animation facilities. The latter is more akin to hardware routes, where it is normal to simulate an abstraction level to spot any problems before proceeding with the design of the next level. Much of the differences between these approaches are owing to two reasons:

- Hardware is much more expensive and time consuming to produce than software. It is not normally desirable to fabricate hardware unless there is a high probability that the design will work. It is important to assess the design beforehand.

- It is often difficult to find the state hardware is actually in—internal values have very poor visibility. Simulation is often required to discover the internal behavior—this is contrasted with software, where it is almost always possible to view the behavior of real programs as they run—using a debugger or in-circuit emulator.

3 JOINT HARDWARE/SOFTWARE DESCRIPTIONS

For hardware/software codesign it is important to be able to describe systems in some form of "joint notation." Having said that, there are several interpretations as to what this actually means, the primary ones being:

- The description of both a processor architecture, in particular, the instruction set, and the software to run on that computer
- The description of systems in terms of modules that may be implemented as either software or hardware: The system may also include modules that have to be implemented as either hardware or software.

The two categories reflect a difference in approach. The first is primarily concerned with the production of new computers, and the second with the production of dedicated application systems, where custom hardware is added to an existing processor. The work described here is aimed at the second category; it is not intended to describe an instruction set, but the algorithms used.

It is perhaps worth considering what would be meant by the concept of software-only and hardware-only modules. Essentially these would have features that rule out either hardware or software implementation. A key feature in software is multiprocessing via time sharing, where processes are created and destroyed as required. Although not, strictly speaking, impossible with direct hardware implementations, it is very costly—the simplest hardware is formed from static state machines, with predictable parallelism, and arbitrary amounts of concurrency are difficult. It is preferable to state that for hardware systems, the logical topology of a system is *static*—with predetermined numbers of processes, and thus processors, and limited fork/join possibilities. Similar arguments apply to dynamic data—it could be implemented, but at seemingly too great a cost to be worthwhile. If modules break these restrictions, they must be implemented in software. Requirements for hardware-only modules are fewer, because software can do most operations. Possible exceptions involve explicit parallelism or highly detailed timing, perhaps relating to external interfacing. However, hardware-only descriptions may be introduced for lower levels of abstraction as a means of including efficient implementations.

The work described here is concerned with the introduction of implementation-independent joint hardware/software systems. It includes how hardware-specific modules might be introduced, because that is part of an efficient design route. It does not really address software-only modules, although their inclusion in this scheme should be relatively simple.

4 BACKGROUND WORK

Previously the group had been involved with several systems or languages that attempted to provide either an implementation-independent route into hardware or joint software/ hardware description as discussed earlier—the main difference being whether software routes were supported. These included using SDL [1] and Occam [2], and led to a custom language called BEADLE [3,4], developed as part of the AIDA Esprit project. BEADLE's aims involved restricting the features to those that allowed both software and hardware development. This was an interesting course, but introduced added problems that were not previously anticipated:

- It was difficult to relate the BEADLE portion with hardware-only or software-only modules. The whole system had to be translated, and existing designs could not be introduced easily.
- Considerable activity was required to support the system as a whole, when the real requirement was to just support the architectural synthesis step—the conversion of BEADLE modules into hardware, which was the primary aim of the work.

Although BEADLE proved costly to support, it was deliberately designed to provide for implementation-independent descriptions—it included type descriptions that allowed users to state the data storage requirements, rather than relying on the underlying structure. Its concurrency techniques were based on Extended-CSP [5], as had earlier been used with Occam, and proved very general, although initial implementations, at least, were costly. The language was developed because the alternatives did not support such features. However, the experience gained did suggest that introducing a new language was to be avoided, if possible.

Subsequent to the BEADLE project, work was undertaken examining VHDL's suitability as a hardware design language [6], with particular emphasis on its usability for implementation-independent design and to represent designs at several abstraction levels— and thus through most or all of the design process. The conclusion to this was that VHDL was a very poor design language: To describe a system, a user has to provide an implementation of the system architecture, because the *signal* concept is singularly weak and too close to the eventual implementation. Furthermore, it was very difficult to link designs described at different abstraction levels.

5 A PROPOSAL FOR IMPLEMENTATION-INDEPENDENT DESCRIPTIONS

From the VHDL work came the idea of flexible interfaces, where the communication between the ports would be flexible. The basic concepts are that a system is described as a set of concurrent modules, each module has a number of ports, and that the associated module ports are connected. This technique, already touched on above, is very common and forms one of the primary methods of system design—not least because it reflects the common step of hierarchical decomposition. It is used in such varied systems as Extended-CSP and VHDL, with the proviso that the system is static, with predetermined numbers of modules/processes. However, several parts of the proposal were to take it beyond that of VHDL:

- The protocol was to be associated with the port, rather than being implemented explicitly in the internal description. For example, a data port might be designated as full-handshake and would consist of several underlying signals: the data, request, and acknowledge. With regard to the module description, initial descriptions would merely indicate to send or receive data to/from a port, with the protocol work being implicit. In most circumstances, the protocol could be changed by merely changing the port description. At lower levels of abstraction, the control signals would be introduced to the module description, and the control portion introduced explicitly. This would reflect the hardware implementation, and could be readily translated into a language such as VHDL, and thus into hardware.
- The system was to have strict types, as with VHDL. However, the connection of types with unlike ports—either in terms of data carried or protocols used—was to be allowed, providing users supplied mapping/conversion functions. These were to be introduced implicitly, with little user intervention.

The latter facility is intended to reflect systems under development, where different protocols and data representation are used at different abstraction levels. It is arguable that it should be possible to turn such a facility off: For the final implementation, it is important that no implicit mapping functions be left, because they disguise hardware. By that time, the structure of the system should be as close as possible to that of VHDL, allowing direct linkage to lower level systems, and allowing systems to include VHDL descriptions would be an advantage, although not easy to arrange.

A range of protocols is envisaged, the most complex of which involve several lower level control or data signals acting together, with perhaps some temporal relationships, such as one data signal per clock cycle. In fact, the most complex scenarios are where, for example, several signals are viewed by module A as being linked, but which are connected separately to modules B and C. It is very difficult to support the situation where A, B, and C have different ideas as to the protocol used, and this problem has not really been addressed. However, it is clear that rather than provide a complete set of data types and protocols, it is necessary to support an environment where users can write their own mapping functions. This inevitably requires them to get into the underlying workings of the system, even if this requirement is minimal. It may be that in a design team, certain members are designated to understand the inner workings of tools, and support the rest where required—that some members of a design team concentrate on simulation has been observed in practice.

6 A BASIC NOTATION

The following notation was developed at an early stage in this project, not really for use in design as such, but to provide a goal at which to aim. Most of the requirements had been derived from the VHDL work mentioned earlier, and will not be justified further here. It does not say anything about the way in which the behaviors of systems are described, only about how they are connected. It is to be expected that a variety of behavioral descriptions styles might be used.

A system consists of a number of processing elements (PEs), which communicate via events. There are two types of events:

Data events.   Which communicate from one place to another—or maybe to several places if required.

Query events.   Which are two-way: some data is sent, processing done, and data are returned. These connections are one/one. (This was the original concept, but actually many-to-one was implemented.)

Events are considered reliable, although some protocols may seek to support cancellation and resend. All data sent via events is typed, although the system should support the sending of several optional fields in the same event, and run-time specification of data type and size—at least in some parts of the language.

As noted later, the PEs may be arranged as a network, as a loose collection, or as a mixture of the two styles. Furthermore, each PE may in turn be a subnetwork. Both dynamic and static processing elements are supported. This was introduced to help with hardware/software codesign, and the intention was that the style be akin to CSP, with ports being addressed by name. However, referring to processes via a pointer or reference may be more appropriate; this has yet to be explored fully.

The events that each processing event can handle are indicated as *input ports* to PEs. Each input port specifies the data representation and protocol the PE expects for that particular event. Input ports can be bundled, to indicate that the system could choose to implement them as some kind of array, but an implementation can choose to ignore this.

There is a static subset of the language, which is intended to describe parts of the system that are or could be implemented in hardware. In this subset, PEs also have output ports, which indicate the events that it can send—again with data and protocol specification. A system here consists of a network of PEs connected via *channels,* which connect one input port to one or more output ports. The processing elements are static; they can neither be created nor destroyed. Representations of these elements are shown in Fig. 1, and an example system is shown in Fig. 2.

As noted earlier, the key thing about the methodology is that disagreement between input and output ports, in terms of the protocols and data types used, does not invalidate a system—the user of the system is allowed to add extra information to bridge the gap. In a simulated system, this might involve a protocol and data conversion function, and in a real system some extra hardware/interface software. However, these *interface elements* (IEs) should be independent of the design proper—the basic picture of the design remains unchanged. This is important, because if one of the design units is replaced by an alternative version, the port types and thus the required IEs may well change. This way, the logical system structure is preserved. The support environment should automatically provide some of the IEs, but others would have to be provided by the users, and the environment would have to decide which to use when.

A similar situation occurs with nonchannel events. Here, however, all events using the same protocol mechanism in the same system are assumed to use a single imple-

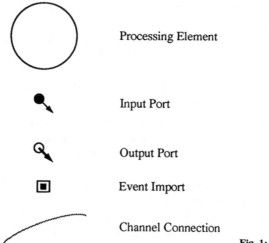

Fig. 1: Network symbols

mentation mechanism—a single protocol converter IE will suffice for each protocol pair in the whole system, rather than for each event separately. Separate data converter IEs will also be required for data type mismatch—but again one per type pair per system. An alternative scheme might limit these dynamic IEs to within particular PEs, or even some other criteria, to allow different schemes to be used to reflect design partitioning. Nonchannel communication is intended for software use.

As noted, this is intended as a system that is independent of description languages—the PEs themselves could be described in C++, VHDL, or whatever is convenient. The idea is to provide a common framework on which to hang these descriptions and to overcome some of the problems in describing multilevel descriptions in languages such as VHDL, which have very fixed process interface specifications.

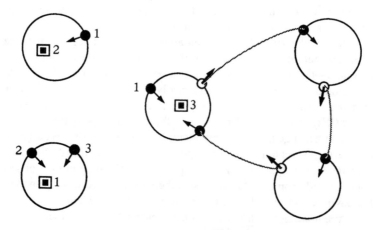

Fig. 2: Example system description

6.1 Extension to Software Descriptions

Most of the preceding discussion is concerned with hardware. To use it for codesign, it is necessary to consider the implications of extending it to cover software. Because the preceding approach grew out of one with a history of considering codesign, this is not a great problem. Essentially the data and query methods discussed are, depending on the protocols used, similar to data communication in CSP, Occam, and Ada. To obtain software descriptions it is merely necessary for the PE descriptions themselves, in other words the behavioral descriptions of the modules, to be in a form that is suitable for simple conversion to software—for example, described using a programming language. However, for real use it is also necessary that efficient implementations be obtained. The assumption in this project is that, providing the communications mechanism essentially reflects those used in concurrent systems programming, it will be *logically* efficient. Whether it is in practice efficient will depend on how good the implementation is—it would obviously be important, for real application, to extensively profile and refine the underlying kernel, but this does not affect the value of the overall approach. As described, the main problem with the kernel would be the protocol/data conversion, which implies that if no conversion takes place then any overheads should be minimized.

Of course, for joint hardware/software systems, methods are required to link hardware and software modules. The obvious way to do this is to extend the concept of the kernel to cover the links to the software, and then to incorporate the basic link as a protocol converter—the software seeing a high-level protocol and the hardware low-level signals. Alternatively, and not mutually exclusive, a communications architecture could be introduced by which the PEs communicate at a high level. This architecture would be extended so that software on a linked processor was logically part of the network. This was the basic proposal of the BEADLE work mentioned, and some work on an equivalent for this system has been undertaken [7].

7 THE USE OF C++

Having decided on our strategy, the decision was made to try to implement some systems this way—or at least derive successful descriptions of the problems turned up by the earlier VHDL work. Because of the experience of the group in supporting new languages, the opposite extreme was decided on—to see how far an existing language could be used without modification. It was further decided to use C++ as a vehicle for experiment [8]. The original reasoning for this was based on some initial work on object orientation—the concept of modules sending messages is central to the object-oriented scheme. C++ was primarily chosen because of its wide availability, but it quickly emerged that the object-oriented style of C++ did not really reflect the concurrency required, nor the concept of protocols. Instead, a run-time library has been produced that allows multitasking from within C++ and supports messages being passed between the tasks. A higher level library provides objects, such as modules and ports, that use the multitasking primitives.

Initially having to provide the run-time kernel seemed a great disadvantage, but has actually proved an asset, because the semantics of the communication are independent of the language used. Using a concurrent language would have restricted the primitives available. Furthermore, it is possible to provide different kernels for different situations—including multiprocessing and linking hardware and software subsystems. The work is solely concerned with supporting the specified primitives, and need not reflect any C++ semantics.

A final advantage of using C++ was not perhaps fully appreciated at the start of the work. This is that C++ is being increasingly used for software implementation in embedded applications, and thus the language is already in use in the application area under question. Having said that, much of this is coupled with CASE tools, which embody different mechanisms—not using multiprocessing to the same extent nor the same flexible protocol structure. However, the links are probably worth investigating.

7.1 C++ Descriptions

As has been mentioned, the key to the C++ descriptions has been the production of library facilities providing multitasking and messages between the tasks. The other facilities are built on this layer. Implementations have so far been written for SunOS and HP/Apollo DomainOS, but the requirements are simple and should be portable to most multithreading kernels—or with some more work, could be mapped to a naked embedded system.

When modeling systems of the type described here, the following concepts must be modeled:

1. Networks of components
2. Communication between the components
3. Internal component functionality.

Since it is derived from C, C++ has features for systems programming, and the latter category seems to go without saying. In fact, it has proved necessary to provide extra facilities for bit manipulation—so that bit vectors can be described of arbitrary sizes. The latter is really for hardware use, where the size of bit vectors needs to be known—possibly being smaller or larger than the word size of the processor. C++ has facilities for a wide range of internal functionality styles. The essential problem is to describe the various components as concurrent objects, which is discussed later.

The aim here is to provide an overview of the core facilities, as they appear to users of the system. The port-to-port facilities are dealt with first, followed by the general query facilities. Although this is really contrary to the way they would be used—with the second set used in the initial design—it seems simpler to describe them in this order.

The central facility is the need to send data from one module to another: The sending module transmits the data, and the receiving module accepts it and processes it. The description for the sending module might look like

```
output (data);
```

where *output* is the name of the signal, to be dealt with later, and *data* is the value to be transferred. In the receiver module, the description could appear as:

```
next = next_action();
assert (next == input); // optional
// data can be read from input.data
input.accept();
```

where *input* is the name of the signal. This may appear overly complex, but the advantage of this approach is that you can write a module that will wait for several inputs at the same time and then proceed accordingly, for example:

```
next = next_action();
if (next == input1) {
    do_something(input1.data);
    input1.accept();
}
else if (next == input2) {
    do_something_else(input2.data);
    input2.accept();
}
else ...
```

The accept( ) call indicates that the "transaction" has been completed. This has proved useful for error detection in the fairly common situations where output is sent before data are accepted—although this is partly related to the underlying run-time system. However, this call is required by some protocols, and it is simpler to adopt the convention of it always being given.

The reference to "some protocols" is an important one here. The preceding fragments are merely those of the communications syntax, and say nothing about the semantics used. This is one of the powers of the system: Similar syntax can be used for several different styles of transaction. In order for the above to be truly meaningful, some extra items must be introduced: modules and signal declarations. What is actually supplied are declarations of module "classes"—generic descriptions of modules for which specific instances can be declared, and which are parameterizable. The signal interfaces are included as fields in these modules. For example, consider a stage in a pipeline—with a single input and a single output. For the example, we use bit vector values, although that is very flexible. Such a module might look like

```
class Stage: Module {
    public:
        Stage (int sze, Protocol *proto = NULL, char *name = NULL)
            Module (name), output (sze, "output"),
            input (sze, this, proto, "input", &Module::PolledInput)
            {}
        BitVectorInput input;
        void attach (BitVectorInput &in) {
            output.attach()
        }
```

```
protected:
    BitVectorOutput output;
private:
    void behav () {
        for (;;) {
            Action *next = next_action(); // must be input
            input.accept();
            tick();
        }
    }
    virtual void tick() = 0;
};
```

In this, member function *Stage* is the constructor, used for initialization, *attach* is used to link the output with an associated input, and *behav* is called when the function has been created—effectively the module function or behavior. Note that in the constructor, *input* is given as a *PolledInput*. This supports the *next_action* clauses thus far described. The default is to remain silent about the arrival and implicitly accept it—this is useful for data signals under handshake control, for example, where data is always accepted, and would otherwise complicate the arrangement. Alternatives allow a user-defined routine to be called instead, for example, for interrupts. The final member function *tick* is not actually described; it is merely defined and given as "=0". This is a C++ trick to say that this is not a real object, but a general definition of a pipeline stage without some functionality. Child classes of this can then be defined with explicit functions. For example, to define a *ShiftStage* class, which shifts the data as they pass through:

```
class ShiftStage: public Stage {
    void tick() {
        output (input.data << 1);
    }
};
```

This ability to declare a general object, and then specific types, is a key one in C++. Although it was not directly identified as such earlier, it is evidently an advantage in system description—reflecting the ability to define both variations of functionality and of implementation.

Having declared modules, the question of communication semantics must once again be asked. The default protocol is intended to be a simplification of VHDL: The output is sent directly to the input, and no synchronization takes place between the modules. No time delays are implied. This is satisfactory for simple combinatorial networks with no feedback, but can break down when memory is introduced. To go beyond this, it is necessary to define the protocols used for different elements, and extra fields were introduced into the design. This is the reason for the Protocol parameter of the constructor, which here indicates the protocol to be used for the input port. Apart from the default, the following are provided:

- *ClockedProtocol:* The signal is delivered a number of clock cycles later.
- *DelayedProtocol:* Similar, but designed to work where the clock is declared explicitly in the user interface. This better reflects lower level hardware.
- *Synchronized:* This is a very different protocol. The sending process waits until the receiving process has accepted the signal.

When used, a main "program" is created that declares these units and then connects them. For example, three shift stages might be declared:

```
ShiftStage stage1 (8, new ClockedProtocol(1));
ShiftStage stage2 (8, new ClockedProtocol(1));
ShiftStage stage3 (8, new ClockedProtocol(1));
...
    stage1.attach (stage2.input); // eg. in main
    stage2.attach (stage3.input);
    stage3.attach ...
```

Stage 3 will be attached to another module. Custom test harness modules are used to generate the initial data and to sink the output. Standard text I/O commands are currently used to generate output reports. This connection technique is but one alternative, and not necessarily ideal. Another possibility would be to declare named signal parameters and pass these as parameters. The underlying mechanism for this would not be particularly different than the current; only the syntax would be different.

Although the protocol is currently passed into the module as a parameter, it is possible that a more useful notion would be to describe the protocol internally to the module description. In practice, the differences are minor—merely being whether the protocol is passed as a parameter or stated internally to the constructor. The advantage of the latter is brevity and the former that it is simpler to introduce complex protocols that link several signals.

As mentioned previously, an alternative form of communication is in the form of query/responses. The syntax used by the receiving module is almost identical to that described earlier—the difference being that the module can read and write data files of the port, in order to receive and return data. The similarity between the styles was deliberate, to allow one module to include both styles if required. The syntax of the sender is again similar, except that the call may send several pieces of data and may return a value, if required. Although mentioned in the basic notation, no protocol has been introduced at this level—it has not so far been required.

As a simple example, consider a memory. This has two "instruction" ports: read and write. The read takes an address—the query—and returns the stored value—the response. The write merely takes an address and data—the response is merely to indicate that the operation has finished. To describe that, one might use:

```
class Memory: Module {
   public:
      Memory (int sze, int bits_per_ele):
         size (sze), bit_mask (1<<bits_per_ele-1),
         data (new int[sze]) {}
      ReadInstruction read;
      WriteInstruction write;
   private:
      int size;
      int *data;
      int bit_mask;
      void behav ()
      {
         for (;;) {
            Action *next = next_action();
            if (next == read)
               read.value = data[read.address];
            else // write
               data[write.address] = write.value & bit_mask;
            next->accept();
         }
      }
};
```

Some examples of this being used are:

```
                Memory mem (100,4);
                mem.write (22,3);
                int res = mem.read (46);
                BitVector addr (7);
                BitVector bv(4) = mem.read (addr);
```

The last line here should give some idea of the flexibility of this system: By declaring conversion functions between bit vectors and integers, it is possible for modules dealing in bit vectors to deal directly with an integer memory. Alternatively, the memory could use bit vectors internally.

Although the syntax of these facilities is similar, the semantics are actually determined by the declarations of particular signals and instructions: *BitVectorInput, BitVectorOutput, ReadInstruction,* and *WriteInstruction* must be declared in practice. This is actually one of the weaknesses and yet one of the strengths of the system. A strength because the semantics are not predetermined. A weakness because their declaration is complex and long-winded—too much so to be described in full here. Having said that, it is actually a very mechanical process, and it should be a simple matter to automate, giving the types of each data field and the direction of travel. The obvious C++ alternative, the use of templates, is not practical because the numbers of function parameters and data fields vary between each example.

8 CONCLUSIONS

This chapter described two notations to support hardware/software codesign: an outline one and a reflection of part of it via C++. The need to support different parts of the system using different data representations and different protocols has been identified, both to support codesign and to support the subsequent development of the hardware. The outline version included the idea of linking ports described in different protocols and using different data representations. The C++ version does include the linkage of ports described using different data representations, but not really ones using different protocols. What it does support is the association of a protocol with the input port, and the automatic use of the output transmission of this port. This is not really the same thing.

It is fairly clear that given a complex enough run-time system, the full system would be possible. What would be required are extra *OutputProtocol* objects, with these and modified protocol objects being responsible for the transmission. More subtle communication would be required than at current, to allow several links to be made to the same object. Although this seems initially feasible there are several obstacles to its use in practice:

- The protocol objects will become more difficult to describe and to use. They will have to send signals to other objects telling them when to send or receive data, and it is not clear quite how this fits in with the existing arrangements.

- Perhaps more importantly, it is less clear how different protocols will be connected. Data linkage is undertaken via C++ data conversion facilities, but for complex protocols the sender will have to register itself with the receiver. This will almost certainly mean that each protocol object would require explicit code for each *OutputProtocol* object that will address it—making the introduction of different protocols expensive since all the other objects may require modification.

These drawbacks show the disadvantage of using an existing language. The experience has shown that the initial description method was produced quickly, and with few problems. A "simulation" environment was gained almost immediately, as the descriptions are executable. The problems arose as the description method required facilities past those of the host language. It is evident that this supports a worthwhile implementation structure: It can be used as a software implementation, and the basis of hardware implementations is also provided, the problem is in bridging the two.

An alternative to this method, which could be viewed as an extension, would be to provide a front-end system, taking either the graphical notation described already or using an extended textual language. The advantage is that the users would be protected from any syntax "funnies" introduced because of the C++ host, and that the protocol conversion routines would be the next step. The disadvantage here is that it is starting to move into the realm of CASE tools, and rather than develop yet another, it would be useful to try to utilize an existing tool.

The next obvious steps for this work are to try to utilize a CASE tool to act as a front end, and to investigate further the run-time requirements of protocol conversion. At the same time, work will investigate the use of these techniques to implement some joint hardware/software systems—probably using a joint microprocessor/FPGA prototyping system that has recently been developed.

As a final comment it should be mentioned that this is not the only system aimed at multiple *domains*—that is, implementation techniques. A known alternative is the Ptolemy system, where systems are constructed of modules that exist in different domains and facilities are provided for them to intercommunicate. The investigation of the use of Ptolemy has been proposed for solving the problems addressed here, although this has not been done due to lack of time. However, it should be understood that much of the purpose here is to support the design of systems, where the association of modules with their implementation and their interface is somewhat dynamic, depending on which description of a module is in use, as much as to how it is implemented. It would appear that Ptolemy is intended to support a more static association, and it is this aspect that does not seem as well suited to this particular problem area. Having said that, Ptolemy aims to go much further—linking in signal processing and other techniques that have not been addressed using the approach described here.

REFERENCES

The following describe the use of software varieties of SDL and Occam, respectively, for the description and subsequent synthesis as hardware structures:

[1] J. Forrest, "A Language and an Architecture for Silicon Compilation," PhD Thesis, University of Manchester, 1987.

[2] G. V. Collis, "Prototype High Level Hardware Synthesis System," PhD Thesis, University of Manchester, 1987.

[3] J. Forrest and M. D. Edwards, "BEADLE: An Algorithmic Language for the Description of Digital Systems," in *Design Methodologies for VLSI and Computer Architecture,* D. A. Edwards, Ed., North Holland, Amsterdam, 1989.

[4] H. Hounat, "The Mapping of BEADLE Descriptions on to Occam," MSc Thesis, University of Manchester, 1989.

[5] K. M. Chandy and J. Misra, "Deadlock Absense Proofs for Networks of Communicating Processes," *Info. Proc. Lett.,* 9(4), pp. 185–189, 1979.

[6] J. Forrest and M. Edwards, "Multiple Level Design Using VHDL," presented at Euro-VHDL Conference, Stockholm, September 1991.

[7] D. Nablis, "Hardware Implementation of C++ Communication Protocols," MSc Dissertation, University of Manchester, 1993.

[8] S. B. Lippman, *C++ Primer,* 2nd ed., Addison-Wesley, Reading, MA, 1991.

PART   II

Frameworks and Environments

The term *framework* in electronic design automation denotes a computer-based, integrated design environment that binds together and supports design tools. In their seminal paper, Harrison *et al.* [1] define a framework as ". . . all the underlying facilities provided to the CAD tool developer, the CAD system integrator, and the end user necessary to facilitate their tasks." The CAD Framework Initiative (CFI) views a framework as a collection of extensible programs/modules used to develop a unified CAD system.

We believe that with the increased interest in codesign, CAD frameworks will emerge that will support common techniques for specifications, developments, and verification of mixed hardware/software systems. Conceivably, such frameworks will incorporate tools to aid in HW/SW formal specification, modeling, for mapping models to physical realizations, validation, and performance, and cost analysis.

The chapters in this part present research and development efforts motivated by these needs. In Chapter 13, Bortolazzi, Tanurhan, and Müller-Glaser discuss an integrative approach that combines the commercially available CAD tools from both hardware and software spectra. Called *DEBYS* (DEsign BY Specification), the methodology is aimed at providing formal, model-based specifications and executable design modules. The next chapter, by Mertens, examines the utility of applying Hatley/Pirbhai system development methods to codesign. The focus is on generating system architectures in a modular, hierarchical fashion.

Chapter 15, authored by Nauber, Scherer, and vom Boegel, presents an emulation-aided design environment that assists designers in functional specification, modeling of architectural alternatives, hardware/software partitioning, rapid prototyping, and verification and evaluation of design alternatives. In Chapter 16, Gandhi and Roberston discuss a conceptual basis for a design framework based on a model for codesign data. Drawing from the conventional concepts of entity-relationship (ER) methodologies, they outline an architecture for a specification-based data model. The architecture has the major modules of specification, implementation, configuration, and manifestation components. A multilevel design is illustrated in the context of such an architecture.

Edwards describes work on system-level synthesis using high-level behavioral description languages. He gives an overview of the description environment called BEADLE and presents an appraisal of approaches to codesign for synthesis. Chapter 18, by Buchenrieder, Sedlmeier, and Veith, focuses on an computer-aided environment called CODES. The system, developed at Siemens in Germany, provides facilities for design data and flow modeling. An electronic motor control unit example illustrates the use and effectiveness of the design environment.

REFERENCE

[1] D. Harrison *et al.*, "Electronic CAD Frameworks," *Proc. IEEE,* 78(2), pp. 393–417, 1990.

CHAPTER   13

Toward an Environment for System Specification and Design

Jürgen Bortolazzi   Yankin Tanurhan   Klaus D. Müller-Glaser
Computer Science Research Center
Electronic Systems and Microsystems Department
Forschungszentrum Informatik (FZI),
Karlsruhe, Germany

Abstract: The goal of research and development efforts in the area of system specification and design is to provide computer support for the formulation of requirements, goals, and constraints, the generation and validation of alternative solution approaches, the analysis and simulation of specification models, and the flowdown of specifications to subsystem design. As a number of recent approaches enable the formal, model-based description of functional and behavioral specification as well as the execution and analysis of the resulting system models, growing hope for a complete specification and system design environment arises. For this purpose, available methods, description formats, and tools have to be combined to describe reactive (i.e., event-driven), and nonreactive aspects of system specification. Furthermore, constraints not contained in the formal descriptions, such as environmental conditions or system quality requirements, have to be acquired, stored, and considered in specific descision processes, such as hardware/software trade-off or function mapping.

The goal of DEBYS (DEsign BY Specification) is to combine commercially available tools such as i-Logix Statemate,™ ISI Matrix$_x$,™ SES/workbench,™ as well as CASE tools, VHDL synthesis, and simulation tools with a rapid prototyping system to provide formal, model-based specification and executable models. Furthermore, major research efforts concentrate on new approaches to complement these tools through proprietary developments in the area of knowledge-based requirements definition, estimation, and project planning. These tools will be encapsulated or integrated into a CAE framework and a number of techniques for code import and simulator coupling are under development. A major research aspect is the area of constraint management, e.g., in the areas of timing, area, speed, power consumption, reliability, and physical interfaces. Knowledge-based acquisition and constraint propagation techniques are used to provide accompanying support for the system specification and design process.

1 INTRODUCTION

The requirements and specification phases are defined as those stages in the system design cycle that precede the design of system architecture. These phases include the formulation and analysis of the functional, behavioral, and data-oriented requirements to the proposed system and nonfunctional requirements, conditions and constraints that must be met and considered, respectively. As shown in Fig. 1, the design process of complex, heterogeneous systems is a hierarchy of specification, design, implementation, and integration processes at different levels of abstraction. At the system and subsystem level, implementation is replaced by a lower level process. At the component level, technology-specific design processes are used to realize the components. Having successfully finished the implementation process at one level, the results are integrated at the next higher level up to the system level.

Within this process, specification, design, verification, and validation are performed at each level and therefore are accompanying the overall system design process. The requirements definition at the system level represents the initial, interactive process of formulating the customer's needs as well as the vendor-specific restrictions and common technical and economical conditions. Feasibility studies are performed to validate the requirements. The formulation, validation, and modification of requirements results typically in a specification document that includes a collection of formal and informal, functional and nonfunctional requirements, goals, constraints, and marginal conditions. These specifications are refined, completed, and transformed during the hierarchical process shown in Fig. 1.

Currently available specification techniques, such as Structured Analysis for Real-Time Systems (SA/RT) [1,2], StateCharts [3], SpecCharts [4], Specification and Description Language (SDL) [5,6], hardware description languages (HDLs) [7], and object-

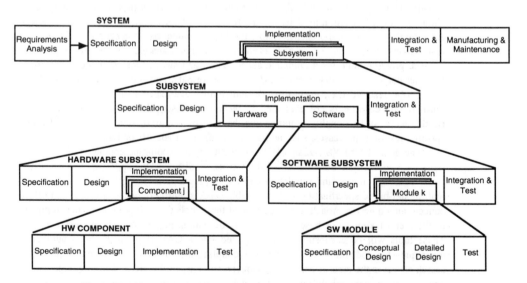

Fig. 1: The hierarchical specification, design, implementation, and integration process

oriented methods [8,9] mainly concentrate on the behavioral specification. However, to guarantee the successful development of a complex system, a great deal more information is required than is given in the functional specification alone. Technical and economical constraints, such as application-specific marginal conditions, maximum ratings, capabilities of available technologies, time-to-market window, and forecasted development and fabrication costs are some of the essential nonfunctional aspects to be considered during the feasibility study, design planning, and design management stages. Table 1 gives an overview of specification domains for electronic systems as defined in [10]. The approaches to computer support for requirement definition and specification can be classified into model-based and knowledge-based approaches.

1.1 Model-Based Approaches

Numerous specification languages have been developed in the areas of requirements and systems engineering, computer-aided software engineering (CASE), and electronic design automation (EDA) [1,4,11]. Widely accepted and used are SA/RT and SDL environments, which integrate formal or semiformal description formats, a specific methodology, and tools for analysis and simulation. The common aspect of these approaches is that the user develops an executable model of the system under development. This model provides the base for analysis and simulation. However, some serious drawbacks of these model-based specification techniques mandate complementary or new approaches:

- Most of the current approaches are suited toward very specific specification domains (e.g., StateCharts for behavioral modeling of reactive systems, VHDL for digital electronics).
- The user is forced to specify precisely all behavioral and functional aspects and therefore handling of uncertain specifications and stepwise refinement of specifications is not supported.
- The description of nonfunctional requirements and constraints is not supported.
- No support is provided for a complete specification and design flow.
- Documentation and history management are incomplete.

1.2 Knowledge-Based Approaches

The drawbacks just listed lead to a number of research activities in the area of knowledge-based requirements and systems engineering. These approaches focus mainly on specification acquisition such as natural language specification, specification knowledge representation [10], early checking of consistency and control [11], and feasibility studies and decision support [12]. Although promising, most of these approaches are still in their infancy and lack executable models and support for analysis and simulation and integration into the overall design flow.

TABLE 1: Specification Domains for Hardware/Software Systems

Interface Specification	Behavioral Specification	Structural Description	System Environment	Design Environment	Test Environment
I/O ports	Functional modeling	Component definition and identification	Temperature	Project planning	Test strategy planning
Maximum ratings	Dynamic modeling	HW/SW partitioning	Humidity	Cost planning	Test systems
Operating conditions	Data modeling	Hierarchical modularization	Mechanical stress	Milestones	Accuracy resolution
Supply conditions	HW/SW description languages	Connectivity	Chemical stress	Personnel	Security margins
Packaging interconnect	Templates	Critical paths	Radiation	Tools	Test links
Static, dynamic, transfer requirements	Transfer functions		Noise sources	Project management	Production test
Tolerances	Graphical description		EMC, ESD	Documentation	Quality assurance
	Parameters		Reliability MTBF, MTTR		AQL, PPM, ZDS

1.3 The DEBYS Project

The DEBYS (DEsign BY Specification) project is intended to develop an integrated design and test environment for the design of electronic systems. In this context, commercial tools are used to support specific acitivities in the design flow, and proprietary tools are developed to fill the gaps. To be able to profit from both knowledge-based and model-based approaches, the following requirements and tasks have been formulated for the DEBYS project:

- Development of a specification and system design environment based on formal methods
- Support for the development of executable, model-based specifications
- Support for analysis and simulation of both system and system components
- Support for test strategy planning
- Integration into an open environment that provides basic services such as tool communication, design, and data management
- Integration of new, knowledge-based methods and tools that are necessary to complement the available functionality
- Development of a methodology that combines these approaches.

Several tasks must be performed by an environment of this type. In this context, it is essential to cope with:

- The acceptance of computer-based methods, especially formal methods, in the early requirement acquisition
- Handling of different ways of system specification (behavioral, functional, and structural)
- The influences and relationships of constraints in different design phases (when and how does a specific constraint influence the design evolution)
- The relationships between requirements description, specification, early specification validation, design planning, and design management
- The development of a common data model.

The approaches to knowledge-based acquisition, management, and checking have been described before [10]. This paper focuses on the concept for the behavioral specification part in Table 1 and shows the benefits of the integration of knowledge-based and model-based specification techniques. It is organized as follows: Section 2 describes the DEBYS environment and the functionality of the integrated system specification, design, and simulation part. A brief overview of the knowledge-based parts and the common specification data model is also given. Section 3 presents experimental applications, and in Section 4 conclusions and future work are discussed.

2 THE DEBYS INTEGRATED SPECIFICATION AND SYSTEM DESIGN ENVIRONMENT

2.1 The DEBYS System Architecture

The DEBYS environment consists of a number of commercial and proprietary tools integrated into a CAE framework. The commercial tools currently available are:

- Interactive Development Environments Software through Pictures^{TM} (StP): a classical SA/RT tool providing data, control, and process as well as object-oriented modeling
- i-Logix Statemate^{TM}: a specification, analysis, and simulation tool based on the graphical formalism of StateCharts
- Integrated Systems Incorporation Matrix$_x$^{TM} and SystemBuild^{TM}: a specification and simulation tool for computer-aided control system design and analog/digital system simulation based on transfer function decription
- Scientific and Engineering System SES/workbench^{TM}: an architectural level design tool that provides statistical analysis and architectural simulation.

The rapid prototyper is based on a commercial rapid prototyping machine (e.g., Quickturn RPM^{TM}) with a hardware modeling capability. A standard microprocessor, controller, or digital signal processor is available for running the compiled C code, whereas ASIC peripherals (designed application-specific integrated circuits mainly for system I/O tasks with hard real-time requirements) are described in VHDL, then synthezised exploratively (using Synopsys^{TM} tools) and mapped into the RPM's programmable logic devices. This leads to an early system emulation capability, which allows one to verify the system function by emulation rather than simulation, so that the overall design cycle is much shorter and more assured.

The proprietary tools include

- Computer-Assisted Specification (CAS): a knowledge-based environment for the acquisition, management, and checking of requirements, goals, and constraints [10]
- Chip Estimation System (CES): a tool for high-level estimation of area, speed, power consumption, and reliability of digital functional blocks [14]
- Project Plan Generator (PGS): a tool for the planning and management of design projects tightly coupled to the CAS and CES tools [14]
- Generator System (GENSYS): a tool for generating reusable code of parameterized standard functions [15].

These tools are encapsulated or integrated into the common JESSI CAE framework [16]. For this purpose, a specification data model is under development that supports different views and different description formats. The approach is very similar to multimedia data models and can be characterized as a semantic network of information containers. This approach helps to handle the problem of combining tool-specific information packages stored in the file system and detailed data models developed for the proprietary tools. For the proprietary tools, tight on-line coupling and common event and message management are used [16].

The underlying design methodology for DEBYS is decribed next.

2.2 Initial System Partitioning and Module Classification

Figure 2 shows the schema for the coarse partitioning of an electronic system. The interface to the real world can be characterized in general by signal-carrying energy forms. For electronic systems the six most important are electrical, magnetic, thermal, mechanical, chemical, and optical (radiant). The knowledge of the energy forms required allows the system designer to select sensor and actuator principles accordingly. Sensors and actuators usually need special interface circuitry to perform energy conversion to or from the preferred system internal signal-carrying energy form, namely, electrical energy. Electrical signals then may be processed in either analog or digital signal processing subsystems. Digital circuitry is used for overall system control and for intersystem communication (electrical or optical signals may be used for communication). A power supply unit is neccessary to make the intelligent system autonomous and a special power electronics subsystem is usually needed to complement actuators.

This partitioning schema should be used at the very beginning of the system design process to identify and classify neccessary subsystems, modules, components, and signal-carrying energy forms. This will be done manually by the designer, because to our belief no computer-aided tool for system partitioning will ever be existent for that design task (a single designer or a team of designers must have an idea of how to implement a system

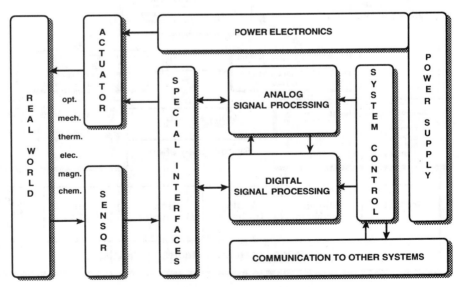

Fig. 2: Principal structure of a heterogeneous system

when only a verbal description is given for what a system is supposed to do—this process really needs human ingenuity and creativity).

If such a system partitioning is given, the selection of methodologies and tools for design, verification, and test as well as possible vendors, technologies, and fabrication methods will be both module and classification specific. Also economic and technical feasibility studies, project planning, and assignments of human and machine resources are easier to do when they are module and classification specific.

2.3 Meet in the Middle Strategy: System Versus Component Design Environments

Furthermore, we believe that there will be no design systems capable of handling all requirements for designing and verifying the complete system as well as all possible system components (e.g., sensors and actuators). Therefore, we suggest a "meet in the middle strategy" for a design environment for overall system design on the one hand and many different design environments for individual system components on the other hand [16] (Fig. 3).

Design environments for components are characterized by tight coupling to certain technologies and vendors, the tools will be dedicated but highly flexible and will be usable by component experts only. They will support component optimization and characterization and will result in quality-assured parameterized component libraries or a single component optimized for a specific system.

Environments for overall system design will include tools for system engineers, e.g., requirement specification tools, tools for estimating critical economical and technical

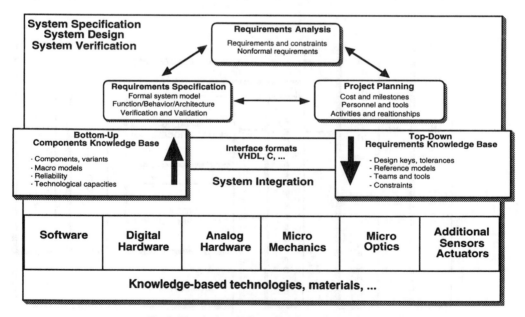

Fig. 3: Meet in the middle strategy for system design

design data, hardware/software trade-off and performance analyses for the evaluation of design alternatives, project and tool planning, software engineering tools, hardware synthesis, simulation, and test tools. The tools should be highly productive, resulting in short development cycles by supporting reusable hardware and software modules (libraries, module generators, synthesis, technology mapping, etc.) and allowing for a vendor and technology independent design as long as possible.

Between the system design environment and the various component design environments, well-defined interfaces and standards for methodology and data models are neccessary. Most essential is the interface for library data, especially for macromodeling to allow system simulation. The component designer must provide parameterized data from component characterization as accurately as possible and may generate a macromodel as accurate as necessary to the system designer [17] (or the system designer has to develop the macromodel). This is only possible if both parties know and exchange information on all critical parameters necessary to decide whether a specific component is usable or not for the design of a specific system and what the macromodel should look like (what data and functions are abstracted and which are modeled or not, which cross sensitivities are existing and modeled or not).

In the following, we describe our current approach for the overall design of an electronic system (component design environments and interfaces according to the meet in the middle strategy are not discussed here).

Figure 4 shows the scenario supported by DEBYS. The left-hand side describes methods and tools that provide support and control for the different development phases and the right-hand side describes results of the phase-specific activities.

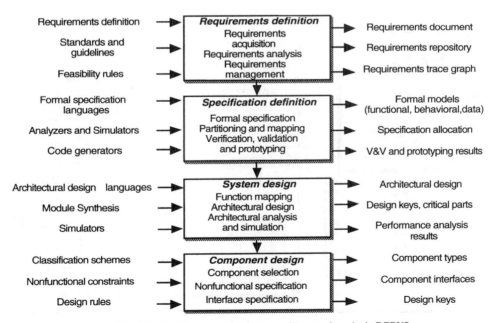

Fig. 4: Computer support, development phases, and results in DEBYS

2.4 Initial Requirements Definition

At the beginning of a system design process, the goals, requirements, constraints, and marginal conditions for a system design are formulated. The information is needed to perform feasibility studies as well as to formulate detailed system specifications. The result is a requirements document that often provides the base for a contract between customer and vendor. As the definition of requirements is mainly based on informal statements, computer support is restricted to management and documentation. However, a number of approaches are used in DEBYS to provide a systematic acquisition of requirements:

- Hypertext-based approaches provide the possibility to organize requirements using information nodes and links. Structure and dependencies within a specification can be described (Fig. 5). Database models are available that support the management of descriptions consisting not only of text, but also of graphics, dynamic data links, etc.

- Predefined plans such as the definition of necessary activities related to an object-oriented model of specification structure including concepts representing specification entitites and methods representing the functionality to produce the specific descriptions. DEBYS/FRESCO (Frame-Based REpresentation of Specification COncepts), a knowledge representation environment currently under development, provides the formulation of concepts based on knowledge representation elements such as frames, constraints and rules.

- Predefined graphics-based templates, classification schemes (e.g., for I/O signal definition), and interactive questionnaires are defined as requirements definition

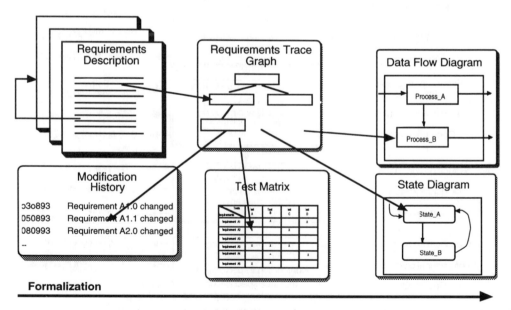

Fig. 5: Hypergraph for stepwise refinement of requirements

methods for specific concepts and are activated automatically. Dynamic updating of default values based on a lazy evaluation technique provides additional support.

- Structured, hierarchical approaches to requirements definition based on a strategy of iterative initial description, allocation to sublevel elements, and flowdown support.
- Rule-based validation of requirement definitions provides early checking of completeness and consistency based on heuristic knowledge.
- Structured, retrievable representation of requirements definitions provides the base for requirements management, i.e., requirements allocation, flowdown, and traceability.

The DEBYS object-oriented specification database consists of a number of container classes for structured representation of requirements as well as programmable constraints to represent relationships and dependencies.

Concept- and hypertext-driven requirements definition and structured representation in a database allow for the analysis of the acquired requirements. Functional requirements are extracted to be refined in the formal specification phase. Nonfunctional requirements, constraints, and conditions can be allocated to specific activities in the specification and design process. They provide the base for decision and planning support, for specification refinement, and validation of results. Last but not least, they are an important part of test strategy planning and test setup.

2.5 Specification and System Design

The development of the specification model is based on a combination of control-oriented and process-oriented descriptions similar to the SA/RT approach and extended by the use of StateCharts for dynamic modeling (control-oriented specification), and by the alternative use of transfer functions, module generators or high-level modeling in VHDL and C for the description of processes (Fig. 6).

The analysis and simulation of the models is based on a variety of techniques:

- Analysis and simulation of system control: deadlock, reachability, nondeterminism, hazards, interactive and batch simulation, performance analysis
- Analysis and simulation of analog and discrete processes: time- and frequency-domain analysis, open- and closed-loop frequency analysis, root locus, parameter extraction.

These techniques are supported by the specific capabilities of tools like i-Logix Statemate and ISI Matrix$_x$ as well as the possibility to build a system simulation model based on generated C and VHDL code. For the simulation of complete systems, a number of techniques can be used:

- Interactive simulation from a control-oriented view through C code import from Matrix$_x$ into the Statemate simulation environment

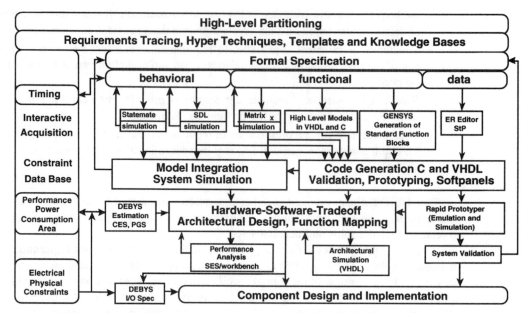

Fig. 6: Integrated computer support for requirements definition, specification, and system design in DEBYS

- Simulation of an overall system model in Matrix$_x$ including control parts imported from Statemate
- Coupling of a VHDL simulator, Statemate, and Matrix$_x$ to support the usage of existing models
- Prototyping based on an integration of generated C and VHDL code.

Partitioning and mapping to architectural blocks is done using synthesis for VHDL and manual mapping for the other parts of the specification. Estimation and project planning as well as prototyping are used to support the hardware/software trade-off. Furthermore, architectural simulation and statistical performance analysis is done using SES/workbench and VHDL simulators.

A simple, pragmatic approach to architectural design can be performed directly:

- The specification of system control using StateCharts enables code generation in C and VHDL. Therefore, the system control part can be realized as software or as ASIC using hardware synthesis.
- The specified processes are transformed into real-time C-code and downloaded onto a standard microprocessor or microcontroller.
- The specified information flows are refined through protocol descriptions in C or VHDL and realized accordingly.
- Finally, the hardware/software interface is developed.

Obviously, this simple approach does not cover the whole spectrum of designs owing to numerous contraints. To support the decisions for hardware/software trade-off, performance analysis, estimations of hardware and software design characteristics (speed, area, power consumption, code length, critical path), and prototyping have to be used. For performance analysis, the formally specified system parts are mapped onto an architectural model including process blocks, resources, communication links, and queues. This model is described using the SES/workbench^{TM} tool. The timing behavior and performance requirements to the different functional blocks are specified using templates. The behavioral specification model is mapped in generating and integrating C code into code blocks on the architectural model. As a result, a mixed-mode behavioral and structural model exists. The architecture is then successively refined in replacing behavioral models by architectural schematics. Analysis and simulation is used for correctness and completeness checking. However, the process of translating specifications into architecture should be supported by formal verification. Currently available tools lack sufficient performance.

To simulate the behavior of the architecture, information tokens traverse through the graph, processes are activated, and resources are used and locked and unlocked. The model allows concurrent, synchronous, and asynchronous behavior of a system. The possibility of associating multiple behavioral blocks in one level to a single block in a lower level of the hierarchy supports the stepwise design of system architecture. For example, several behavioral communication links can be mapped to a bus and several behavioral blocks can be mapped to a single functional unit. Having finished the architectural description, C and VHDL code can be generated.

The requirements and constraints described in the nonfunctional part of the requirements definition influence the design flow in different transformation and optimization steps. The specification environment must provide support for the acquisition and management of this information and should assist the user in applying it at the right time in the specification and design flow. Some of these associations are

- Timing constraints are considered in high-level behavioral specifications such as StateCharts.
- Requirements to the data flow (type of information) must be considered in functional specification and functional partitioning.
- Area, speed, and power constraints are considered in architectural design.
- Physical constraints, such as electrical ones, are considered at the physical interface specification.

As an example for a computer-based link between functional and nonfunctional specification, the detailed specification of hardware interfaces is supported by DEBYS I/OSpec, a knowledge-based tool for electrical interface specification that uses information from the functional interface description (extracted from architectural models) and nonfunctional physical requirements and constraints (such as voltage and current requirements) for interactively completing the specification.

Currently, the approaches to architectural design are by far not complete or sufficient. However, they provide support for an interactive transition form specification to design.

3 EXAMPLE

The following example is used to demonstrate the application of the different methods described here to support the requirements description and specification of an automotive cruise control system. The cruise control system represents a relatively simple automotive control system with a low priority in the overall automobile systems functional hierarchy. Being a comfort function, its interaction with other control systems, such as the engine control or the antiblocking system, must be immediately stopped in case of a brake or accelerator pedal signal. The original requirements description consisted of 60 pages of text, tables, and diagrams.

1. *Requirements description:* The acquisition of the requirements description is done using the DEBYS/CAS Hypertext-based front end (Fig. 7). The tool provides a predefined description of specification contents for automotive control systems stored in the FRESCO knowledge base. Functional as well as nonfunctional requirements and constraints are completely entered via text and table editors. A table-based acquisition supports structured and traceable descriptions of the different functional requirements as well as related test procedures. Currently, this information is used to create checklists for the following formal specification of the system model and the test procedures.

2. *Formal environment description:* A complete system specification must include the relevant parts of the system environment such as sources and sinks of information as well as feedback loops. The environment is described by a data flow diagram called a *context diagram.* The context diagram represents the top-level system description including the environmental processes, the information flow, and the system interface. Figure 8 shows at the top the cruise control as one process in the top-level context diagram.

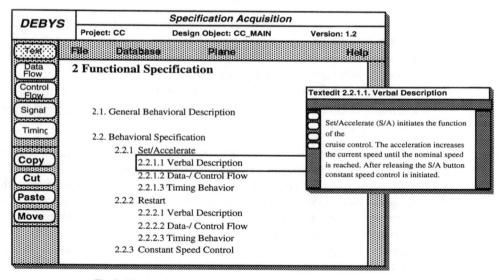

Fig. 7: User interface to the Hypertext-based requirements acquisition

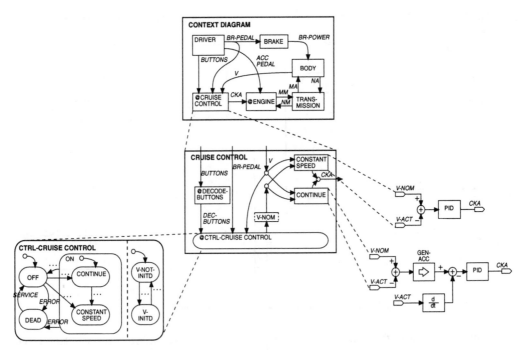

Fig. 8: Simplified integrated specification model of the cruise control

3. *Stepwise refinement and formal control specification:* The functional specification of the system to be designed is refined by a hierarchy of data flow descriptions. Each function described in the requirements definition is represented by a black-box process and a number of interconnecting data and control flows (Fig. 8, middle). Existing behavioral models are also represented as processes and are linked into the corresponding black box. System control is described at each level of the data flow hierarchy. For this purpose, a single control process is described using the visual formalism of StateCharts (Fig. 8, bottom left). Therefore, complex control processes can be described as concurrent, hierarchical state machines. State machine communication is based on broadcasting events and actions throughout the whole model. The activation/deactivation of processes is described formally and related to the transitions in the state machine model.

4. *Formal process specification:* Algorithms for process control are described using transfer functions (Fig. 8, bottom right). Therefore, the process interfaces from the data flow diagrams are imported into ISI Matrix$_x$. A library of functions and parameterizable blocks is used to describe continuous or discrete processes in the *s*- or *z*-domain. Within the cruise control example, 23 different processes reaching from simple PID controllers to complex engine models have been described. Figure 9 shows a combination of a State-Chart description and a transfer function to model the set/acceleration behavior of the cruise control.

5. *Prototyping:* Finally, the data flow hierarchy and the control and process specifications are used to generate C code and to intergrate the code fragments together with a user interface into a complete, executable system model. This software prototype is

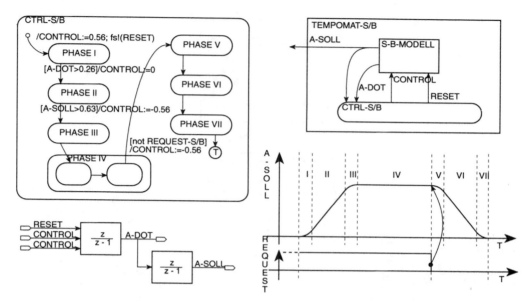

Fig. 9: Control and process model of set/acceleration function

used to validate the behavior of the model on a workstation. After the validation and correction of the model, it is downloaded into a test environment consisting of a standard microprocessor and I/O components in a test car or a engine test environment.

The advantages of the DEBYS approach recognized during this project were

- The systematic approach to the acquisition and refinement of the specification
- The possibility of concurrently formalizing the control and process specifications after having fixed the functional interfaces in the data flow diagrams
- The related significant decrease of inconsistencies and development time (the decrease in development time is estimated to be one-third of that in comparable designs)
- The different levels of analysis and simulation from rule checking to rapid prototyping that led to a high quality of the specification model
- A common, well-organized, and highly interrelated documentation of the requirements, constraints, the formal models, and the prototype.

However, a number of limitations and drawbacks were considered during this and other different applications of our approach:

- The lack of real integration of commercial and proprietary tools
- The well-known problems of the SA/RT approaches: diverging data flow hierarchies, acceptance problems, lack of support for reusability
- The imperative, control-oriented view of a system (a complex state machine controls all processes)

- The lack of freedom in the formal specification phases (weak requirements have to be replaced by detailed formal models and therefore design space is unnecessarily restricted)
- Lack of support for real back annotation because of the use of commercial tools.

However, a number of severe problems were addressed and successfully handled and possible approaches suggested for problem solving in the near future:

- Computer-aided support from the very beginning of the system design process
- Consideration of functional as well as nonfunctional requirement and constraints
- Support for iterative refinement on the requirements, specification, and architectural design level
- A restricted selection of different methodologies that is necessary to address various system designs.

The ongoing application of the environment in different projects will provide the base for gaining experience and insight into the existing problems that have to be addressed.

4 CONCLUSIONS AND FUTURE WORK

The DEBYS environment for requirement definition, specification, and system design combines commercial and proprietary tools as well as a CAE framework to provide computer support for the early design phases of complex, heterogeneous systems. Model- and knowledge-based techniques are used to support the initial requirements definition as well as the development of executable models for analysis and simulation. System-level simulation is provided by a number of concepts for simulator coupling and code import. Furthermore, prototyping is an essential feature of the environment. The integration of knowledge- and model-based techniques represents an important step in the development of an environment of the early design phases. As a result, some of the drawbacks and limitations of isolated approaches can be managed. A number of serious problems are still left and therefore represent the subject of future research and development efforts. These include

1. The extension of computer support for planning and decision support in the early requirements definition
2. Support for feasibility studies including packaging and interconnect constraints, e.g., multichip modules
3. Investigations of a well-supported transisition between requirements definition and model-based specification
4. Improved consideration of constraints within the system specification and design phases
5. Improved support for a stepwise refinement approach to requirements and specification development.

REFERENCES

[1] D. J. Hatley and I. A. Pirbhai, *Strategies for Real-Time Specification,* Dorset House Publishing, New York, 1988.

[2] T. DeMarco, *Structured Analysis and System Specification,* Prentice-Hall, Englewood Cliffs, NJ, 1979.

[3] D. Harel, A. Pnueli, J. P. Schmidt, and R. Sherman, "On the Formal Semantics of StateCharts," in *Proc. 2nd Symp. Logic in Computer Science,* pp. 54–59, 1987.

[4] S. Narayan, F. Vahid, and D. D. Gajski, "System Specification and Synthesis with the SpecCharts Language," in *Proc. ICCAD,* pp. 266–269, 1991.

[5] R. Saracco, J. R. W. Smith, and R. Reed, *Telecommunications Systems Engineering Using SDL,* North-Holland, Amsterdam, 1989.

[6] CCITT Recommendation Z.100, "Specification and Description Language SDL."

[7] VHDL System Design, The VHDL Consulting Group, Version 2.1, 1991.

[8] P. Coad and E. Yourdon, *Object Oriented Analysis,* Prentice-Hall, Englewood Cliffs, NJ, 1991.

[9] J. Rumbaugh, P. Blaha, W. Premerlani, F. Eddy, and W. Lorensen, *Object-Oriented Modelling and Design,* Prentice-Hall, Englewood Cliffs, NJ, 1991.

[10] K.D. Müller-Glaser and J. Bortolazzi, "An Approach to Computer Aided Specification," *IEEE J. of Solid-State Circ.,* 25(2), pp. 335–345, April 1990.

[11] M. Dorfman, "System and Software Requirements Engineering," in *System and Software Requirements Engineering,* R. H. Thayer, M. Dorfman, Eds., IEEE Computer Society Press, Los Alamitos, CA, 1990.

[12] A. Borgida, S. Greenspan, and J. Mylopoulos, "Knowledge Representation as the Basis for Requirements Specifications," *IEEE Computer,* pp. 82–90, April 1985.

[13] D. W. Knapp and A. C. Parker, "The ADAM Design Planning Engine," *IEEE Trans. Computer-Aided Des.,* 10(7), July 1991.

[14] K. D. Müller-Glaser, K. Neusinger, and K. Kirsch, "A Knowledge Based Project Plan Generation and Control System for ASIC Design Management," in *Proc. CICC,* pp. 25.4.1–25.4.4, 1991.

[15] M. Selz, R. Zavala, and K. D. Müller-Glaser, "Gensys—ein mehrstufiges Generatorsystem," in *Proc. of ITG/GI Workshop Entwurfsmethodik für Integrierte Schaltungen und Systeme,* 1992.

[16] J. Bortolazzi and K. D. Müller-Glaser, "Framework Integration of an Environment for Microsystem Design," in *Proc. Microsystem Technologies,* Berlin, pp. 153–160, 1991.

[17] P. Nagel, R. Scharf, W. Wolz, and K. D. Müller-Glaser, "A Generation Environment for Simulation Models for Micro System Components," in *Proc. Microsystem Technologies,* Berlin, pp. 233–240, 1991.

CHAPTER 14

System Architecture Design Using Structured Methods

Peter Mertens
Siemens AG
Erlangen, Germany

Abstract: Our definition of the term *system architecture* is the system's decomposition into modules and their connections and interfaces, together with appropriate specifications of these elements. A good system architecture is very important for product quality and development productivity. It is therefore desirable to be able to evaluate an architecture's quality regarding not only performance, but also flexibility-related properties such as reuse potential or adaptability to new requirements or new technology. To that end, we would like to have architecture models that are detailed enough to allow evaluation along the above lines, and general enough to be suitable for HW/SW systems.

For modeling system architectures, we are investigating the usability of the Hatley/Pirbhai architecture models by participating in actual development projects. This lesser known part of the Hatley/Pirbhai systems development method considers both HW and SW and contains architecture flow diagrams and architecture interconnect diagrams plus textual descriptions (architecture dictionary and interconnect specification). The diagrams form a structured hierarchy, which corresponds to the eventual system's hierarchy, and have well-defined semantics. The interconnect diagram is especially useful for discussions between HW and SW engineers, and so the models help defer HW/SW partition. The step from requirements to architecture is eased by a *requirements-to-architecture template,* which also helps to define the modules as black boxes, thereby promoting information hiding. To ensure traceability of requirements, a traceability matrix is used that can also be employed for simple architecture quality assessments.

Thus, these models contain all types of information important for architecture and have several features that ease the way from requirements to architecture and for heuristic architecture quality assessments. In our project work, the most important immediate impact was on the understandability, consistency, and completeness of the system documents involved.

Other results include the applicability of the method down to the HW/SW interface and useful additions to the methodology.

In future work, we would like to find measures for the flexibility-related architecture properties and to develop templates for the textual part of the models that help provide the information needed in these measures. The eventual goal is a catalog of good system architectures fit for reuse.

1 INTRODUCTION

1.1 Definition

System architectures are a very important issue in systems engineering. Before we start explaining the reasons, we need a definition of *system architecture* that is precise enough for working with it, yet general enough to be applicable to software, hardware, and embedded systems. Since the definitions in the literature are not sufficient, we use our own: Architecture =

- The decomposition of a system into subsystems, called "modules"
- The (functional) specification of these modules
- The (data) interfaces between the modules
- The modules' interconnections = the channels on which the data flow.

Each module can in turn be described as a system with its own architecture. The complete system architecture will form a hierarchy of modules, which in general is different from the hierarchy defined by the system's functional decomposition.

1.2 Location in the Development Process and Importance

A system's architecture is defined when going from the requirements phase to the design phase of the development process. In the large projects we are addressing, the module decomposition and the ensuing system hierarchy will correspond to the project organization in terms of groups that develop individual components (see Fig. 1). A good decomposition into modules and clear interfaces will give a clear description of who is to do what and which information is needed as an input from other groups. Therefore, a good architecture helps channel communication and collaboration between the groups and reduces overhead owing to poorly defined technical responsibilities. This is an important issue in enhancing development productivity. The architecture as the system's structure also influences the structure of the documentation.

Regarding the system as a product, we note that the architecture determines important system properties such as

- Performance
- Flexibility-related properties such as adaptability to changes in requirements or technology, potential for reuse, maintainability, and many more.

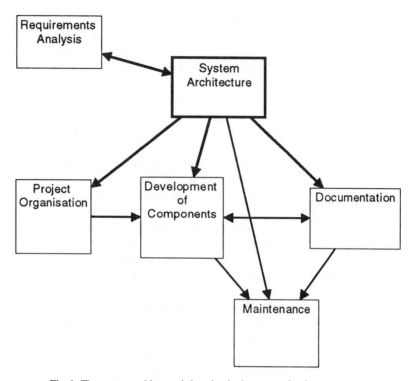

Fig. 1: The system architecture's location in the system development process

For example, maintenance, which accounts for a substantial portion of system costs [1], depends on the structure of the documentation and a clear system decomposition in order to be able to locate and remove failures quickly and correctly (Fig. 1).

A system's performance can be expressed in numbers, and can be estimated using methods such as simulation or timed Petri nets. For this purpose, tools are available (see, e.g., [2]). We do not discuss this issue any further.

For the flexibility-related properties, however, no generally accepted measures exist. Yet, it is paramount to make these system properties measurable early in the design phase. Once we can decide about an architecture's quality, we will be able to accumulate a catalog of good architectures that can be reused to get better productivity and quality.

To be able to measure an architecture's properties, we must first describe the system architecture precisely. This architecture modeling is the topic of the main body of this chapter. In the last part, we describe some preliminary results from our project work.

1.3 Goal

In our working group, we help enhance development productivity by working in actual development projects with the engineers to coach them on the use of new methods and tools. Although we use input from academic research, our approach is to provide the engineers with ready-to-use methods. Our demands on methodology are therefore substantially driven by the acceptance and standardization of the methods and tools.

To be easily readable and accessible, we require the architecture modeling methods to be graphics oriented. To be able to bind the architecture to system requirements, we demand a method that works well with established structured methods used in requirements analysis. We found such a modeling method in the Hatley/Pirbhai architecture models [3–5]. We decided to use these models in a project together with the development engineers to find out about the real-world problems of using it and how to adapt it to the specific project's needs.

The model's elements are described using the example of programmable logic controls (PLCs; see, e.g., [6]) in the next section. In Section 3, the potential benefits of using the models are described. Section 4 offers some observations from our participation in an actual development project.

Some remarks are in order about the role these methods play in HW/SW codesign. First, the systems we consider contain both HW and SW, and the methods are applicable to both. System-level architecture design can be viewed as a high-level HW/SW codesign. Second, many of the architecture components appearing in the models are typical subjects of HW/SW codesign, such as PCBs with both standard microprocessors and ASICs. So, the architecture model is an important input for HW/SW codesign. Third, being neutral to HW/SW partitioning, the methods are useful for doing HW/SW codesign, e.g., for delaying HW/SW partitioning or for defining several alternative ways of partitioning that can then be evaluated. The general ideas and the conceptual framework the method provides are a good guidance for using the possibilities of tools like Statemate^{TM}.

2 THE ELEMENTS OF THE HATLEY/PIRBHAI ARCHITECTURE MODELS

2.1 Functional Model

We start with a functional model of our fictitious PLC (Fig. 2). To describe the functions, we have used structured analysis [7] with real-time extensions (SA/RT) [3,4] as an example. This methodology stems from SW engineering. There are two main ideas: First, to specify the system precisely by decomposing the system's functions into more elementary ones using a data flow point of view. Each decomposition yields a set of functions, sometimes also called *processes* or *transitions,* that are connected through a network of data flows. Second, we need to cope with complexity by hierarchically decomposing each function further until an elementary level is reached, at which each function is defined in a suitable specification language. Thus, a hierarchy of networks is generated that must fulfill consistency conditions and rules that guide development of the model and allow automatic checks in CASE tools. The real-time extensions mainly consist of describing the behavior of the functions by states and transitions, very similar to the ones used in HW design.

The model in Fig. 2 shows the flow of data between processes (bubbles) that perform the PLC's functions, plus terminators and stores. Rectangles with broken lines denote *terminators,* i.e., entities outside the system with which it communicates. Solid arrows

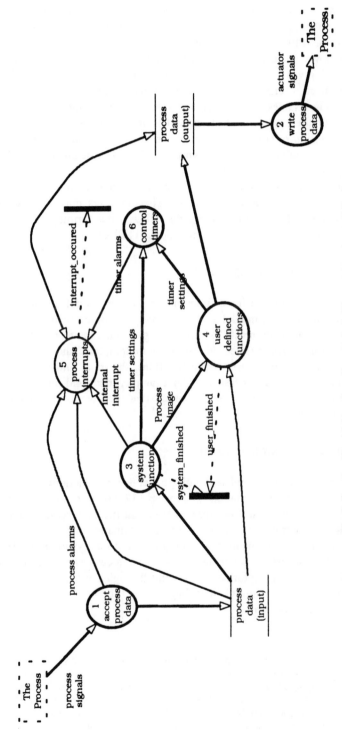

Fig. 2: Functional model (data flow diagram, including context and control flow)

are data flows, broken arrows are control flows. "Bubbles" denote "processes" that use and transform data, parallel lines are data stores, and the vertical bars denote the control specification (CSPEC).[1] For further explanation of symbols, see [3,4]. In the CSPEC, the control flows are used to determine which of the processes is active at a certain time. Figure 3 gives an example. The CSPEC tells one how the control flows (here: interrupt_occurred, user_finished, and system_finished) affect the behavior of the system. Process activation tables show which functions are active under certain conditions in a certain state of the system. The states and their transitions are described in the STD. When the condition or control flow above the line comes true, the action below the line is taken, and the state changes as shown in the STD. For details on CSPECs, STDs, and PATs, see [3,4].

The graphical model is to be accompanied by a requirements dictionary, containing descriptions of all data and control flows. The processes must be described by either detailing them in further data flow diagrams (DFDs), thus forming a functional hierarchy, or by describing them in process specifications (PSPECs).

2.2 The Architecture Template

If one tries to allocate these functions to specific modules, one will notice that a system containing nothing more than there is in Fig. 2 wouldn't work. To take into account the system's communication with its surroundings and the maintenance and self-test tasks, Hatley and Pirbhai have invented the "architecture template" shown in Fig. 4. It contains boxes for the control or user-interface functions, the input and output processing, and the maintenance and self-test tasks. In our example, input and output to the process the PLC is supposed to control are so important that they were already considered in the functional diagram.

2.3 Enhanced Functional Model

The template is now completed to give the enhanced functional model of Fig. 5. (The circled "M" here is an abbreviation for process #12, "monitor system," in order to avoid even more crossings of data flow arrows.) Note that it was necessary to include two new terminators: the control network that supplies information from other parts of the plant and from other PLCs, and the user, who programs and surveys the PLC. The user must be able to monitor the system, hence the necessity of process #12, "monitor system," which has access to almost any information flowing through the PLC. (In the pure approach, the context diagram, the control flow diagram, and the control specifications also have to be enhanced at this step).

---

[1] In fact, for conciseness, we have put information into one diagram that would go into three different, yet connected, diagrams in the pure Hatley/Pirbhai method [3]: A context diagram would contain just the terminators and our system as a single bubble. The DFD would contain the data flows, stores, and process bubbles, but no terminators, control flows, or control specification bars. The control flow diagram (CFD) would contain the bubbles, control flows, and control bars, but no data flows, terminators, or stores. Hatley and Pirbhai call the DFDs+PSPECs the *functional model,* and CFDs and CSPECs the *control model.*

305

Interrupt_occured	P 4 user defined functions	P 3 system functions
1	–	see STD
0	see STD	–

Process activation tables (PATs)

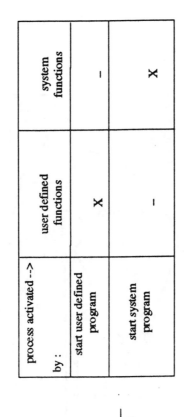

process activated --> by :	user defined functions	system functions
start user defined program	X	–
start system program	–	X

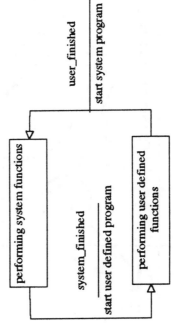

State-transition-diagram (STD)

Fig. 3: Control specification (CSPEC) for the functional model in Fig. 2

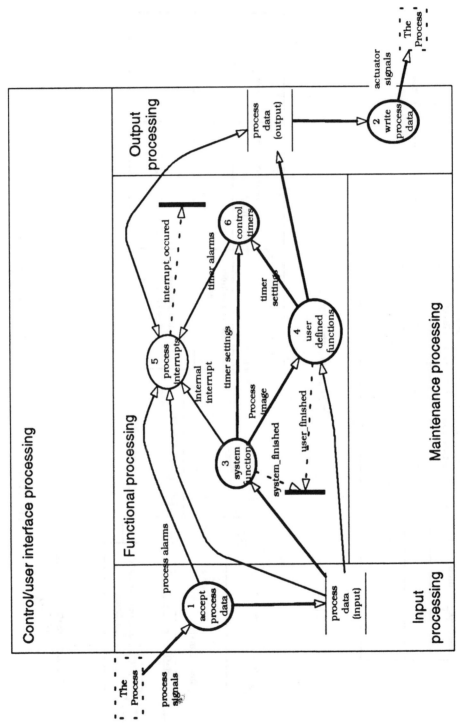

Fig. 4: Functional model with architecture template

306

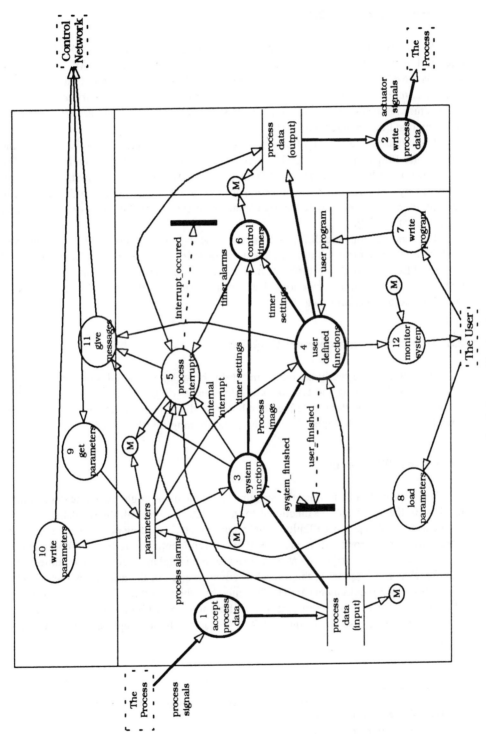

Fig. 5: Enhanced functional model

2.4 Architecture Flow Diagram

We are now ready to allocate functions to modules. This has been done in Fig. 6 by circling functions that will be implemented by a certain module. Two "M" abbreviation symbols are contained in the IU and OU encirclings, indicating that part of the monitoring activities are to be implemented by these two modules. It is not necessary to respect the architecture template boxes. For example, the CPU module has processes from both the functional and the maintenance parts.

The modules and the data flows between them that are defined this way go into the architecture flow diagram of Fig. 7.[2] Here, rounded rectangles denote the modules. The data flows have been grouped together to give an easier-to-read diagram, but are still described by solid line arrows, while control flows are denoted by broken line arrows. In general, more than one module can be contained in each template box (see also the later schematic of Fig.10).

The module icons are different from the process bubbles in order to keep one from confusing the functional with the architectural description, because in general these will be very different and define different hierarchies. Note that a power supply is included that does not perform any functions that appear in the data flow description, because it does not use or transform data.

2.5 Architecture Interconnect Diagram

We still have to specify the interconnections between the modules on which the data flow. This is done using the *architecture interconnect diagram* of Fig. 8. The interconnections are shown with user-defined symbols (solid and heavy lines for the bus, broken lines for power, a dash-dotted line for the programming interface line).[3]

2.6 Traceability Matrix

It is very important to trace the system requirements through the whole development process. In the step from the functional to the architecture model, the traceability matrix can be used for this purpose (Table 1). All requirements, including processes, CSPEC, and stores, are listed in rows. All modules that have been identified are listed in columns, and an "X" means that the requirement on this row is to be implemented by the module on this column. Being more precise, the traceability matrix and not the allocation diagram (Fig. 6) defines which requirements are implemented by which module. To ensure the covering of all requirements, *every* requirement must be implemented by *at least one* module [3]. However, we have also found the matrix to be useful for a simple architecture quality control.

---

[2] In the pure Hatley/Pirbhai approach, an architecture context diagram, in most cases identical to the functional context diagram, is added (see [3]).

[3] Some different conventions have been suggested in [3–5].

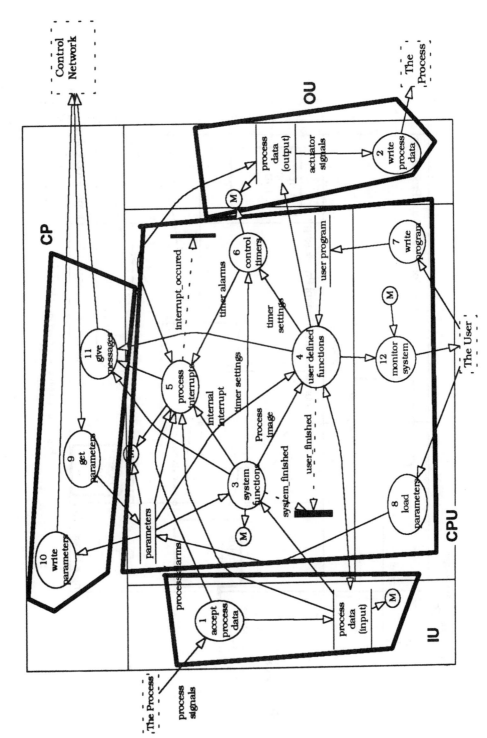

Fig. 6: Functons-to-modules allocation

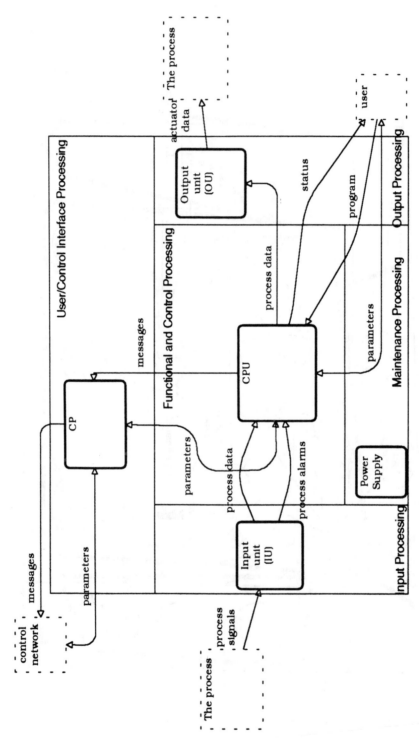

Fig. 7: Architecture flow diagram (AFD)

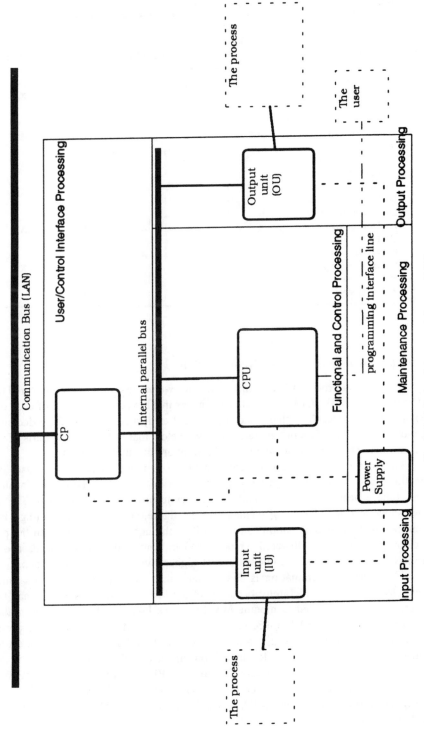

Fig. 8: Architecture interconnect diagram (AID)

TABLE 1: Traceability Matrix for PLC Example

Process #	CP (Communication Processor)	IU (Input Unit)	CPU	OU (Output Unit)
1. Accept process data		X		
2. Write process data				X
3. System functions			X	
4. User-defined functions			X	
5. Process interrupts			X	
6. Control timers			X	
7. Write program			X	
8. Load parameters			X	
9. Get parameters	X			
10. Write parameters	X			
11. Give messages	X			
12. Monitor system		X	X	X
CSPEC			X	
Process data (input) store		X		
Process data (output) store				X
Program store			X	
Parameter store			X	

2.6.1 Further Functional Decomposition

If we look at process #12, "monitor system," we see that it has been allocated to three different modules: IU, CPU, and OU. This means that the responsibilities of each of these modules are not clearly defined, and that we better detail process #12 by decomposing it, thus introducing a functional hierarchy level below that of Fig. 5. The parts of process #12 can then be allocated separately to different architecture modules.

This idea is depicted schematically in Fig. 9. It is an example of the fact that the functional and the architecture hierarchy do not run in parallel: Functions in hierarchy level 1 have been allocated to modules in architecture hierarchy level 0. The dashed lines show correspondences of elements in the figure, such as processes (e.g., P4) and their hierarchical decomposition (processes P4.1 through P4.4), or between the polygon encircling the processes allocated to module M3 and that module itself. The dashed circles are intended to show the decompositions of higher level processes as a group.

The process denomination is chosen such that the difference between functional hierarchy and module hierarchy becomes clear: for example, process P3 has become process M3–P1, allocated to module M3. Processes P4.2 and P4.4 have been allocated as processes M3–P2 and M3–P3, respectively. Module M3 has been decomposed into three sub modules, M3.1 through M3.3. Processes M3–P2 and M3–P3, identical to P4.2 and P4.4 from the functional decomposition, are not further decomposed and become M3.3–P1 and M3.3–P2, respectively. Process M3–P1, however, identical to P3 from the functional decomposition, had to be further decomposed, so that P3.1 and P3.3 could be allocated as M3.1–P1 and M3.1–P2, respectively. Similarly, P3.2 and P3.4 are allocated as M3.2–P1 and M3.2–P2.

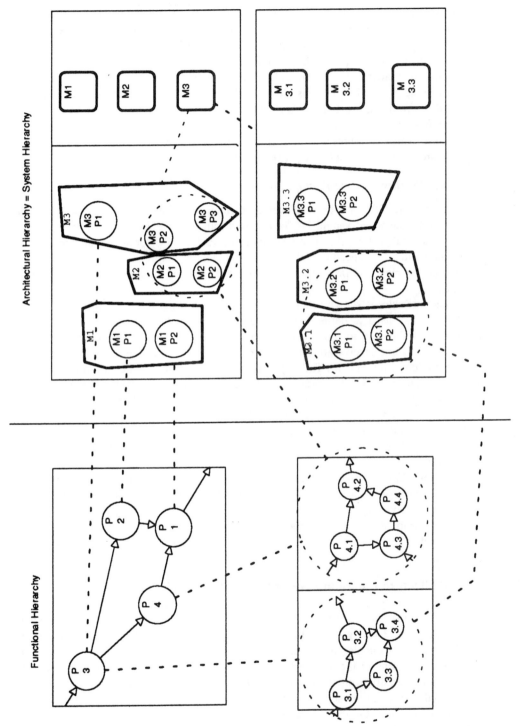

Fig. 9: Schematic illustration of the difference between functional and architecture hierarchy

313

This is also an example of a functional decomposition driven by architectural considerations and shows that both descriptions are interdependent and need not be developed one after the other, as in the waterfall model of the system life cycle, but can well be developed iteratively, as in the Boehm spiral model [8].

Note also that the use of the architecture template in decomposing modules into submodules helps develop them as clean black boxes: a layer of interfaces is wrapped around the core functions. If later some interface or interconnection has to be changed, the functions can be left intact and vice versa. In software engineering, two heuristic architecture quality measures that go with this are *information hiding* and *data abstraction* [4]. The architecture template thus helps incorporate some of the heuristics.

2.6.2 Further Module Decomposition

The module CPU has been allocated so many functions that it is a full-fledged, complex subsystem that should be decomposed into separate architectural units. To do this, it is helpful to take the functions allocated to the CPU, draw a template around them, and build an enhanced model of the CPU functions before allocating them to CPU submodules. It may also prove necessary to detail some of the processes, as in the last paragraph.

This procedure is shown schematically in Fig. 10. (First row: the steps of Sections 2.1 through 2.5, used to define the modules N.1 through N.5. Second row: enhancing the functions allocated to module N.1. Denomination of modules is similar to that of Fig. 9. Broken line arrows are logical correspondences, solid line arrows are steps in the completion of the model.) This figure is an example of an architecture-driven system specification process: The functional model does not exist independent of the architecture model, as on the left-hand side of Fig. 9, but only as a module specification that is attached to each module on a given module hierarchy level. However, one has to be careful to make clear connections (e.g., data flow balancing) between the functions on different levels of module specifications to ensure a consistent functional model embedded in the architectural one.

This development process idea [9] is well suited for large projects. The architecture and module descriptions, i.e., the design, on level N make up the requirements specification for the next lower level N+1. It is therefore important to always state which level one is talking about before one starts discussions: one person's design is another person's requirement.

2.7 Architecture Dictionary and Interconnect Specification

The architecture model is not complete without written descriptions of the data and interconnections. These go into the architecture dictionary and the interconnect specification (see the examples in Tables 2 and 3). It is important to include references to the interconnections in the architecture dictionary, which is the most conspicuous difference to the requirements dictionary. These parts of the architecture model allow us to detect bottlenecks and can serve as a starting point for performance evaluations. They are absolutely necessary for actually building the system, because they contain the detailed information on the interfaces one has to take into account.

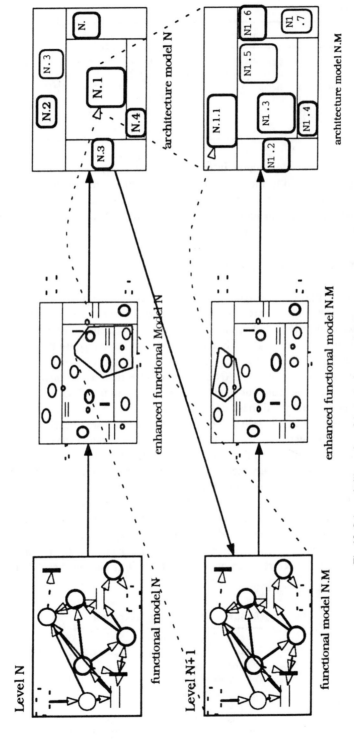

Fig. 10: Schematic illustration of decomposing a module by reconsidering the functions allocated to it using the architecture template

Level N

functional model N

enhanced functional Model N

architecture model N

Level N+1

functional model N.M

enhanced functional model N.M

architecture model N.M

N.

N.3

N.2

N.1

N.4

N.3

N1.6

N1.7

N1.5

N.1.1

N1.3

N1.4

N1.2

TABLE 2: Architecture Dictionary

Name	Consists of	Origin	Destination	Channel
Process data (input)	Analog process data (input) + digital process data (input)	Input unit (IU)	CPU	Internal parallel bus
Analog process data (input)	1{real number}36	-"-	-"-	-"-
Digital process data (input)	1{bit}128	-"-	-"-	-"-
Parameters	...	External	CP	Communication bus (LAN)
...	...	...	...	...

However, *which* particular information must be contained in these specifications, especially with regard to the flexibility-related architecture properties, is not clear at the moment. The layout of these specifications (an architecture dictionary template and an interconnect specification template) must be developed for each actual project. We are currently working on this issue.

2.8 Some Remarks on the Example

For the purpose of explaining the methods in this chapter, we have chosen a rather high-level hardware/software system as an example (not a Siemens PLC, but a fictitious one modeled after [6]). It has an architecture that is almost completely determined by hardware considerations: The CP, IU, and OU are necessary units, because the process bus connecting the PLC to sensors and actuators has to be electrically decoupled from all other connections, and the LAN control network requires an intelligent CP to connect to the PLC. All other functions have been allocated to the CPU.

The principle behind these decisions, which are obvious from hardware considerations, is called *communicational cohesion* in the software engineering architecture heuristics [4]: "group together functions that talk with one particular terminator or one specific part of one's system." From this example we expect that the use of architecture diagrams will help software engineers incorporate this heuristics in their designs, because all communication interfaces are described graphically in the model.

Another example of hardware-driven architecture is the use of the internal parallel bus (Fig. 8): This is dictated by the requirement that the user may configure a PLC as he or she wishes by adding more modules that connect to this bus. The analogue in software would be "soft buses," or, more generally, standard data formats or masks. This example indicates that architecture interconnect diagrams will also be helpful in pure software development.

TABLE 3: Interconnection Specification

Internal parallel bus
64-bit parallel bus
Protocol: ....
Electrical properties: ...
Baud rate: ...
(Optional): available controllers ....

Another point to make is that these architecture models form a hierarchy of networks and thus ease the step from requirements in the form of network-like data flow diagrams to design in the form of purely hierarchical structure charts (described, e.g., in [4]), which is still a major issue in software engineering.

2.9 The Complete System Specification and the Development Process

The modeling methods described here are *structured methods,* as indicated by the name *structured analysis.* This means that

- They allow for a hierarchical description of the system.
- Each hierarchy level, however, has a network structure.
- The leveling leads to consistency requirements that the models have to fulfill (balancing of flows).
- The models are interconnected by mutual references and by written documents (dictionaries).
- The models lend themselves to automatic consistency control, as in CASE tools.

Pirbhai [9] stresses that one cannot build the system unless one has completed one's specification *including the architecture.* The specification consists of the functional and control model (context diagram, DFDs, PSPECs, CFDs, CSPECs, and the requirements dictionary), the enhanced functional model (enhanced versions of each part mentioned), and the architecture model (context diagram, AIDs, AFDs, module specifications, architecture dictionary, and interconnect specifications).

The structure of the finished model—architecture model plus module specifications in the form of functional models attached to each module—allows for a consistency check, because all dependencies between different documents are spelled out: One knows where to look for some specific piece of information, and one is guided in all of the analysis steps by the prescribed structure of the model.

However, it is not necessary to proceed along any prescribed development process model. Rather, process models are there to know what one eventually has to do until one has finished the specification. Different scenarios are possible, some of which were described in Section 2.6. This approach of not taking the process model too seriously is called the "fake it" approach [10].

3 BENEFITS

3.1 Benefits of the Architecture Models

As explained in Section 1, the benefits of architecture models in general are that they form the basis for measuring an architecture's properties. They formalize the design process, lead to a better architecture simply by making one think about architectural issues, and are basic for structuring all later development steps.

The Hatley/Pirbhai models in particular help defer hardware/software partition and enhance communication between HW and SW engineers. This becomes clear by a look at the architecture interconnect diagrams: They are very similar to the block diagrams that are used in hardware descriptions. However, they are linked to the architecture flow diagrams, and these, in turn, to the data flow diagrams, which are used by software engineers. Thus, putting both descriptions on equal footing and connecting them via written specifications and consistency requirements, the architecture model lends itself as a basis for discussions between the hardware and software sides.

Partitioning algorithms to evaluate design alternatives can be used once the architecture dictionary and the interconnect specifications contain all information needed by the chosen algorithm.

3.2 Benefits Regarding the Development Process

Most of these benefits are related to the flexibility of the methods. For example, no specific development process is enforced. In fact, one can move back and forth freely between the functional and the architectural model. The architecture models can be used to incorporate existing modules into one's design, thus enhancing reuse. The methods allow incorporation of other tools, like different functional models (e.g., state charts) or existing (CASE) tools to draw one's diagrams. One can also tailor the symbols and dictionary templates to one's specific needs. The models lend themselves to consistency checks and so enhance one's system documentation quality. Most of these issues were dealt with in Section 2.

3.3 Benefits Stemming from the Architecture Template and the Traceability Matrix

The template helps develop the modules as clean black boxes, to promote information hiding and data abstraction, and to take into account the system's communication with its environment, as well as maintenance and self-test tasks. This was demonstrated in Section 2.6.

The traceability matrix allows for simple architecture quality assessments and helps not to allocate a process to more than one module (note, however, that this may be inevitable with CSPECs!), and not to allocate too many requirements to a module that is not further decomposed (see Sections 2.6, 2.8, and 2.9).

4 OBSERVATIONS FROM THE ACTUAL PROJECT AND OUTLOOK ON FURTHER WORK

4.1 First Observations from a Real-Life Project

When using the Hatley/Pirbhai models in an actual project, the first benefit that was substantiated was the impact on document consistency. Most of the other benefits will only turn up in later stages of the project. However, some interesting issues have been identified that are of general interest.

4.1.1 Tool Support

Apart from preliminary work [5], there is no tool support for the architecture diagrams. We currently use a graph editor that allows for user-defined symbols and supports hierarchies. Although a tool that provides extensive consistency checks, even across different model parts and including the written specifications, would be useful, we remark that all structured methods have been invented and their applicability and benefits shown by means of just pencil and paper.

4.1.2 Architecture Interconnect Context Diagram

This has not been suggested by Hatley and Pirbhai, but we find it to be a useful addition to the architecture context diagram, which is almost identical to the functional context diagram (see [3]).

4.1.3 Modeling Interconnections as Modules

Indeed, we have already done this by including the CP module in Fig. 5. Since the same logical data go in and out of this module without being used (Fig. 7), we have in fact violated a rule put forth in [3]. The reason is that in later stages we will also have to model the behavior of the CP by decomposing and detailing it, which is not possible with interconnections (as opposed to other architecture description approaches, like CMU's UniCon).

4.1.4 Changing Views When Detailing the Model

The CP problem of the last section is already an example of changing views: On the highest level, it could as well be described as an interconnection, but on lower levels we want to detail it and therefore model it as a module. Another example that is not as easily resolved is the fact that software modules of high levels become just data being moved from storage to processor and back when one models the CPU hardware or the operating system. Somewhere in between a break has to occur.

4.1.5 Using SDL Sequence Charts for Describing Timing in Scenarios

Since the CSPECs have been allocated to the modules, the timing of the functions is sometimes hard to see in the models. We have found it useful to provide SDL sequence charts [11] with architecture diagrams to describe scenarios of system operation. This makes the models easier to understand and can also be a first step toward detailed design or implementation using SDL.

4.2 Open Questions and Further Work

Besides addressing the open issues of Section 4.1, our efforts go mainly in two directions.

4.2.1 Applicability of the Models to the Hardware/Software Interface and Operating System Level

Since for hardware/software codesign we want continuous, coherent model support, this is an important question. To describe HW/SW interfaces, some of the hardware has to be modeled, preferably with the same method as the software. This issue is connected to Section 4.1.4.

4.2.2 Implementing Architecture Measures

In Sections 2.6, 2.8, and 2.9 it was shown that, up to now, there are only heuristic measures for the flexibility-related architecture properties. We hope to learn about better approaches from software measures and hardware/software partitioning algorithms. Once we find promising measures, we can develop templates for the architecture dictionaries and interconnect specifications that have entries for all information needed for the algorithms to work.

5 UPDATE

Since this paper was written, several points could be substantiated, and several new directions have evolved.

5.1 Term Definitions

It has proved to be important to make the following points to avoid confusion.

1. *Hatley/Pirbhai SA/RT* is a well-known method to describe the *functional* requirements for a system (see Section 2.1 and Figs. 2 and 3).
2. *Hatley/Pirbhai architecture model* is a method to describe a system's architecture, that is its *physical* characteristics. It is as old as the SA/RT method, but not nearly as well known (see Sections 2.4 through 2.7 and Figs. 7 and 8).
3. *Hatley/Pirbhai system specification* is the combination of the above two, together with the architecture template and the traceability matrix. It has all been published *together* in [3] (see Section 2.3 and Figs. 4, 5, and 6).
4. *Pirbhai system development process* is a development process that guides one to develop the Hatley/Pirbhai models [9]. It states explicitly that you need both a functional and an architectural model, but it does not force you to use Hatley and Pirbhai's methods. Thus, it has a flexibility that allows for adaptations (see Sections 2.3, 2.6, 2.8, and 2.9 and Figs. 4, 5, 6, 9, and 10).

5.2 Progress in Using the Methods in a Development Project

As mentioned in Section 4, the most immediate impact of using the method was that we were able to find missing or inconsistent definitions in the preliminary stages of the system papers. It was very important to model the system while developing it. The diagrams were favorably regarded by the system engineers as a means to present and defend the architecture they had developed.

5.3 Enhancing and/or Changing Model Specifics

To accommodate a layered view of the architecture that many SW engineers have become used to, the architecture flow diagrams in our real-life project were drawn in a manner that reflected the layered structure in the arrangement of the modules on paper. To enhance understanding, two additional features were used in the diagrams: Data interface submodules, such as queues and buffers, were drawn into the modules instead of being shown on the next hierarchy level. This idea, taken from the SW architecture diagrams of [4], leads to a better understanding of the model and has also proved useful when preparing the architecture for implementation along the lines indicated by [12].

To show the dynamics of the architecture without having to build a full functional SA/RT model (which was impossible due to lack of time at the advanced stage of the project), SDL sequence charts were used as indicated in Section 4.

In another project with object-oriented SW development, the traceability matrix was adapted to show dependencies between the functional requirements and the classes that implement them.

These examples show that the models fulfill a very important requirement: They are flexible enough to be adapted to the problem and environment at hand. They can also be introduced in a step-by-step fashion, first concentrating on major trouble spots before trying to build a complete model.

5.4 Modeling a PLC CPU Board

A PLC CPU board with three processors was modeled to build a complete Hatley/Pirbhai system specification [13]. It was found to be possible to use the methods on the HW level, as mentioned in Section 4. Some specific HW modeling problems were solved and can be used in further hardware models. Among others, the models had the following results:

- The models lead to a very thorough understanding of the workings of the board. Some requirements on the operating system that depend on the specifics of the board were singled out.
- The model is a good starting point to write the HW-specific parts of the operating system.
- The time required to learn the methods and apply them to a completely unknown system, including writing it all up, was about three months. With experience with this type of CPU and with the modeling method, and by modeling parallel to or in HW design, this time can no doubt be shortened substantially.
- When modeling hardware, the architecture interconnection diagram is a good starting point, since it can be directly drawn from the circuit plan. However, the complicated control, which is necessary between the processors and which is distributed between the processors, forces one to write several different control

specifications for the board. Also, the engineer found Ward and Mellor's "activate/deactivate" arrows [14] to be helpful.

6 CONCLUSIONS

We have chosen the Hatley/Pirbhai architecture modeling method for use in an actual system development project. We believe that it leads to architecture models that complete a consistent system specification. This is supported by first observations in real-life projects. The method is general enough to be used by hardware and software engineers, and it can probably be extended far enough to serve as a continuous, coherent modeling technique throughout the hardware/software codesign process. It contains instruments (architecture template, traceability matrix) that help take some heuristic architecture quality measures into account.

Our main directions for further work, on which we would appreciate input from the academic community, involve the questions of the different views of system architecture, the applicability of the methods down to the HW/SW interface, and the use of practical architecture quality measures.

REFERENCES

[1] M. Pressman, *Software Engineering—A Practitioner's Approach*, p. 326, McGraw-Hill, New York, 1982.

[2] G. Forte, *IEEE Software*, pp. 70–79, esp. 73, May 1992.

[3] D. Hatley and I. A. Pirbhai, *Strategies for Real-Time System Specification*, Dorset House, New York, 1987.

[4] K. Shumate and M. Keller, *Software Specification and Design*, Wiley, New York, 1992.

[5] T. Nicinski, "Extending Teamwork for Architecture Diagrams," *IEEE Software*, p. 54, May 1992.

[6] P. Wratil, *Speicherprogrammierbare Steuerungen in der Automatisierungstechnik*, Vogel, Würzburg, 1989.

[7] T. DeMarco, *Structured Analysis and System Specification*, Prentice-Hall, Englewood Cliffs, NJ, 1978.

[8] B. W. Boehm, "A Spiral Model of Software Development and Enhancement," *IEEE Computer*, p. 61, May 1988.

[9] I. A. Pirbhai, *A Process for System Development*, Seminar by Systems Methods, Inc., Seattle, WA, 1991.

[10] D. L. Parnas and P. C. Clemens, "A Rational Design Process: How and Why to Fake It," *IEEE Trans. Software Eng.*, SE-12(2), p. 252, Feb. 1986.

[11] SDL Specification, CCITT Blue Book, Geneva, 1989.

[12] M. Nagl, *Softwaretechnik—Programmieren im Großen,* Springer-Verlag, Berlin, 1990 (in German).

[13] O. Brunn, "Anwendung der Hatley/Pirbhai-Modellierungsmethode auf Mikrocomputersysteme am Beispiel einer AG-CPU inklusive Hardware und Betriebssystem," Diplomarbeit, Fachhochschule für Technik Esslingen, 1992/93 (in German).

[14] P. T. Ward and S. J. Mellor, *Structured Development for Real Time Systems,* 3 vols., Prentice-Hall, Englewood Cliffs, NJ, 1985.

CHAPTER 15

First Strategies, Concepts, and Tools for Hardware/Software Codesign in an Emulation-Aided Design Environment

Petra Nauber   Klaus Scherer   Gerd vom Boegel

Fraunhofer-Institute of Microelectronic Circuits and Systems

Dresden, Germany

Abstract: An emulation-aided design environment for complex HW/SW systems consisting of a rapid prototype emulator and a set of appropriate design tools that was under development in 1992 is introduced. The underlying design methodology is discussed on general aspects and approaches to HW/SW codesign. Open problems and possible solutions are worked out. The rapid prototype emulator is an open, user configureable system. The functionality of the design is carried out by different types of modules that can be integrated in the emulator. This allows for a fast and cost-effective verification of the design and different alternatives in a real-time system environment. In the meantime, the work has been progressed resulting in a PC-based emulation system.

1 INTRODUCTION

The growing functionality and complexity as well as restrictive requirements on time to market, costs, performance and quality make tremendous demands on the design and verification of complex hardware/software systems (HW/SW systems). In particular, the specification of information processing units, which are carrying the main functional-

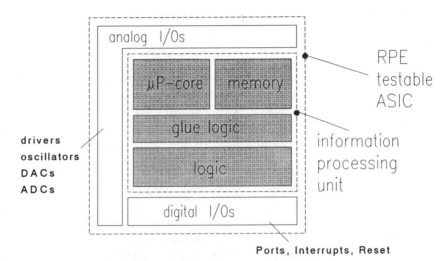

Fig. 1: Centralized information processing unit as special case of an ASIC design

ity of such a system (see Fig. 1), can be very problematic. The reason for this is the heterogeneous nature of the system and its embedded environment.

Design tools have to take into account and must be able to handle such features as

- Behavior, structure, causal relations
- Concurrency, distributed functionality, distributed control, distributed resources
- Hierarchy
- Communication, synchronization.

At the Fraunhofer Institute of Microelectronic Circuits and Systems (IMS) an emulation-aided design (EAD) environment for application-specific HW/SW systems is under development [14]. Its objective is to shorten design time and to improve design quality supporting the designer at the following steps:

- Functional specification of the information processing unit at the behavioral level
- Modeling of various architectural concepts
- Partitioning the design into hardware and/or software components
- Fast realization of real-time prototypes (rapid prototyping)
- Verification and evaluation of design alternatives
- Design transfer into the target technology (e.g., gate array, ASIC, PLD, etc.).

For fast and cost-effective verification of the design in a real-time system environment, a rapid prototype emulator (RPE) is integrated in the EAD environment. The RPE is a useful tool for the functional verification and performance evaluation of complex HW/SW systems [17].

2 DESIGN METHODOLOGY AND HW/SW CODESIGN: GENERAL ASPECTS, OPEN PROBLEMS, AND APPROACHES

To make use of the benefits of EAD, a fast and cost-effective transformation of the design task into the RPE is necessary. Within the EAD environment an appropriate methodology and suitable tools for a mainly computer-aided design flow from a verbal description to its realization on the RPE is available, where the main emphasis is on the support of both system-level design and functional design verification and performance evaluation within the real-time environment.

2.1 Design Methodology

HW/SW systems tend to become more and more application specific because of the demand for continuously growing system functionality. Distributed system components and heterogeneous hardware implementations characterize such systems. On the other hand, the customer's demands for a short time to market and cost efficiency require a flexible design environment that incorporates design flow from behavioral description to implementation as well as tools for managing design changes and redesigns and for investigating advantages and disadvantages of design alternatives.

The tools integrated in the EAD environment (Fig. 2) support the designer starting at the system level. After specifying the requirement and environment descriptions and constraints of the design task, synthesis steps are carried out to transform the design into a structure of communicating hardware and/or software modules, which itself can be designed by means of conventional design tools. With RPE integrated in the EAD environment the designer is able to verify the functionality of the design within the system's real-time application environment. This can be done at a very early phase of development when no assumption about implemention has been made yet. Therefore, changes in design and corrections of the prototype can easily be carried out using the design tools and the software configurable RPE hardware. The RPE is also an appropriate tool for weighing different hardware/software design alternatives.

2.2 Specification and Modeling

Specification is the process of working out a formalized model and the design constraints that make up the base of all further design steps, verification, testing, and finally putting it into operation. It is an essential part of system-level design (see Fig. 3).

The specification process is strongly connected to the underlying model. From a verbal, informal description of the design task a formalized description consisting of a requirement and environment definition and design constraints is generated on the base of a suitable modeling approach. No unique modeling or specification method exists [15]. On the contrary, the choice of a specific modeling approach is problem specific and depends on its efficiency regarding

- Modeling power
- Validation and verification including simulation

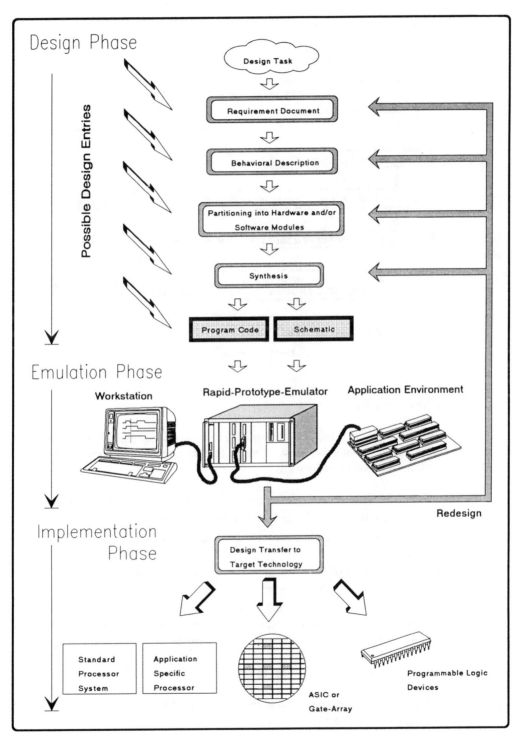

Fig. 2: EAD of information processing units

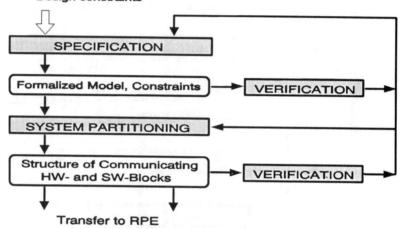

Fig. 3: System-level design

- Analysis support
- Model transformations (synthesis)

and is influenced by the designer's knowledge and experience as well as by significant modeling aspects. On the other hand, a formal description of a heterogeneous design task has to fulfill such general requests as

- Representation of functionality and/or structure at different abstraction levels
- Implementation-independent specification of complex systems
- The means for describing the essential requirement definitions and design constraints
- Equal treatment of hardware and software tasks without fixing their realization at this abstraction level
- Support of all following design steps
- Support of the design of complex heterogeneous HW/SW systems by means of hierarchy, concurrency, communication, synchronization, and distributed resources.

Modeling approaches that are relevant in system design are

- Various classes of graphs, including Petri nets [4,8]
- Communicating FSMs
- Sequential processes.

Many textual and graphical descriptions are based on these formal models. In designing complex systems, different descriptions for modeling subtasks can be useful. Behavioral description languages and hierarchical nets seems to be appropriate formal descriptions for complex design tasks.

In the EAD environment an extension of Petri nets, the so-called "information processing" nets, will be integrated. The information processing net [10] is a directed bipartite graph

$$N = (\mathbf{R}, \mathbf{S}, \mathbf{E}, \mathbf{F}, \mathbf{I})$$

with

- two distinct node sets $\mathbf{R}$ and $\mathbf{S}$
- a set $\mathbf{E}$ of edges: $\mathbf{E} \subseteq (\mathbf{R} \times \mathbf{S}) \cup (\mathbf{S} \times \mathbf{R})$
- a set $\mathbf{F}$ of mappings of net elements into a set $\mathbf{W}$ of (abstract) attributes of abitrary complexity $\mathbf{F}_i : \mathbf{R} \cup \mathbf{S} \cup \mathbf{E} \longrightarrow \mathbf{W}_i$
- an interpretation $\mathbf{I}$, which maps the net elements into components of the system.

The set $\mathbf{F}$ has been inserted to improve the modeling power of Petri nets. By means of $\mathbf{F}$ the formal model can be held open to application-specific adaptations and model extensions later. With regard to HW/SW codesign attributes can be defined that allow, for instance, the modeling of design constraints such as

- Timing conditions
- Energy requirements and power dissipation
- Request and release of resources
- Implementation requirements.

The specification process has to be supported by several verification steps. Besides the proof of correctness the formal description is analyzed to derive the design parameters (e.g., timing conditions, degree of concurrency, amount of functionality, etc.) from the requirement definitions and the design constraints [9]. These parameters are the basis of criteria for controlling the following design steps and will be updated over the whole design process by including further design information.

Based on the information processing net a structural analysis of the system can be carried out as well as investigations of its dynamic aspects and the analysis of design complexity [10]. Because there isn't any verified formal model when entering the specification phase, the formal description has to be reflected on the demands of the verbal requirement document. This process is called *validation* and until now has been supported mainly by system-level simulation [1]. To improve the design efficiency, this simulation should be supported more and more by performance, testability, and feasibility analyses.

2.3 System Synthesis and HW/SW Codesign

System synthesis means the iterative process of carrying out transformations on the formal model. The starting point is the formalized and verified model, including design

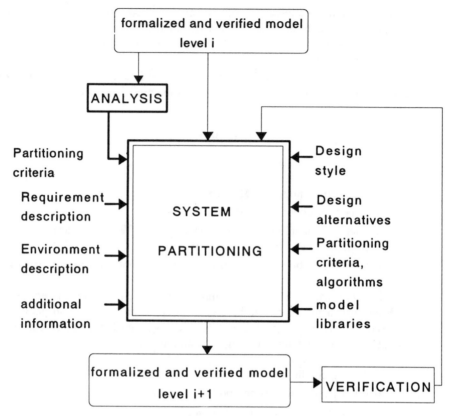

Fig. 4: System partitioning

constraints, which is generated in the specification phase. HW/SW codesign is an essential part of system synthesis. It indicates the process of partitioning the complex system into communicating hardware and/or software modules, which then can be separately designed using conventional tools (see Fig. 4).

Several system architectures can be derived and their properties can be investigated in the EAD environment by carrying out different partitioning steps. These architectures can vary from pure hardware modules over mixed hardware and software structures to pure software modules. The behavioral description of the synthesized hardware modules will then be refined stepwise until logic synthesis tools can be applied. The source code of the software modules is also generated from the behavioral description using a compiler, which converts the structural terms of the behavioral description into adequate terms of the used programming language, especially C language.

The objective of HW/SW codesign is to achieve a global, nearly optimum solution for

- Cost efficiency regarding design, implementation, and operation of the system
- Flexibility of the system regarding functionality, design alternatives, changes in technology and implementation
- Design amount regarding design time, time to market, manpower

- A given target architecture, in particular the architecture and functionality of the RPE

while meeting the design constraints and ensuring the desired functionality of the system under development.

The process of HW/SW Codesign is driven by design constraints. At each level of the partitioning:

- The model has to be analyzed regarding the constraints.
- Partitioning criteria have to be derived from the design constraints.
- Appropriate partitioning algorithms must be chosen.
- The quality of the partitioning must be evaluated by cost functions.

Design constraints are more than simple cost functions. They must take into account all aspects of a design and can contain the following:

- *Functional requests* such as I/O behavior, operations to be executed, initialization requirements
- *Nonfunctional requests* on quality: performance, feasibility, portability; interfaces: to system environment and components; system environment; realization/implementation: models, libraries; test/diagnosis: testability, reproduceability; design management: time, costs, resources.

Important problems to be solved are the determination of significant design constraints for each partitioning level and the definition of the associated partitioning criteria. In particular, behavioral criteria must be developed because at this abstraction level criteria can only be estimated values. Appropriate analysis tools supporting this process must also be developed. But the formalization of partitioning criteria, which is an essential requirement for the algorithmic support of the partitioning and evaluation process is still an open problem. Most of them will not be—will only be with difficulty—formalizable. In this case, we must distinguish between nonformalizable and, at a particular design level, no available criteria.

Nonformalizable criteria should be handled by providing verbal sets of rules, in which the designer's experience should also be incorporated. For criteria that are not available at particular design levels (e.g., the chip area at the behavioral level), libraries should be generated that include design experience and design estimations of already implemented designs.

Other criteria can be managed using more or less complex attributes of the information processing nets.

Furthermore, causal connections between criteria that are mutually dependent (e.g., chip area and the degree of concurrency) must be taken into account along with criteria excluded from each other (e.g., minimal chip area and minimal system delay) [2].

Known approaches to system partitioning are mainly used in designing hardware systems [5,11,12,13]. Here the meeting of the time constraints has priority over all other partitioning criteria. Also area/timing trade-offs are more deeply investigated. For HW/SW codesign, multiple-constraint partitioning using evolution techniques is a helpful method [7,16]. Starting with an initial solution of the partitioning task with regard to the timing constraints (e.g., implementation of the whole system in software or hardware depending on the desired timing), an improvement will be derived by eliminating bad characteristics and generating better ones. Taking into account the feasibility of the current partitioning and its components will lead to an adequate solution of the partitioning problem.

Open problems that must be solved yet are

- Formalization of all essential optimizing criteria (algorithmic or rule driven)
- Weighting of the optimizing criteria regarding their significance for a given partitioning problem
- Choosing an appropriate application sequence of the criteria.

Fuzzy tools seems to be very useful in handling design steps that are difficult to formalize. Therefore further work should also investigate fuzzy approaches to the problem of generating partitioning criteria from various design constraints.

3 VERIFYING HW/SW CODESIGN ALTERNATIVES THROUGH RAPID PROTOTYPE EMULATION

Within the EAD design environment under development at the Fraunhofer IMS the advantages of emulation in a real-time embedded system environment are related to the flexibility of the RPE modules and a mainly computer-aided design methodology, which together create a powerful tool for the design of complex HW/SW systems.

The RPE is the central part of system verification and evaluation, which enables an effective use of the emulation benefits that follow:

- Short time to first prototype
- Short redesign cycle time
- Identical functionality with target system
- Form and timing of emulated signals close to those of the target technology
- Prototype operation in its application environment
- Cutting of design and cost risks through complex verification before implementing in silicon.

3.1 The RPE Concept

The RPE [3] is an open emulation system that allows interactive design specification and design verification in the embedded system environment under real-time conditions. Verification of HW/SW codesign can be realized in relation to functionality and performance.

In the current version, hardware modules generated through HW/SW codesign are transferred to the RPE by using netlists. Such modules are implemented into the prototype

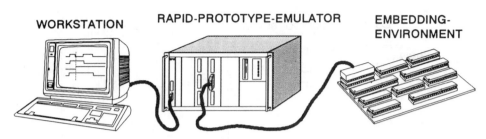

WORKSTATION   **RAPID-PROTOTYPE-EMULATOR**   **EMBEDDING-
                                                                ENVIRONMENT**

Fig. 5: General view of the RPE system

by means of programmable logic devices. To analyze software functions (program code), processor modules with standard microprocessors (e.g., Motorola 68000, Intel 8051) and memory modules are available. Programmable interfaces make the connection to the hardware modules and the system environment so that an identical behavior and real-time prototype is offered to the designer. The embedding system environment is connected via a plug and an emulator cable to the RPE system (see Fig. 5). After that the emulation, e.g., the functional verification and performance evaluation of the design, can take place within the system environment. It can be supported by programs for emulation control and emulation result monitoring that run on a workstation and by additional analyzing tools (e.g., a logic analyzer).

3.2 The Global Structure of the RPE

To reach a high adaptability to the environment of a variety of designs, the RPE has a modular structure. The hardware functions to be implemented in the emulator will be divided into blocks and allocated to specific modules such as logic modules, processor modules, and analog modules (see Fig. 6).

The logic modules consist of interconnected FPGAs (LCAs of the type XC3090-70/XILINX). Depending on the complexity of a circuit, up to four logic modules can be used. To increase the emulation power in HW/SW codesign, additional processor modules can be used for running software functions of the design. For integrating sensors and actors into the emulation process A/D and D/A converters, each with eight channels, are available.

The RPE can easily be integrated in the design tool environment. The interface between design tools and RPE is a standard netlist format (e.g., EDIF), so design capture on multiple levels (e.g., schematic, behavior) is possible.

3.3 Structure of the Logic Module

One RPE logic module contains only four FPGAs. That is a very small number compared with other emulation-systems [6]. Figure 7 shows the hard-wired structure of the modules. The user port (I/O) represents the interface with the surroundings (environment, logic analyzer, etc.), while the module port (M) provides the connection to further modules.

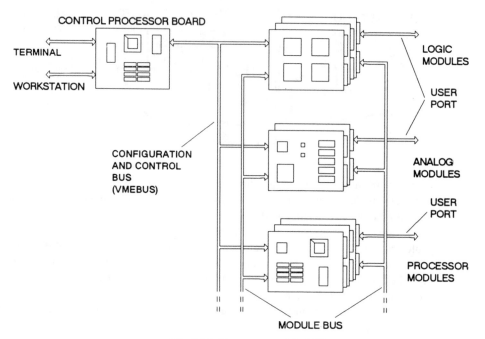

Fig. 6: Modular structure of the RPE

The architecture of an RPE logic module is a result of the extensive examination of a variety of LCA arrays with different numbers of LCAs (up to 36 LCAs per module) and connection structures. Most of the routing channels of the chosen structure represent connections between two LCAs and the user or module port (see Fig. 7). This particular structure allows us to route a direct connection from any LCA to each other LCA within the RPE, which minimizes the number of bypasses, so a drastic increase of utilization of LCAs is possible. The timing behavior becomes determinable and the maximum emulation clock rate is calculatable.

The concept of the RPE logic module aspires to the following improvements:

- Utilization of LCAs up to 60%, which leads to aproximately 20.000 usable gates per module
- A high routing flexibility based on the special kind of routing channels
- A calculatable emulation clock rate dependent on the design
- A short implementation time for the prototype.

3.4 Implementing the Design

After its functional verification on the RPE, the design can be transferred into various implementations on various resource bases. Starting with the netlists the hardware modules are implemented by means of conventional design tools. The software modules

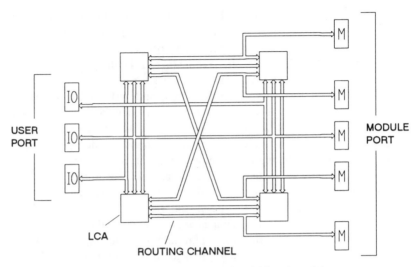

Fig. 7: Connecting structure of the RPE logic module

are already available in the form of C program code and can easily be transferred to the target processor if it is of the same type as in the emulation system.

Possible implementations could be, among others,

- Standard PCB designs or full custom ASICs for pure hardware modules
- Application-specific processors for mixed hardware/software modules
- Program code on a standard microprocessor system for pure software modules.

4 CONCLUSIONS

The EAD design environment represents a powerful tool for the design of complex HW/SW systems. The underlying design and verification methodology makes it particularly useful for functional specification and design at higher levels of abstraction. The RPE, which is integrated in the design environment, allows for the functional verification and performance evaluation of systems under development in its real-time application environment. At that time neither assumptions about realization as hardware and/or software modules nor fixing of any implementation and technology are necessary. Therefore modeling inaccuracies and design faults can be detected early and easily corrected without expensive, time-consuming changes in silicon. This provides the user with an effective and cost optimal redesign tool.

The integration of the RPE within the EAD environment allows the designer to make extensive use of the advantages of HW/SW codesign. Design alternatives can be investigated and the functionality and performance of systems and system components can be compared in an effective manner. Especially when designing complex and heterogeneous HW/SW systems, problems can arise in completely specifying the desired behavior including the system environment and the interfaces. The EAD design environment in conjunction with the RPE makes it possible to transfer the specification into a real-time prototype so that at least parts of the validation process (e.g., the functional verification of the specification against the requirements) can take place in the system's environment supporting the system simulation in the difficult task of pattern generation.

A first working version of the EAD design environment has been developed at the Fraunhofer Institute of Microelectronic Circuit and Systems. Design entry is possible with behavioral description and schematics but further extension integrating extended Petri nets is under development. Manual interventions are still necessary, especially in partitioning the design. This version allows the designer to transfer a design task into the logic modules of the RPE, analyzing it and implementing it in hardware. For the design of mixed hardware and software systems based on application-specific processors, special tools for the synthesis of application-specific CPUs can be used. The processor description, which is generated as a result of a specific compiler developed at IMS Duisburg, is the starting point for high-level synthesis. By means of existing synthesis tools and hardware generators, the design can be structured, optimized and processed for the transfer to the RPE. For software components running on standard microprocessors, a hardware platform is also available on RPE.

ACKNOWLEDGMENTS

Parts of this work were prepared within a research programme supported by the German Society of Application of Microelectronics.

REFERENCES

[1] M. Altmäe, P. Gibson, L. Taxen, and K. Torkelsson, "Verification of Systems Containing Hardware and Software," in *Proc. Euro-VHDL*, pp. 149–156, Stockholm, 8.-m.g., 1991.

[2] T. Amon and G. Borriello, "Sizing Synchronisation Queues: A Case Study in Higher Level Synthesis," in *Proc. 28th ACM/IEEE Design Automation Conference*, pp. 690–693, IEEE, 1991.

[3] G. vom Bögel and K. Scherer, "An Optimized Architecture for an Rapid-Prototype Emulator," *Microproc. Microprog.*, 37, pp. 211–214, 1993.

[4] C. Charlton, P. Leng, and M. Ribers, "Object-Oriented Modelling in Digital Circuit CAD Systems," *Microproc. Microprog.*, 32, pp. 93–100, 1991.

[5] Y. Y. Chen, Y. C. Hsu, and C. Ta. King, "MULTIPAR: Behavioral Partitioning for Synthesizing Application-Specific Multiprocessor Architectures," in *Proc. EDAC 92*, pp. 14–18, IEEE, 1992.

[6] M. D'Amour, S. Sample, and T. Payne, "Risc Emulation Cuts Design Risk," *High Performance Syst.*, CMP Publishing, pp. 28–37, Oct. 1989.

[7] R. K. Gupta and G. De Micheli, "System-Level Synthesis Using Re-programmable Components," in *Proc. EDAC 92*, pp. 2–7, IEEE, 1992.

[8] J. Haufe, M. Kieser, M. Leisenberg, K. Matzdorff, P. Nauber, E. Oberst, and S. Rülke, "Ausbau und Erweiterung der Arbeitsversion zur Nutzerversion SESAD," Forschungsbericht, Akademie der Wissenschaften, Zentralinstitut für Kybernetik und Informationsprozesse, 1984.

[9] Y. C. Hu, A. Verschueren, and M. P. J. Stevens, "Object Oriented System Analysis for VLSI," *Microproc. and Microprog.,* 32, pp. 101–108, 1991.

[10] R. König, "Analyse von Informationsverarbeitungsnetzen,'" Internal Paper, Fraunhofer-Institute of Microelectronic Circuits and Systems, 1992.

[11] D. C. Ku and G. De Micheli, "Relative Scheduling Under Timing Constraints: Algorithms for High-Level Synthesis of Digital Circuits," *IEEE Trans. Computer-Aided Des.,* 11(6), pp. 696–718, 1992.

[12] K. Kücükcakar and A. C. Parker, "CHOP: A Constraint-Driven System-Level Partitioner," in *Proc. 28th ACM/IEEE Design Automation Conference,* pp. 514–519, IEEE, 1991.

[13] E. D. Lagnese and D. E. Thomas, "Architectural Partitioning for System Level Design," in *Proc. 26th ACM/IEEE Design Automation Conference,* pp. 62–67, IEEE, 1989.

[14] E. Oberst and K. Scherer, "Neue systemtechnische Entwurfsmethoden und werkzeug für mikroelektronische Systeme und Komponenten," in *Kongressbericht Gerätetechnik und Mikrosystemtechnik,* Band 1, pp. S301–312, VDI Berichte 960, 1992.

[15] F. J. Rammig, "Approaching System Level Design," in *Proc. Euro-VHDL,* pp. 6–23, Stockholm, 8.-m.g., 1991.

[16] Y. Saab and V. Rao, "An Evolution-Based Approach to Partitioning ASIC Systems," in *Proc. 26th ACM/IEEE Design Automation Conference,* pp. 767–770, IEEE, 1989.

[17] K. Scherer and O. Rettig, "Rapid Prototyping mikroelektronischer Hardware-Software-Systeme—Eine Alternative zu Simulation und Breadbording," in *Rechnergestützter Entwurf und Architektur mikroelektronischer Systeme,* pp. S285–296, Springer Verlag, Berlin, 1990.

CHAPTER 16

SBDM as a Model for Codesign Data

Munish Gandhi   Edward L. Robertson
Computer Science Department
Indiana University
Bloomington, Indiana, USA

Abstract: The specification-based data model (SBDM) is a unifying framework to model configurations of systems that contain components from differing engineering disciplines. SBDM views the hierarchy of components as layers of alternating specification and implementation. This allows the system to be designed without presupposing a specific type of implementation for its components. The design phase is followed by a configuration phase, where a choice mechanism picks those implementations that are most suitable for assembling the system. Finally, a manifestation phase materializes the chosen implementations for each component in the system.

1 INTRODUCTION

Each discipline has modeling mechanisms that must be unified in order to support heterogeneous development environments. A framework that takes a unified approach to modeling not only supports design with a variety of implementations but also allows the design to proceed without presupposing a specific type of implementation for its components. For example, the model would allow the description of an algorithm that could be implemented using firmware or an ASIC.

We present a minimal model that unifies mechanisms for system design, system configuration, and system instantiation. We regard the model as an *engineering asset*, which may be appropriately extended for purposes of a specific design environment. For example, the PMDB project [1] has modeled the data relating to the software development life-cycle process used at TRW. Though the scope of the PMDB project was much larger, it too attempted to develop a model that was not tied to specific methodologies and techniques. Rather, it produced a generic model that excluded implementation issues [2]. Another work with objectives similar to ours is the data model (DODM) in the DAMOKLES project [3].

The presented model considers the specification for each component of a product as being closely linked to its implementation. The need for such an integration has been felt before. Swartout and Balzer [4] argue that even though software process models view specification and implementation as successive steps, in reality they influence one another. In other words, as software evolves both specifications and implementations undergo change. In fact, systems that integrate specifications in the design process are being developed currently. For example, the DEBYS (DEsign BY Specification) project intends to develop an integrated design and test environment for the design of electronic systems [5].

Our effort has been guided by a few general objectives. We explicate these as the following principles:

P1: The model should be general and flexible.

P2: Both the modeling notation and the model itself should be minimal.

P3: The model should represent designed objects.

P4: Specifications should be preeminent in the model.

Principles *P1* and *P2* are obviously intimately related. A minimal framework holds the fewest possible conflicts with a wide range of applications and offers the least resistance when adapted to a particular domain. Since familiarity and common acceptance complement minimality in facilitating adaptability, we use entity-relationship techniques as our notation. Likewise, *P3* and *P4* are related in their focus on design. Designed objects clearly arise because of an active process, but a data model should record the consequences of these activities rather than model the activities themselves. Hence the model captures only the structural relationships between the components of the product. Other interactions, especially those that are process oriented, are outside the core model. On the other hand, *P3* and *P4* sometimes require that certain aspects often considered incidental to the design process must be made explicit in capture and representation.

The development process is conceptually separated into design, configuration and manifestation stages. Each stage builds a distinct hierarchy. The components built during design constitute a design hierarchy, during configuration a definition hierarchy, and during manifestation an instance hierarchy. Thus we have the following process considerations during each stage of development:

- During design, development proceeds using alternate layers of specification and implementation. Modifications are accommodated using the versioning mechanisms for both specifications and implementations.

- During configuration, a choice mechanism is provided to pick those versions of implementation most suited for assembling a system.

- During manifestation, the design for each component in the system assembly is materialized. This results in each materialized component getting an identity of its own.

The remainder of this paper presents the Specification-based Data Model (SBDM) using an E-R diagram. Before we present the SBDM, we introduce the general concept of data modeling and the entity-relationship approach to data modeling. Section 2 reveals the entities and relationships needed to manage an evolving system design. Section 2.1 presents the specification entity, Section 2.2 presents the implementation entity, and Section 2.3 discusses how a system may be designed using the relationships between these entities. The configuration entity presented in Section 2.4 is used to configure the system and the manifestation entity in Section 2.5 allows configurations to be instantiated. Section 3 illustrates these concepts by modeling a toy CAD application, modeling a codesign application, and outlining an approach to model an object-oriented software system. Finally, Section 4 concludes the report by summarizing some implications of the presented model.

1.1 Data Modeling and the ER Approach

The data modeling approach has been an important milestone in the development of database systems. In this subsection, we indicate how designers could benefit from using such an approach to model the structure of the systems they are building.

A *data model* is a unified conceptual view of the information maintained and used by an organization. A conceptual view of the data, as opposed to a physical view, offers critical advantages to the users of the information.

CONCEPTUAL INDEPENDENCE. Design tools that use similar data need not hard-code the structure of the data into the tool. Thus, the data structure could easily evolve without making the design tool obsolete. Conversely, design tools could evolve without necessitating a reorganization of the data.

IMPLEMENTATION INDEPENDENCE. Design tools, in fact, need not even concern themselves with operations to store, maintain, and retrieve the information. Data management platforms could be used to handle these data. Since the operations on the data have been abstracted, the same data model may be implemented in different ways.

COMMUNICATION. A carefully expressed data model is a concise way to communicate the "architecture" of the data, and because a data model is only conceptual, the communication does not get clouded with implementation details.

A data modeling *approach* is a formalism to specify data models. The *entity-relationship* (ER) [6] approach is a popular data modeling formalism. An ER model classifies the real world into *entities* and *relationships* between entities. Both entities and relationships may have *attributes*. As an example (Fig. 1), consider the ER schema to model project assignments in a company. The schema consists of two entities—*Engineer* and *Project*. An engineer is related by the *is_assigned_to* relationship to a project. Engineers and projects have their names as attributes. Furthermore, certain constraints on the relationship may be specified. This is done using a pair of numbers *(min, max)*, which indicate the minimum

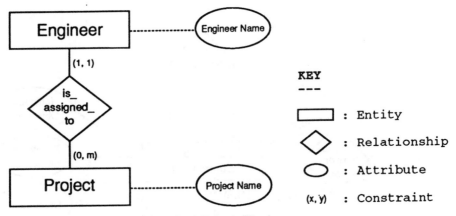

Fig. 1: Example ER schema

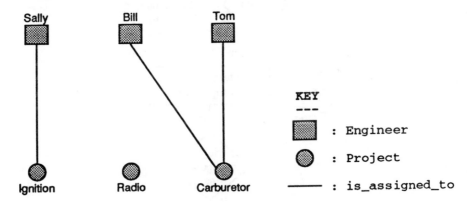

Fig. 2: Example ER instance

and the maximum number of times that one instance can participate in the indicated relationship. In our example, an engineer may be assigned at the minimum and at the maximum to one project. The project may at the minimum have no one working on it. At the maximum, there may be an arbitrary number of people working on it.

Figure 1 is an abstraction that shows only the structure of the data, hence, the title *schema*. When we have actual values that fit into a schema we have an *instance* of the schema. Figure 2 shows an instance of the schema in Fig. 1. In Fig. 2, Sally, Bill, and Tom are engineers. Sally is assigned to the ignition project, while Bill and Tom are assigned to the carburetor project. Note that there is no one working on the radio project. This is consistent with the constraints specified in the schema.

2 DESIGN COMPONENTS IN SBDM

This section presents the SBDM using the ER formalism (Fig. 3). The entities in the figure correspond to four important components in SBDM:

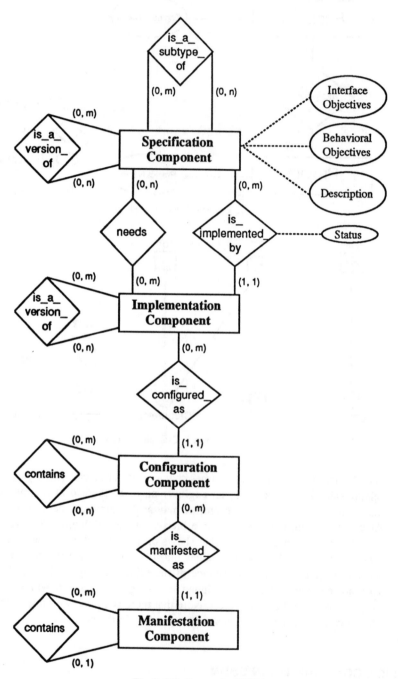

Fig. 3: E-R diagram for SBDM

1. *Specification Component:* Encapsulates a formal statement of the objectives satisfied by its implementations and may be versioned to reflect an evolving design, or subtyped to represent a generalization hierarchy.

2. *Implementation Component:* Implements the objectives as specified by the specification component. This component may also be versioned.

3. *Configuration Component:* Selects implementations for a desired configuration. The containment of the configuration components specifies the relative placement of the implementations in a configuration.

4. *Manifestation Component:* Permits a distinction between those elements in the final product that have the same definition, yet are distinctly instantiated. This is done by considering each element in the final product as a manifestation of the components in a configuration hierarchy.

2.1 Specification Component

A *specification component* (SpecC) is a precise statement of objectives expected to be satisfied by some objects. This statement has three parts: interface objectives, behavioral objectives, and a description (Fig. 3). *Interface objectives* define the protocol of the interaction between the objects and the external world. *Behavioral objectives* define the functional characteristics expected of the object. The above two objectives should necessarily be syntactically or semantically verifiable. The *description* section informally states nonverifiable and other miscellaneous objectives.

A specification may be versioned to reflect a maturing design. A SpecC *is_a_version_of* another if the former is directly derived from the latter. The graph formed by SpecCs and the *is_a_version_of* link between them is assumed to be a directed acyclic graph. The nodes of a connected component of this graph form a *specification set*.

SpecCs may also be arranged in a subtype hierarchy. A *is_a_subtype_of* B indicates that A is a specialization of B, or, alternatively, B generalizes A. The structure formed by considering SpecCs as nodes and *is_a_subtype_of* relationships as directed edges is again a directed acyclic graph.

2.2 Implementation Component

A specification component *is_implemented_by* an *implementation component* (ImpC) (Fig. 3). This object necessarily satisfies the interface objectives of its specification. However, it only attempts to satisfy the behavioral objectives and the description sections of its specification. The degree to which the ImpC satisfies the behavioral objectives is reflected in the *status* of the *is_implemented_by* link. As with specifications, the relationship *is_a_version_of* may be used to version implementations.

Implementations are not shared by specifications. If an ImpC A meets the functionality of two distinct SpecCs, then those SpecCs should be abstracted into a single SpecC, which is implemented by A. This makes explicit the "union" of the two specifications. A specification set together with implementations for its elements constitute a structured group meeting similar objectives. Elements in this group of plans and implementations form a cohesive unit called a *functionality*.

2.3 Multilevel Design

A system is usually designed as a component hierarchy with "lower" levels refining or decomposing "higher" ones. In SBDM, SpecCs and ImpCs are fundamental to the design process and we refer to them collectively as *design components*. A single-level design organizes these design components to construct various functionalities. A multi-level design, in turn, organizes the functionalities hierarchically to form subsystems. This is done by linking an implementation of a higher functionality with specification of its constituent functionalities. Thus, an ImpC of the higher functionality *needs* SpecCs of the lower functionality (Fig. 3).

The *needs* relationship between an implementation and a specification corresponds to those relationships among modules that define the software architecture. The semantic richness of such relationships necessitates at least two kinds of *needs*. The first, *uses*, indicates that an implementation uses the facilities promised by the specification. A procedure call in a software system is a good example of this. The second, *is_composed_of*, indicates that a module is a part of another. This may occur, for example, in a mechanical assembly. An obvious difference between the two is that the *uses* link between functionalities may form a cycle, the *is_composed_of* link may not.

Conceptually, the *needs* relationship could be considered to link functionalities. However, linking functionalities rather than design components would result in a rigidly structured system. Designers must be free to allow different implementations within a functionality to decompose into different lower level functionalities. A direct link like the *needs* relationship between ImpCs and SpecCs furnishes the model with such a flexibility. In Fig. 4, for example, F_2^1 and F_2^2 need only G_1; F_2^3 needs both G_1 and H_3. We also allow multiple *needs* from an ImpC to a SpecC. These links indicate that several copies of the object specified by the SpecC are required. For example, H_3^1 requires two copies of I_2. The issue of copy identification is obviously relevant only for some technologies.

The structure of a multilevel design is similar to an AND-OR graph.[1] In Fig. 4, the assembly of F_2^3 requires both G_1 and H_3. At G_1 and H_3 exactly one of the implementations is chosen, say, G_1^2 and H_3^1, respectively. Thus, SpecCs in multilevel design correspond to OR nodes and ImpCs correspond to AND nodes.

Systems that are built using alternating implementation and specification layers have significant advantages:

• A specification is part of the design and may be versioned with increasing knowledge about the system. This may be contrasted with the conventional viewpoint, which essentially puts *all* specifications before implementations. Hence an evolving system is difficult to model, making the system difficult to manage. Furthermore, since a specification is in close proximity to its implementations it is easier to keep up with changes.

• Abstracting the requirements into the SpecC and having multiple implementations for the requirements allows one to experiment concurrently using different implementations.

---

[1] The structure is not exactly an AND-OR graph because a subtype hierarchy may be present.

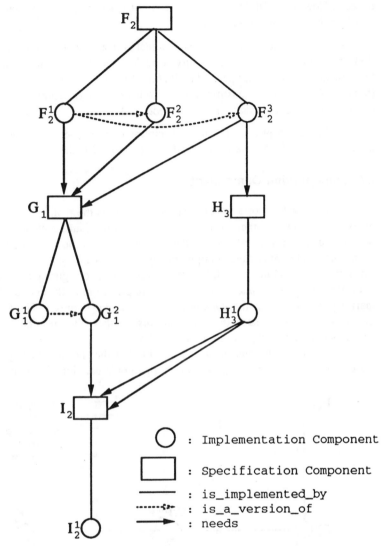

Fig. 4: Multilevel design

• Version percolation is effectively controlled. A SpecC succinctly describes what is expected of its ImpCs. In Fig. 4, the fact that there are two implementations of G_1 does not cause there to be two versions of F_2^3. Multiple versions of a specification are a different situation. Say G_1 has a version G_2. Since the contract between G_1 and F_2^i is still valid, there is no need for other versions F_2^*; but, by the same token, any attempt to use G_2 would require a new version. Even in this case, however, the versioning would (normally) stop at F_2.

On the process side, the designer of F_m^n may feel the need to be notified if G_2 is created. A design method using SBDM may easily incorporate such a notification process. However, SBDM does not mandate it since it attempts to define only structural relationships among components.

• A decision as to whether a new object is just a version of a previous implementation or belongs to a new functionality is made rather trivially. If the new object satisfies the objectives stated in a SpecC then it should be in the implementation set of that specification. Otherwise, it constitutes a new functionality (and hence a new SpecC should be created to accommodate the new object).

• The design process becomes disciplined simply because new ImpCs are not allowed in the model before their specifications are defined.

2.4 Configuration Component

A configuration for a system may be defined as the relative functional arrangement of its subsystems. In other words, a configuration mechanism must not only identify the relevant subsystems but also specify their placement in the system structure. In SBDM, each functionality may have multiple implementations and each implementation may need yet other functionalities to fulfill its objectives. Thus, configuring a system would require a marking of an ImpC and, recursively, the ImpCs from each functionality it needs. This marking is done using the *configuration component* (ConfC). The ConfCs themselves link to other ConfCs such that one *contains* another. This results in a structure which parallels that of the ImpCs in the system design.

We illustrate the mechanism by considering the scenario in Fig. 5. To assemble a system with specification F_m, we mark an implementation F_m^n as being of interest by

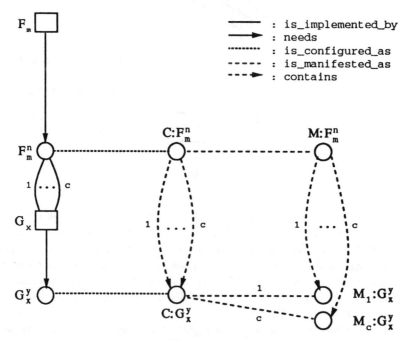

Fig. 5: Configuring and instantiating a system

using a ConfC, say $C : F_m^n$.[2] This is denoted by saying F_m^n *is_configured_as* $C : F_m^n$. For each specification G_x needed by F_m^n, a design version G_x^y is chosen and $C : F_m^n$ is linked to the ConfC for G_x^y, say $C : G_x^y$. Thus, $C : F_m^n$ *contains* $C : G_x^y$. If G_x^y *needs* other functionalities we repeat the above for specification G_x, where G_x^y is the ImpC of interest for G_x. Else, we are done.

Of course, it may not be necessary to create ConfCs explicitly and link them to get the desired configuration. A method of defaults may derive the configuration hierarchy automatically. The idea here subsumes that used in [7]. For each specification one may designate a distinguished object from its design set as *current*. To configure an object, we recursively construct it using the current versions of each functionality linked by the *needs* link. An atomic ImpC is configured using the ImpC itself. Obviously, configurations resulting from this method depend on the designations of current versions at configuration time.[3]

2.5 Manifestation Component

Reference [8] refers to the need for distinguishing an instance hierarchy and a definition hierarchy. The *manifestation component* (ManC) entity in SBDM together with the *contains* relationship enables us to create explicitly an instance hierarchy. Furthermore, the *is_manifested_as* relationship links the instance hierarchy with the definition hierarchy, which is built using the ConfC entity.

The instance for a ConfC, say $C : F_m^n$, is manifest as a manifestation component, say $M : F_m^n$. Because F_m^n (and hence $C : F_m^n$) is a composite, $M : F_m^n$ contains other manifestation components. These satisfy the following constraints:

• For each *contains* link from $C : F_m^n$ to $C : G_x^y$, $C : G_x^y$ *is_manifested_as* $M_1 : G_x^y$, $\ldots$, $M_c : G_x^y$, where c is the number of *contains* links. Each manifestation of $C : G_x^y$ is then related to $M : F_m^n$ by *contains*.

• Given a manifestation $M_a : G_x^y$, the ConfC from which the manifestation's parent in the instance hierarchy is manifest, is the same as the parent of the ConfC in the definition hierarchy from which $M_a : G_x^y$ is manifest.

3 EXAMPLE APPLICATIONS

SpecCs, ImpCs, ConfCs, ManCs and the structural relationships between them constitute an important part of SBDM. This section illustrates the wide applicability of these concepts by structuring systems from different engineering disciplines.

We first consider a hardware design and represent it using SBDM. Next, we indicate the correspondence of software design concepts to SBDM concepts. It should be clear from these that the SBDM approach is applicable to both hardware and software

---

[2] Note that there may be many ConfCs for an ImpC. Thus, $C : F_m^n$ does not represent a unique ConfC for the ImpC F_m^n. The same holds true for the ImpC G_x^y.

[3] To configure current versions for different platforms, a constraint mechanism may be used. We do not elaborate on that mechanism here.

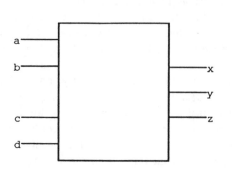

Interface Objectives
input : a b c d
output: x y z

Behavioral Objectives
x = (a+c) MOD 2
y = ((a+2b+c+2d) MOD 4) DIV 2
z = (a+2b+c+2d) DIV 4

Description
  The input lines a,b and c,d
encode two 2-bit numbers. The
adder outputs on x,y,z the
3-bit encoded sum of these
numbers

Fig. 6: Adder specification: $Adder_1$ (step a)

components. Having shown the universal applicability of SBDM, we are in a position to represent designs with mixed hardware and software components. Thus, we finally use SBDM to represent a system requiring codesign.

Section 3.1—involving the design of a hardware adder—is more elaborate than the following sections so as to illustrate the fundamental concepts. Specifically, the internals of a SpecC and an ImpC are specified to show their influence on the versioning and configuration mechanisms. Section 3.2—involving an object-oriented software system—illustrates the power of the model in designing products in a domain with a rich set of structural relationships. Finally, Section 3.3 demonstrates the applicability of SBDM as an organizing tool for codesign components.

3.1 Hardware Design

We model a CAD application using a toy example similar to that used in [9]. Consider the design of an adder which outputs the sum of two 2-bit numbers. To illustrate the versioning mechanisms of our model, we assume a hypothetical scenario consisting of the following steps:

- a. We begin by specifying our objectives for the adder (Fig. 6). That we begin by defining a SpecC reflects the importance of specifications in our model.
- b. Assuming that a half adder would be useful in implementing the 2-bit adder, we create the specifications for an adder slice (Fig. 7). Since this is the first version of the adder slice we call it $AdderSlice_1$.
- c. $Adder_1$ is now implemented using the $AdderSlice_1$ as a subcomponent (Fig. 8). Since this is the first implementation of $Adder_1$ the ImpC is named $Adder_1^1$.
- d. $AdderSlice_1$ may be improved to handle an extra carry input. The new adder slice, $AdderSlice_2$, is a full adder and a version of $AdderSlice_1$ (Fig. 9).
- e. $Adder_1$ is now implemented using the full adder (Fig. 10).

Figure 11 summarizes the relationship between the components used in the adder design. The figure also shows the implementations for the adder slices. These may be completed any time after the specifications for the adder slices have been finalized.

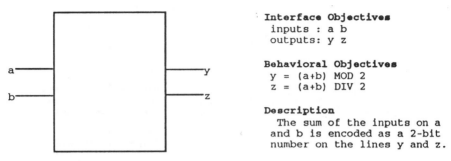

Interface Objectives
  inputs : a b
  outputs: y z

Behavioral Objectives
  y = (a+b) MOD 2
  z = (a+b) DIV 2

Description
  The sum of the inputs on a
  and b is encoded as a 2-bit
  number on the lines y and z.

Fig. 7: Half adder: *AdderSlice*$_1$ (step b)

3.2 Software Design

In this subsection, we suggest how SBDM could be used to model data in object oriented software systems. We use principles represented in the design approaches of Booch [10] and Meyer [11].

A specification for a family of objects in SBDM is very close to the notion of a class interface in object-oriented systems. It defines the communication protocol used to interact with the objects, the behavior expected of the objects, and other important

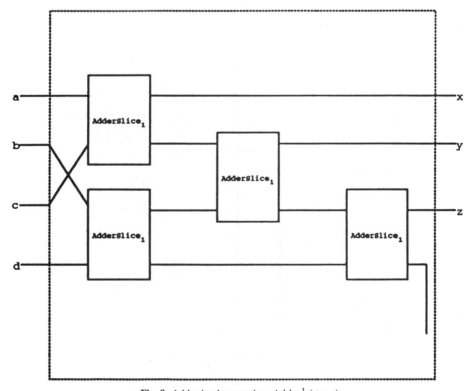

Fig. 8: Adder implementation: *Adder*$_1^1$ (step c)

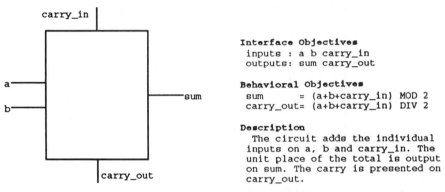

Interface Objectives
  inputs : a b carry_in
  outputs: sum carry_out

Behavioral Objectives
  sum   = (a+b+carry_in) MOD 2
  carry_out= (a+b+carry_in) DIV 2

Description
  The circuit adds the individual
  inputs on a, b and carry_in. The
  unit place of the total is output
  on sum. The carry is presented on
  carry_out.

Fig. 9: Full adder: *AdderSlice$_2$* (step d)

information regarding the objects. And since most design methods define how exactly
the class interface is specified, we can reuse the class interface as the SpecC for a class
in SBDM.

For example, Booch defines a "class template" as a "means of documenting the
meaning of each class." Among other elements, the class template contains fields and
operations. Furthermore, for each operation the parameters, result type, preconditions,

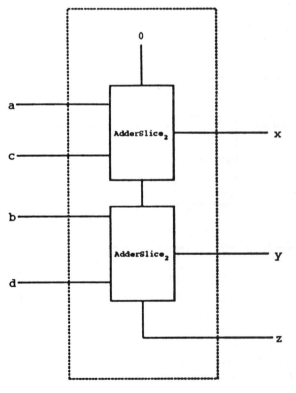

Fig. 10: Adder implementation: *Adder$_1^2$* (step e)

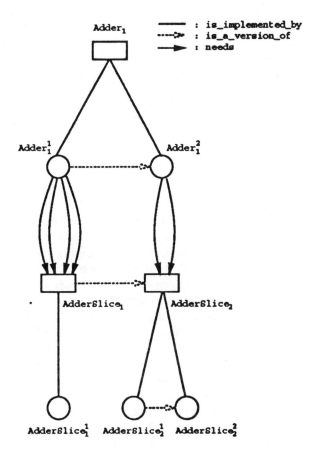

Fig. 11: SBDM instance for adder

postconditions, action, documentation, etc., are defined. Since these elements include the necessary elements required in a SpecC, the creation of a SpecC for each class in the Booch model of object-oriented design requires no additional effort. In fact, this equivalence of a class template and a SpecC has some advantages. First, as shown before, the presence of specifications controls version percolation. Second, the integration forces the class documentation to be in tune with the implementations. Third, it represents a more realistic view of the design process as it closely ties specifications and implementations.

An object-oriented system is usually a complex structure embedding in itself at least two hierarchies. The first, a structural hierarchy, defines the structural composition of the system. The second, a class hierarchy, defines the inheritance relationships among classes. In SBDM, the structural hierarchy is represented by *is_implemented_by* and *needs* relationships and the class hierarchy by *is_a_subtype_of* relationship. That there is no subtype relationship between ImpCs reflects the level of abstraction at which a class hierarchy should be defined.

Conventionally, the structural hierarchy of components in a system is drawn separately from the class hierarchies in which the components participate. This may incorrectly suggest that the hierarchies are independent of one another, which of course they

are not. Since class hierarchies are defined on specifications and specifications are integrated in the structural hierarchy, SBDM models the two hierarchies as complementing
one another.

The ImpC and the *is_implemented_by* relationship have obvious parallel in object-
oriented systems. An implementation component may simply be the module that implements the class. For example, in ADA if each class is placed in a separate package, the
package implementation may be considered an ImpC for that class (and the specification
package a part of the SpecC).

3.3 Codesign

The major advantage of a high-level model-based approach is that it is independent of
the implementation medium and thus naturally supports codesign. Having considered pure
hardware and software designs, we now consider the codesign of a process monitoring
system. Figure 12 displays the three stages in building the process monitoring system—
design, configuration, and manifestation. The key provides the representations used for
the entities and relationships in SBDM.

Consider the design. The *process monitor* is specified in the SpecC at the top of
the design. This has one implementation, represented by one ImpC, which uses a *report
generator* and two identical *machine monitor*s to monitor two machines. The latter results
in the double link between the implementation and the *machine monitor*. The *machine
monitor*, in turn, has two implementations. The first version uses an *embedded microprocessor* and *software* to implement the *machine monitor*. The embedded microprocessor
can be bought off the shelf and hence is presumed to have one implementation. The *software* ImpC is also assumed to have one implementation. The second implementation of
machine monitor is a *discrete realization*.

A few points may now be noted about the design subtree under the *machine monitor* SpecC. The machine monitor has two ImpCs. The versioning link between them
represents the coexistence of an alternative rather than a replacement. In general, this
interpretation of the versioning link is valid for all designs using SBDM. (For example,
the previous version may coexist for historical reasons.) The coexistence of versioned
components has implications for codesign. Specifically, one may create a SpecC for a
particular functionality. This SpecC may then be implemented in hardware or software
to create ImpCs that satisfy the SpecC. Thus, a design may try out both hardware and
software implementations in parallel. In our example, the *discrete realization* and the
software based implementations may proceed independently of one another.

Furthermore, note that the *machine monitor* and the *report generator* SpecCs capture
their respective functionalities. This allows the subtree rooted at *report generator* to be
developed in parallel with the subtree rooted at *machine monitor*. As in the above, this
allows the parallel development of codesign components. However, in this case, the components being developed in parallel interact with one another rather than being alternative
implementations of a single specification.

Now consider the configuration phase. A subset of the ImpCs may be chosen to
configure the *process monitor*. Assume that we are interested in the *discrete realization*.
Since the SpecCs are the choice points, we now chose an implementation for each spec-

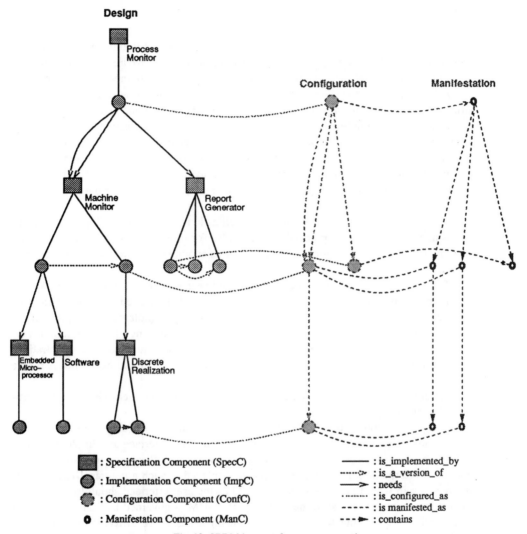

Fig. 12: SBDM instance for a process monitor

ification in this subtree. The figure shows the configuration that uses the only ImpC for the *process monitor*, the second ImpC for the *machine monitor*, the second ImpC of the *discrete realization*, and the first ImpC of the *report generator*.

This configuration may now be manifested. Since there are two *machine monitors* needed by the *process monitor*, the *process monitor* and its *discrete realization* are manifested twice. This brings up an important difference between software and hardware: Separate copies of hardware implementation must exist in the manifestation when there are several links to a ConfC in the configuration. On the other hand, a software manifestation normally requires only one manifestation. Such requirements may be enforced by constraints for which we are currently developing a formalism.

4 CONCLUSION

We have presented a model that uses a minimal set of concepts to unify mechanisms for system design, system configuration, and system instantiation. We also demonstrated the generality of the model using examples drawn from differing engineering domains.

A key concept is that a design hierarchy may be considered as a structure of alternating specifications and implementations. Either of these components may be versioned to realistically reflect an evolving system design, and keep specifications and implementations consistent with one another. The versioning mechanism may further be used to delay a hardware/software decision. For example, the first version of a specification may specify a functionality without committing itself to hardware or software. Later, one may commit newer versions of the specification to be implemented in either hardware or software.

Abstracting the requirements into a specification and having multiple implementations allows the design to proceed concurrently. For example in Fig. 12, a group may work on the *discrete realization* at the same time as another group working on monitoring *Software*.

The versioning mechanism permits an intuitive configuration mechanism. A configuration simply selects desired implementations from the required functionalities. This mechanism allows for concurrent development of alternative implementations, and thus a choice between hardware/software need be made only at the time of configuration. Furthermore, we do not make any real distinctions between static and dynamic configurations [2,7]. In fact, we consider the difference to be process-oriented and hence not part of a data model.

Finally, manifestations are used to distinguish the instance hierarchy from the definition hierarchies [2,9].

Our presentation of the SBDM model has concentrated on conceptual aspects, but effective use of such a model requires a perspicuous user interface and implementation. Looking at the toy example in Fig. 11, it is obvious that there are limitations to the amount of information that can effectively be displayed in such a diagram. The instance of a real design would far exceed this limit. Thus the user interface should provide ways for restricted viewing. Because the topology of SBDM is governed by conceptual rather than Euclidian space, the windowing mechanism needs to be different and under the user's control. Facing this issue in a larger context is one factor in our definition and implementation of a general system that supports but goes beyond SBDM. As a result, the system generalizes the entity-relationship approach by allowing entities to be contained within other entities. This containment levels the system into abstraction layers that may be viewed at the desired level of detail.

ACKNOWLEDGMENT

This work was partially supported by the Indiana Business Modernization and Technology Corporation.

REFERENCES

[1] R. Ahmed and S. B. Navathe, "Version Management of Composite Objects in CAD Databases," in *Proceedings of the 1991 ACM SIGMOD International Conference on the Management of Data,* pp. 218–227, May 1991.

[2] D. Batory and W. Kim, "Modeling Concepts for VLSI CAD Objects," *ACM Transactions on Database Systems,* 10(3):322–346, September 1985.

[3] G. Booch, *Object Oriented Design with Applications,* Benjamin/Cummings, Redwood City, California, 1991.

[4] P. P. Chen, "The Entity-Relationship Model—Toward a Unified View of Data," *ACM Transactions in Database Systems,* 1(1):9–36, March 1976.

[5] H. T. Chou and W. Kim, "A Unifying Framework for Version Control in a CAD Environment," in *Proceedings of the 12th VLDB Conference, Kyoto, Japan,* pp. 336–346, August 1986.

[6] K. R. Dittrich, W. Gotthard, and P. C. Lockemann, "DAMOKLES—A Database Systems for Software Engineering Environments, in *Proceedings of an International Workshop on Advanced Programming Environments, Trondheim, Norway,* pp. 353–371, June 1986.

[7] R. H. Katz, *Information Management for Engineering Design,* Springer-Verlag Computer Science Survey Series, Heidelberg, Germany, 1985.

[8] R. H. Katz, "Toward a Unified Framework for Version Modeling in Engineering Databases." *ACM Computing Surveys,* 22(4):375–408, December 1990.

[9] D. McLeod, K. Narayanaswamy, and K. BapaRao, "An Approach to Information Management for CAD/VLST Applications," in *Proceedings of the SIGMOD Conference on Databases for Engineering Applications, San Jose, California,* pp. 39–50, May 1983.

[10] B. Meyer, *Object-oriented Software Construction,* Prentice Hall International (UK) Ltd., Hertfordshire, HP2 4RG, 1988.

[11] K. D. Mueller-Glaser, J. Bortolazzi, and Y. Tanhuran, "Towards a Requirements Definition, Specification, and System Design Environment," in *EURO-DAC Proceedings (to appear),* 1992.

[12] M. H. Penedo and E. D. Stuckle, Integrated Project Master Database IR&D Final Report, Technical Report TRW-84-SS-22, TRW, December 1984.

[13] M. H. Penedo and E. D. Stuckle, "TRW's SEE Saga," in *Software Engineering Environments—International Workshop on Environments, Chinon, France,* pp. 25–56, September 1989.

[14] W. Swartout and R. Balzer, "On the Inevitable Intertwining of Specification and Implementation," *Communications of the ACM,* 25(7):438–440, July 1982.

CHAPTER 17

Hardware/Software Codesign: Experiences with Languages and Architectures

M. D. Edwards
Department of Computation
University of Manchester Institute of Science and Technology (UMIST)
Manchester, United Kingdom

Abstract: This chapter describes the research work carried out at UMIST in the area of system-level synthesis. This activity was undertaken as part of two recent ESPRIT projects: AIDA (888) and ASAC (2394). In both cases, systems were specified, using high-level behavioral description languages, independently of their implementations in either hardware or software. For purely software solutions, it was possible to translate the high-level descriptions into a form that could be executed on conventional single and/or multiprocessor systems. For purely hardware solutions, it was feasible to synthesize suitable chip architectures from their high-level specifications. For mixed hardware and software solutions the synthesized chips, plus interface components, could be used as coprocessors in standard computer systems.

A critical appraisal of the approaches taken to system-level synthesis, incorporating hardware and software codesign, is presented. Particular emphasis is placed on the close interrelationship between the chosen behavioral specification language and the system implementation architecture. Based on both the positive and negative aspects of these projects, avenues for possible future work are discussed.

1 INTRODUCTION

The design and development of large-scale real-time systems invariably results in implementations that include the integration of both hardware and software components. The development of applications software to be executed on standard or customized microcomputer systems is now commonplace—a software solution. Improvements in VLSI technology have led to the widespread use of ASIC components, which may be used to realize a complete system, including processor, application code, and input/output—a hardware solution. Alternatively, ASICs can be developed to implement special-purpose hardware to support a software application running on a computer system—a mixed solution. Whatever the result, there must be coherent mechanisms for specifying the behavior of mixed hardware and software systems independently of their final implementations, and for subsequently synthesizing all or part of such systems from their high-level specifications. In addition, specific techniques are required for evaluating the potential trade-offs between hardware and software alternatives in order to optimize system performance and cost.

This chapter describes experimental work performed at UMIST in the area of system-level synthesis. This work was undertaken as part of two recent ESPRIT projects: AIDA (888) and ASAC (2394). In both cases, systems were specified, using high-level behavioral description languages, independently of their implementations in either hardware or software. For purely software solutions, it was possible to translate a high-level system description into a form that could be executed on a conventional computer system. For purely hardware solutions, it was possible to synthesize suitable chip architectures from their high-level specifications. For mixed hardware and software solutions, the synthesized chips, plus interface components, could be used as coprocessors in standard computer systems.

In the AIDA project, the initial specification of a real-time digital system was given in the language BEADLE [1] as a network of concurrently active, communicating, sequential tasks. A prototype simulation system was developed for the language in order to perform implementation-independent analyses of an application system. A generic single-chip hardware architecture was developed to support BEADLE specifications of systems. The architecture consisted of a network of node processors—one per task—interconnected via a communications network. An important aspect of this work was the development of a synthesis system, which customized the generic hardware architecture for a particular application. The resulting architecture was defined in VHDL [2], which was used as an input to both simulation and lower level synthesis tools. Thus, it was possible to synthesize a purely hardware solution for a system. A set of transformation rules was developed to translate a BEADLE description of a system into an OCCAM [3] description. The OCCAM program could be executed on a transputer network for simulation purposes. Thus, it was possible to synthesize a purely software solution. As an intermediate arrangement a special-purpose "communications" chip was designed to permit a synthesized chip solution to be interfaced to a standard VME bus. It was then possible to have a mixed hardware/software system with some BEADLE tasks running on the synthesized hardware and the remaining tasks being executed on a conventional microprocessor.

An overview of the BEADLE language, the generic hardware architecture, hardware architecture synthesis system, and system implementation options are presented in Section 2. Experiences with the use of BEADLE as a system description language, together with the inherent advantages and disadvantages of the chosen implementations, are presented.

The work performed in the ASAC project was designed both to build on the experiences gained in the AIDA project and to enhance the capabilities of the synthesis system. Ada [4] was chosen to specify a system in terms of both its hardware and software components. The work carried out at UMIST was the synthesis of chip architectures from

Ada descriptions of the identified hardware components. Note that Ada was not used as a conventional hardware description language but as a specification language for input to a high-level architecture synthesis system. In an approach similar to that taken in the AIDA project, a generic physical architecture was developed, which was customized by the requirements of an application system. Again the synthesized hardware architecture was specified in VHDL. A side effect of using Ada as a system specification language is the fact that a purely software solution is readily achieved. An overview of the generic hardware architecture, the architecture synthesis system, and the restrictions applied to Ada in order to permit hardware synthesis is presented in Section 3.

A summary of the lessons learned in the two ESPRIT projects, stressing the close interrelationship between the chosen specification language and system implementation architectures, is presented in Section 4. Finally, avenues for possible future work are discussed in Section 5.

2 BEADLE: ARCHITECTURE SYNTHESIS

The major goal of this work was to develop a high-level synthesis system that accepted a description of an application and generated—via a number of intermediate stages—a customized VLSI single-chip architecture, which implemented the specified application. It is well known that the automatic synthesis of VLSI circuits can be achieved using a silicon compiler [5], which is a software tool that accepts a description of an application, processes it, and translates it into a physical layout of a chip in a particular technology. Compilers may be classified according to the kinds of input descriptions they allow: structural or behavioral [6]. With a structural compiler, the input description is in the form of a set of interconnected components, where the compiler instantiates the layout of each component by either extracting it from a library or invoking component assembler software tools. The component layouts are subsequently placed and routed on a chip to achieve the final physical layout [7].

A behavioral compiler accepts a description of a system expressed as the relationships between its inputs and outputs over time, together with a set of design constraints, for example, performance requirements. There are two types of behavioral compilers: The first automatically generates layout directly from an input description, and the second employs high-level synthesis techniques to produce the input for a structural compiler [8–10]. Compilers that generate layouts immediately are normally limited to the generation of circuits for particular application domains, for example, digital signal processors [11,12] and microprocessor-type devices [13–15]. In fact, in the case of behavioral compilers, there is a strong link between the application domain, the associated chip architecture, and the application description language.

To produce silicon compilers for specific application areas, it is necessary to develop appropriate target architectures, chip topologies, and physical layout styles [11–15]. The selection of a suitable architecture, together with a complementary application description language, is pivotal to the quality of the circuits produced by the associated compiler. The wrong choices of languages and architectures can have disastrous effects, as outlined in Section 3.

Our work was concerned primarily with the derivation of chip architectures targeted at the implementation of embedded real-time control systems, for example, engine management processors and industrial robot controllers. One commonly accepted way to specify the behavior of such systems is to define networks of cooperating sequential tasks, which communicate via message passing on logical links. In our case, the system-level specification of an application is defined in the BEADLE language, and the target architecture by a set of processors—one per BEADLE task—interconnected via a generalized communications network. The synthesized architecture is defined in the hardware description language VHDL, and is used as an input to lower level synthesis and physical layout tools. Therefore, our architecture synthesis system forms the first stage of a true silicon compiler. Later work was concerned with the realization of BEADLE tasks in either hardware and/or software, as discussed in Section 2.4.

Other researchers have derived specific target architectures, as part of silicon compilation tools, to match embedded real-time systems defined in high-level software programming languages such as OCCAM [16–19] and Ada [20,21]. Although these languages also permit an application to be defined by a network of cooperating sequential processes, there are a number of major drawbacks to these approaches: the chosen, fixed, target architectures are unsuitable for the realization of large systems; a restricted subset of the language has to be defined for synthesis purposes; and the semantics of the language usually have to be modified in order to permit hardware synthesis. Our approach attempts to overcome these inadequacies by providing an application description language that is aimed specifically at hardware synthesis, together with an extensible generic target architecture, which may be customized for the particular application.

2.1 BEADLE Language Overview

The BEADLE language has been designed to allow the description of embedded, real-time control systems to be expressed in an algorithmic manner. This is achieved by defining the behavior of an application as a set of concurrent, sequential processes in such a way that features difficult or impossible to implement in hard-wired structures are omitted, for example, dynamic process creation/destruction and recursion. There is, therefore, a synergy between the constructs of the BEADLE language and the associated synthesized architecture.

In BEADLE, sequential processes, known as *tasks,* are grouped into networks, which may also contain subnetworks—a system description. The two separate descriptions, tasks and networks, ensure that neither dynamic processes nor shared variables can be described. A task, therefore, exists for the lifetime of a system. Intertask communication is by means of extended-CSP constructs [22]; that is, via typed, point-to-point channels. A graphical representation of a notional system, described in BEADLE, is given in Fig. 1.

Figure 1 indicates that System S has five external channels connected to its environment, and contains a single top-level network, Network 1, which contains two subnetworks, Network 1.1 and Network 1.2, and two internal channels, which are used to connect the two subnetworks. Network 1.1 contains three tasks, A, B, C, and three internal channels, which are used to connect its local tasks. Finally, Network 1.2 contains two tasks, D, E, and two internal channels.

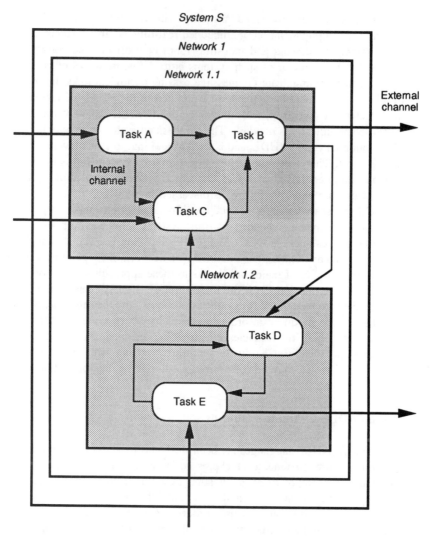

Fig. 1: AIDA: networks of BEADLE tasks

The definition of a task, and its associated network, indicates the channels connected to it—the number of channels, their direction (input or output), and the data type each carries. The body of a task can be considered to be equivalent to a single program in a high-level software programming language such as Pascal. As such, a task body will contain the data type definitions and a list of sequential statements, which are of two kinds: those concerned with the behavior of the task and those related to task communications. The behavioral statements are similar to those found in most high-level programming languages and include assignment, case, do, loop, and subprogram statements.

Remember that BEADLE has been designed with hardware synthesis in mind and does not contain any features that cannot be reflected directly in hardware. This is especially true for the data types provided in the language where certain types intended for use on standard computer systems have been omitted; for example, pointer and file types. The basic data types are enumerated type and integer subtype, together with array, record, and channel structured types. Examples follow:

```
enumerated type TYPE traffic_light = (red, amber,
                                       green, red_and_amber);

integer subtype TYPE data_value    = SUBTYPE integer
                                     RANGE 0 .. 65535;

array           TYPE data_buffer   = ARRAY [1 .. 50] OF
                                     data_value;

record          TYPE sensor        = RECORD
                                       maximum,
                                       minimum,
                                       current: temperature;
                                       status : sensor_status
                                     END_RECORD;

channel         TYPE button        = CHANNEL;   -- a dataless
                                                   channel

                TYPE light_state   = CHANNEL OF
                                     traffic_light;
```

In the preceding examples, the synthesis system will assign, by default, an ordered set of numerical values to the type members—starting at zero, with a unit increment between consecutive elements, and employing the minimum number of bits. For example, the data representation for the type traffic_light, encoded in 2 bits, would be: red = 00, amber = 01, green = 10, and red_and_amber = 11. Although the format of data transferred on internal channels is irrelevant, data transferred on external channels usually has a predefined physical representation, which is dictated by the system environment. It is important that this information be conveyed to the synthesis system in a clear and unambiguous manner. This can be accommodated in BEADLE as shown here:

```
TYPE traffic_light = UNORDERED (red           = 1,
                                amber         = 2,
                                green         = 4,
                                red_and_amber = 3
                               ) WIDTH 3;
```

This definition encodes the type values, in three bits as defined by WIDTH 3 as red = 001, amber = 010, green = 100, and red_and_amber = 011.

Three classes of communications statements occur within the bodies of BEADLE tasks: simple input/output (I/O); conditional input; multiple I/O. Simple I/O refers to intertask communication on a single channel connecting two tasks. An out statement (!) in the sender task will indicate a value to be sent on a specified channel to the receiver task. A matching in statement (?) in the receiver task will name the variable that receives the value sent on the specified channel. The communication is synchronous in that both tasks must wait until the channel transfer is complete before continuing. A simple example is given next for two tasks A and B connected via a communications channel, channel_3:

TASK A	TASK B
channel_3 ! (x * y) / 2;	channel_3 ? average;

Simple I/O statements do not cover all the intertask communications requirements. A task must be able to handle several potential data transfers arriving simultaneously, in an unknown order, on several input channels, and one must be chosen for input before continuing—conditional input. Constructs similar to those found in OCCAM—such as ALT and PRI ALT—are provided to manage these situations. Multiple I/O statements are also included in BEADLE to allow a set of simple input and output statements to be performed both concurrently and independently. In normal circumstances they would be executed sequentially. In this case, the complete set of I/O transfers is completed before normal processing continues.

Simple primitives have been provided to allow channel performance requirements to be stated by a designer. These requirements would normally relate to channels that interface to the external environment of a system—the environment dictating constraints on system performance. In fact, interfacing external channels to an alien environment raises complex issues; for example, the single channel data transfer protocol may not be suitable for a range of peripheral devices in a system, for example, temperature sensors, simple switches, and plasma panel displays. Two different, but related, performance measures can be given for a channel of a particular type: the maximum throughput of the channel and the data transmission time.

The maximum throughput states the largest number of allowable data item transfers per second, and the data transmission time indicates the worst case time (in seconds) allowed for the transfer of a single data item. These measures state the constraints for single channels only; they do not declare how the performances of different channels are related. In addition, there is no mechanism in the language for specifying the performance of individual tasks. This is a difficult problem due to the synchronous nature of intertask communication, where it is nontrivial to predict how long a task may have to wait for a data transfer to occur [20]—such information is usually application and data dependent. The channel performance constraints, however, may be used to guide the architecture synthesis process in choosing a suitable physical interconnection structure for the tasks.

The following example defines a channel type that has a maximum throughput of 200 data transfers per second, each with an allowable worst case transmission time of 10 μs. Its data format is also given:

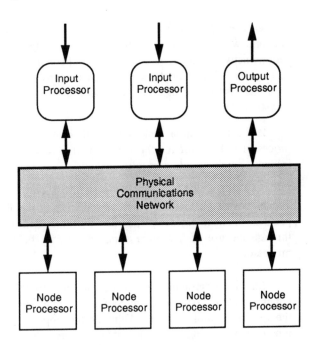

Fig. 2: AIDA: generic target architecture

```
CONST micro  : real = 0.000001;

TYPE status  = UNORDERED (active = 1, inactive = 2,
                         in_error = 4)
             WIDTH 3;
plant_status = CHANNEL OF status
             RATE 200
             TIME 10*micro;
```

It is self-evident that any derived hardware architecture must directly support the BEADLE description of a digital system. The implementation of the intertask communications statements will have the greatest impact on the choice of architecture. It is the physical realization of the logical channels, including their data transfer protocols, that provides the necessary flexibility in the definition of alternative target architectures. By investigating different trade-offs in an architecture, it is possible to produce a range of feasible solutions for a particular application.

2.2 Generic Hardware Architecture

The BEADLE description of an application is mapped onto a generic target architecture (Fig. 2), which will support networks of tasks communicating through logical, point-to-point, typed channels. The objective is to customize this architecture for an application. When synthesizing a feasible architecture, the following design decisions will have a significant impact on the chosen solution:

1. The set of logical channels must be mapped onto a physical communications network, which interconnects the communicating tasks. The topology of the communications network must be such that any channel performance requirements can be met. In fact the efficient implementation of the physical communications channels, together with their associated data protocols, is the overriding consideration in the realization of a system.

2. Each sequential task is realized on its own customized node processor. A node processor will reproduce the behavior of a task both in terms of its functionality and intertask communication requirements.

3. The external interface of a system is specified through a set of external channels. Techniques must, therefore, be derived to map the BEADLE channel communications protocol to those protocols specified by the system environment. This will be achieved through the use of I/O processors, which may be considered as special-purpose node processors.

Intertask communication is specified in BEADLE via dedicated, one-way channels, which results in tasks being interconnected in an *ad hoc,* irregular manner as dictated by the specification of a system. Although this approach is suitable for describing task communications in a logical manner, it is not normally practical to mimic this interconnection structure in the physical implementation of a system due to the potentially high communications costs that can be incurred by implementing many point-to-point links. For systems where tasks operate in a relatively independent manner—a fundamental attribute for the chosen application domain—it is possible to tolerate a low communications bandwidth compared to the corresponding task computation bandwidth. This implies that alternative communications networks can be employed that are more cost effective in terms of task communications. In effect, there is a trade-off between the wiring overheads of direct links and the increased interface logic generated by time-multiplexing multiple channels onto shared links.

A large number of connection topologies are possible for linking networks of node processors [23]. Not all of these topologies, however, are suitable for our problem domain; for example, regular connection structures such as hypercubes, trees, and arrays are not considered to be appropriate due to the inherent "irregular" nature of the task network interconnections. It was decided, therefore, to work with a small set of seemingly more suitable topologies in order to gain experience with the architecture synthesis system at the expense of not having optimized networks. We wished to experiment with the synthesis system while adopting a pragmatic approach to the selection of flexible topologies.

The first such topology is a single, global bus, which can be used to interconnect each node processor to any other node processor in a system [Fig. 3(a)]. To increase the amount of parallelism, in terms of communications transactions, a multiple bus structure [Fig. 3(b)] may be included. The use of multiple local buses connecting networks of related tasks together with a single global bus is an attractive proposition. The final possibility is to provide direct links, [Fig. 3(c)], between tasks in order to satisfy the performance constraints imposed on particular channels that cannot be satisfied using shared bus structures. It is, of course, possible to construct a hybrid of these topologies, [Fig. 3(d)].

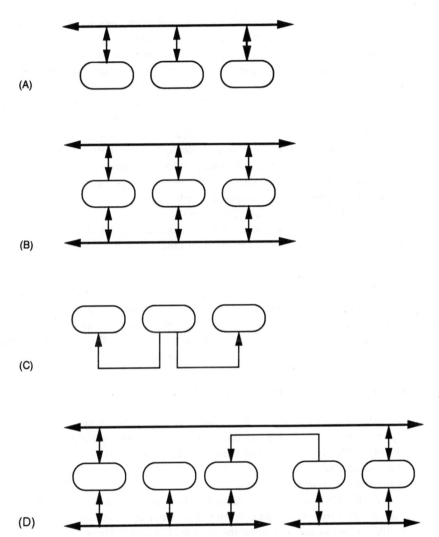

Fig. 3: AIDA: communications network topologies: (a) global bus; (b) multiple buses (for example, two); (c) direct connections, and (d) a hybrid network.

The architecture used in the prototype system was chosen to be a single, bit-parallel global bus in order to minimize the wiring requirements for systems and to simplify the synthesis task. A global bus can be considered to be the most general type of communications network and, as such, may suffer from a lack of performance—the other networks are, in reality, optimizations of a global bus in order to alleviate local performance bottlenecks.

Each sequential task is implemented on its own customized node processor, which is synthesized directly from a BEADLE description. The structure of a synthesized node processor, together with its associated behavior, is defined hierarchically in VHDL as an interconnected set of submodules. A node processor consists of two subprocessors: the function processor and the communications processor.

The function processor is responsible for implementing the sequential behavior of a BEADLE task, and the communications processor realizes the channel data transfers. The communications processor is itself composed of two subprocessors: the protocol processor and the network processor. The protocol processor provides a standard implementation of the BEADLE communications protocols independently of the chosen physical communications network and is customized for the particular application by the synthesis system. The protocol processor provides queues for buffering incoming and outgoing message packets. A network processor provides the necessary interface to the communications network and implements the low-level message passing protocols. Note that for expansion purposes, there are well-defined interfaces between the bus network/protocol processors, and the protocol/function processors.

A BEADLE description of a system defines the external channels, but does not indicate how they are interfaced to an external environment. The channel protocols are designed for internal intertask communications and, in general, will be incompatible with the requirements of the system environment; consider, for example, the interface to an industry-standard bus. In fact the restriction of a single-channel protocol in BEADLE proved to be a major obstacle to the synthesis of high-quality systems. Techniques were, however, devised in the prototype tool to interface these channels—data plus protocols—to an external environment by defining special-purpose I/O processors to realize specific external data transfer protocols, for example, latched-input and latched-output processors.

2.3 Hardware Architecture Synthesis System

The objective of the hardware architecture synthesis system is to generate a customized, single VLSI chip version of the generic target architecture for a particular application. The synthesized architecture is defined in VHDL and is used as the system specification for lower level synthesis tools. A simple block diagram of the synthesis system is shown in Fig. 4.

A BEADLE behavioral description of an application is entered into the design database of the synthesis system. A prototype BEADLE simulator is available in order to verify the intended behavior of the system. The simulator is based on the use of UNIX "processes" and "pipes" in order to mimic the structure of a network of communicating tasks.

The architecture synthesis core forms the heart of the system and is responsible for constructing a structural VHDL description of the chip architecture from a set of VHDL component models. The architecture database contains the VHDL models of the node processors, I/O processors, and global bus. Individual models are either fixed for all architectures, for example, finite state machines, or customized—via generic parameters—according to the number of tasks, number of channels and related data types. The models are described in either register transfer or sequential VHDL subsets.

The resulting chip architecture specification may be verified using a conventional VHDL simulator and is subsequently used as an input to other logic synthesis tools. These synthesis tools accept the register transfer and sequential VHDL descriptions of the architecture components and generate equivalent networks of logic gates.

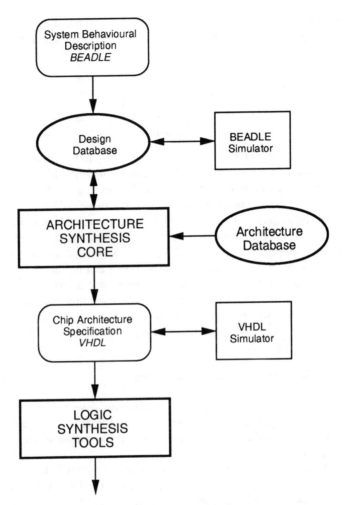

Fig. 4: AIDA: hardware synthesis system

To provide insight into the quality of the architectures generated by the system, the results of synthesizing a simple example are presented. The chosen example, which is considered to be a typical application, is a taxi cab meter controller. The system consists of two concurrent tasks—control and meter—with 15 channels: 9 external input, 3 external output, 3 internal. The synthesis system produced a solution based on two node processors, nine latched-input processors, and three latched-output processors connected via a single global bus. The prototype synthesis system was written in Pascal and runs on Apollo workstations. The VHDL specification of the chip architecture was synthesized in under 10 s—the synthesis of the complete system obviously took much longer to complete!

The BEADLE description consists of approximately 200 lines of code; the synthesized VHDL description of the customized architecture comprises nearly 10,000 lines of code; the synthesized chip contains roughly 250,000 transistors. Because of the excessive number of transistors required to implement such a simple system, it is instructive to ascertain how the transistors have been allocated among the different types of processors connected to the single bus:

Input processors	33%
Output processors	11%
Node processors	
Sequential functions	25%
Communications	31%

These figures indicate that 75% of the transistors are required to support the communications network in the synthesized architecture—44% of the transistor count is needed to realize the very simple I/O data transfers. This example indicates that the implementation of the fixed intertask communications protocol of BEADLE dominates the quality of the synthesized architecture. There is, therefore, a requirement either to modify the implementation of the communications protocol or to have different protocols for internal and external channels or to adopt both options. A detailed discussion of both this example and the hardware architecture synthesis system can be found in [24].

An order of magnitude reduction is necessary in order to gain wider acceptance of this approach to system-level synthesis. Whatever this overhead, however, it represents the necessary price that must be paid in order to generate a feasible chip architecture, which has been synthesized automatically within a short time scale—the classical performance/design time trade-off.

2.4 System Implementation Options

Whereas the original synthesis system was design to produce purely hardware solutions for an application described in BEADLE, it is also feasible to produce either a purely software solution or a mixed hardware/software solution from the same single description, as depicted in Fig. 5.

A set of rules was developed to translate a BEADLE description of a system into an OCCAM description [25]—a software solution. The OCCAM program could be executed on a transputer network for simulation purposes. Although it proved relatively straightforward to translate the BEADLE communications structure—including nondeterminism—into OCCAM equivalents, significant problems were encountered when translating BEADLE types into OCCAM due to the poor typing mechanisms in OCCAM. Restrictions caused by the communications structure of transputer components caused additional problems.

As an intermediate arrangement, a special-purpose "communications" chip was designed to permit a synthesized chip solution to be interfaced to a standard VME bus [26]. The interface chip effectively provided a mapping between the communications protocols of the VME bus and the global bus within a synthesized chip architecture. This allowed BEADLE tasks running on an ASIC to communicate with other BEADLE tasks being executed, in software, on a conventional computer system. A major problem encountered was that no "quantitative" mechanism existed for partitioning BEADLE tasks between hardware and software implementations. This gave rise to the strange situation that, although a partitioned solution could be realized, a suitable technique was not available for the generation of such partitions.

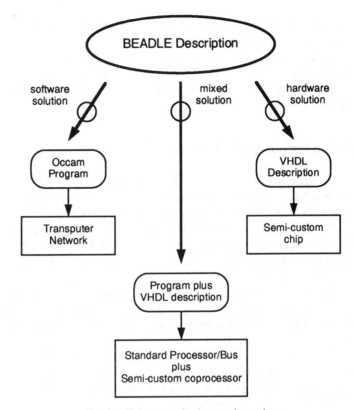

Fig. 5: AIDA: system implementation options

3 ADA: ARCHITECTURE SYNTHESIS

The major objective of this work was to build on the knowledge gained in the BEADLE-based architecture synthesis project. The original idea was that the BEADLE language would also be used in the new project to specify the hardware components, which were to be synthesized as part of a complete system. The decision was made, however, to specify the high-level behavior of both the hardware and software components of a total system in the programming language Ada. The main reason for this decision was that Ada is a general-purpose real-time programming language and, as such, widely used in a number of industrial applications. The decision to discontinue with a "home-grown" language and adopt a standard language, with its associated development environment, is an important one and has significant repercussions on the synthesis philosophy. For example, one of the previous rules was broken to allow a subset of Ada to be chosen for hardware synthesis purposes (see Section 3.1).

In this context, Ada is not being used as a conventional hardware description language, for example, to describe networks of logic gates, but as a specification language for describing systems for input to a high-level synthesis tool. A network of Ada tasks will be input to the synthesis system and an optimized physical architecture will be generated (see Sections 3.2 and 3.3). The behavior of a "hardware" task, and its interface semantics, will be preserved so that it can operate concurrently with other system tasks implemented in either hardware or software.

Note that although the AIDA project produced "real" tools and results, the work performed in the ASAC project was limited. As a consequence, the ideas presented in this section represent the results of a feasibility study and not the outcome from a complete program of work.

3.1 Ada Language Restrictions

A system hardware specification is expressed in the form of a network of Ada tasks. Each task has a task entry specification and a task body. The entry specification defines a task's interface to the other tasks in the system. The task body specifies the executable behavior of the task. A subset of the language was chosen to permit hardware synthesis. Although this approach contradicts the original aim of having "pure" specification languages with no restrictions for hardware synthesis, a pragmatic approach had to be taken for practical reasons.

For synthesis purposes, the Ada task communications primitives are of particular interest. Based on the experiences of synthesizing VHDL descriptions of the sequential behavior of BEADLE tasks, we assumed that a similar approach could be taken with Ada tasks.

Task interaction in Ada is handled by treating each task as a sequential process that communicates with other tasks. Task communications are explicitly synchronized in time by means of a rendezvous mechanism. If task A wishes to send a message to task B, the following protocol is observed:

1. Task A calls the appropriate entry in task B, thus signaling that it is ready to communicate. Note that other tasks in the network can also call the same entry in task B; this provides a many-to-one communications structure.
2. When task B is ready to accept the entry call, a message is passed—in one or both directions—and the two tasks resume their independent actions.

This simple rendezvous can be achieved with a pair of entry/accept statements, as shown next. Note that the task that reaches the rendezvous first must wait for the other one to arrive at the corresponding point in its execution.

```
TASK B IS
   ENTRY receive_message(M : IN string);
END B;

TASK BODY B IS
   .
   ACCEPT receive_message(M : IN string);
   .
END B;
```

```
TASK BODY A IS
    .
    B.receive_message(my_message);
    .
END A;
```

Ada provides extra facilities for more complex intertask communication mechanisms:

1. *Selective wait:* A receiving task must accept a single entry call from two or more possible active calls or wait until one of the entry calls becomes active.

2. *Selective wait with an "Else" part:* A receiving task must accept a single entry call from two or more possible calls if an immediate rendezvous is possible, or perform an alternative sequence of actions if none of them is currently active.

3. *Select with guards:* Possible entry calls may have guards. If an entry does not have a guard or the Boolean expression for the guard is true then the entry is "open"; otherwise it is "closed." If an entry is closed it is not considered for selection. Guards are evaluated once at the "beginning" of the statement. There must be at least one open entry or an "Else" part in the statement. This is similar to item 2.

4. *Select with a delay alternative:* A receiving task must accept a single entry call from two or more possible calls within a specified time period otherwise an alternative sequence of actions is performed.

5. *Timed entry call:* A calling task waits for a rendezvous with a corresponding receiving task for a specified delay period. If the delay period expires, the call is cancelled and an alternative sequence of actions is performed.

6. *Conditional entry call:* This is semantically equivalent to a timed entry call with the delay period set to zero.

The proposed synthesis system was expected to handle all of the Ada task communications constructs except for the "timed entry call" and "conditional entry call" cases. It was believed that the realization of these constructs in hardware would, in the first instance, prove to be too inefficient due to the complexity of "cancelling" entry calls in the called tasks.

3.2 Generic Hardware Architecture

The Ada description of a system hardware component may be mapped onto a generic target architecture, which supports networks of communicating tasks. This is a similar approach to the one adopted in the AIDA project where:

1. There will be a finite number of Ada tasks in any system specification—the dynamic generation/termination of tasks is not permitted.

2. Each Ada task is implemented on its own node processor, which is customized in terms of its communications requirements and functionality.

3. Each node processor is synthesized using a small number of parameterized modules. The behavior of a node processor will be specified using models expressed in sequential VHDL, with module interconnections defined in structural VHDL.

4. Each node processor needs to have different types of communications links, for example, a bidirectional bus and a direct connection. Each processor needs different numbers of communications links in order to permit the construction of nontrivial physical communications networks.

5. A message-based communications mechanism is needed where incoming messages can be queued for later processing by a node processor. A node processor only deals with incoming messages when it expects to perform a rendezvous with another node processor.

6. Input/output interfaces to industry-standard buses will be provided.

7. It is assumed that the physical architecture may have to be partitioned across a number of ASICs. The chip partitioning process may be constrained to permit partitions at well-defined boundaries, that is, where there is not a dramatic loss of communications bandwidth. This process is driven by ASIC I/O pin limitations and off-chip path delay considerations. To overcome one of the major problems identified in the BEADLE synthesis system—in which the implementation of the fixed intertask communications protocol dominated the quality of the synthesized architecture—a different protocol was adopted for message transfers between node processors. It was found that by increasing the number of address bits in a message packet to include task and entry identification, constructing a single-bounded FIFO queue for message packets in each node processor, and incorporating explicit hardware acknowledgments to signal the successful transfer of packets between node processors, an order of magnitude reduction in the total transistor count for a hardware component could probably be achieved. In effect, there was a trade-off between an increase in the number of wires needed in a communications path with a reduction in the functional complexity of a communications interface.

3.3 Hardware Architecture Synthesis System

The objective of the hardware architecture synthesis system is again to generate a customized, possibly multiple, VLSI chip version of the generic target architecture for a particular application. The synthesized architecture is defined in VHDL. A block diagram of the synthesis system is given in Fig. 6.

An Ada behavioral description of a hardware module is entered into the architecture synthesis core. The Ada description can be compiled and verified using "normal" software engineering techniques. Note that a side effect of using Ada as a system specification language is that a purely software simulation is readily achieved.

The synthesis core is responsible for constructing a structural VHDL description of the physical architecture from a set of VHDL component models. These are models of the node processors and communications networks. Again, individual models will be either

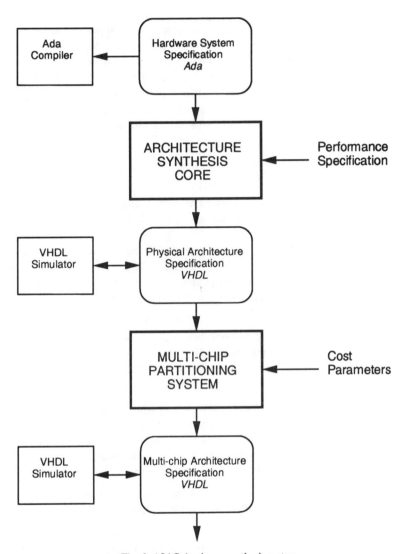

Fig. 6: ASAC: hardware synthesis system

fixed for all architectures or customized—via generic parameters—according to the number of tasks, number of task entries, and associated data types. The models are mainly described in sequential VHDL subsets. It is assumed that the hardware synthesis task is driven by the communications frequency for each task entry. The communications frequency information was to be derived by a systems modeling tool, which was developed outside of this project.

The resulting physical architecture specification was to be verified using a conventional VHDL simulator and subsequently used as an input to a multichip partitioning tool. The objective of the chip partitioning tool is to analyze a VHDL description of a hardware module (subsystem) and to produce an estimate of the number and types of

ASICs required to implement the subsystem. The output of the partitioning tool would be a VHDL description of the interconnected ASICs, together with their internal hardware module allocations. The complete process is driven by a number of parameters, for example, silicon area and number of external pins for different ASICs. A prototype partitioning tool was developed to determine the feasibility of this operation [27].

Finally, the resulting multichip architecture specification may be verified using a VHDL simulator and subsequently used as an input to lower level synthesis tools.

4 LESSONS LEARNED

A number of significant lessons have been learned from the work performed in both ESPRIT projects. The main points are outlined below:

1. Despite all temptations, be aware of the consequences of developing "homegrown" languages to specify hardware/software systems. Due to the high cost of developing and supporting new languages, it is usually more advisable to adapt existing, possibly industry-standard, languages. Such languages normally have a set of well-defined development tools.

2. When adapting an existing language to specify both hardware and software subsystems, care must be taken not to alter the semantics of the language in any way—this guarantees that existing specifications remain valid. The choice of a suitable language subset is crucial.

3. Be aware of the "hidden" costs in synthesizing a hardware/software architecture. In an architecture with multiple, communicating processes the trade-off between the implementation complexity of the communications protocol and the choice of a process communications structure represents a critical decision. Communications costs must not be allowed to dominate the final implementation.

4. Care must be taken to realize the external I/O requirements of a system in an efficient manner. Consideration should be given to the adoption of industry-standard interfaces.

5. The symbiosis of the system description language and the corresponding hardware and software architectures should be maximized. This will result in better quality hardware/software systems.

6. Efficient mechanisms are required to perform the hardware/software partitioning task. Experience has been gained in the synthesis and implementation of mixed hardware/software systems, but little work has been performed in exploring hardware/software trade-offs.

5 FUTURE DIRECTIONS

As a result of undertaking research work in the general area of hardware/software co-design and the specific area of language-to-architecture synthesis, the following suggestions are made regarding future possible avenues of work necessary to enhance the quality of hardware/software systems:

1. A unified development environment is needed to support the concurrent design of a system's hardware and software [28].

2. A multiple-level modeling environment is required for "hardware," "software," and "undecided"—hardware or software—system modules. This is especially true for intermodule communication protocols. The use of reusable software and hardware modules should be incorporated into such an environment.

3. The need to develop high-quality hardware/software partitioning tools is paramount [29,30]. Cognizance needs to be taken of developments in the area of "pure" hardware partitioning tools [31].

4. The ideas developed in this work can be extended to the use of synchronous, reactive real-time programming languages, for example, ESTEREL [32]. Such languages are defined by a formal semantics and permit the use of formal techniques to specify, implement, and verify hardware/software systems in an integrated manner.

Current work is targeted at the use of synchronous, reactive languages for the design and implementation of hardware/software systems.

ACKNOWLEDGMENTS

The work described in this chapter has been undertaken as part of the AIDA and ASAC ESPRIT projects. The author greatly values the assistance of colleagues at Bull, ICL, Olivetti, SGS-Thomson, Siemens, and UMIST. Special thanks are due John Forrest of UMIST without whom much of this work would not have been possible.

REFERENCES

[1] M. D. Edwards and J. Forrest, "BEADLE: An Algorithmic Language for the Description of Digital Systems," in *Design Methodologies for VLSI and Computer Architecture,* D. A. Edwards, Ed., North-Holland, Amsterdam, 1989.

[2] "IEEE Standard VHDL Reference Manual," IEEE Std 1076-1987, 1988.

[3] *Occam Programming Manual,* Prentice-Hall, Englewood Cliffs, NJ, 1984.

[4] "The Programming Language ADA Reference Manual," ANSI/MIL-STD-1815A, 1983.

[5] D. Johannsen, "Bristle Blocks: A Silicon Compiler," in *Proc. 16th Design Automation Conference,* pp. 303–310, IEEE, 1979.

[6] B. M. Pangrle and D. D. Gajski, "Design Tools for Intelligent Silicon Compilation," *IEEE Trans. Computer-Aided Des.,* CAD-6(6), pp. 1098–1112, 1987.

[7] "CHIPSMITH: A Random Logic Compiler for Gate Arrays and Standard Cell Implementations," Lattice Logic, Edinburgh, 1985.

[8] M. C. McFarland, A. C. Parker, and R. Camposano, "Tutorial on High-Level Synthesis," in *Proc. 25th Design Automation Conference*, pp. 330–336, IEEE, 1988.

[9] G. Borriello and E. Detjens, "High-Level Synthesis: Current Status and Future Directions," in *Proc. 25th Design Automation Conference*, pp. 477–482, IEEE, 1988.

[10] P. Duzy, H. Kramer, M. Neher, M. Pilsl, W. Rosentiel, and T. Wecker, "CALLAS—Conversion of Algorithms to Library Adaptable Structures," in *VLSI89*, G. Musgrave and U. Lauther, Eds., Elsevier Science Publishers, Amsterdam, 1989.

[11] P. Denyer, and D. Renshaw, *VLSI Signal Processing: A Bit-Serial Approach*, Addison-Wesley, Reading, MA, 1985.

[12] H. De Man, J. Rabaey, and P. Six, "Cathedral II: A Synthesis and Module Generation System for Multiprocessor Systems on a Chip," in *Design Systems for VLSI Circuits: Logic Synthesis and Silicon Compilation*, G. De Micheli, A. Sangiovanni-Vincentelli, and P. Antognetti, Eds., Martinus Nijhoff Publishers, Dordrecht, 1987.

[13] A. Jerraya and B. Courtois, "The Syco Silicon Compiler and Its Environment," in *Design Systems for VLSI Circuits: Logic Synthesis and Silicon Compilation*, G. De Micheli, A. Sangiovanni-Vincentelli, and P. Antognetti, Eds., Martinus Nijhoff Publishers, Dordrecht, 1987.

[14] T. Blackman, J. Fox, and C. Rosebrugh, "The SILC Silicon Compiler: Language and Features," in *Proc. 22nd Design Automation Conference*, pp. 232–237, IEEE, 1985.

[15] M. Hirayama, "Silicon Compiler System Based on Asynchronous Architecture," *IEEE Trans. Computer-Aided Des.*, CAD-6(3), pp. 297–304, Bristol, 1987.

[16] D. May and C. Keane, *Compiling Occam into Silicon*, Inmos, 1987.

[17] G. V. Collis and M. D. Edwards, "Automatic Hardware Synthesis from a Behavioural Description Language: OCCAM," *Microproc. Microprog.*, 18(1–5), pp. 243–250, 1986.

[18] R. Dowsing, R. Elliott, M. Templeton, G. Williams, and F. Woodhams, "A Framework for the Synthesis of Hardware from Occam," *Microproc. Microprog.*, 27, pp. 373–380, 1989.

[19] E. Brunvand and R. F. Sproull, "Translating Concurrent Communicating Programs into Delay-Insensitive Circuits," Computer Science Research Report CMU-CS-89-126, Carnegie Mellon University, 1989.

[20] E. J. Girczyc, R. J. A. Buhr, and J. P. Knight, "Applicability of a Subset of Ada as an Algorithmic Hardware Language for Graph-Based Hardware Compilation," *IEEE Trans. Computer-Aided Des.*, CAD-4(2), pp. 134–142, 1985.

[21] E. I. Organick, T. M. Carter, M. P. Maloney, A. Davis, A. B. Hayes, D. Klass, D. Lindstrom, B. E. Nelson, and K. F. Smith, "Transforming an Ada Program Unit to Silicon and Verifying Its Behaviour in an Ada Environment: A FIRST EXPERIMENT," *IEEE Software*, 1(1), pp. 31–48, 1984.

[22] K. M. Chandy and J. Misra, "Deadlock Absence Proofs for Networks of Communicating Processes," *Info. Proc. Lett.*, 9(4), pp. 185–189, 1979.

[23] L. D. Wittie, "Communication Structures for Large Networks of Microcomputers," *IEEE Trans. Computers*, C-30(4), pp. 264–273, 1981.

[24] M. D. Edwards, "A Generic Hardware Architecture to Support the System Level Synthesis of Digital Systems," *Microproc. Microprog.,* 40, pp. 255–240, 1994.

[25] H. Hounat, "The Mapping of BEADLE Descriptions onto OCCAM," MSc Thesis, University of Manchester, 1989.

[26] V. G. Stokoe, "VME Bus to BEAST Bus Converter," Third Year Project Report, Department of Computation, UMIST, 1989.

[27] A. Tardif, "Multiple ASIC Partitioning Project," MSc Dissertation, University of Manchester, 1991.

[28] J. O. Coplien, "Ishmael: An Integrated Software/Hardware Maintenance and Evolution Environment," *AT&T Tech. J.,* pp. 52–63, 1991.

[29] T. Juntunen, J. Kivela, A. Reinikka, M. Sipola, J. P. Soininen, K. Tiesyrja, and T. Tikkanen, "Real-time Structured Analysis in System Level Design of Embedded ASICs," *Microproc. Microprog.,* 24, pp. 449–454, 1988.

[30] E. Barros and W. Rosentiel, "A Method for Hardware Software Partitioning," in *IEEE COMP EURO,* pp. 580–585, IEEE, 1992.

[31] K. Kucukcakar and A. C. Parker, "CHOP: A Constraint-Driven System Level Partitioner," in *Proc. 28th ACM/IEEE Design Automation Conference,* pp. 514–519, IEEE, 1991.

[32] G. Berry and G. Gonthier, "The Esterel Synchronous Programming Language: Design, Semantics, Implementation," INRIA Report 842, 1988.

CHAPTER 18

CODES

A Framework for Modeling Heterogeneous Systems

K. Buchenrieder   A. Sedlmeier   C. Veith

Corporate Research and Development

Siemens AG

Munich, Germany

Abstract: This chapter describes a CAx environment/framework for designing hardware/software systems concurrently. We describe a codesign manager that provides the neccessary infrastructure for design flow, data, and task management. The codesign manager regulates the codesign process as a whole. Major design steps such as modeling and simulation as well as hardware integration worked out with a knowledge-based hardware configuration tool are described. Furthermore, it is shown that hardware/software codesign stems from a theoretical basis and can be proved by an abstract model of parallel random access machines. A real-life application proves the feasibility of the approach.

1 INTRODUCTION

Intelligent and heterogeneous systems are generally constructed from many tightly coupled hardware (HW) and software (SW) components. Traditionally, these components are designed by several different engineers or even departments and finally integrated to result in a product. The motivation for CODES (COncurrent DESign environment) arises from the increasing SW and HW complexity of controller-based systems and from the intent to narrow the gap between the designer's intent and the behavior of the resulting prototype or system implementation.

By looking at numerous designs it became clear that the development of concurrent HW and SW components must be based on a formal computational model. Furthermore, an interactive codesign philosophy requires a framework within which tools can be freely embedded, and also noncomputer-related design steps supervised. The design environment described in this chapter provides task, flow, and data management by means of a dedicated framework that encapsulates CAD tools for the development of time-discrete and time-continuous components. It has the following properties:

- It provides tool encapsulation mechanisms to integrate external units via task-oriented service interfaces.
- It supports the concurrent development of units according to predefined strategies or policies.
- Special services establish the easy connection of modules to a running application.
- It manages complexity by using high-level models consisting of hierarchical components.
- It facilitates the integration of new HW or SW components.
- It helps to trace back user actions and system states to experiment with different versions of the work.

One objective of this framework is to support verification on all possible levels of design. Verification ensures design consistency. The framework is also expected to ensure data consistency and compatibility. To reduce design costs as far as possible, the design engineer produces models of design sections for each level of representation in advance, and then stores them in libraries for reuse or goes back to existing model libraries. We distinguish between design libraries and verification libraries. Design libraries contain models or programs previously designed. These are the building blocks used by the design engineer for the final run-time system. Verification libraries contain simulation or test modules, which make it possible to automatically translate the design into the input language of simulators. They also contain collections of design rules for each design level.

Traditional means of HW/SW development are based on a divide-and-conquer strategy. Here, SW and HW subsystems are worked on separately and integrated in the last step. Many successful products have been developed with this method, and the advantages need not be discussed. However, superfluous steps are inherent to the process, such as one group designing features of an interface that must be reversed or adapted by another group. Many institutions have realized that traditional HW/SW development methods are no longer adequate and the demand for a codesign environment has grown. In the following, codesign is used as a synonym for concurrent or cooperating design, denoting two principal research directions: parallelizing tasks for faster turnaround and streamlining HW/SW communications to eliminate redesigns.

The CODES prototype, developed in our labs, is primarily a research platform for the development of codesign principles. It offers researchers from different design disciplines an open architecture to integrate commercial and proprietary design tools and to carry out small to medium designs. Our research effort in developing CODES was driven by two demands: First, a user must be able to model, analyze, and simulate the complete system regardless of the implementation of individual components. Second, it must be possible to treat the design process as a system of its own right. This means that both HW and SW designers alike must be able to comprehend all aspects of the system model.

CODES features parallel random access machines (PRAMs) as abstract models for the HW/SW systems, and Petri nets for design process modeling. To demonstrate the CODES environment we designed a motor control unit. It consists of some time-discrete and several time-continuous components implemented as HW or SW components depending on the designers' choice. A small team of designers created the system model, designed the individual modules and integrated all into a working prototype. Additionally, we developed the model of the design process using a codesign manager for use in later projects.

The reminder of this chapter is organized as follows: First we give an overview of the CODES environment. The next section shows how a design approach is supported by the underlaying framework. Section 4 shows the principal design phases in CODES. SIDECON, a knowledge-based configuration tool for hardware components, is introduced in Section 5. Section 6 discusses PRAMS and in Section 7 we give some examples in which we tested parts of CODES. In Section 8 we draw some conclusions and describe possible extensions of CODES in the future.

2 SYSTEM OVERVIEW

CODES is designed to develop an integrated HW/SW prototype for mixed-module systems that contain time-discrete, time-continuous, and specialized HW and SW modules. Modules are engineered either with tools within the CODES environment, or imported from external sources, existing projects, or libraries. Designs are composed of communicating units each representing a behavior. Figure 1 shows specifications of the complete system, which are captured with tools based on structured analysis, refined, and then partitioned into manageable units. From the descriptions of these units, C is generated for software and VHDL for hardware modules. These descriptions are then compiled,

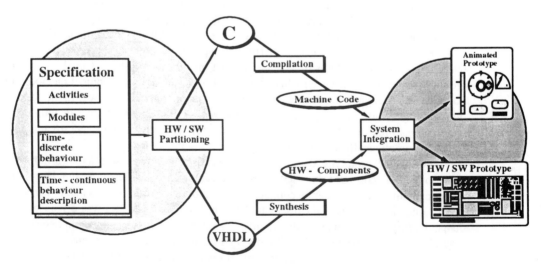

Fig. 1: System overview

synthesized, or handcrafted. In the system integration step, all components are put together, resulting in a visual or real prototype. Visual prototypes behave like the desired HW/SW system but provide the user with some "touch and feel." Positions of physical control elements such as buttons, switches, and displays can be experimented with. The purpose is to improve the supplier/customer interaction. Real prototypes are actual HW/SW systems for performance evaluation, measurement, and use. Simulators at the system and algorithmic level are provided for validation and rapid prototyping of the HW/SW system.

CODES is a high-level environment that builds on methods and tools that are themselves design environments, e.g., synthesis systems and PCB design tools. The shortcomings of our prototype are propagated by the underlying components; algorithmic synthesis, for instance, is an ongoing research topic, but for now we just take a working algorithmic synthesis system for granted. As researchers gradually complete the specialized design tools, current shortcomings will disappear. The most important feature of CODES is its open architecture supported with our codesign manager [1] for the convenient inclusion of new tools and new design styles. This manager assists users in the design flow management, tool management, and configuration file management of HW/SW projects. Based on the idea of conventional frameworks, it not only assures the consistency of design data, but also keeps the entire design flow consistent. Whenever a designer changes one or more parts of a design, the codesign manager suggests the proper sequence of actions and, if possible, performs those actions automatically. Currently, CODES targets the design of processor-based systems emphasizing the optimal cooperation between SW and HW.

Components of the generated system are synchronized through hard interrupts, ensuring the smooth interaction of HW and SW. Within the CODES environment, complete interrupt control synthesis is provided, thus enabling the design of systems with more than one processor.

3 THE CODESIGN MANAGER

The codesign manager serves a twofold purpose: First, it provides infrastructure and support for CODES users with facilities for data management, tool integration, and design flow management. Second, we use it to model and analyze codesign processes. In this chapter, we describe the use of the codesign manager as a framework for the modeling and execution of CODES.

In its current state, the codesign manager consists of a graphical net editor, a rule compiler, and flow management components as shown in Fig. 2. It also includes hierarchical process models, a graphical interface for the flow manager, and a communication mechanism for the tool manager.

The codesign manager is able to capture both the static and dynamic behavior of systems. Note that in this context *system* means "design environment" or "design process," and is clearly distinguished from the system that is specified, designed, and implemented. The codesign manager uses Petri nets for modeling the design process. This technique is powerful enough that we model completely different and more or less technical, processes (see also Fig. 3).

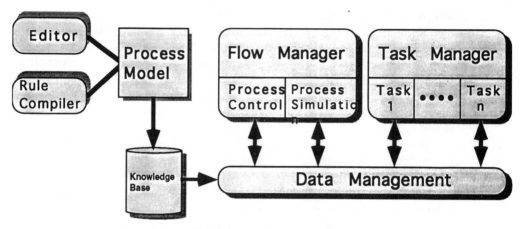

Fig. 2: The codesign manager

In CODES, a special form of Petri nets, called *predicate transition nets* (Pr/T nets) with some extensions [2], is used as the basis of our modeling technique. From the graphical net representation, the system generates OPS83 production rules to control the design process. The rules characterize actions depending on conditions. Production systems are built from a set of condition-action rules and a working memory containing facts. Production rules fire and perform the related actions if the associated conditions yield. They model dynamic knowledge and govern conflict resolution, parameter selection, and error handling. If several rules fire in parallel, a resolution strategy is invoked for the selection of an appropriate rule. Actions alter the contents of the working memory, and thus new matches may occur.

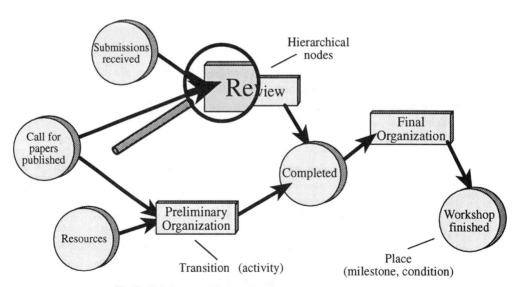

Fig. 3: High-level model of the first HW/SW codesign workshop

A net syntax checker examines the correctness of the predicate-transition net syntax and also keeps track of isolated symbols and open connections. After the creation of the net model, a rule compiler is started that translates nets into a set of OPS83 rules. The compiler checks the net semantics against continuity of the control token flow and performs a deadlock analysis. Additionally, it generates three rules in OPS83 syntax. Rule 1 provides and checks the availability of input tokens. This rule suggests executable tools to the designer. Another rule performs the status modification and starts the task manager tool, which supervises the appropriate tool. If a designer decides to start a tool, input tokens are removed and selected tools invoked. Rule 3 handles output tokens and releases variable bindings. After that the design process continues.

4 PRINCIPAL DESIGN STEPS

A CODES prototype with two alternative branches for design specification consists of a multifacet core, built from readily available tools such as Statemate^{TM} [3], Matrix$_x$^{TM} and in-house design software packages such as SDL, KLAR, and SIGRAPH-SET$^{\textregistered}$, enriched with interfaces and instruments for convenient intertool communications. Since CODES is primarily a research platform, the development of codesign principles was emphasized and almost no time spent on tool development.

4.1 Structure of the CODES Environment

CODES consists of three main parts:

- Tools for specification and system-level design, which directly support the abstract PRAM model
- Tools for component design, implementation, and integration; they indirectly support the abstract model by operating on the models created with the system-level design tools
- A framework for design process modeling, data modeling, and design flow management. This framework is based on high-level Petri nets.

The philosophy of CODES is that specifications and system models serve as an intermediate format between the theoretical PRAM model on the one hand, and design and implementation on the other. Algebraic PRAM specifications are inconvenient to deal with for most designers. It is also difficult to generate code directly from PRAM specifications. This bears a certain analogy to the structure of compilers, which usually consist of a front end and a back end.

Our selection of tools for specification and system-level design was based on the degree of support for our theoretical model. We found that with both Statemate^{TM} and SDL we can almost, but not quite, get a full coverage of all aspects of our model. The fact that we did not start to implement the "perfect tool," but used Statemate^{TM} and SDL instead, reflects the nature of the CODES project. Statemate^{TM} and SDL—and their shortcomings with respect to the PRAM model—are described in Section 6.

For the design, implementation, and integration of components we have chosen the tools Matrix$_x$^{TM}, SIDECON, traditional programming tools (editor, compiler, debugger), hardware synthesis tools based on VHDL, Statemate^{TM}, and SDL. SIDECON is a knowledge-based configuration tool for printed circuit boards. Statemate^{TM} and SDL are included in this list, because their capabilities exceed specification and system-level design and reach out to the lower levels of design as well. For all of the "component" tools, no *a priori* restrictions exist except that they have to match the Statemate^{TM} or SDL design philosophy.

4.2 Specification and System-Level Design

The CODES design approach starts with a verbal specification of the desired HW/SW system (requirement analysis). After the specification is captured, it is translated into a PRAM model using either Statemate^{TM} or SDL, a CCITT standardized [4,5] specification and description language and then checked for inconsistencies. Figure 4 shows the branching of the CODES environment into two paths. Statemate^{TM} and SDL are equivalent with respect to their power to generate system models, but each of them offers exclusive features for the convenience of system designers. Therefore, we decided to provide the Statemate^{TM} route and the SDL route as distinct alternatives in CODES.

Statemate^{TM} is based on the StateChart formalism developed by D. Harel [6], and SDL is based on Hoare's CSP model [7]. Both models are, in principle, parallel finite-state machines, and they both allow the use of storage. They both support our abstract PRAM model. The most fundamental difference between them is the way they treat communication: Statemate^{TM} uses broadcast communication, whereas SDL uses point-to-point communication. Further, SDL provides (conceptually infinite) message buffers, a feature that must be explicitly modeled within Statemate^{TM}. Theoretically, both tools can emulate the communication mechanism of their counterpart: In SDL, every message a process sends can be made available to every other currently existing SDL process. In Statemate^{TM}, point-to-point communication can be implemented by suitable encoding of signals. With these emulation strategies, however, one loses much of the elegance of the model specifications in Statemate^{TM} and SDL.

Regarding the clarity of specifications, Statemate^{TM} edges SDL: Statemate^{TM} allows hierarchical models (SDL models are "flat") and provides a concise syntax for the generation of events in the form event/condition/action (this must be explicitly modeled in SDL). SDL has the advantage over Statemate^{TM} when it comes to the dynamic generation of processes (RAMs). SDL provides a mechanism for it, whereas Statemate^{TM} does not. We stress that this is just a practical, not a theoretical, advantage because any real-world computation is finite, and we can therefore avoid dynamic generation of RAMs by just providing "enough" RAMs in the Statemate^{TM} model. Along the same lines, hierarchical descriptions in Statemate^{TM} achieve no theoretical advantage either, because every hierarchical RAM can be described by an equivalent "flat" RAM. (Note that both tools provide a variety of simulation and analysis methods that we do not describe here.)

When it comes to the conversion of system models to component designs and implementations, we believe that Statemate^{TM} and SDL are equivalent. Both tools provide code generators for C on the software side and for VHDL on the hardware side.

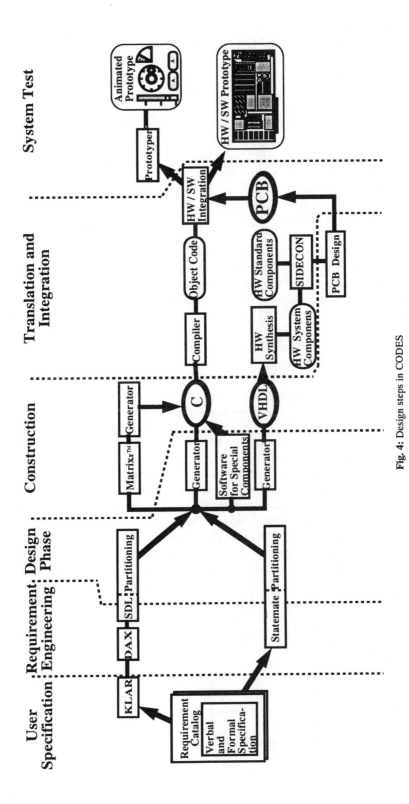

Fig. 4: Design steps in CODES

5 HARDWARE INTEGRATION BASED ON SIDECON

Components of the system are designed with either Matrix$_x$^{TM}, SIDECON, or a traditional system specification and programming environment, such as SDL or Statemate^{TM}, as discussed in the last section.

Statemate^{TM} and SIGRAPH-SET SDL are powerful tools for the design of time-discrete components. Time-continuous (i.e., conceptually analog, but discrete implementation) components are constructed with Matrix$_x$^{TM}. It provides a convenient environment for control system design and provides standard graphical symbols for all necessary control elements. With Matrix$_x$^{TM}, two tasks can be performed: First, time-continuous components can be designed and simulated on an individual basis. Second, CODES users can observe the behavior of their system in its target environment by creating models of the (usually continuous) environment with Matrix$_x$^{TM}.

CODES provides an interface between Matrix$_x$^{TM} and Statemate^{TM}. Through this link, time-continuous components can be bound to Statemate^{TM} descriptions, and Statemate^{TM} descriptions can be bound to time-continuous modes of their environment. An equivalent link does not yet exist for SIGRAPH-SET SDL, but because Statemate^{TM} descriptions and SIGRAPH-SET$^®$ descriptions are equivalent, the implementation problem is simplified.

Additional components, such as foreign C routines, VHDL models, or existing hardware, can also be added through a similar mechanism. Existing hardware components are identified in the system model and integrated into the system using SIDECON [8].

SIDECON is a collection of tools to synthesize printed circuit boards. It is based on the MICON system [9–12], developed at Carnegie Mellon University.

SIDECON uses standard chips, programmable integrated circuits such as ASICs and PLDs, passive electronic components, and mechanical components. The result is a netlist that can be further processed by design tools for placement and routing.

SIDECON is a knowledge-based system. Its synthesis tool designs a schematic diagram and a netlist of components, chosen from a library, a task that is often called *configuration*. The synthesis task is performed in a hierarchical stepwise refinement process. The refinement is controlled by a hierarchical structure of components (functional hierarchy, Fig. 5) that expresses the functional relationship between parts on different levels of abstraction. The root node represents the highest abstraction level, and the leaves correspond to parts on the lowest abstraction level, the physical parts. The hierarchy comprises two types of links, AND and OR links. An AND link indicates, that the more abstract part has to be replaced by a combination of all parts that are linked to it. An OR link designates the refinement to exactly one part that has to be selected.

Parts are represented by part models. The models contain characteristics that describe properties of the part and specifications. These describe requirements for parts on the next lower level in the hierarchy.

The mapping to the successor parts is done by templates that are represented as rules. In the CODES system, SIDECON's task is the integration of newly generated HW and SW components on a microprocessor-based design. Figure 2 shows the configuration of hardware components and the integration of generated machine code into a complete HW/SW prototype. The final prototype, a board, resembles the platform to carry the

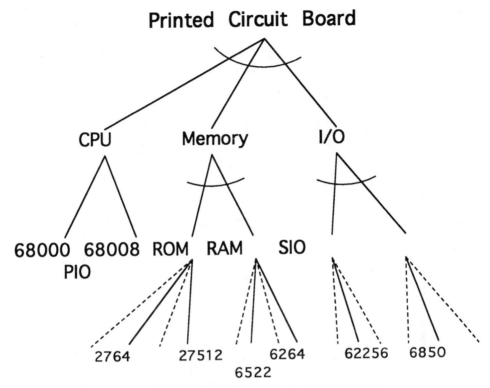

Fig. 5: AND-OR structure from board to components

software. It is composed of a processor, memory, and standard off-the-shelf components, enhanced with some special synthesized hardware. Generated software executes on this platform.

6 PARALLEL RANDOM ACCESS MACHINES

The abstract model of parallel random access machines [13,14] is the baseline of our work. The RAM formalism suits codesign needs well because it is as powerful as the Turing formalism (refer to theorem 7.6, pp. 166–167 in [13]). It consists of a finite-state machine (FSM) and some finite random access store. For this reason, RAMs can accept context-sensitive languages (theorems 9.5 and 9.6 of [13]). Depending on the FSM model chosen, access to the store is carried out either on a transition or state visit. Computations are designed top down in a modular fashion regardless of a later implementation. Since RAMs are computationally equivalent to bounded-tape Turing machines, any existing computer or algorithm can be described using RAMs. This is especially advantageous because powerful theoretical methods exist for the analysis of Turing transducers [13]. As shown in Fig. 6, the PRAM's I/O frame encapsulates several RAMs and thereby

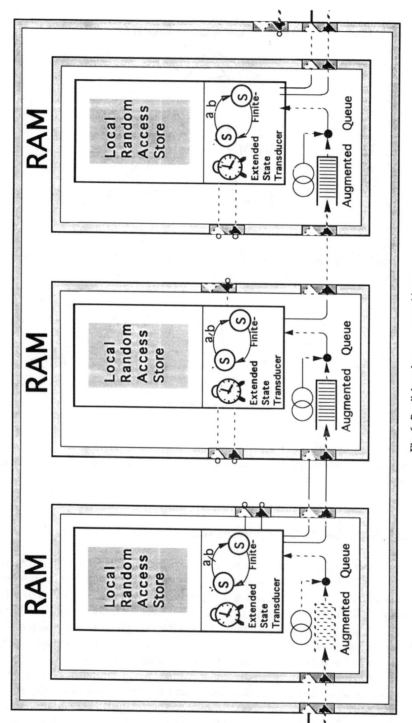

Fig. 6: Parallel random access machine

supports an explicit model of the environment in which the designed system is assumed to function. For this reason, RAMs can be viewed as embedded systems, which can be effectively designed so that reuse of designed modules can be more reliably exercised.

RAMs encapsulated in the I/O frame consist of an extended finite-state transducer, some local storage of limited size, and one or more I/O ports. Transducer extensions relate to:

- The handling of external activities such as program start and termination
- Access of the local store and state-history management
- Postponement of signals and events
- Timing-related behavior and timing-conditions.

To ensure that the final design is composed of well understood and functioning building blocks these are treated as separate units until realization.

All communication activities in the model are carried out using ports and channels. A port may be connected via a channel to one or more appropriate ports. These may be located at another RAM or attached to the embracing frame that represents the system's environment. Ports in the model are composed of a data and a synchronization terminal that can be typed and attributed for proper exchange of data between ports and for simulation and connection to the prototyper. The model supports point-to-point as well as broadcast communication. These modes are distinguished by either a line connect between ports or a bubble connect attached to the sender's terminal. Synchronous and asynchronous communication is differentiated by the presence or the omission of connects at respective synchronization terminals. So-called "short-pulse catching problems" [15] are effectively avoided with augmented queues, which buffer incoming signals. Because parallel finite-state transducers may consume more than one symbol at a time, in an order possibly different from arrival, the symbol or event at the head of the queue is considered first. If no transition can be carried out, all elements in the queue are considered and possible transitions performed. This mechanism ensures that neither messages nor events are lost or postponed indefinitely.

The RAMs in the model are special with respect to an instantiation mechanism. It provides each RAM with the power to instantiate a copy of any RAM enclosed in the environment frame. Some tasks, such as *mail distribution* or *runway scheduling* [16] seem to require dynamic instantiation capability, at least this is what some of our users demand. However, we have reason to believe that this is mainly a matter of convenience to ease system specification than a lack of computational power.

7 EXAMPLE

To demonstrate the usefulness of CODES, we chose an electronic motor control unit as an example. We settled for this example because it represents typical projects of our product divisions.

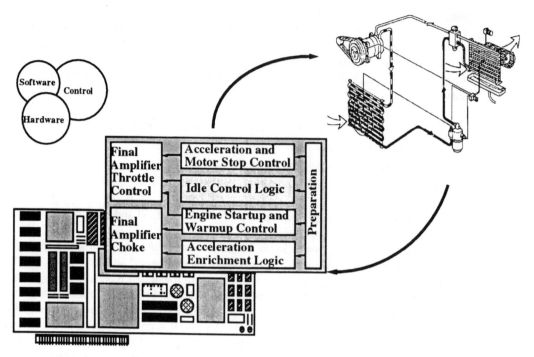

Fig. 7: Microprocessor-based implementation of a motor control unit

7.1 Testbed Description

The motor control unit (called Ecotronic) is a closed-loop system that consists of a controlled engine, several sensors, and a microprocessor-based brain box, as shown in Fig. 7. The controller itself is composed of time-discrete and time-continuous control sections.

An Ecotronic motor controller consists of four subunits:

- Acceleration and motor-stop control
- Idle control logic
- Engine startup and warm-up control
- Acceleration enrichment logic.

In the design process we concentrated on developing the underlying time-discrete, event-driven controller for subcomponent interaction, and the time-continuous idle-speed module. We selected this combination of hierarchical components because it demonstrates true codesign of an event-driven state machine that interacts with a time-continuous component (not even considering our attempt to improve the world's energy savings since almost 30% of a motor vehicle's fuel consumption in heavy traffic occurs during idling).

Consequently, the idle speed should always be as low as possible. At the same time, it should be adjusted so that the engine can sustain electrical loads, air conditioning, or power steering without stalling.

7.2 Results

Using CODES, we prototyped and designed large portions of the example described in Section 7.1. In the process, a HW/SW system along each of the two routes, as depicted in Fig. 2, was developed. The design effort resulted in a working visual prototype, a synthesizable VHDL module for the controller, C code for the idle-speed module, and abstract components for SIDECON mapping.

Starting with a verbal specification from an autoelectronic data book, we designed a set of StateCharts and SDL charts. The conversion of the specification to either a Statemate^{TM} model or an SDL model was an inherently manual step, because no translation facilities of this kind can be expected in the near future.

The resulting charts correspond to the structure of the system as described in Section 7.1 and Fig. 7. In this step, we also settled for the final architecture of the system, consisting of the controller (implemented in dedicated HW), several specialized hardware components, and the idle-speed module, to be implemented in SW. According to Fig. 2, the idle-speed module, which is a time-continuous component, was developed with the control systems tool Matrix$_x$^{TM} and implemented in SW. Once we had made the decision as to which modules should be implemented in software and which in hardware, the HW and the SW design processes for the components followed traditional routes. The desired level of codesign was achieved by employing the codesign manager, which controlled all dependencies between both design domains and all processes and subprocesses.

After component design, we generated synthesizable VHDL for the controller and C code for the idle-speed module. The remaining components were designed so that an easy mapping to SIDECON's part libraries become possible.

8 CONCLUSIONS AND FUTURE WORK

We have developed a complete HW/SW codesign environment. Its usefulness was shown with several example designs. By exercising the example of the idle-speed controller we found that a small team of engineers was able to carry out the design and to integrate the controller into an existing HW/SW model. The emphasis of the project was not on the improvement of design time. Instead we wanted to demonstrate that an integrated design for HW and SW is possible. The CODES environment enabled engineers from different disciplines (software, electronics, control systems) to work together and communicate effectively. It took the team about one week to develop the controller. With CODES, they validated the system model in a stand-alone fashion within a model of its environment. This, and the use of SIDECON, led to a smooth integration of all components. Parallel to the work of the team, we used the codesign manager to model the design process that is typical for the design of HW/SW systems.

We are not claiming that the team using our prototype environment was faster than it would have been using a conventional approach; this was not a primary goal of our work. This project clearly shows that true HW/SW codesign is possible even though special tools need to be developed to overcome existing problems. The CODES prototype is far from being a marketable product, but it is a first step, and it works.

With respect to future work, we will elaborate on the process model achieved with the codesign manager, so that it eventually will converge to a standard process model for HW/SW codesign. We will also provide tools to transform formal SDL specifications to Statemate^{TM} models. Another part of our work is the ongoing enhancement of the SIDECON knowledge base. In general, there is much to do to automate the interfaces between the components of CODES.

REFERENCES

[1] F. Bretschneider and H. Lagger, "Design-Flow Modeling and Knowledge Based Management," *Appl. Artificial Intell.,* 6, pp. 45–57, 1992.

[2] F. Bretschneider *et al.,* "Knowledge Based Design Flow Management," in *Proc. Int. Conference on Computer-Aided Design (ICCAD-90),* pp. 350–353, IEEE, 1990.

[3] M. Seifert, "Statemate^{TM}: A New Method for the Design of Complex Systems," in *Proc. Echtzeit '91 Conference on Real-Time Systems,* June 1991 (in German).

[4] CCITT Recommendation Z.100: Specification and Description Language (SDL), Geneva, 1992.

[5] F. Belina, Ed., "SDL Methodology Guidelines," Appendix I to CCITT Recommendation Z.100, Geneva, 1992.

[6] D. Harel, "On Visual Formalisms," *Comm. ACM,* 31(5), pp. 514–530, May 1986.

[7] C. A. Hoare, *Communicating Sequential Processes,* Prentice Hall, Englewood Cliffs, NJ, 1985.

[8] K. Buchenrieder and A. Pyttel, "System zur wissensbasierten Konfigurierung von Leiterplatten," in *CADS-Fachzeitschrift für Design-Automation in der Elektronik,* pp. 52–59, Sep. 1992.

[9] W. P. Birmingham, A. P. Gupta, and D. P. Siewiorek, "The MICON System for Computer Design," in *Proc. 26th ACM/IEEE Design Automation Conference,* pp. 135–140, IEEE, 1989.

[10] W. P. Birmingham, A. Kapoor, D. P. Siewiorek, and N. Vidovic, "The Design of an Integrated Environment for the Automated Synthesis of Small Computer Systems," in *Proc. Hawaii Int. Conference on System Sciences,* 1989.

[11] W. P. Birmingham and D. P. Siewiorek, "Capturing Designer Expertise," in *Proc. 26th ACM/IEEE Design Automation Conference,* pp. 610–613, IEEE, 1989.

[12] W. P. Birmingham and D. P. Siewiorek, *Automated Knowledge Acquisition for a Computer Hardware Synthesis System,* Academic Press, Boston, 1989.

[13] J. Hopcroft and J. Ullmann, *Introduction to Automata Theory, Languages and Computation,* Addison-Wesley, Reading, MA, 1979.

[14] E. Gurari, *An Introduction to the Theory of Computation,* Computer Science Press, Rockville, MD, 1989.

[15] W. Fletcher, *An Engineering Approach to Digital Design,* Prentice-Hall, Englewood Cliffs, NJ, 1980.

[16] F. Hofmann, "Betriebssysteme: Grundkonzepte und Modellvorstellungen," Leitfäden der Informatik, Teubner Verlag, Stuttgart, 1991.

PART   III

Case Studies

The chapters in Part III present three codesign case studies. Kalavade and Lee demonstrate the application of the Berkeley Ptolemy environment to the design of a telephone channel simulator. In Chapter 20, Taxen and Ostman discuss coverification issues in the context of a telephone exchange design problem. Herpel *et al.* transcend the conventional electronic design focus and present prototyping of embedded controllers in mechatronic systems, i.e., mechanical systems with embedded information processing elements.

CHAPTER 19

Hardware/Software Codesign Using Ptolemy
A Case Study

Asawaree Kalavade   Edward A. Lee
Department of Electrical Engineering
and Computer Sciences
University of California
Berkeley, California, USA

Abstract: Ptolemy is an environment for simulation and prototyping of heterogeneous systems. By supporting the coexistence and interaction of different models of computation, Ptolemy facilitates mixed-mode system simulation, specification, and design as well as generation of DSP assembly code from a block diagram description of the algorithm. These features render Ptolemy suitable for hardware/software codesign. This case study demonstrates the use of Ptolemy for hardware/software codesign. The test case is a telephone channel simulator that generates EIA-specified channel impairments for voice-band data modem testing, where the hardware comprises custom hardware coupled to programmable DSP chips, and the software is the code running on these programmable processors. The codesign methodology using Ptolemy is illustrated via the development and evaluation of a sequence of designs for this telephone channel simulator. These designs address multiprocessor communication, scheduling and code partitioning issues, as well as issues of system-level hardware/software partitioning of functionality.

1 INTRODUCTION

1.1 What Is Codesign?

In a traditional design strategy, the hardware and software partitioning decisions are fixed at an early stage in the development cycle and the hardware and software designs are developed separately from then onward. With advancements in technology, however,

397

it becomes possible to obtain special-purpose hardware components (ASICs) at a reasonable cost and development time. Some designs also call for some programmability in the end product. This suggests a more flexible design strategy, where the hardware and the software designs proceed in parallel, with feedback and interaction occurring between the two as the design progresses. The final hardware/software split can then be made after the evaluation of alternative structures with respect to performance, programmability, nonrecurring (development) costs, recurring (manufacturing) costs, reliability, maintenance, and evolution of design. This design philosophy, which helps reduce the time to market, is called hardware/software codesign.

1.2 Scope of Codesign Strategies

Codesign strategies can be applied to designs at different levels:

1. *Processor design:* An optimized application-specific processor can be achieved by jointly designing the hardware, the instruction set, and the program for the application.

2. *System-level design:* Codesign methodology is applicable at the system level, where an algorithm must be partitioned between custom hardware and software running on commodity programmable components. The hardware would typically include discrete components, ASICs, DSP cores, microprocessors, microsequencers, microcontrollers, or semicustom logic developed using FPGAs or logic synthesis tools. There are many possibilities for partitioning a given design between hardware and software components. Evaluation of these alternatives using system-level simulation of the hardware and software is a key aspect of codesign.

3. *Application-specific multiprocessor system design:* Design of an application-specific multiprocessor system is challenging because it involves selection of the appropriate number of processors, the interprocessor communication (IPC) strategy, and the design of the software for the application. Software synthesis requires partitioning and scheduling of the code over the processors, so scheduling techniques must be capable of adapting to changing hardware configurations. Thus, design of such an application-specific multiprocessor system is an iterative process—it involves trade-offs associated with the selection of the optimal hardware structure and software partitioning.

With the help of a case study, this work presents a study of a codesign methodology at the second and third levels. We do not address processor design, but instead assume that the programmable components are commodity parts.

1.3 Codesign for DSP Applications

In this study, we restrict the scope of codesign to digital signal processing (DSP) applications. DSP applications have the desirable feature that their implementation is simple, yet demands high performance and throughput. A variety of commercial DSP microprocessors can be used for most of the sophisticated signal processing required in these applications. Two frameworks for the development of software for such DSPs (particularly using the Motorola DSP 56000 and 96000 families) have been developed by the Berkeley DSP Design group; they are called Ptolemy [1,2] and Gabriel [3,4], and these can be extended for the simultaneous design and simulation of hardware and software, as is shown in this chapter.

2 A CASE STUDY

This section describes the telephone channel simulator that has been selected for this case study, and justifies its selection as a suitable case to demonstrate the use of Ptolemy for hardware/ software codesign [5].

2.1 The Telephone Channel Simulator

A telephone channel simulator models the response of a telephone channel by generating impairments such as linear distortion, frequency offset, phase jitter, nonlinear distortion, and noise [6] (as characterized by the EIA-496-A standard [7]). It is used by voice-band data modem designers to test the performance of modems. Satisfactory performance of modems under these impairment conditions provides robust assurance of modem performance on most telephone lines in the public-switched network of the United States. The algorithm for the telephone channel simulator is shown in Fig. 1.

The simulator could be designed using Motorola DSP56000s for most of the signal processing. The hardware model for such a system would typically require, besides DSPs, components such as codecs and glue logic.

2.2 Selection of Test Case

The telephone channel simulator, shown in Fig. 1, requires a modest amount of signal processing and represents a "real" system that would benefit from the advantages that codesign offers—low development and production costs and a reduced time to market, yet it meets required performance goals. Under technology available today, it may need multiple processors for the signal processing, hence it also brings up many of the issues involved with the design of hardware and software for multiprocessor DSP systems. It is hence critical to design the hardware, generate the software from the algorithm, and simulate the hardware system that executes this software—all within a unified environment. Commercial systems can independently either generate code for DSPs or permit the design and simulation of hardware—they do not provide much interaction between these two capabilities. Ideally, the software synthesis should be retargetable; it should support iteratively changing the hardware configuration and the algorithm. Ptolemy can support all of these requirements. For all these reasons, the telephone channel simulator has been selected as the test case for the hardware/software codesign study under Ptolemy.

The organization of the rest of the paper is as follows: Section 3 briefly describes the Ptolemy simulation environment and its modeling and synthesis capabilities. The

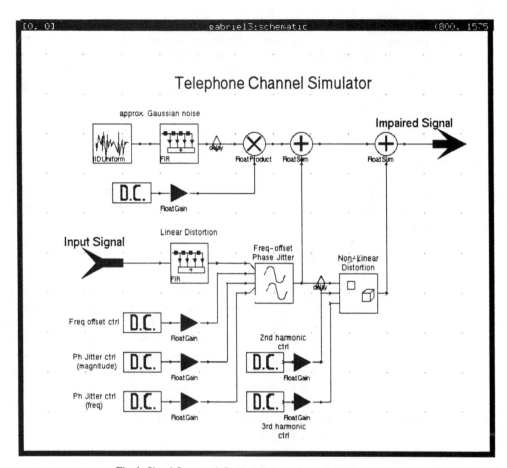

Fig. 1: Signal flow graph for the telephone channel simulator

codesign methodology is explained (with respect to a case study) in some detail in Section 4. Finally, conclusions are drawn in Section 5.

3 THE PTOLEMY SIMULATION ENVIRONMENT

Ptolemy is an environment for simulation and prototyping of heterogeneous systems. It uses object-oriented software technology to model each subsystem in a natural and efficient manner, and has mechanisms to integrate these subsystems into a whole.

3.1 Internal Structure of Ptolemy

Figure 2 shows the structural components of Ptolemy. The basic unit of modularity in Ptolemy is the *block*. *Portholes* provide the standard interface through which blocks communicate. A block contains a module of code [the "go( )" method] that is invoked at run time, typically examining data present at its input portholes and generating data

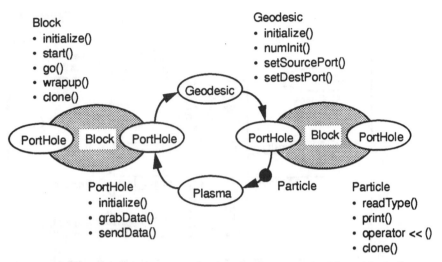

Fig. 2: Block objects in Ptolemy send and receive data encapsulated in particles to the outside world through portholes; buffering and transport is handled by the Geodesic and garbage collection by the Plasma

at its output portholes. The invocation of "go" methods is directed by a *scheduler* that determines the operational semantics of a network of blocks. Blocks communicate using streams called *particles,* which form the base type for all messages passed. The *Geodesic* class establishes the connection between portholes. The *Plasma* class manages the reclamation of the used particles.

The lowest level (atomic) objects in Ptolemy are of the type *star,* derived from a block. A *galaxy,* also derived from a block, contains other blocks internally. A galaxy may contain internally both galaxies and stars. A *target,* also derived from a block, controls the execution of an application. In a simulation-oriented application, it will typically invoke a scheduler to manage the order in which star methods are invoked. For a synthesis-oriented application it can synthesize assembly code for a programmable DSP, invoke the assembler, etc. A *universe,* which contains a complete Ptolemy application, is a type of galaxy.

3.2 Heterogeneous Simulation Using Ptolemy

Ptolemy accomplishes the goal of multiparadigm simulation by supporting a plethora of different design styles called *domains.* A domain realizes a computational model appropriate for a particular type of subsystem. A domain in Ptolemy consists of a set of blocks, targets, and associated schedulers that conform to a common computational model—the operational semantics govern how blocks interact with one another. The domain and the mechanism of coexistence of domains are the primary features that distinguish Ptolemy from otherwise comparable systems such as Comdisco's SPW and Bones and Mentor Graphic's DSPstation. Some of the domains that are currently supported include Synchronous Data Flow (SDF) [8], Dynamic Dataflow (DDF), Discrete Event (DE), and the

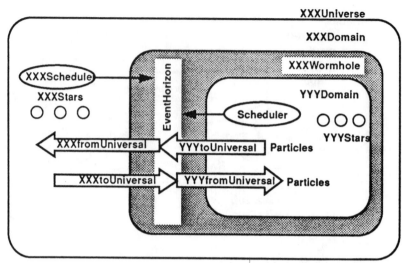

Fig. 3: The universal EventHorizon provides an interface between the external and internal domains

Digital Hardware Modeling Environment (Thor [9]).The SDF and Thor domains that are used in the application discussed in this chapter are now described in further detail.

SYNCHRONOUS DATA FLOW (SDF) DOMAIN.   SDF [8] is a data-driven, statically scheduled domain. *Data-driven* means that the availability of particles on the inputs of a star enables it. Stars with no inputs *(sources)* are always enabled. *Statically scheduled* means that the firing order of the stars is determined only once during the start-up phase and this schedule is periodic. The SDF domain supports simulation of algorithms, and also allows functional modeling of components such as filters and signal generators.

THOR DOMAIN.   The Thor domain implements the Thor simulator, which is a functional simulator for the simulation of digital hardware [9]. It supports the simulation of circuits with abstraction levels from the gate level to the behavioral level. Thor hence provides Ptolemy with the ability to simulate digital components ranging in complexity from simple logic gates to programmable DSP chips. The Thor domain could be replaced by a VHDL domain that could support hardware simulation and synthesis.

The domain class by itself gives Ptolemy the ability to model different types of systems in a natural and efficient manner. It also possible to mix these descriptions at the system level to develop a heterogeneous system. Toward this end, Ptolemy allows different domains to coexist at different levels of the hierarchy. Within a domain, it is possible to have blocks containing foreign domains. The manner in which these domains coexists is now described.

Figure 3 shows the top view of a universe associated with a certain domain XXX, associated with which are the XXXStars and the XXXScheduler. A foreign subsystem is added to this, which belongs to domain YYY and has its own set of YYYStars and a YYYScheduler. This foreign subsystem is called an XXXWormhole. A *wormhole* is essentially a block, which appears externally to be a star (it obeys the operational semantics of the external domain and appears to be atomic to the external domain), but which internally consists of an entire foreign universe (scheduler and stars). A wormhole can be introduced into the XXXDomain without any need for the XXXScheduler to know of the existence of the YYYDomain. The key to this interoperability is the interface between the internal structure of a wormhole and its external environment. This interface is called the *EventHorizon.* By providing a "universal" EventHorizon, each domain needs to take care of just the conversion to and from itself to the universal type. More details on the operation of EventHorizons can be found in [1,2].

3.3 Hardware Modeling Under Ptolemy

Ptolemy supports the modeling and simulation of a variety of hardware components using multiple domains. The Thor domain is used to model digital components—ranging in complexity from simple logic gates to DSP chips [3].

A Thor model for the Motorola DSP56000 has been developed under Ptolemy. The "start()" method of the DSP Star under Thor simply establishes a socket connection with *Sim56000,* Motorola's stand-alone simulator for the DSP56000. *Sim56000* is different from most other processor simulators. It is a complete "behavioral simulation" of the processor, not just an "instruction set simulator" or a "bus functional model." This means that it accurately models the behavior of each of the processor's signal pins, while executing the code. Instruction set simulators do not support this feature of modeling the pin-level behavior. Bus functional models merely emulate a given pattern of the bus activity; they do not execute any code.

During its "go()" method, this star translates the logic values present at the processor's pins into values meaningful to the simulator, transfers them to *Sim56000,* and commands the simulator to advance the simulation by one step. It waits for the simulator to transmit the new logic values back to the processor pins and continues with the rest of the simulation. The simulation can be halted at any time by interrupting the simulator window and intermediate register contents can be examined.

Figure 4 illustrates this behavior. The figure represents the simulation of a single DSP system within Ptolemy. The hardware design consisting of a single processor is developed using the Thor and SDF domains of Ptolemy (lower left). The *Sim56000* that is invoked when the system is run can be seen on the lower right. The window in the top left corner shows a Thor logic analyzer monitoring the output on the serial port of the DSP. The Ptolemy code for the DSP block is shown at the top right corner.

Besides processors and digital logic, it is also necessary to model analog components such as A/D and D/A converters and filters that operate in conjunction with this digital hardware. These analog components can most conveniently be represented by their "functional models" using the SDF domain. It can be observed that abstract functional modeling of components such as filters is sufficient—detailed behavioral modeling is not needed—because in the final product it is very likely that an off-the-shelf component will be used. So, a filter can be easily modeled by an abstract model in the SDF domain, which merely models the response of the filter in terms of the transfer function and is not concerned with the physical implementation of the filter.

The wormhole mechanism discussed in Section 3.2 is used to mix the data-driven, statically scheduled SDF models of analog components with event-driven, logic-valued Thor models of digital components within a single simulation. This concept is used,

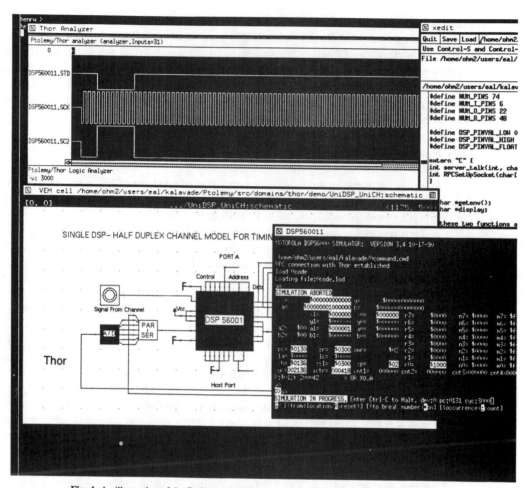

Fig. 4: An illustration of the Ptolemy simulation environment. A hardware design (bottom left) containing a programmable DSP can be developed using the Thor and SDF domains. When the DSP Star (c++ code can be seen in upper right window) is run, it invokes the Motorola DSP56000 Simulator (bottom right), which executes the code. Timing verification is possible using the Thor Logic Analyzer (top left)

for instance, for the modeling of an A/D converter within a Thor domain application containing DSPs and glue logic. Thus, analog and digital hardware modeling at different levels of abstraction is possible using Ptolemy.

3.4 Software Synthesis Under Ptolemy

Ptolemy is capable of synthesizing reasonably optimized assembly code for programmable DSPs using techniques developed in the Gabriel system [4,10]. Descriptions of the hardware (the number of processors, their connectivity, the IPC strategy, and the IPC delays) and the algorithm block diagram are inputs to the code generator. The code generator contains a retargetable scheduler [11] and a mechanism for DSP assembly code synthesis for multiple processors. The scheduler performs scheduling and routing simultaneously to account for irregular interprocessor interconnections and schedules all computations and communications to eliminate shared resource contention. The code generator thus partitions the program to match the available hardware, and schedules it after considering the physical hardware and the IPC and synchronization overhead. This is also retargetable—the hardware description may be changed, and code will be generated automatically for this new configuration, taking into account the changed number of processors or their connectivity.

More highly optimized code generation than that accomplished by Ptolemy has been shown to be viable [10].

4 CODESIGN METHODOLOGY

A general approach to codesign is first discussed with reference to Fig. 5. Based on this codesign methodology, the design of the telephone channel simulator is next explained in Sections 4.1 and 4.2.

The first step in the general design approach (step 1 in Fig. 5) is to obtain the specifications for the application. This is followed by a high-level algorithmic and functional

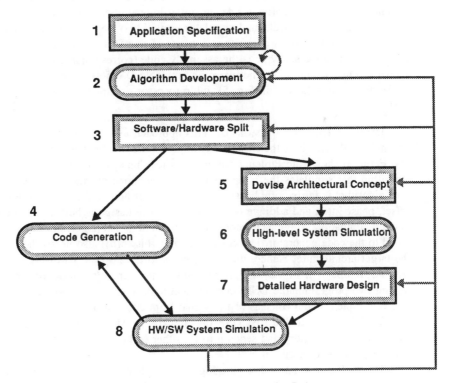

Fig. 5: Codesign methodology using Ptolemy

simulation (step 2 in Fig. 5) using the SDF domain. The functional block diagram (such as that shown in Fig. 1) is simulated to verify algorithmic correctness. A hardware/software split (step 3 in Fig. 5) is then carried out and parts of the algorithm are assigned to hardware and others to software. A hardware simulation (steps 5, 6, and 7 in Fig. 5) for the configuration is developed, and using this hardware configuration information, software is synthesized (step 4 in Fig. 5). The combined hardware/software system is then simulated (step 8 in Fig. 5) and verified for functional and timing correctness.

The process may be repeated and various designs for the system can be iteratively developed. The Ptolemy framework allows simultaneous software and hardware development, as well as simulation and evaluation (on the basis of timing constraints and functional correctness) of alternative candidate design configurations.

The following subsections focus on applications of this codesign approach to *the design of a full-duplex telephone channel simulator.* In the process, issues and trade-offs associated with the design of multiprocessor systems and system-level partitioning of functionality are studied. The final design choice is made after evaluating the trade-offs associated with each design option.

4.1 Multiprocessor Options

The specifications of the algorithm (steps 1 and 2 of Fig. 5) are first obtained. As a first cut, the algorithm is partitioned (step 3 of Fig. 5) such that the DSPs execute the entire algorithm in software. As an initial logical choice, we design the full-duplex (bidirectional) telephone channel simulator around two DSPs, each impairing the signal in either direction. The hardware thus consists of two DSPs as well as codecs and other glue logic, while the software is the assembly code (corresponding to the block diagram shown in Fig. 1) running on the two programmable DSP56000s. As a part of the design of the architecture (step 5 in Fig. 5), interprocessor communication issues are explored next.

DESIGN 1 (SHARED MEMORY).   This approach uses two DSPs for the full-duplex channel simulator, where the DSPs are configured to communicate through a shared memory. Figure 6 shows the Ptolemy components for this system. The top level only of the algorithm that simulates the impairments of a telephone channel is shown in Fig. 6(a). This algorithm is fairly complicated, including linear and nonlinear distortion, frequency offset, phase jitter, and additive Gaussian noise. The design is built in a code generation domain compatible to the SDF model of computation. The algorithm description is provided to the code generator. The code generator [Fig. 6(b)] also needs the description of the target architecture. Hence, the next step is to develop the hardware for the system (steps 5, 6, and 7 of Fig. 5). Figure 6(c) shows the hardware model of the system containing two programmable DSPs communicating through a dual-ported shared memory. The full-duplex model consists of the signal from one end of the channel being filtered, quantized, and sent to the first DSP that impairs it. The second DSP reads these data from the shared memory and sends it to the other end of the channel. Similar processing is done in the reverse direction.

The DSP, clock, and other glue logic are implemented in Thor, the parent domain. The A/D and D/A comprising the codec are modeled functionally as SDF blocks nested

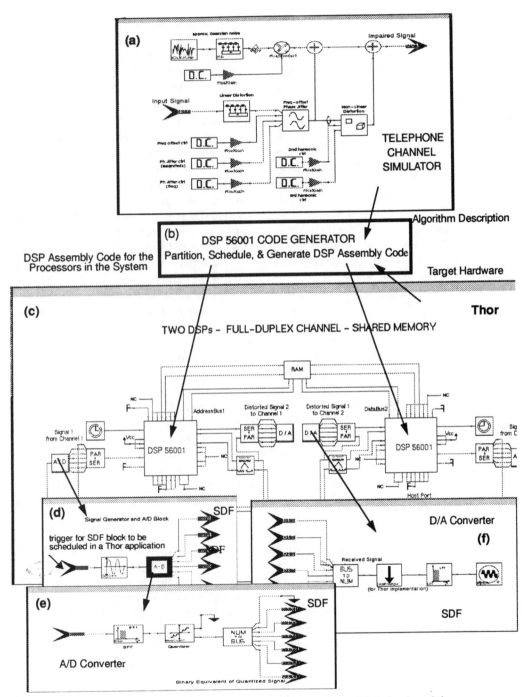

Fig. 6: (Design 1) Ptolemy configuration: hardware model for the full-duplex channel simulator using two DSPs and a shared memory, algorithm description, and the Code Generator

as Thor wormholes. Such functional modeling is sufficient because an off-the-shelf codec will be used in the final design. The A/D abstracted as a transmit filter followed by a quantizer is shown in Fig. 6(e). Figure 6(f) shows the functional model of the D/A converter, which is essentially a low-pass filter. The filter coefficients are designed such that its response matches that of the receive filter in the D/A. The Stars NumToBus and BusToNum, as shown in Figs. 6(e) and (f), provide a conversion between the integers sent/received by the SDF domain and the logic-valued bits recognized by the Thor domain.

The algorithm description along with the hardware description is used by the code generator (step 4 of Fig. 5) to partition and schedule the blocks and generate assembly code for the processors in the system. The output of the code generator is assembly code corresponding to the algorithm that runs on the two processors. This hardware system is then simulated (step 8 of Fig. 5) with the two processors running the code generated by the code generator. As discussed in Section 3.3, running the system invokes the Motorola simulator for each DSP and the simulator runs this synthesized code.

Thus we can see the close interaction between the algorithm description and simulation, code generation, and hardware development and simulation. The hardware itself is modeled at different levels of abstraction using the various domains of Ptolemy.

The development of such mixed-domain applications calls for consideration to datatype compatibility and scheduling issues between domains. For instance, the SDF domain deals with integer and floating point particles, whereas the Thor domain can interpret only 0, 1, Z (float), and U (undefined) data types. So, any data passed between SDF and Thor need to be converted to a binary representation such as that done by the SDF NumToBus block. Also, SDF is a data-driven scheduler, which means that an SDF block gets triggered for execution only when the right number of particles is available on all of its inputs. An SDF "source" star, however, is always ready for execution when in an SDF universe. Thor, on the other hand, is event driven, which means that the arrival of any particle on any input triggers a new event. When an SDF source block is nested as a ThorWormhole, hence, it needs to be externally triggered [as can be seen by the input provided to the signal generator block in Fig. 6(d)]. These input data are used solely for the purpose of triggering the wormhole for execution—the data themselves are discarded. This system can be evaluated and verified by simulation. This multiprocessor implementation is but one option to the design of the telephone channel simulator.

DESIGN 2 (SERIAL PORT).   An alternative design shown in Fig. 7 is developed by iterating through steps 4 through 8 in Fig. 5, where the DSPs now communicate using their serial port instead of the shared memory. As seen in the figure, the signal from one end of the channel is received by the first DSP (DSP1), which impairs it and sends it over the serial port to the second DSP (DSP2), which sends it out to the other end of the channel. Meanwhile, a similar impairment is carried out on the reverse direction for the signal transmitted by DSP2 and received by DSP1. The other blocks such as the A/D and D/A are identical to those developed in Design 1 [shown in Figs. 6(e) and (f)].

The changed hardware configuration (i.e., the modified IPC delay) is provided to the code generator and the code generator partitions and schedules the code again (step 4 in Fig. 5). This system can be simulated and its functional correctness can be verified.

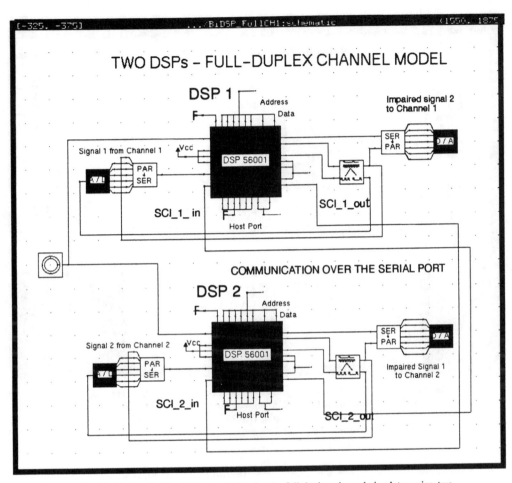

Fig. 7: (Design 2) The hardware design for the full-duplex channel simulator using two DSPs and the serial port for communication

These designs illustrate the ease with which various IPC strategies (and the subsequent code partitioning) can be handled within Ptolemy. These two multiprocessor systems (Design 1 and Design 2) are evaluated with respect to performance, IPC overhead, and system cost. These evaluations are discussed further in Section 4.3.

4.2 System-Level Partitioning Options

To reduce the cost of the design, an alternative hardware design possibility, using a single DSP, is now explored. Preliminary timing analysis shows that one DSP cannot handle the computational load of the bidirectional impairments for the full-duplex channel simulator. So, retracing to the hardware/software split (step 3 in Fig. 5), the algorithm partitioning is redone. The computationally intensive blocks such as linear distortion and

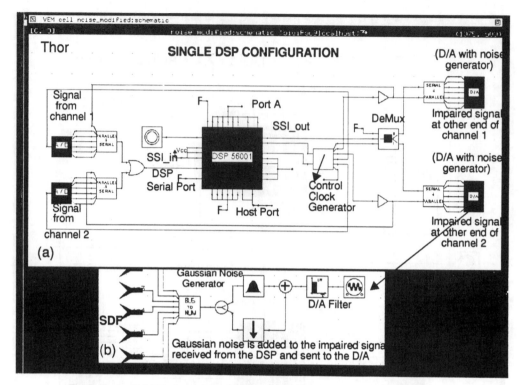

Fig. 8: (Design 3) (a) Hardware design for the full-duplex channel simulator using a single DSP. The noise generator is implemented in hardware. (b) For simulation, the noise generator is implemented as an SDF block generating Gaussian noise. This noise is superimposed on the impaired signal received from the DSP and sent to the D/A.

noise generation are possible candidates for migration from DSP software to custom hardware. Designs based on such alternative partitioning are then developed (steps 5, 6, and 7 in Fig. 5) within the same framework.

DESIGN 3 (HARDWARE NOISE GENERATION). As one alternative, the Gaussian noise generator is shifted to hardware and is implemented by using special-purpose diodes. Generating Gaussian noise is expensive in software, but very inexpensive in analog hardware. This functional migration provides sufficient computation cycles for a single DSP to impair the signal in both directions.

Figure 8 shows such a single-processor model. The signals from two ends of the channel are multiplexed and sent to the DSP, which runs the impairment code. The impaired signals from the DSP are then routed to the corresponding ends of the channel. The Gaussian noise generator is implemented in hardware using Gaussian noise-generating diodes. For the purpose of simulation, however, it is sufficient to model the Gaussian noise generator as an SDF block [Fig. 8(b)]. The output Gaussian noise from this block superimposes the impaired signal, and this "noisy" signal is then passed to the D/A.

Thus, shifting the noise generation to hardware makes it possible to use a single processor for the full-duplex channel simulator. Note that a functional model of the noise generator is sufficient to demonstrate the functionality and verify the specifications—a "physical" model of the diodes is not necessary. The simulation of this design shows that it meets the timing requirements and still performs the functions of the full-duplex channel simulator.

DESIGN 4 (LINEAR DISTORTION VARIANT).   Shifting much of the linear distortion block to hardware provides another design option (not shown). Much of the linear distortion imposed by a telephone channel is due to switched-capacitor filters in codecs that provide the interface to the digital network. By using similar codecs, we can avoid having to replicate this distortion in software. A much lower order filter is implemented in software to emulate other sources of distortion. The consequent reduction in the filter order reduces the computation load of the DSP. This makes it possible to develop yet another single-processor design where the Gaussian noise block is added back to software and linear distortion is moved to hardware.

The hardware model for this system is similar to Fig. 8 with the noise generator being moved to software. The filter used in the A/D is different—it models the linear distortion in the channel.

The new algorithm is provided to the code generator (4) to develop code for these configurations and the resultant systems may be simulated (8) verified for timing and functional correctness. By merely changing the "target architecture" description, software can be automatically generated for these different system configurations.

4.3 Observations

Earlier sections illustrate that alternative multiprocessor-system designs and system-level partitions can be developed with reasonable ease using Ptolemy. Issues of hardware design, code partitioning, and scheduling can be analyzed. Alternative IPC schemes can be evaluated for cost/performance trade-offs.

The serial communication design (Design 2) has the advantage that it overcomes the need for the expensive dual-ported memory needed by the shared memory design (Design 1); however, it suffers from the drawback that it is not flexible in terms of code expansion. The relatively slow speed of the serial communication between the DSPs places an upper bound on the performance of the serial communication design. The shared memory design is relatively more flexible and can support higher inter-DSP communication throughput, though at an increased hardware cost. Also, communication through the shared memory requires semaphore synchronization, which imposes an additional burden on the software. Thus, the final design choice may be made on the basis of demands of the user.

System-level design issues regarding the migration of functionality between hardware and software have also been studied. Different components of the algorithm can be implemented either in hardware or software. The trade-offs involved in the use of special-purpose hardware against programmable processors with respect to board space, component cost, and programmability can be compared and contrasted. The single-DSP designs using either the noise-generator diodes (Design 3) or the codec filters (Design 4) are desirable for their low component cost as one processor and its associated hardware is eliminated. The price paid is loss of flexibility in changing these hardware impairments.

The four cases described here indicate the codesign methodology employed under Ptolemy for application-specific system design. Once the design space is explored, the final choice can be made by the user as per the requirements and resources available.

5 CONCLUSIONS

A case study illustrating the use of Ptolemy for codesign has been presented. Ptolemy is seen to be a flexible environment for the development and simulation of functional and behavioral models of hardware and generation of assembly code for the system. DSP-based hardware designs can be developed and provided to the retargetable code generator, which produces assembly code corresponding to the block diagram of the algorithm. Alternative multiprocessor hardware configurations using different IPC schemes as well as different system-level designs with alternative hardware/software partitions can be iteratively developed, simulated, verified, and evaluated.

These designs can be compared within a unified design environment. All options are available at a given time to the user. Without the need to build a hardware prototype, the evaluation of the combined software/hardware system is possible. As the software and hardware developments proceed with close interaction, the software is ready at design time. This reduces the time to market.

The key property in Ptolemy that supports this style of design is heterogeneity. Software synthesis, hardware modeling, and algorithm simulation are embodied in a single design environment. Different components of a design can be specified using the design style best suited to them, and yet these components can be mixed.

Work is in progress toward extending this hardware/software design framework for embedded system design, where the hardware consists of DSPs with custom logic, or DSP cores, and the software is the program running on these programmable processors. A netlist description of the hardware configuration can be fed to logic synthesis tools to develop semicustom ASICs, or used with DSP core designs.

ACKNOWLEDGMENTS

This work has been sponsored by the Semiconductor Research Corporation (contract 92-DC-008) through its Berkeley Center of Excellence in CAD/IC, and Cygnet, a division of Everex.

REFERENCES

[1] "The Almagest: Manual for Ptolemy Version 0.4," Department of EECS, University of California, Berkeley, Jan. 1993.

[2] J. Buck, S. Ha, E. A. Lee, and D. G. Messerschmitt, "Ptolemy: A Framework for Simulating and Prototyping Heterogeneous Systems," *Int. J. Computer Simulation,* special issue on "Simulation Software Development," 4, pp. 155–182, April 1994.

[3] J. Bier, "FRIGG: A Simulation Environment for Multiple-Processor DSP System Development," Master's Report, Department of EECS, University of California, Berkeley, 1989.

[4] J. Bier, E. Goei, W. Ho, P. Laplsey, M. O'Reilly, G. Sih, and E. A. Lee, "Gabriel: A Design Environment for DSP," *IEEE Micro Magazine,* 10(5), pp. 28–45, Oct. 1990.

[5] A. Kalavade, "Hardware/Software Codesign using Ptolemy: A Case Study," Master's Report, Department of EECS, University of California, Berkeley, Dec. 1991.

[6] E. A. Lee and D. G. Messerschmitt, *Digital Communications,* pp. 128–135, Kluwer Academic Publishers, Boston.

[7] "Interface Between Data Circuit-Terminating Equipment (DCE) and the Public Switched Telephone Network (PSTN)," Electronic Industries Association Proposed Standard EIA-496-A, prepared by EIA Technical Subcommittee TR-30.3, 1988.

[8] E. A. Lee and D. G. Messerschmitt, "Synchronous Data Flow," *IEEE Proc.,* Sept. 1987.

[9] "Thor Tutorial," VLSI/CAD Group, Stanford University, 1986.

[10] D. B. Powell, E. A. Lee, and W. C. Newman, "Direct Synthesis of Optimized Assembly Code from Signal Flow Block Diagrams," *Proc. ICASSP,* '92, San Francisco, CA, March 1992, vol. 5, pp. 553–556, IEEE, New York.

[11] G. C. Sih, "Multiprocessor Scheduling to Account for Interprocessor Communication," PhD Thesis, Electronic Research Laboratory, University of California, Berkeley, Apr. 1991.

CHAPTER 20

Hardware/Software Coverification of a Telephone Exchange
A Case Study

Fredrik Östman   Lars Taxén
ELLEMTEL Telecommunication Systems Laboratories
Älusjö, Sweden

Abstract: Large hardware/software systems can be modeled in C and VHDL and functionally completely verified early in the design process. This means that errors can be detected early and that continuous modeling and coverification can be done during the entire design process. The models will act as a contract between software and hardware design departments, and thus contribute to the quality of the design.

1 INTRODUCTION

This chapter presents experiences from the functional verification of a large hardware/software system, modeled at high abstraction levels. The modeling and simulation of a telephone exchange jointly in C and VHDL using proper interface modules is described. Some implications of cross-discipline development and design domain interaction on the design process are also discussed.

We have adopted here a rather naïve definition of hardware and software: By hardware we mean something designed at a telecommunications hardware department or a team using hardware tools and methods, and by software we mean something designed at a telecommunications software department or a team using software tools and methods. The hardware is thus not the computer on which the software is run, but some functionality intended to be implemented to the largest part as ASICs, rather than by execution on a computer. Hardware in this sense, however, might contain embedded processors, possibly with software that can be downloaded. With these definitions, a telephone exchange is an example of a large hardware/software system.

414

Using VHDL, we can model even quite large hardware systems at a high level of abstraction, much in the same way as software systems. If the hardware is implemented as ASICs, implementation is as straightforward as implementation of real-time software for a microprocessor. In a telecommunications project, hardware and software teams may produce roughly the same amount of source and implementation code each to describe their part of the total function of the system and also have the same need for code management and maintenance support. We therefore foresee a common environment for the functional design of real-time microcircuit systems, without prejudice as to what kind of circuits will eventually be used for implementation. Of course, we have not reached that state yet, and this work was intended to overcome some of the deficiencies with today's methodologies.

A way of overcoming the present gap between hardware and software development is to join them in a common simulation. High-level hardware/software cosimulation introduces new possibilities for top-down system design. Mixed systems can be verified early in the design process, immediately after hardware and software parts have been identified. It is well known that errors introduced early are very expensive to correct at later stages. Furthermore, rather than splitting the design in separate hardware/software paths, and verifying their joint functionality after design completion, cosimulation makes it possible to keep track of hardware/software designs continuously as the design proceeds. The coverified models at one abstraction level can be used as specifications of hardware/software interaction for later design stages.

Using an extended VHDL simulator, we have cosimulated hardware models with software models. This case study of the functional verification of a telephone exchange was performed at ELLEMTEL Telecom Systems Labs in cooperation with the Swedish Institute of Microelectronics in the autumn of 1991. The project was sponsored by CAD-LAB of Ericsson Telecom.

2 THE TELECOM NETWORK CONTEXT

To place the telephone exchange verification into its proper context, we briefly describe the telecom network and its evolution. We also briefly touch on the technology impact in this area.

2.1 The Network Impact

Today, the telecom services are implemented in connected but separate networks such as PSTN for ordinary speech, ISDN for speech, data, text and images, GSM for mobile telephony, and LAN for high-speed data communication. It is expensive to operate and maintain those networks, and therefore a long-term vision has been to use an integrated, single network in which all the telecom services are realized, as shown in Fig. 1. It was hoped that ISDN would become that network, but the introduction of ISDN has been slower than expected. One impeding factor is the enormous costs associated with the replacement of existing equipment. The new networks will have to reuse existing equipment.

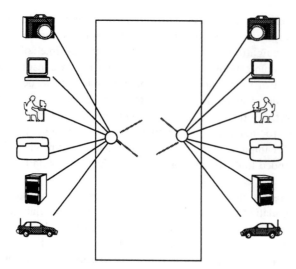

Fig. 1: An integrated network for transmission of speech, data, text, and images

The current trend in telecommunications development is thus a separation of the network into a logical service provider network and a carrier network realizing the transmission. The task of the exchange is becoming more complex and intricate in this scenery. The switching point characteristics, such as capacity, bandwidth, and type of connections, will vary widely. In all of these cases, the exchange will be realized as a combination of software executing on processors and exchange access hardware modules—often new software on old hardware. With the typically high requirements on the dependability of telecommunications equipment, verification of the hardware/software functionality becomes a most important task.

2.2 The Impact of Technology

The implementation of the desired functionality will greatly affect the properties of the system. Moreover, the rate of change in a certain technology may have a major influence on the system design. As an example, Fig. 2 shows a forecast of how implementation of the layers in the OSI protocol will be done. Note that even the highest layer, which is the applications layer, may be implemented in hardware. In a situation like this, it is obviously difficult to establish a fixed implementation strategy. The design process and the modeling must be done in such a way that it is possible to exchange swiftly ASICs for microprocessors and still secure and reuse the verified functionality. Again, a very important building block in such a strategy will be the possibility to coverify the interaction between software and hardware.

3 A NEW DESIGN PROCESS

The traditional way of designing large hardware/software systems has been to specify each part early and assign the implementation of the software and hardware to design teams organized in separate disciplines (Fig. 3). This strategy has several disadvantages:

OSI layer

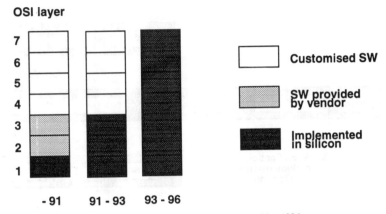

Fig. 2: ISDN semiconductor trends, 1991–1996

- The overall verification is not done until the integration phase, which means that the cost of detecting hardware/software interaction errors is very high.
- The system specification is not formalized in an executable model, which leads to ambiguities and interpretation problems, especially since the designs are usually carried out in separate disciplines with different cultures.
- The verification of the software during the implementation is dependent on a testbench representing the hardware. The same goes for the hardware. These testbenches, which may be regarded as proper models of colleagues' designs, are usually written in the same language as the design itself. For example, if the software is written in C++, there is usually a response model of the interacting hardware written in C++ as well. On the hardware side, the software driver might be modeled in terms of VHDL stimuli. This means that we have double models of the design objects. Effort is spent on duplication, misunderstandings are not discovered, and errors are easily introduced.

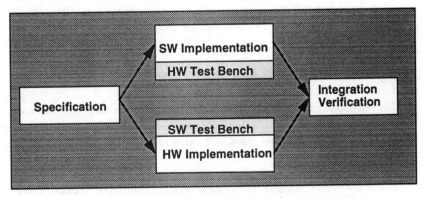

Fig. 3: Traditional hardware/software design process

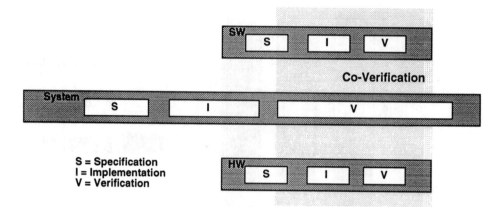

Fig. 4: New hardware/software codesign process

- In the light of the technology scene outlined earlier, it is obvious that a redesign with a different partitioning will have to be started very early in the process, and thus will take too long.

A design process that will better meet the new requirements might look like that outlined in Fig. 4. After implementation-independent system design has happened, a partitioning into software and hardware is done according to trade-off considerations regarding performance, cost, and so on. The software and hardware is then designed and verified against each other at suitable abstraction levels, including the highest one. We then have a re-entrant sequence of specification, implementation, and verification at each abstraction level, which hopefully will greatly reduce the need for a system integration phase at the end of the design process.

In the described scenario, the hardware and software models will test bench each other. As such, they will also act as a contract between the software and hardware design departments. This is very important in large organizations where designs are usually carried out at separate places in the organization and at different locations around the world. Moreover, the use of cross-discipline modeling will hopefully improve understanding and cooperation between the members of the separate disciplines. Obviously, in such a design process, hardware/software coverification plays an important role.

4 COVERIFICATION OF A TELEPHONE EXCHANGE

The telephone exchange was modeled at an abstraction level showing only the functional, or traffic, characteristics of a family of modern synchronous transfer mode exchanges. The model is configurable and modular in size and speed to accommodate several members of the family.

In the exchange, control software is connected to control channels via several processor stations (PSs). The telephone trunks are connected to data channels via exchange terminals (ETs) (see Fig. 5).

Fig. 5: Overall structure of the modeled system (principal view)

4.1 Multiple-Model Structure

To model this mixed system, four different models were used. The model structure, its mapping onto the modeled system, and the language domains are shown in Fig. 6.

A software model was written in C. This model is the actual control software, and it does not have to be modified for verification purposes. The exchange hardware and a simple telecommunications testbench were modeled in VHDL. Using the testbench, different traffic patterns can be sent through the exchange to investigate its behavior.

The hardware/software interface is a model of the hardware/software interaction schemes implemented in a processing system. It has one part written in C and one part written in VHDL, and it is intimately coupled to the VHDL simulator. To write this interface, access to simulator internals was necessary. The supplier of the simulator, the Swedish Institute of Microelectronics, aided us in this task, and used this experience to design generic tools, which are now integrated into their VHDL simulator, MINT [1].

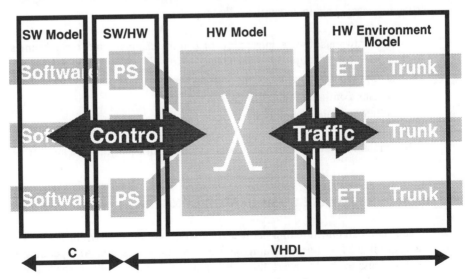

Fig. 6: Model structure and mapping

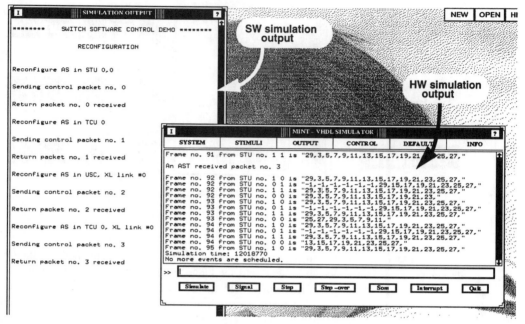

Fig. 7: Example of cosimulation output

4.2 Verification Results

The screen dump in Fig. 7 shows the various actions from the control software in one window, and the corresponding response from the hardware in another window.

The results were a complete functional verification of the exchange at a high abstraction level. This included the following:

- Hardware/software interaction of control channels and metachannels (channels used for start-up of the exchange)
- Connection handling of the traffic channels
- Link configuration
- Internal queues and buffers.

The simulation system is then used as a testbench for both software and hardware design.

5 HARDWARE/SOFTWARE COSIMULATOR CONCERNS

The general architecture of a hardware/software system is shown in Fig. 8. The hardware is controlled by software running on a number of processors. An operating system provides access to the hardware through commands, which result in various actions on the processor bus.

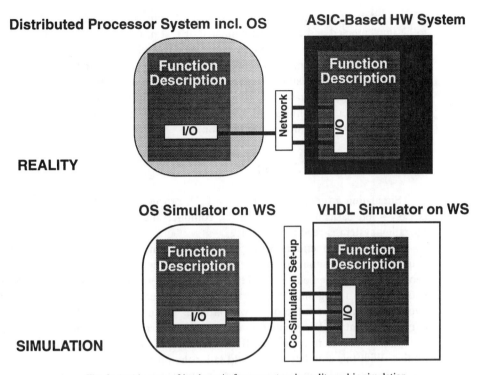

Fig. 8: Architecture of hardware/software system in reality and in simulation

Also shown in the figure is the cosimulation system. What is of interest is the core of each system, describing the function. In the models, we want to use as high an abstraction level as possible so as not to include too much implementation information. This means that we do not want to model the processor at the instruction set or bit level, just as we do not want to model the ASICs at the gate level. Either scheme would make the simulations prohibitively slow. At this level we assume that the hardware and the software are to be implemented correctly with proper verification toward specifications, and those specifications will be the coverified models.

By compiling the source code to run on the workstation used for simulation rather than emulate the instruction fetch scheme, a simulation speed-up of at least two orders of magnitude is achieved [2,3].

5.1 Simulation Synchronization

The simulation environments for hardware and software cannot be easily joined to form a cosimulator; something has to be added to make them go together. Both simulators will have a simulation core that thinks it is in charge. Either the simulations must be externally synchronized, or one of them must be the master and make procedure calls to the other.

We have found that with today's technology, there is little use in trying to synchronize a hardware and a software simulator, because software has little notion of time and a several orders of magnitude bigger time scale. For timing-critical parts, the software has to be implemented and run on an emulated or real processor. Although in the high-level hardware models timing is based on causality, due to the fact that a full-grown hardware implementation environment is used, timing could be added without too much trouble.

The remaining decision is which simulator should be in charge. Our choice to let the software be in control was based on the specific conditions of our project, rather than on a notion of either discipline's superiority or inferiority. It did mean we had to get control in some way over the hardware simulation.

5.2 VHDL Simulator Access

Simulating a functional description for a processor, i.e., a program, on a computer is easy—you basically just change the compiler and run. Access to the workstation's operating system is readily available.

Simulating a functional description for one or more ASICs is more difficult because you need a special simulator. These simulators are not intended to be part of a heterogeneous design environment; instead they are intended for an all-hardware one. Most simulators do have a programming interface, but it is intended for the introduction of models into the simulation, not the other way around. The programming language interfaces of our commercial VHDL simulators did not allow us to take control in a straightforward way, and we therefore used the MINT simulator of the Swedish Institute of Microelectronics. With this simulator, we could tailor the programming language interface to our needs. The cosimulation was performed, in practice, by linking the software to the VHDL simulator and using the interface to access and control the hardware from the software [1,3].

Linking the hardware and software into a common workstation process has serious limitations, and an obvious improvement would be to let the hardware and software tools run in their own processes, communicating rather than interfering with each other.

6 WHY IS HARDWARE NOT SOFTWARE?

Inspection of high-level VHDL code shows that it looks like software. It would be easy to translate the model into C and get away from all cosimulation problems, but we do not want to do this. We need to keep the ASIC programs in VHDL to be able to track the implementation into netlists and finally silicon. On the other hand, it ought to be as easy to interface high-level VHDL as it is Pascal or Ada—but it's not.

Today's ASIC designers are not designing manufacturable hard equipment, but human artifacts, computer files that are sent to an ASIC vendor. With field-programmable logic, the files can be delivered to the customer in exactly the same way as for software. They face the same problems with code and release maintenance, etc., as software designers, and should use the same tools and techniques—but they do not.

To be able to develop functional hardware specifications efficiently, we need some software constructs that are still missing in VHDL. Most of all we need some kind of objects or abstract data types to encapsulate code and data without introducing delta events and process synchronization for every procedure call. Only with these types of constructs available can hardware and software reach up to a common formal specification level.

7 DESIGN DOMAIN INTERACTIONS

The hardware/software codesign task is part of a more general picture, where the interaction between design domains will play an increasing role. This is partly due to the push toward technology limits, such as higher frequencies, which for example make it necessary to solve analog problems in digital design. Another reason for this interaction is that the system performance may be greatly increased not only by the trade-off between software and hardware, but also between, for example, analog and digital hardware.

7.1 Theoretical Foundation Needed

The interaction between different design domains must be better understood and modeled. Such a model must characterize each domain according to its signal structure, and an interpretation function must be assigned to each interaction between the domains (Fig. 9).

A similar problem is that of translating signal information between abstraction levels in a certain design domain. An example of such a translation is between abstract data types and the representation of those types by two- or multivalued logical data types in VHDL.

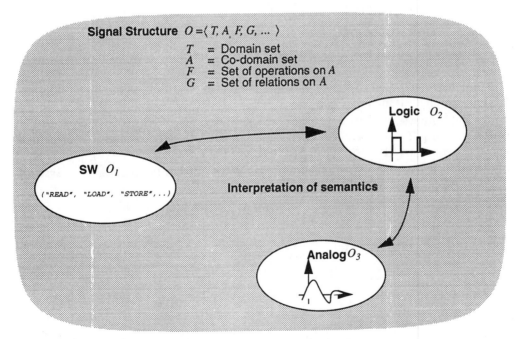

Fig. 9: Interaction between design domains

Each interpretation function must be modeled in a suitable design formalism such as VHDL (even if VHDL is not very well suited to describe such models, mainly due to the weak time abstraction construct). Due to the great span between the model domains, it is not likely or even desirable to try to express the models or the interpretation functions in one formalism.

7.2 The Process Structure Will Change

The common waterfall model for the process flow will not be adequate. With a high degree of interaction between design domains and abstraction levels, the pure top-down design flow cannot be maintained. Instead, the process structure must allow for a more irregular flow between design domains and abstraction levels.

The process structure must then express the information states of the design rather than being a task flow description, since the design may be carried out at various abstraction levels and in different design domains simultaneously. A consequence of this is that the project process and the design process must be clearly separated.

7.3 Support System Interchangeability a Must

A further consequence of the increased design domain interaction is that the interaction between the CAE tools will be tighter. So far, CAE systems have been by and large isolated islands, and it is unrealistic to imagine a CAE framework that will cover all needs. Thus there is a great need for a standardized way of exchanging information between CAE tools. The CFI (CAD Framework Initiative) recommendations may be one way of handling this problem.

REFERENCES

[1] M. Altmäe, "IPL—Generic Interface to Programming Languages," Swedish Institute of Microelectronics, 1992.

[2] M. Altmäe, P. Gibson, L. Taxén, and K. Torkelsson, "Verification of Systems Containing Hardware and Software," *Proc. Second European Conference on VHDL Methods, EuroVHDL '91,* September 1991, pp. 149–156.

[3] P. Gibson, "Integration of Software and VHDL Models for Verification of Systems," Swedish Institute of Microelectronics, 1992.

CHAPTER 21

Computer-Aided Prototyping of Application-Specific Embedded Controllers in Mechatronic Systems[1]

A Case Study

H.-J. Herpel   N. Wehn   M. Glesner
Institute for Micorelectronic Systems
Darmstadt University of Technology
Darmstadt, Germany

Abstract: This chapter presents a methodology and a design environment to support validation and design space exploration of application-specific embedded controllers through computer-aided prototyping. Our approach to prototyping uses a specification language integrated with a set of software tools and an execution-support system. System partitioning into a set of software and hardware modules is done at the system description level. User-guided and automated synthesis tools generate a fully functional prototype, which can be connected to real-world processes to validate system design and to estimate system performance.

1 INTRODUCTION

The overall system performance of machine tools, vehicles, and aircraft can be improved significantly by applying embedded information technology and, in particular, artificial intelligence to it. Mechanical systems with embedded information processing elements are usually referred to as *mechatronic systems*. According to [1], mechatronics (MECHAnics and elecTRONICS) can be defined as an emerging engineering discipline concerned with the design, manufacturing, and operation of machines capable of intelligent behavior. The spectrum of intelligence may vary from programmed behavior and self-regulation over

[1] This research work is sponsored by the DFG through SFB241 "Integrated Mechano-Electronic Systems"

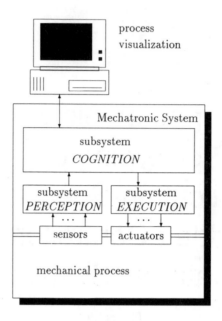

process
visualization

Mechatronic System

subsystem
COGNITION

subsystem
PERCEPTION

subsystem
EXECUTION

sensors   ...   actuators

mechanical process

Fig. 1: Mechatronic system architecture

self-diagnostic, self-repair to learning, self-organization, and giving advice to their own users. Accordingly, a mechatronic system consists of a *controlling system* and a *controlled system.*

For example, in a car, the controlled system is the combustion engine with its ignition system, combustion chamber, clutch, and gear box, whereas the controlling system is the board computer and human interfaces that manage and coordinate the behavior of the car. Thus, the controlled system can be viewed as the *environment* with which the computer interacts.

The controlling system interacts with its environment based on the information available about the environment, say, from various sensors attached to it (see Fig. 1). It is imperative that the state of the environment, as perceived by the controlling system, be consistent with the actual state of the environment. Otherwise, the effects of the controlling systems' activities may be disastrous. Hence, periodic monitoring of the environment as well as timely processing of the sensed information is necessary. The controlling system has at least the following three functional subsystems: perception, cognition, and execution.

Perception is concerned with collecting relevant information and building an internal model of the environment in which the system operates. Major components of this subsystem are sensors, information storage/information processing elements, and communication subsystems.

Cognition is concerned with planning actions that the system should undertake based on tasks given to the system, requests from the user, and the state of the environment as derived from the perception subsystem. Conventional processors, neural nets, and fuzzy processors are some of the elements capable of information processing, learning, negotiation, and decision-making.

Execution is concerned with implementing actions decided by the cognition subsystem and reporting back. Actuators, manipulators, and controllers are the main components of an execution subsystem.

Also, controlling systems have a substantial amount of knowledge concerning the characteristics of the application and the environment built into the system. A majority of today's controlling systems assume that much of this knowledge is available *a priori* and, hence, are based on *static* designs. The next generation of controlling systems must be designed to be *dynamic* and *flexible*.

As mentioned before, most controlling systems are special purpose and thus, we use the expression *application-specific embedded controller* (ASEC) for such systems.

Before we go into details of the design methodology and tools we would like to define some expressions frequently used in the area of real-time information technology. Concurrent execution of functions is required to perform the information processing of today's mechatronic systems. In the field of computer science, concurrently executable functions are called *processes*. The expression *task* is used for a software implementation of a concurrently executable function embedded in a real-time operating system. In the following text, we use the word *task* instead of process to allow a clear distinction between the *mechanical process* and concurrently executable functions of the controlling system. A task refers to the execution of a number of sequential statements. Several tasks can be executed *concurrently*. Concurrent tasks can be either mapped onto a single processor or onto a multiprocessor system where one processor executes only a single task. A node processor in such a multiprocessor system can be either a conventional processor or dedicated hardware for high-performance data processing. Both homogeneous and heterogeneous multiprocessor systems are possible. We use the term *homogeneous* in the sense that only one type of processor is used (e.g., transputer systems), whereas a heterogeneous system is built from different types of processors, e.g., general-purpose microprocessors, digital signal processors (DSPs), fuzzy processors, and application-specific processors.

In a multitasking environment, *intertask communication* plays an important role in the overall system performance. As described in [2], many mechanisms exist for intertask communication and *synchronization* of tasks. In some of them, communication is performed by shared data, which implies that only one task may access these data at any point in time. Semaphores, conditional critical regions, monitors, and path expression belong to this group. Other mechanisms are based on *message passing*. Here, tasks send messages to other tasks and, thus, perform synchronization and data exchange. Message passing may use *direct naming*, i.e., the name of the task to receive data is specified.

The selection of the physical communication structure for intertask communication has a large impact on performance and area. Most multiprocessor environments are based on a single bus (e.g., VME bus) or point-to-point links (e.g., transputer systems). LANs and field bus systems are commonly used in distributed multiprocessor systems. Bus-based systems require a lot of synchronization overhead to transfer data between different node processors. Point-to-point connections can be realized as serial links or parallel bus structures. Parallel point-to-point connections may be fast, but it is expensive to implement them—in terms of number of pins/ports. Serial links, in turn require high clock frequencies but only a few lines between the node processors. Transputers, e.g., have several serial links to build a 2-D array of node processors.

2 DESIGN METHODOLOGY

The growing complexity of control systems in mechatronic applications (e.g., combustion engines, shock absorbers, etc.) requires improved system design technology. According to [3], rapid computer-aided prototyping (CAP) is a promising approach that makes this improvement possible. Figure 2 shows the major difference between the traditional approach to system development and an approach using rapid prototyping.

As described in [4], the traditional life cycle [Fig. 2(a)] starts with an informal behavioral abstraction of *what* is computed. This abstraction is progressively refined and eventually transformed into an operational specification of *how* the computation takes place. Therefore, a discontinuity in the process results in which a behavioral specification of the embedded system is turned into an operational specification from which source code or netlists are derived. This makes it difficult to verify that the source code/netlist matches the behavioral specification, let alone the more informal requirements description.

The alternative approach of the system design cycle [Fig. 2(b)] has been well known for many years in the field of computer-aided software engineering (CASE) and replaces the traditional system development cycle with a life cycle having two phases: rapid prototyping and automated implementation support.

From the earliest design stages of the operational life cycle, the product is an executable abstraction of *how* the system is supposed to work. This abstraction is as formal as a behavioral specification, but the behavior is specified implicitly via a set of ex-

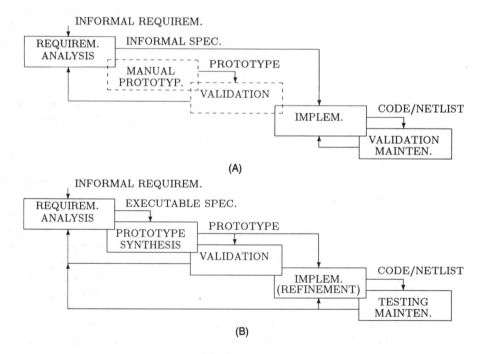

Fig. 2: Design flow

ecutable specifications instead of explicitly in an implementation-independent fashion. This executable model (prototype) of the embedded system can be checked against the user requirements. Early feedback to designers and users is thus possible. The generated prototype can be seen as a very first implementation of the embedded system, which only has to be fine tuned to achieve full performance. Automatic tools may help to further reduce this manual process of fine tuning and adaptation to the real-world requirements (physical size, power consumption, etc.).

The computer-aided prototyping system reduces the designer's efforts by automating time-consuming tasks in conventional prototyping, such as turning specifications into prototypes, modifying prototypes, and performing a search in the design space.

At this point one could argue that all functional aspects in mechatronic systems engineering can be covered by simulation. But simulation heavily depends on the quality of simulation models. Modeling of mechatronic systems is quite a complex task. Sometimes it is even impossible to build a model for the mechanical part of the system. Another problem with system simulation is deciding from where a wrong system response results. Is it due to an error in the controlling part or does it result from an incomplete or not correctly implemented process model?

However, according to [5], software-based simulation systems will always lack *the tyranny of time imposed by signal processing systems*. Finally, designers of an embedded control system want to see the results of their design. They cannot judge much on the basis of bit patterns.

Currently, rapid computer-aided prototyping is done at two different levels: at the device and system levels. At the device level, it means two things: first, shortening the time between netlist shipment and delivery of ASIC prototypes through direct e-beam writing and, second, ASIC prototyping through reprogrammable hardware, e.g., field programmable gate arrays (FPGAs) before any netlist is shipped for fabrication. In this contribution we focus on the second point only, ASIC prototyping with reprogrammable hardware. This kind of prototyping is used relatively late in the design cycle, when system design and partitioning into hardware and software functions is almost done and the user wants to speed up system integration. A prototype of the ASIC is available long before it is fabricated and software can be written and tested before the actual circuit is fabricated. Both hardware and software can be debugged concurrently, which speeds up system design. This is very important for ASIC-based systems where a redesign of the ASIC can delay product delivery by months.

Rapid prototyping at the system level means quick realization of ideas.

3 REQUIREMENTS FOR A CAPtool

Software tools and hardware are needed to support this automated prototyping method. The major parts of such a system are:

- A system description language
- User interfaces, synthesis and analysis tools to speed up design entry and design evaluation

- An execution-support system to demonstrate and measure prototype behavior and to perform static analysis of the prototype design.

A good language for expressing design thoughts in terms of a precise model is important for rapid prototyping. It is impossible to create a good design without a language designed especially for this purpose. A powerful easy-to-use language is a critical part of a computer-aided prototyping system. Such a language is needed before tools in the system can be built. As mentioned before, prototyping of real-time systems requires concurrent execution of system functions to perform the data processing. Accordingly, the prototyping language for real-time systems must comprise features to describe this concurrency. Ada, ConcurrentC, SDL, OCCAM, etc., all support concurrency through corresponding language structures. A trade-off has to be made between the use of one of these introduced languages and the development of a new language tailored to a specific application domain.

Just as important as the language is the user interface to enter a design. The trend is toward graphic-oriented design entry systems. System designers like to describe their ideas more in block diagrams than in alphanumerical form. As a consequence, design entry should be at this block level. Design analysis and verification should be supported through interactive simulation. Simulation results should be presented to the user in a way he or she is familiar with, i.e., line graphics, colored 3-D plots, etc. Another important requirement is that a simulation tool should support real-time simulations with the real process attached to it. This imposes an execution-support system with real-time features such as analog and digital interfaces and processing power capable to perform the necessary data processing.

The majority of the application-specific embedded controllers are heterogeneous systems. Some functions are implemented in hardware (ASICs), others in software executed on standard processors (μP, DSP), and due to the fact that these systems are interfacing with the real world, some part of the system is asynchronous and analog. Accordingly, an execution-support system that supports hardware-in-the-loop simulation should reflect this heterogeneous structure. It should be based on standard processors and on reprogrammable hardware to emulate ASIC functionality.

Some tools are already available that support rapid prototyping either at the system level or device level. Good examples for system design tools are SystemBuild/MATRIX$_x$, Xanalog, SimuLink, SPW (Signal Processing Workbench), StateMate/ExpressVHDL, etc. They all support block-oriented graphical design entry and, to some extent, hardware-in-the-loop simulations (e.g., SystemBuild, Xanalog). SPW and StateMate/ExpressVHDL support prototype implementation through code generators for C and/or VHDL. High-level synthesis tools such as the Synopsis Design Compiler are required to transform the behavioral VHDL description into a netlist for a specific ASIC library.

At least two products are already available on the market that support prototyping at the device level: Quickturn's Rapid Prototyping Machine (RPM) and InCA's Virtual ASIC (VA). All of these products follow the same approach: A given ASIC netlist is recompiled for an FPGA-based prototyping system. Both the Quickturn and the InCA system are based on an array of Xilinx SRAM-based logic cell arrays (LCAs). Another approach to device prototyping followed by many small companies is as follows: They start with an FPGA design and do all the testing and integration with this device to lower the risk for the ASIC itself. In the next phase the FPGA design is mapped onto an ASIC library. This mapping can be done either manually or automatically through technology mappers offered by many ASIC vendors. This technique is very useful as long as the design fits onto a small number of FPGAs, say, up to four. When a design is more complex then partitioning becomes a major problem. The third way to accomplish device prototyping is to use migration tools, where an ASIC is designed based on a generic library. After design verification at this level, it can be compiled into either an FPGA or a standard cell design. This approach is very similar to the previous one except that switching between different technologies can be done simply through recompilation.

4 OUR APPROACH: CAPtools

As mentioned in the previous sections, very good tools are available for rapid prototyping at the device level, when the ASIC architecture is fixed on a netlist level, and for implementation-independent rapid system prototyping. Very few system design tools support ASIC implementation through a VHDL interface. To our knowledge, no tool is currently available that supports heterogeneous system design from specification down to prototype implementation and hardware-in-the-loop simulation.

Our approach to rapid computer-aided prototyping is based on the following life cycle model:

- Algorithmic description of the system behavior
- System analysis through software simulations of the specified algorithms
- Algorithm refinement with respect to VLSI implementation
- Automated prototype synthesis
- System verification through hardware-in-the-loop simulations.

A set of hardware and software tools has been developed to support this life cycle model (see Fig. 3).

The design flow from a high-level description to an executable prototype is as follows: First the user has to decompose the system into a set of concurrent tasks using IHL. Next a compiler checks the input file for consistency and completeness and generates source code for every task specified in the system description. In the last step these source files are compiled to executable code and mapped onto the execution-support system.

4.1 The Language

Imes High-Level Language (IHL) was designed together with the prototyping method to ensure the most efficient use of the language at the specification or design level and has special features for real-time system design. IHL is a state machine-oriented language for real-time systems and allows concurrent tasks to be specified as a collection of sequential subspecifications.

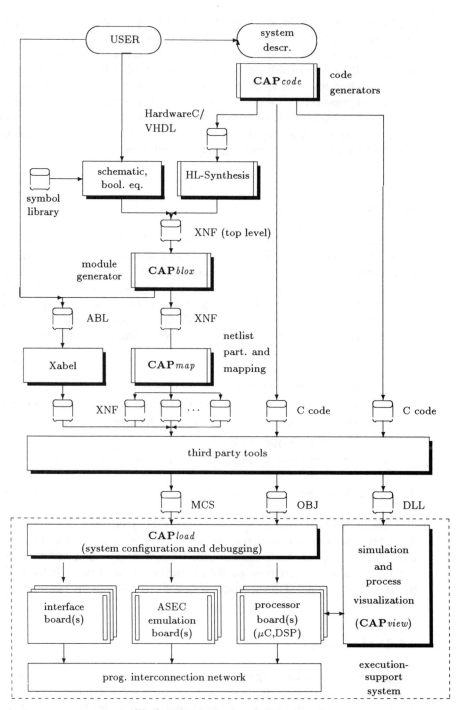

Fig. 3: Configuration of our CAP environment

IHL provides two basic building blocks for prototypes: communicating tasks and communication channels. Communicating tasks exchange information through common data areas synchronized by mailboxes. Tasks in an IHL program consist of a data declaration part and a set of macros. The data declaration part defines the direction of the data flow from/to the task in terms of imported and exported data. Each macro describes the sequential processing on imported or internal data. The sequence in which the macros are executed is data driven or determined by external events. This mechanism is modeled as a behavioral finite state machine (BFSM). The following IHL code segment tries to illustrate this. It is part of the description of a parameter estimation system that we comment on later in this text.

```
SYSTEM ParameterEstimation;
DECLARATION
  Svf_i              : TASK ATTRIB="IMPL=TMS32030";
  Svf_o              : TASK ATTRIB="IMPL=HardwareC";
ENDDECLARATION;
IMPL
  TASK Svf_i;
  DECLARATION
    xi_c             : EXPORTED DATA LONGFIX [4] := [0,0,0,0];
    x                : IMPORTED DATA FIX := 0;
    a                : IMPORTED DATA LONGFIX [4,4];
    b                : IMPORTED DATA LONGFIX [4,4];
    sha              : IMPORTED DATA LONGFIX [4,4];
    shb              : IMPORTED DATA LONGFIX [4,4];
    bio              : IMPORTED MAILBOX LONGFIX;
    xi_k_1           : INTERNAL DATA LONGFIX [4] := [0,0,0,0];
    xi_k             : INTERNAL DATA LONGFIX [4] := [0,0,0,0];
    xk               : INTERNAL DATA LONGFIX [4] := [0,0,0,0];
    ma               : INTERNAL DATA LONGFIX [4,4];
    mb               : INTERNAL DATA LONGFIX [4,4];
    sa               : INTERNAL DATA LONGFIX [4,4];
    sb               : INTERNAL DATA LONGFIX [4,4];
    n                : INTERNAL DATA LONGFIX;
    i                : INTERNAL DATA FIX := 1;
    j                : INTERNAL DATA FIX := 1;
    WaitADC          : STATE;
    Calculate        : STATE;
    CalcSvf          : MACRO;
  ENDDECLARATION;
  IMPLEMENTATION
    MACRO CalcSvf;
    IMPL
      xk[4]   := xk[3];
      xk[3]   := xk[2];
```

```
    xk[2]   := xk[1];
    xk[1]   := FIXTOLFIX(x);
    WHILE 'i < 5' IMPL
      xi_k_1[i] := 0;
      WHILE 'j < 5' IMPL
        xi_k_1[i] := xi_k_1[i] + ((ma[i,j]*xi_k_1 [j]) >> sa[i,j])
                               + ((mb[i,j]*xk[j]) >> sb[i,j]);
         j := j + 1;
      ENDIMPL;
      xi_k_1[i] := xi_k_1[i] << n;
                   i := i + 1;
    ENDIMPL;
    [xi_k] := [xi_k_1];
    [xi_c] := [xi_k_1];
  ENDIMPL;
  STATE WaitADC;
  TDEF
    NEXT STATE WaitADC    CONDITION 'bio = 1';
    NEXT STATE Calculate CONDITION 'bio = 0';
  ENDTDEF;
  STATE Calculate;
  IMPL
    EXECUTE CalcSvf;
  ENDIMPL;
  TDEF
    NEXT STATE WaitADC;
  ENDTDEF;
ENDIMPL;
```

4.2 Prototype Synthesis

When the system behavior is described in IHL, a retargetable compiler (*CAPcode*) transforms this description into different destination languages. *CAPcode* currently supports three implementation paths:

- Generation of a software model to support software simulations during early design phases
- Generation of code for digital signal processors
- Generation of a hardware description language to support hardware implementation.

Every task in the IHL description can have a different attribute assigned to it, specifying the destination language, e.g., HardwareC and C code for the TMS320 digital signal processor family. Since code generators have been well known for so many years, the main emphasis in this contribution is devoted to hardware synthesis. But before the synthesis

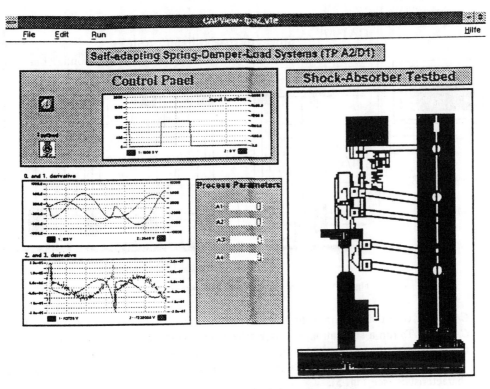

Fig. 4: *CAPview* simulation environment

process is described in more details, the underlying execution-support system is presented here for better understanding.

The Execution-Support System

An executable model of an embedded system that supports hardware-in-the-loop simulation has to provide real-time features such as analog/digital interfaces and processing power capable of real-time data processing. As stated before, concurrent execution of functions is required to perform this data processing.

Our execution-support system is based on two major components:

- A simulation and process visualization unit (*CAPview*)
- A user-programmable hardware environment (*CAPrt*).

CAPview serves as a software prototype (no real-time features) in the first step of requirements validation and as a quick-look display for hardware-in-the-loop simulations. Figure 4 shows a hardcopy of the screen.

CAPview includes predefined modules to display simulation results (analog instruments, line graphics, etc.) and modules to adjust system parameters. Programmable function generators and files of measured data can be used to simulate the external environment. A serial communication module allows us to connect external instruments to

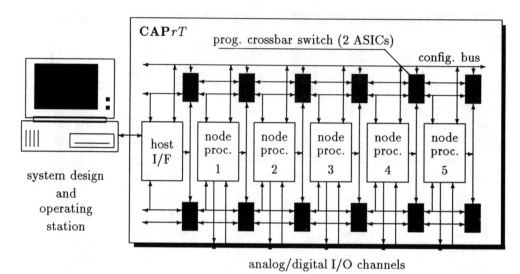

Fig. 5: Architecture of the execution-support system

CAPview. User-defined simulation modules can be added easily and executed within *CAPview*. To run a simulation, the user selects all necessary modules from a given list, places them on the screen, and defines the communication channels between them.

CAPrt is based on the demands of our application domain and has the following characteristics (see Fig. 5):

- A network of four segmented 32-bit-wide busses provides the connectivity structure for six node processors.
- The connectivity structure is software programmable.
- Each node can be connected to any other node in the network (either point-to-point connections or broadcast mode).
- The communication channels are unidirectional.
- Each node has two input ports and one output port.
- Dual-ported RAMs and FIFOs are used for intertask data exchange.
- Mailboxes and semaphores are used to synchronize data exchange.

Such an architecture has several advantages:

- Pipelining is established automatically when two functions are connected via a communication channel.
- Processors of different types and different configurations (memory, coprocessors, etc.) can be used in the system. Functions with very short response time can be realized with application-specific processors.

All node processors have the same architecture (see Fig. 6): A motherboard provides program memory (32k × 64) and data buffers (Dual-port RAM, mailbox, and semaphore

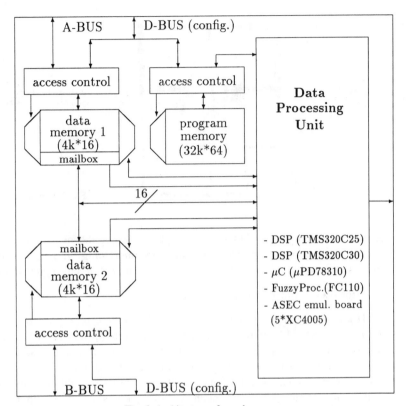

Fig. 6: Architecture of a node processor

logic) as download and debugging circuitry for the plugged-in data processing unit. The data processing unit (DPU) can be either processor based (e.g., TMS320C30 DSP, FC110 fuzzy processor) or it can be an ASEC emulation unit (AEU). The emulation unit consists of five programmable gate arrays, of which 4 can be configured as application-specific data paths. The controller is formed by the fifth programmable gate array and the program memory (see Fig. 7). Xilinx LCAs have been selected for this task because they combine high complexity (up to 20,000 gates for the XC4020) with in-system reprogrammability. The XC4000 series allows us to configure the configurable logic blocks (CLBs) as on-chip RAM, which further increases their flexibility. The connectivity structure between the four LCAs has been derived from an analysis of current digital signal processor architectures and an analysis of algorithms used in actual research projects in the field of mechatronics (state variable filter, clutch control, etc.).

The FPGAs on the emulation board allow us to perform complex operations on data stored in front of the unit. For example, matrix and vector operations are directly supported through corresponding memory structures (FIFO, ring buffers) on the motherboard.

Five emulation boards can be connected via the programmable interconnect structure in many different ways, allowing complex data processing—either sequential or parallel.

The manipulation of data on each node processor is data driven, i.e., each node processor waits until all data are available before the operation starts. The results of

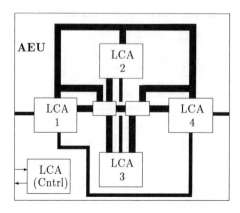

Fig. 7: Emulation board configuration

the data processing are written to the input buffer of the next node processor, which performs further processing. Sensors/actuators interfacing with the mechanical system can be connected to every node processor through analog and digital I/O channels.

High-Level and Structural Synthesis

High-level synthesis techniques on the microarchitectural level are used to map specific tasks on an AEU of the execution-support system. Starting with a HardwareC description [6], an automatic synthesis onto the AEU is carried out. Since the tasks to be executed on the AEU are usually data flow dominated, we try to exploit the inherent parallelism as much as possible. The target architecture is highly multiplexed with only a small number of functional units such as ALUs, adders, etc. The output of the high-level synthesis process is an abstract XNF netlist, which is mapped by a subsequent structural synthesis onto the 5 LCAs of the AEU.

Structural synthesis finalizes the prototype implementation of the application-specific processors. A module generator and a partitioning tool tightly interact to generate a prototype of the ASEC running on the emulation board of the execution-support system. In a first step the module generator (*CAPblox*) estimates the complexity of the blocks specified in the top-level netlist and writes this information back to the netlist. Next, the partitioner (*CAPmap*) performs partitioning at the top level under the constraints given by the prototyping hardware, introduces additional I/Os where necessary, and generates several XNF netlists. These netlists are expanded to gate-level representation by the module generator, which supports more than 20 macros, including adders/subtracters, ALUs, and different types of multipliers (from serial to fully parallel).

5 DESIGN EXAMPLE

The design of an application-specific digital signal processor for the evaluation of a state variable filter equation is presented here. Those filters are used for real-time parameter estimation of dynamic systems (see Fig. 8). Real-time parameter estimation is based on the least-squares algorithm, which requires the derivatives of the measured signals. In most cases it is difficult to obtain these signals directly from sensors attached to the

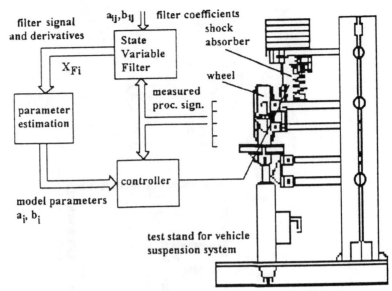

Fig. 8: On-line parameter estimation system for adaptive shock absorbers

process. State variable filters (SVFs) now perform a low-pass filtering of the measured signals and generate the derivatives automatically. For more detailed information about SVFs see [7].

The function of the SVF may be described by the following equation:

$$\xi(k) = A * \xi(k-1) + B * x_k(k) \tag{1}$$

with $x_k(k)$ = vector of the last signal samples
A = system matrix
B = input matrix.

The state variable vector $\xi(k)$ has to be interpreted in the following way:

$$\xi(k) = \begin{pmatrix} \xi_0(k) \\ \xi_1(k) \\ \vdots \\ \xi_n(k) \end{pmatrix} = \begin{pmatrix} \text{reconstructed (filtered) input value } X_{F0} \\ 1. \text{ derivative of the filtered input value } X_{F1} \\ \vdots \\ n. \text{ derivative of the filtered input value } X_{Fn} \end{pmatrix}$$

The system matrix A and the input matrix B are dependent only on filter design parameters and thus may be calculated before process identification starts.

CAPview was used to verify the implementation of the SVF equation using a simplified software model of the shock absorber testbed. The model was provided by engineers from the control department and integrated into the *CAPview* environment. The filter algorithm was specified in floating-point representation, which is not well suited to VLSI

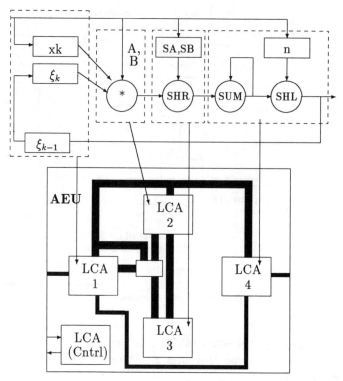

Fig. 9: Data path structure and its mapping onto the emulation hardware

implementation. Even with submicron technology it is costly to implement floating-point arithmetic units. Thus, a fixed-point version was derived from the original algorithm [8]:

$$
\xi_i(k) = \left[\sum_{j=1}^{n} (a_{ij}^* * \xi_j(k-1)\text{SHR shift\_}a_{ij}) \right. \tag{2}
$$
$$
\left. + \sum_{j=1}^{m} (b_{ij}^* * x_j(k)\ \text{SHR shift\_}b_{ij}) \right] \text{SHL } n
$$

Validation of the design transformations was performed by running simulations on *CAP-view* with the floating-point version as a reference.

In the next step, hardware-in-the-loop simulations took place in order to ensure that the modified filter algorithm produces correct results under real-world conditions. Two identical DSP boards were used to calculate the filter equations for either input and output of the process. For each board, 490 lines of TMS assembler code were generated, and a data acquisition rate of 1.7 kHz was achieved.

In the final step of the validation process the data path and controller synthesis for an application-specific processor was carried out followed by the prototype implementation on an emulation board. Figure 9 shows the data flow for the SVF algorithm and its mapping onto the emulation board.

CONCLUSIONS

Modern mechatronic systems engineering refers to engineers from mechanics, electronics, control, microelectronics, software, marketing, manufacturing, etc., cooperating in product development. This requires communication across the different disciplines, which all have their own terminology and culture. Experiences in the past have shown that communication across cultural boundaries is difficult and inefficient.

Methodologies and tools have to be developed that can help narrow this communication gap between the different engineering disciplines. But tools alone won't help much to increase design productivity significantly if they are not embedded into an efficient project management scheme.

Engineers of different disciplines have to cooperate from the very beginning of a project to make the most efficient use of their specific skills and know-how. A set of system engineering tools (sometimes also called concurrent or simultaneous engineering tools) with well-defined interfaces between the individual modules has to be provided that allows the team members to enter their design data (down to a certain level of detail) and to obtain the results of a simulation in a manner familiar to them.

The design of various mechatronic systems has shown that rapid prototyping is a very useful technique during early design phases to validate the functional requirements and to derive implementation specifications for the embedded electronic system. A fully functional prototype can be generated very early in the design process and checked against the user requirements through hardware-in-the-loop simulation. Thus, the implementation specifications are based on reasonable figures about required processing power and memory as well as hardware complexity. Based on these numbers, cost and design time estimations can be more precise than without the support of such a tool.

Efficient code generators and high-level synthesis tools are mandatory to support both the prototype synthesis and automized implementation of the specified embedded electronic system. In the past high-level synthesis has stressed the problem of generating a specific (hardwired) architecture for one specific algorithm. However, a shift in high-level synthesis becomes obvious. In the future high-level synthesis has to target programmable architectures, which are tuned to a class of algorithms. The reasons are manifold and are not discussed further. Programmability in this context means that either the hardware itself is programmable, e.g., by the use of FPGAs, or software determines the final functionality. The data paths of these architectures typically imply a lot of parallelism [for example, *Very Long Instruction Word* (VLIW) architectures].

As far as our work is concerned, we will look for a generic architectural processor model with appropriate software support, which is tuned to our application domain. Special emphasis will be devoted to an efficient microcode generation that is able to exploit fully the parallelism of the processor architecture. We will also provide an interface to VHDL-based synthesis systems in the near future to simplify the synthesis process and to automate the migration from ASEC emulation to ASEC implementation with cell-based design systems, for example. Presently, the initial partitioning of the embedded system into a set of software and hardware functions is mainly based on the experience of the designer. Future work will concentrate on system synthesis mainly on automated partitioning of a behavioral system description into a set of concurrent tasks.

REFERENCES

[1] G. Rzevski, "Mechatronics at the Open University," in *Proc. ISATA,* Florence, May 1991, pp. 15–22.

[2] P. A. Laplante, *Real-Time Systems Design and Analysis,* IEEE Press, New York, 1992.

[3] Luqi and M. Ketabchi, "A Computer-Aided Prototyping System," *IEEE Software,* pp. 66–72, Mar. 1988.

[4] R. Balzer, T. Cheatham, and C. Green, "Software Technology in the 1990's: Using a New Paradigm," Computer, pp. 38–45, Nov. 1983.

[5] H. DeMan, "Design Technology Research for the Nineties: More of the Same?" in *Proc. Euro-DAC '92,* Hamburg, September 1992, pp. 592–596.

[6] N. Wehn, H.-J. Herpel, T. Hollstein, P. Poechmueller, and M. Glesner, "High Level Synthesis in a Rapid Prototype Environment for Mechatronic Systems," in *Proc. Euro-DAC '92,* Hamburg, September 1992, pp. 188–193.

[7] K. Peter and R. Isermann, "Parameter-Adaptive PID-Control Based on Continuous-Time Process Models," in *Proc. IFAC Symp. on Adaptive Control and Signal Processing,* Glasgow, 1989.

[8] H.-J. Herpel, P. Windirsch, M. Glesner, J. Fuehrer, and J. Busshardt, "A VLSI Implementation of a State Variable Filter Algorithm," in *Proc. First Great Lake Symp. on VLSI,* Kalamazoo, MI, March 1991, IEEE, New York, pp. 138–143.

Index